T0301699

Supply Chain Construction

The Basics for Networking the Flow of Material, Information, and Cash

Series on Resource Management

RECENT TITLES

Supply Chain Construction: The Basics for Networking the Flow of Material, Information, and Cash
by William T. Walker
ISBN: 978-1-4822-4046-7

Directing the ERP Implementation: A Best Practice Guide to Avoiding Program Failure Traps While Tuning System Performance
by Michael W. Pelphrey
ISBN: 978-1-4822-4841-8

Building Network Capabilities in Turbulent Competitive Environments: Business Success Stories from the BRICs
by Paul Hong and YoungWon Park
ISBN: 978-1-4665-1575-8

Principles of Supply Chain Management, Second Edition
by Richard E. Crandall, William R. Crandall, and Charlie C. Chen
ISBN: 978-1-4822-1202-0

Supply Chain Risk Management: An Emerging Discipline
by Gregory L. Schlegel and Robert J. Trent
ISBN: 978-1-4822-0597-8

Supply Chain Optimization through Segmentation and Analytics
by Gerhard J. Plenert
ISBN: 978-1-4665-8476-1

Vanishing Boundaries: How Integrating Manufacturing and Services Creates Customer Value, Second Edition
by Richard E. Crandall and William R. Crandall
ISBN: 978-1-4665-0590-2

Food Safety Regulatory Compliance: Catalyst for a Lean and Sustainable Food Supply Chain
by Preston W. Blevins
ISBN: 978-1-4398-4956-9

Driving Strategy to Execution Using Lean Six Sigma: A Framework for Creating High Performance Organizations
by Gerhard Plenert and Tom Cluley
ISBN: 978-1-4398-6713-6

Supply Chain Architecture: A Blueprint for Networking the Flow of Material, Information, and Cash
by William T. Walker
ISBN: 978-1-57444-357-8

Supply Chain Networks and Business Process Orientation: Advanced Strategies and Best Practices
by Kevin P. McCormack and William C. Johnson
with William T. Walker
ISBN: 978-1-57444-327-1

Series in Resource Management

Supply Chain Construction

The Basics for Networking the Flow of Material, Information, and Cash

William T. Walker, CFPIM, CIRM, CSCP

CRC Press is an imprint of the
Taylor & Francis Group, an **informa** business

CRC Press
Taylor & Francis Group
6000 Broken Sound Parkway NW, Suite 300
Boca Raton, FL 33487-2742

Printed on acid-free paper
Version Date: 20150727

International Standard Book Number-13: 978-1-4822-4046-7 (Hardback)

Library of Congress Cataloging-in-Publication Data

Walker, William T.
Supply chain construction : the basics for networking the flow of material, information, and cash / William T. Walker.
pages cm
Includes bibliographical references and index.
ISBN 978-1-4822-4046-7 (hardcover : alk. paper) 1. Business logistics. 2. Materials management. I. Title.

HD38.5.W3453 2015
658.7--dc23 2015027381

Visit the Taylor & Francis Web site at
http://www.taylorandfrancis.com

and the CRC Press Web site at
http://www.crcpress.com

This work is dedicated to Henry, my grandson,
and to Elise, Maddie, and Ella, my granddaughters.

Contents

Foreword

William T. "Bill" Walker has spent his entire business career designing, building, and managing supply chains for Hewlett-Packard, Agilent, Siemens, and most recently StarTrak. His experience shows in his latest book, *Supply Chain Construction: The Basics for Networking the Flow of Material, Information, and Cash*. As readers will see, Bill writes from firsthand knowledge of what works and what pitfalls to avoid.

Readers should be prepared to concentrate when reading this book. It will not only inform, it will also challenge you; it is not a collection of warm and fuzzy thoughts that sound nice but leave much to the imagination. Bill provides a logical approach to supply chain construction and illuminates the progression with comprehensive, nontrivial examples and illustrations. He blends words, stories, and diagrams that explain the concepts clearly and concisely.

The book can be of value both to readers who want to start a business and to those who are working in existing companies and who recognize the need or opportunity to improve their already existing supply chains. A look at the Table of Contents shows the chapters are arranged in a logical sequence. While each chapter can stand alone, together they provide a holistic look at the myriad activities required to build effective, and efficient, supply chains.

After introducing the basic blueprint, Bill explains that supply chain success depends on building relationships with customers and suppliers—relationships that foster collaboration among supply chain partners to ensure the success of all participants. Supply chains involve multiple, and sometimes disparate, entities that must be brought together into a cohesive, compatible enterprise. Too often, supply chain disruptions result from fragile or ill-advised relationships.

After explaining the need for building relationships, Bill stresses the need for maintaining a positive cash flow. This is especially important for start-ups or small businesses that sometimes try to expand faster than their resources can support. A positive cash flow is essential for a business to survive. Of course, profits are also important, and the book shows that building a profitable business starts with understanding the customer and developing products that meet the needs of the marketplace, in both performance and pricing.

The book approaches supply chain construction from the perspective of two primary tasks: building the network container—the supply chain framework—and filling it with product contents. Chapters 5, 6, 7, and 8 on "Make," "Source," "Deliver," and "Return," respectively, address how to construct the network container. Chapters 9, 10, 11, and 12 on "Demand Planning," "Inventory Management," "Performance Measures," and "Risk Management" address how to fill the network container with its product contents.

I have known Bill for a number of years and have learned to respect what he says. He is direct, succinct, and truthful. He is also extremely knowledgeable about supply chains and their management, as I am sure the readers will find out as they explore the contents of this book.

Richard E. Crandall, PhD, CSCP
Appalachian State University

Preface

People ask why I'm so passionate about supply chains. My answer is really exemplified by the life experiences of my students. Upon graduation, my students have followed one of five career paths:

1. Joe became an entrepreneur and helped launch Sollega, a company providing solar panel racking solutions. My courses raised awareness that every entrepreneur has to develop and operate a supply chain as part of his or her business plan.
2. Sui went to work for his parents' company, becoming the general manager of Wood Flooring by Design. My courses provided the tools to explicitly identify the current supply chain and improve its competitiveness.
3. Elizmar went to work for Corporate America to become an operations analyst at FreshDirect. My courses provided a methodology to integrate processes for material, information, and cash flows across functional and geographical boundaries.
4. Talha went on to PhD studies in supply chain management at Northeastern University. My courses stimulated his desire to learn more and to contribute to the growing body of knowledge in our field.
5. Silvy chose an unrelated professional life in public relations and communications. My courses raised awareness that supply chains are found in every aspect of our lives.

The primary purpose of this book is to teach those unskilled in the art the basics of how to construct a new supply chain from scratch and begin its operation successfully. A secondary purpose of this book is to teach those with some practical business experience the basics of how to successfully modify an existing supply chain and continue its operation competitively.

How This Book Is Organized

Supply Chain Construction is organized in the following manner. The first 10 chapters teach how to make a supply chain work from the ground up. It answers the basic questions of where to start, what to do, and how to do it to build the network container and to fill it with product contents. Each new concept is discussed three times: once in its relevant chapter, once in a very detailed forward network construction example found in Chapter 2: "The Blueprint," and once in a very detailed reverse network construction example found in Chapter 8: "Return." The application of information technology is considered within each chapter rather than being consolidated into a separate chapter. This is because *Supply Chain Construction* takes a principles-based basic approach. While modern information technology applications demonstrate a rate of change at a dizzying pace, these principles remain the principles. The last two chapters explore the diagnostics necessary to bring a new supply chain online and the discipline of risk management to keep the new supply chain viable.

Make It Work

- *Chapter 1: Eight Steps*
  How to understand customer requirements, how to write the Supply Chain Construction Requirements Specification, and how to get started on a supply chain construction project.
- *Chapter 2: The Blueprint*
  How to construct a forward supply chain. Includes a detailed step-by-step example of how to apply the Supply Chain Construction Blueprint to build a forward supply chain.

Chapters 3 through 8 Detail Constructing the Network Container

- *Chapter 3: Building Relationships*
  How to build trusting relationships and collaboration in the midst of change.
- *Chapter 4: Cash Flow*
  How to determine end-to-end product pricing/landed cost and how to maintain cash flow during a supply chain construction project.
- *Chapter 5: Make*
  How to select the best factory and midbound logistics to meet supply chain requirements.
- *Chapter 6: Source*
  How to select the best suppliers and inbound logistics to meet supply chain requirements.

- *Chapter 7: Deliver*
  How to select the best distributor and outbound logistics to meet supply chain requirements.
- *Chapter 8: Return*
  How to construct a reverse supply chain. Includes a detailed step-by-step example of how to apply the Supply Chain Construction Blueprint to build a reverse supply chain.

Chapters 9 and 10 Detail Filling the Network Container with Its Product Contents

- *Chapter 9: Demand Planning*
  How to forecast demand and fulfill customer orders.
- *Chapter 10: Inventory Management*
  How to determine the inventory investment, how to place inventory with appropriate lot sizing, reorder points, and safety stock, and how to determine end-to-end inventory turns.

Make It Work Well

Chapter 11 is dedicated to making the supply chain work well. It uses a basic set of performance measures and diagnostics to tune up the new or the modified supply chain for peak performance.

- *Chapter 11: Performance Measures*
  How to measure, diagnose, and validate a supply chain the performs as expected. Includes an Appendix on how to use Excel to plot the Value Circle.

Make It Work in a Flexible and Risk-Tolerant Manner

Chapter 12 is dedicated to making the supply chain work in a flexible and risk-tolerant manner. It separates what can be controlled from what cannot be controlled with strategies to manage risk.

- *Chapter 12: Risk Management*
  How to address supply chain risk under extreme operating conditions.

Special Features in This Book

This work, *Supply Chain Construction*, follows the format of my earlier work, *Supply Chain Architecture.* The storyline is a special feature of this format. The storyline does more than set up each chapter for the reader; it also engages the reader with the intrapersonal and interpersonal conflicts that are typical in a supply chain construction project.

The storyline is contiguous from chapter to chapter; it can be read piecemeal or all at once. The storyline and case studies in this book are composites of personal experiences based on more than 40 years of working as a practitioner. In addition to straight text, *Supply Chain Construction* contains The Blueprint, logical sequences, bullet lists, checklists, 53 figures, 100 formulas, and 103 tables with detailed numerical examples and a reference bibliography.

William T. Walker, CFPIM, CIRM, CSCP
Practitioner and Author

Acknowledgments

I want to acknowledge the love and support of my wife, Linda, and especially all that she has taught me about teaching others. My family, Stacy, Andy, Elise, Maddie, Nicolle, Ralph, Ella, and Henry, has given me their loving support through this year of writing my latest book. Special thanks go to my son Ralph, an accomplished and licensed architect, for the front cover design.

I want to acknowledge the contribution of my publisher, Rich O'Hanley, and my editor, Lara Zoble. Special thanks go to my fellow author, good friend, and subject matter expert, Dick Crandall, for reading and commenting on the entire manuscript and for his many significant suggestions.

I want to acknowledge the inquisitive minds of my graduate students at New York University Polytechnic School of Engineering and my undergraduate students at the Rutgers Business School, especially for their courage in telling me when they did not really understand a supply chain concept.

Finally, I want to salute my professional colleagues worldwide, who gave me new opportunities to learn and challenged my thinking since my last book was published, especially Joe Aiello, Bob Albano, Ryan Armasu, Valerian Arva, Maziar Baharfar, John Banfield, Kevin Barnett, Clara Benarto, Peter Black, Preston Blevins, Daniel Bourbeau, John Boyer, Joshua Branock, Trevor Brougham, Damian Bucovsky, Scott Burchell, Hans Calis, Rick Cathers, Chaya Channakeshava, Swati Chiney, Linda Clark, Harold Clark, Lloyd Clive, Tom Cluley, Rick Coble, Bob Collins, Brian Collins, Steve Cokinos, Gary Cokins, John Costello, Jim Cox, Dick Crandall, Rick Crandall, Donna Dargel, Mark DeLessio, Greg DeMetro, Jolly Rasesh Desai, Tony DeVincenzo, Tom DiAngelis, Evan Dickinson, David Dobrzykowski, Ron Dolan, Reed DuBow, Rick Elder, Ray Farrelly, Rich Ferri, Carl Foehner, Howard Forman, Deepthi Polasa Gandhi, Anne Gatewood, Richard Gawron, Jim Gelose, Rajiv Ginde, Dennis Goldensohn, Mike Greenstein, David Gsell, Pat Hanley, Omer Haroon, Todd Heacock, Delfin Herras, Joni Holeman, Paul Hong, Clete Hugens, Mike Hutwelker, David Jacoby, Dave Jankowski, Bill Johnson, Hemal Kacharia, Venky Karuppanan, Arnie Kennedy, Doug Kelly, Jerry Kilty, Wally Klatch, Jeff LeClair, Lei Lei, Ken Lidman, Ben Lowe, Elizmar Arriojas Maldonado, Monica Marchaterre, Kevin McCormack, Pablo Mesa, Alan Milliken,

Dean Miller, John Miller, Russ Miller, Dan Moore, Peter Murray, Gerald Najarian, Steve Neiman, Jim Nering, Jerry Neuner, William Nickle, Constance Nyman, Young Won Park, Mike Pelphrey, Kristine Perry, Herb Perten, Rob Peterson, Gary Pezutti, Gerhard Plenert, Paul Pittman, Virginia Vogel-Polizzi, Carol Ptak, Lian Qi, Ron Redling, Don Reed, Todd Reed, Terry Rettig, Dave Rivers, Tom Robinson, Maryanne Ross, Bob Schicke, Greg Schlegel, Jim Semerad, Art Shaffer, Tim Slifkin, David Shaw, Joe Shedlawski, Gary Smith, Ray Snyder, Bob Sismilich, Judy Sjo-Gaber, Eric Somers, Edgar Sosa, Starr, Jerry Steinberg, Steve Talis, Dave Tootill, Robert Trent, Michael Trocchia, Tom Ulincy, Irvin Varkonyi, Jegan Vincent, Joseph Walden, Michael Walsh, Rosaline Wang, John Watzka, Patricia Wickham, Blair Williams, Mark Williams, Matt Williams, Xiaowei Xu, and Lee Zimmerman

About the Author

William T. Walker, CFPIM, CIRM, CSCP

This is my story. I am a supply chain practitioner, a book author, and most recently an adjunct professor.

My professional life in supply chain management began with learning the logistics of moving heavy artillery through the jungles of Vietnam. It continued through 33 years of employment with the Power Products Division of Hewlett-Packard, which then became Agilent Technologies; through learning about fire detection systems distribution at Siemens Building Technologies; to seven years as director of Supply Chain Management for StarTrak Information Technologies, LLC, a small telematics company that instrumented refrigerated containers, which then was bought by ORBCOMM. My experience includes years of time in each of the following roles: army lieutenant, design engineer, production engineer, manufacturing section manager, production and inventory control manager, software project manager, hardware engineering section manager, division purchasing manager, division materials manager, supply chain architect, and director of supply chain management. Over the years, I participated on large corporate teams to install Oracle and SAP enterprise resource planning systems and on a small company team preparing a Consona ERP system installation. My work travel led to exposure to cultures around the world in 29 countries on 5 continents.

In addition to a bachelor of science in electrical engineering and a master of science in industrial engineering with a concentration in operations research both from Lehigh University, I hold lifetime certifications from APICS: Certified Fellow in Production and Inventory Management (CFPIM), Certified in Integrated Resource Management (CIRM), and Certified Supply Chain Practitioner (CSCP). George Plossl spoke at the very first APICS event I ever attended; that was in 1980. From 1989 through 1998, while working full time, I served at the APICS society level as a volunteer professional association executive. This included years as the APICS vice president of Region 2 over the membership education chapters in New York and New Jersey, years as the APICS vice president of education for Specific

Industry Groups providing relevant education across a range of industries, and years as treasurer and then president of the APICS Education and Research Foundation awarding small grants for supply chain management education research. In 1999, I was awarded the society level APICS Volunteer Service Award. Later, I became part of a team of eight volunteer subject matter experts that created the first APICS supply chain education, APICS Advanced Supply Chain Management, delivered in 2000 on a CD-ROM. My APICS volunteer service included speaking at more than 20 APICS international conferences and exhibitions and travel to APICS events in 42 states.

My first book, published in 1985, *Managing the Growing Plant*, was an Institute of Business Planning desktop reference for manufacturers. In 1997, I was invited to add a chapter on logistics to the *Third Edition of the Production and Inventory Control Handbook*, edited by Jim Greene and published by McGraw-Hill. In 1998, I coauthored the monograph *Supply Chain Management: Principles and Techniques for the Practitioner* with Karen Alber while she was with Quaker Oats. Beginning in 1999, Barry Jacobs at Montgomery Research invited me to contribute white papers to five of his volumes on *Achieving Supply Chain Excellence through Technology* (ASCET). I was honored by The Logistics and e-Supply Chain Forum as one of "The Top 20 Logistics Executives of 2000" for my education contributions. In 2003, I was invited to write a chapter on supply chain networks for *Supply Chain Networks and Business Process Orientation* by Kevin McCormack and Bill Johnson, published by CRC Press. My second book, *Supply Chain Architecture: A Blueprint for Networking the Flow of Material, Information and Cash*, was written during a period of unemployment and was published by CRC Press in 2004. Additionally, Publisher Rich O'Hanley recruited me to be series editor for the *Resource Management Series* published by CRC Press/Taylor & Francis. I have been instrumental in helping other authors publish 18 of their own books on supply chain topics.

My teaching experience began in 1999 with two-day workshops on supply chain management delivered through the University of Dayton Center for Competitive Change. I then developed a series of focused one-day seminars, which morphed into full-semester courseware on supply chain engineering based on my second book. Beginning in 2010, I have taught supply chain engineering to more than 100 graduate students of industrial engineering at the New York University Polytechnic School of Engineering in Brooklyn, New York. In addition, I have taught demand planning and fulfillment to some 80 undergraduate students of supply chain management and marketing sciences at the Rutgers Business School in Newark, New Jersey. While my teaching reinforced the approach of principles-based basic supply chain education, I found that students struggled with some of my material because it was too theoretical. This book, *Supply Chain Construction*, represents a significant improvement in the presentation of my material culled from a lifetime of practitioner application and learning. The approach has been perfected by my students.

Supply Chain Construction: The Basics for Networking the Flow of Material, Information, and Cash is my third book. This work is a distillation of a lifetime of self-learning with a lot of help from my business associates. I like to think that my contribution to the field is my deep understanding of supply chain management that along with some teaching ability helps others, such as you, connect the dots. I can be reached at: wt_walker@verizon.net.

Chapter 1

Eight Steps

Every successful supply chain construction project follows a process that builds to a blueprint. This chapter begins the journey with an explanation of the Eight-Step Process to a successful supply chain construction project. The project might be to build a new supply chain or to modify an existing one. The project might be a forward supply chain that manufactures and distributes products to markets or a reverse supply chain that accumulates product from the field for remanufacturing and recycling. No matter, the Eight-Step Process described in this chapter and the Supply Chain Construction Blueprint detailed throughout this book covers all such projects.

Prologue

"Is this all you can give me? I see just another lousy quarter of declining sales and missed profit targets," Steve, the young capable president of the Power Products Division, stared at his staff across the boardroom table in the Barnegat Room. Each conference room had been named after a state park.

Alice, the vice president (VP) of Finance, started to explain certain underlying assumptions, "Look, the economy has been particularly bad, especially in Europe, and we expect..."

Steve cut her off, "Alice, with all due respect, Finance cannot fix the problem. Engineering and Marketing has got to come up with new products and new markets, soon!"

This division of a larger corporation was looking to rejuvenate its stalled revenue growth. The Power Products Division had been an independent east coast manufacturer of power supplies before being acquired by the west coast electronics giant. The Power Products business was a tough business. Their precision, computer-controlled power supplies were designed, marketed, manufactured, and distributed from a single location. Competition was plentiful, especially internationally. Some markets appeared to be saturated. Old, previously loyal customers said that they did not need such exotic specifications, and they certainly could not afford such high prices.

Just then Jerry, VP of Marketing, walked into the meeting and took his seat.

"You're late, as usual!" snapped Steve.

Jerry was new to the division and destined to move onward and upward. He viewed this position as a stepping stone to greater achievement. This hotshot marketer said, "Oh, hi Steve. My team just completed our review of an exciting new market opportunity. Let me tell you about it."

The others around the table were relieved to take a break from Steve's tirade. Besides, maybe Jerry really had some new opportunity.

"Remember how we learned last quarter that our sister division, Computer Products, is planning to launch a new family of midmarket computer servers to complement the big mainframes? My team thinks there's a unique opportunity for our division to piggyback on this initiative."

Herb, VP of Engineering, interjected, "The last time we tried to sell our power supplies through the Computer Products Division, it was a disaster. In spite of all our investment, our manufacturing could never achieve their cost target. …Been there, done that!"

"If you would stop making your designs so darn complex, we could have had a fighting chance in manufacturing," said Tom, the VP of Manufacturing.

Jerry regained control of the meeting, "I'm not talking about power supplies. I'm talking about something new…uninterruptable power supplies, or UPS. This is a device that provides battery backup, when the power line goes down. My team thinks we should deliver a family of three products to match the three server sizes being offered by Computer Products. Our UPS products would be sold to the same set of customers buying the new Computer Products servers."

"Maybe there's something to be said for Jerry's idea," said Herb, aligning himself with Jerry. "You know my engineers are experts when it comes to power control and even digital interfacing. We would only have to learn a little about battery technology to pull this off."

"Now you are talking!" replied Jerry. "My team thinks the UPS should tie directly to the server. When the line voltage sags or is interrupted, the UPS could trigger a graceful shutdown before the server loses all power. The UPS could sense line voltage recovery and trigger the server to restart in the right sequence."

"How would we sell such a product?" asked Steve. "Our Instrument Sales Force sells to engineers; it does not call on the same set of customers as does the Computer Products Sales Force."

"Yes, that will be a challenge to be overcome," responded Jerry.

"Manufacturing cost is another significant challenge to overcome," said Tom, determined to make his point heard above the increasing enthusiasm for Jerry's pet project.

Once again, Jerry headed off the objection, "Oh, we wouldn't manufacture here. As you said before, Tom, it's too expensive. We would use a contract manufacturer probably in another country."

"We would have to work carefully through the financial implications of that decision," said Alice.

Up until now George, the VP of Quality, had listened intently to Jerry's remarks. George was a deep thinker with considerable business experience in several functional areas while at previous employers. But he was not well understood by the others in this leadership circle. "While we are listing critical success factors, there are a couple of others to consider," began George.

"What's that?" asked Jerry.

"First, I'm concerned that I'm not hearing much in your plan in the way of what customers want. The conversation so far seems to center around what the technology can provide."

"Yes, and what else?"

"To be successful, our approach to entering a new business segment needs to follow a process," explained George. "We need to agree on an objective that provides value to our customer. And we need to select a project team, and then hold them to a timeline and a budget."

"And, I suppose you just happen to have such a process?" remarked Jerry.

"In fact, I know someone who does."

"We don't have a budget for any such project," Alice interjected.

"Yes, and my engineers are all committed to other ongoing projects," said Herb.

"Before getting all tied up in knots, let's discuss our objective," said Steve. "I like Jerry's entrepreneurial spirit in suggesting that we move into a different product area in a different market. We have certainly beaten our heads against the wall in the power supply market for years and years. I like Herb's thought that, from a product perspective, our technology investment would be mostly around battery technology. I'm concerned that Jerry and his Sales Team have never sold into this new market segment. I'm concerned that if we decide to outsource manufacturing to meet a cost target, then what does that mean for our employees here? Alice is right that we don't have any budget today, but that's where Corporate might be able to help. And, George has a point about needing good project management to achieve a quality outcome. But what is our real objective?"

Each of the vice presidents remained silent in thought about their own functional areas of responsibility and about their own career ramifications of success or failure.

"We need to get our revenue line back on track to meet Corporate's profitability target. Otherwise, none of us will have jobs six months from now. I don't like the undercurrent of squabbling at this meeting, but I recognize that each of you is concerned about your future. So are our employees; let's not forget that. The only way out of this downturn is to pull together as a team," continued Steve. "When we know a little more, our objective can be turned into a performance specification for a new business."

"OK. Let me take a stab at a bold objective," replied Jerry, since it was his idea from the start. "Our objective is to introduce a family of UPS products to be sold with servers from the Computer Product Division to customers throughout the United States before the end of next year."

"But we don't have a product!" said Herb.

"But we don't know if we can be competitive in manufacturing!" said Tom.

"But we don't have extra cash to invest!" said Alice.

"Yes, yes, and yes. Is there anything else this team thinks we will need?" asked Steve.

Once again, George spoke from experience, "Yes, there is one more thing. We will need a new supply chain to deliver our new products to our new set of customers. This supply chain is the bridge between the customer needs of a market segment and the value-added of a product. If we can't connect the two, then we have a show stopper."

Name Your Supply Chain Scenario

All too often, entrepreneurs start their new businesses unaware of the need for a supply chain network design. All too often, large companies are acquired and their product lines merged with no regard for supply chain network integration and rationalization. All too often, mature products die with the birth of the next product generation, and supply chain networks are abandoned, when companies divest with complete disregard of the need for customer support and environmental sustainability.

Goods and services supply chains touch every aspect of our lives. Competing supply chain networks are everywhere, from the supermarket checkout counter at Pathmark to the FedEx delivery of an Apple iPad to the more subtle restocking of $20 bills in a Bank of America ATM to the automotive maintenance service performed at Jiffy Lube. In our increasingly complex global society, engineering undergraduate and graduate students, executive MBAs, project managers, factory teams, distributors, architects, construction bosses, service bureaus, business executives, and small business entrepreneurs the world over need to understand the construction of supply chain networks to perform competent work.

All supply chains operate within a life cycle context. A life cycle includes the elapsed time of four phases: conception, growth, maturity, and decline. Your business scenario may be dominated by a market life cycle, a product life cycle, or a business life cycle. For example, the introduction of a new product line may necessitate building a new supply chain network to reach a new market segment. Or, competitive market pressures in a business causes the realization that the current approach is no longer viable. Or, the onset of process maturity in a business causes the realization that the business needs to compete as a supply chain. Whatever is the dominant life cycle reason when you are reading this book, your supply chain construction project will fall into one of four possible scenarios:

- *Building a new supply chain from scratch*—Whether you know it or not, every business has some kind of supply chain. This fact is often overlooked by entrepreneurs. This book explains everything you need to know when you build your first supply chain from scratch.
- *Expanding the products and/or the network in an existing supply chain*—New product introductions plus company mergers and acquisitions are just two common causes to expand your supply chain. This book tells you how to do it effectively and efficiently.
- *Contracting the products and/or the network in an existing supply chain*—Winning combinations of products and market segments change over time. Sometimes, businesses shrink. This book details how to resize your supply chain to meet the requirements of your business.
- *Ending and disassembling an old supply chain*—Over time, products become obsolete, suppliers go out of business, and markets are abandoned. This book explains why the termination of a supply chain should be carefully planned and executed especially for the sake of the human resources and environmental sustainability.

In today's world, professionals are driven to grow revenue, add products, add services, cut costs, grow profits, avoid risk, shrink inventory, accelerate cash flow, improve investment returns, and generally do much more with much less. Entrepreneurs start new businesses. Midlevel professionals face the challenge of implementing mergers and reorganizations. Business owners on the verge of a disaster, self-inflicted or natural, have little choice but to rebuild from the ruins. Supply chain construction is the common thread through each of these stories. Consider the following three typical examples.

An Entrepreneur Starts a New Business

An entrepreneur decides to open a pastry shop and on-site bakery. She rents 2,400 square feet of space on the corner of a busy intersection with a bus stop for New York City. This corner shop has large street-level windows, where people walking by can see the baked goods being made and can read the signage. While all the people who pass by the shop each week represent a market, only a segment of this market is interested in baked goods. Specifically, people getting on the bus each morning would like to purchase something for their 45-minute ride into the city. These folks need to be able to come into the pastry shop to make a quick purchase just before their bus arrives. They do not want to fuss with a lot of coin change. The entrepreneur decides to limit her baked goods to just three kinds of pastries each to be sold for an even $3. She makes sure two employees are scheduled to work the cash register during the morning rush. As time goes by, the entrepreneur plans to add new pastries at the same price and drop old pastries to keep her product offering fresh.

Later in the day, shoppers like to come into the pastry shop for a little refreshment. This is a different market segment that wants to be served and is willing to wait a couple of minutes for one of the shop's employees to serve them. They want to get off their feet by sitting at the small round tables; they want to relax by watching the world go by through the large windows. It is important that the signage meant to attract the bus crowd does not obscure the view of the shopping crowd. Otherwise, there will be a channel conflict. The shopping crowd appreciates reading sales blurbs from other local merchants. They need something to drink for a dollar. The entrepreneur understands that she cannot compete directly with the Starbucks down the street; she decides to offer a lemonade drink.

The entrepreneur's supply chain network consists of the retail store to deliver product with an attached bakery to make the product. The flour, butter, and other essential ingredients are sourced from local wholesale outlets. Two-day-old goods are donated to a local food bank. Garbage and trash are recycled weekly through a municipal contract.

The product delivered consists of the three types of $3 baked goods and the $1 lemonade drink. The pastry chef, who starts work at 4 a.m., must have storage space for enough inventory of raw materials to bake a day's worth of finished goods. The baked goods are stored in plain view of customers under a heat lamp. Some inventory is given to a food bank after the second day without a sale.

Sales revenue equals the sales volume times the price per product. The sales revenue must be large enough to cover the cost of goods sold (COGS), plus employee wages, plus the storefront rental, plus the loan for baking equipment, plus garbage pickup fees, plus all taxes, plus a small profit for the owner. If the pastry shop is open 50 weeks a year 6 days a week, and if the business needs to generate $300,000 per year to stay viable, then the business needs to attract an average of 250 $4 sales per day. This is a throughput of 75,000 pastries per year. The cost structure and throughput of the supply chain network must be able to support these requirements. Otherwise, the product, the supply chain network, and the market segment are mismatched.

Starting a new business takes an investment. The entrepreneur needs to know how much cash is needed up front and what to expect in regular cash flow. This is exceedingly hard to do without a plan and good record keeping. When the entrepreneur gets around to looking at the books a week after the store has opened, she is shocked by the state of her finances. At the end of the first week, she has purchased $7,500 in materials and $11,000 in equipment; she owes $1,200 in rent and $1,300 in wages. Daily cash register receipts for the first week were $300, $620, $440, $100, and $700, for a total gross weekly revenue of $2,160. Her receipts do not begin to cover her expenses, and her cash gap is growing. The supply chain relationships with suppliers, customers, employees, and the owner will need to be quickly stabilized to achieve a sustainable business.

A Business Merger Jeopardizes the Operating Model

A small, highly successful custom jewelry manufacturer is looking to expand. Clients schedule a time to bring their necklaces and bracelets to a dozen retail stores in the tri-state area. Artists work in-person with the customer to design a personalized customization and jewelers perform the intricate work to modify each piece. As a side benefit, the customer may borrow a piece of "equivalent" high-end costume jewelry during the time their piece is being crafted. Once completed, the customized piece is appraised at the store, and the customer has the option of purchasing insurance at the time of delivery. The customers love to brag about their one-of-a-kind jewelry creations. Such word-of-mouth advertisement has helped to grow the business, and this has drawn the attention of a national department store chain.

The large department store chain wants to offer their customers a jewelry customization service through a merger with the small manufacturer. The department store operates a jewelry department in each of its 600 stores nationwide. The department store envisions its customers choosing a design from a catalog and shipping their jewelry overnight to the factory. Once modified, the jewelry would be returned, and the customer would be notified to make their pickup at the department store. If the premise of such a merger is accepted, it would completely change the culture of the current business model. Table 1.1 compares the envisioned "to-be" operating model with the current "as-is" operating model.

There is considerable risk in such a merger. A 50× rapid growth in throughput is unrealistic because of resource constraints, cash flow constraints, and the time it will take to hire additional skilled jewelers. Key question number one is, "What is the cash constrained rate of growth the custom jewelry manufacturer can sustain?" Key question number two is, "After the novelty wears off, what is the average demand and seasonality that the 600 national department stores will generate month after month?" A more practical supply chain construction plan would be to run a pilot with the 10 closest department store locations. When the pilot has proven successful, split the remaining department store locations into six to eight

Table 1.1 "As-Is" to "To-Be" Operating Model Comparison

Operation	*The "As-Is" Business*	*The "To-Be" Business*
Send	The customer brings jewelry to one of a dozen local jewelry stores.	The customer brings jewelry to one of 600 national department stores.
Customize	An artist works one on one with the customer. The jeweler customizes the piece.	The customer picks a design from a catalog. The jeweler customizes the piece according to a standard plan. Artists are needed only to create the catalog. Many more jewelers are needed to handle the volume of throughput.
Deliver services	Costume jewelry is loaned to the customer. The one-of-a-kind jewelry is appraised and insured at delivery.	Appraisal and insurance services are eliminated.
Return	The customer comes to the jewelry store for pickup.	The customer comes to the department store for pickup.

implementation phases. Then implement the network expansion a phase at a time over a period of two years.

An Established Manufacturer Depends Too Much on One Customer

An electronics contract manufacturer, who has been in business for 25 years, needs to improve his cash flow. His business currently has an annual revenue of $6,000,000. However, his largest customer is 50% of the business, or $3,000,000. This represents a high risk should this customer ever decide to move on or become dissatisfied with the manufacturer's performance.

The contract manufacturer asks his Sales Department to break out the sales, his Finance Department to break out the cost of goods sold (COGS), and his Materials Department to break out customer-specific inventory for the largest customer. From this, the owner learns that his largest customer drives $1,850,000 of $3,850,400 in COGS, or 48%. The largest customer is responsible for $835,000 of the $1,540,000 in inventory, or 54.2%. The largest customer provides $90,000 of the annual $145,000 in net profit for the business, or 62.1%. Without additional customer diversification, the contract manufacturer is driven by the whim of this one customer.

The contract manufacturer has significant debt and thin margins from which to pay off his debt. Since he owns the building outright, he realizes that his debt is mostly financing inventory and accounts receivable. His largest customer runs a high mix business. This customer is always pushing for more inventory to improve delivery performance across the mix. Frankly, the forecast information that the contract manufacturer receives is nearly worthless. His inventory has grown so large that he only gets about 2.5 turns per year. The fact that this customer takes 45 days to pay just compounds the situation. The hand-to-mouth cash flow to refinance inventory is a constant drag on the business.

Yesterday, his largest customer asked to have a private meeting. He was told that the customer was moving its business to a first-tier electronics manufacturing services (EMS) company within the next three months. This decision was driven by the customer's need for lower costs and a higher level of manufacturing engineering services. A contract had already been signed with the new EMS. He was told that arrangements would be made to buy and transfer the inventory. He was wished "good luck" in his future endeavors. The owner suddenly faced the stark reality that while he would recoup most of his inventory investment, half of his production employees would lose their jobs in three months.

Let's Get Started

As you begin to read this book, you probably have a cup of coffee or tea at hand. The cup is a kind of container. The coffee or tea is a kind of contents. You could have selected a glass or a mug container to be filled with water or soda as contents, but you selected a cup and filled it with coffee or tea. Likewise, a supply chain has two parts: a container and some contents. The container is the supply chain network, and the contents are the products held within the container.

Supply chain construction is completed in two phases. The first phase is to build the network container according to The Blueprint. The first phase follows from a network design. The second phase fills the network container with product contents, or inventory, from which deliveries are made to customers. The second phase follows from an operations strategy.

Your customer always comes first. To get started, you should have a clear picture of who you expect to be your customer. Your customer is part of a market segment having common product needs, common pricing expectations, and common delivery expectations. You have to alert potential customers that you have such a product and/or service for sale that they might want to buy. You have to decide exactly how your supply chain network will deliver the product to the market segment.

Complete This Eight-Step Approach

When you set out to accomplish something, you need a plan. You might call this your "plan A". As you progress along the journey, your understanding will change, your assumptions will change, and your resources will change. At some point, you may decide that plan A will just not accomplish the objective. So you dream up "plan B" or "plan C"...or "plan K." Whether you are new to the concept of supply chains or a seasoned business professional, the project approach and The Blueprint presented in this book will teach you how to be successful building a new supply chain or modifying an existing one.

Build and Validate Layer by Layer

How do you go about constructing a supply chain network to connect your market with your product? An important lesson that I learned in the 1970s as an analog hardware design engineer at Hewlett-Packard (HP) is the methodology of developing a solution in layers and then validating the performance of each layer through measurement. When a layer is not performing to specification, diagnostics are applied to identify and fix the problem. But it is often the case that the plan A solution is just not capable of the desired performance. Under such circumstances, the project team iterates back through earlier decision points until evolving a workable plan B.

The first layer included a specification, a block diagram, and an incomplete list of expensive components. A crude estimate of the cost per feature was judged against a competitive cost target. If this incomplete cost rollup already exceeded the target, the design approach taken in the block diagram had to be abandoned. The second layer involved the development of a complete schematic and parts list for the product. A total cost was computed, and an estimate of the product's reliability was calculated from an analysis of parts count commodity by commodity. The third layer involved the layout of a printed circuit assembly. Prototypes were constructed or simulated by computer, and the feature performance of the circuit was measured. Additionally, worst-case tolerance analysis and statistical analysis of published specifications were performed. A revised total cost that now included the expensive multilayer printed circuit board was computed. The fourth layer evaluated the dynamic performance of the design, looking for large signal distortions and possible oscillation triggers. Often, additional components had to be added to the design to dampen oscillations; again, there was a total cost impact. The fifth layer involved the mechanical packaging and thermal design of the product. The enclosure usually consisted of sheet metal and plastic wrapped around the printed circuit assembly. Heat sinks and fans were added, with great emphasis on making measurements to validate that the worst-case temperature rise on certain critical components did not exceed some limit. Enclosures, heat sinks, and fans were high-cost additions to the total cost. When these components were not included in earliest cost estimates, the total cost by the fifth layer sometimes made the product design unworkable. Again, a design iteration was required. The final layer involved third-party evaluation and validation of the product design under extreme environmental conditions. Prototypes were tested against shock, vibration, ambient temperature extremes, humidity, electrostatic discharge, plus conducted and radiated electromagnetic interference. When a product failed its environmental testing, some portion of the product design had to be reworked along with the cost implication of the solution. In the end, a go/no go competitive cost measure was considered for every layer, while other measures, like distortion and temperature rise, were layer specific.

The methodology of layering to a complete solution is fully applicable to supply chain construction. This book takes a three layer approach.

- *Layer 1: Make it work*—Your supply chain construction project formally begins with a written requirements specification. Follow The Blueprint to pull together the margin targets; the SOURCE, MAKE, DELIVER, and RETURN relationships; and the forecasts and inventory management to just make the supply chain work. Measures of throughput capacity, price/landed cost, and inventory turns dominate this layer.
- *Layer 2: Make it work well*—Optimize the processes, develop the relationship trust, and deploy the measurements to bring your supply chain to peak performance under normal operating conditions. Throughput diagnostics, price/landed cost diagnostics, and inventory turns diagnostics are used to tune performance in this layer.
- *Layer 3: Make it work in a flexible, risk-tolerant manner*—The supply chain construction project formally ends with a validation of demonstrated network performance. Know the extent to which your supply chain can respond to abnormal conditions without breaking. Know its risk tolerance for events outside your control that might sink the business. The liquidity of cash-to-cash cycles dominates this layer.

The Eight-Step Approach

Supply chains are everywhere. Every business requires one, yet many people do not think about their business in such terms. The primary purpose of this book is to teach those unskilled in the art how to construct a new supply chain from scratch and begin its operation successfully. The secondary purpose of this book is to teach those with some practical business experience how to successfully modify an existing supply chain and continue operations competitively.

This book is organized for easy implementation of the Supply Chain Construction Blueprint (The Blueprint) within the context of a layered Eight-Step Approach to be followed by the project team. Successful supply chain construction projects follow this approach step by step to completion (see Table 1.2). Unsuccessful projects attempt steps out of sequence, fail to iterate steps on unachievable performance, or just never end.

Table 1.2 The Eight-Step Approach

Step	*Action*	*Reference*
1	Start the supply chain construction project with a focused objective connecting the market and the product	Chapters 1 and 3; Blueprint Step A
2	Formally staff a project team document the project timeframe and project budget	Chapter 3; Blueprint Step B
3	Write the supply chain construction requirements specification (SCCRS)	Chapters 1 and 11; Blueprint Steps 1 and 11
4	Layer 1: make it work—construct the network container; iterate steps as necessary	Chapters 2 and 4–8; Blueprint Steps 2–9
5	Layer 1: make it work—fill the network container with product contents; iterate steps as necessary	Chapters 2 and 8–10; Blueprint Steps 12–17
6	Layer 2: make it work well—validate performance, run diagnostics, fix or iterate steps as necessary	Chapter 11; Blueprint Steps 10, 18, and 19
7	Layer 3: make it work in a flexible, risk-tolerant manner	Chapter 12; Blueprint Step 20
8	Formally end the supply chain construction project	Chapters 3 and 11; Blueprint Step 19

An Important Note to the Reader about Enterprise Resource Planning, Quality, and Sustainability

Some readers may feel that the technical details on information technology, quality, and sustainability as related to supply chain management are underrepresented in this book. This book reflects lifelong learning about the practical application of basic concepts. It is important to understand how my work experiences shaped decisions on what to include in the book's content.

The rate of change in enterprise resource planning (ERP) application software and information technology, in general, eclipses the rate of change in writing and publishing books. Basic concepts are valid for long periods of time; technology specifics are not. Yet, at the same time, information technology is the great enabler that ties the various supply chain trading partners together. I participated on large ERP implementation teams within huge corporate settings for a conversion to Oracle at HP and for a conversion to SAP at Siemens Building Technologies. I also participated on a never completed Consona ERP implementation project within a very small company setting at StarTrak Information Technologies, LLC. This ERP implementation project was never completed because StarTrak was bought out; the ERP project was not an investment priority for the new owner. In my experience, these ERP applications encapsulated business rules, process flows, and operations data very well, but they obscured the end-to-end transparency of how the business was run. Once the ERP application was in place, functional training aside, it was difficult for employees to understand how and why the supply chain dots had been connected.

This book takes the approach that it is necessary to understand the basics of what is going on under the covers, to be followed later by layering on the most appropriate, most modern information technology system available at the time. Each chapter in this book discusses the role of connected information, but the book does not detail specific commercially available information technology products. Just to make my point, a technical explanation of the following sampling of recent advances in information technology would require its own book but would do little to explain the construction of a supply chain.

- *Virtual private networks with remote login*—These give geographically distant employees and external trading partners, having proper password protection and role rights, access to the ERP application and its data.
- *Client-server architecture*—An application software master resides on the server with client personal computers licensed to download copies of the program such as Microsoft Office. Software upgrades need only be applied once to the master.
- *WMS, TMS, APS, SCM, SRM, CRM*—Warehouse management system, transportation management system, advanced planning and scheduling, supply chain management, supplier relationship management, and customer relationship management are all specialized software applications that bolt-on to enhance ERP.
- *Data warehousing*—This is the ability to share dissimilar data elements through a report writer across different functional areas, geographical regions, and time periods.
- *Web portals*—These are websites that provide seller/buyer information exchange interfaces between trading partners; also used for the purpose of electronic auctions.
- *Cloud computing pay per use*—This is used when you cannot afford your own hardware and software systems and are willing to risk placing all your private business data into the hands of a third party.
- *Social media and mobile devices*—These are instantaneous, but not necessarily universal, 24 × 7 anywhere sense and respond access to information networks.
- *Big data*—At the time of this book's publication, the definition and application of the merits of big data were being debated.

Quality is a business philosophy. HP embraced quality best practices. In my experience, most of HP's, Siemen's, and StarTrak's suppliers were ISO certified and passed annual quality audits. StarTrak drove quality deep into its supply base because its product had to endure extreme environmental conditions in the field. Quality is about a product's fitness for use. It is about repeatable conformance to specification in a manufacturing process. It is about customer satisfaction in distribution. It is about continuous process improvement. It is about the reduction of all waste. These are certainly worthy attributes of a robust supply chain. This book is very much about the reduction of waste in that following The Blueprint will enable you to get your construction project done right the first time. Providing competitive pricing and competitive delivery lead time are necessary but insufficient elements of customer satisfaction. Forecasting and planning network inventory and cash flow properly and the decisions made around returns management are keys to minimizing cumulative product and process waste. However, the specific technical intricacies of quality product design and quality manufacturing process design are outside the context of this book.

Finally, sustainability is both a business philosophy and a life philosophy. Sustainability is about the choice of raw materials used in product design and in its packaging for logistics design. Sustainability is about the carbon footprint for source, make, deliver, and return processes in a supply chain. Sustainability is about the relative emissions from the transportation mode selected for inbound, midbound, and outbound logistics. Sustainability is about clean air and clean water. Sustainability is about the environmentally responsible handling, recycling, and disposal of product and process waste. Sustainability is about humane human resource management. Sustainability was just coming onto the radar screens of HP, Siemens, and StarTrak at the times that I worked for them; consequently, my work experience with sustainability is limited. While this book lifts up decision points where sustainability should enter into the equation, such as in trading partner selection, transportation mode selection, staff rightsizing, and material recycling, it is light on exactly how to go about implementing sustainable products and processes.

Set a Focused Objective to Connect the Market and Product

A supply chain connects the supply of a product and/or service with market demand. The starting point for any supply chain construction is its context. You will want to have a clear picture of what market segment is to be joined with what product and/or service. One without the other is doomed to fail. If you build it without serving a need, they will not come. If you identify a market need without having a product solution, nothing will happen. Again, you should know both the product and the market segment, both supply and demand. This book teaches you how to successfully connect the two together through a supply chain network. Let us start by looking at the pastry shop example in more detail.

Market Demand

While your supply chain network may be designed and operated to deliver to several different market segments, focus on one market segment at a time. Use the following set of attributes to describe each one.

- *Name the market segment*—Give each market segment a unique and descriptive name: Example 1: The "Bus Commuter" market segment; Example 2: The "Downtown Pedestrian Shopper" market segment.
- *Clearly state the customer need*—You expect to be able to satisfy the same need among all the potential customers in this market segment. It is helpful to have some anecdotal evidence of this customer need. Example 1: All the commuters getting on the bus want a little "pick-me-up" for their morning commute. Example 2: The downtown pedestrian shoppers want some nourishment plus a little break to get off their feet.
- *Define the pricing expectation*—All potential customers in this market segment see your pricing similarly as a fair value. Example 1: The bus commuters who come into the pastry shop are willing to spend $3 for a pastry and $1 for a lemonade relative to spending $15/day on bus fare. Example 2: The downtown shoppers who come into the pastry shop are willing to spend $3 for a pastry and $1 for lemonade relative to spending $2 for two hours of parking.
- *Define the delivery expectation*—All potential customers in this market segment consider your delivery lead time and delivery methods to be competitive. Example 1: Bus commuters encounter two sales clerks and no coin change, enabling them to make a quick, easy purchase and still get into the bus queue. Example 2: Downtown pedestrian shoppers get timely service while seated at a table.
- *Identify any temporal boundaries*—Understand if any time or seasonality boundaries drive this market segment. Example 1: Buses arrive and depart at the stop between 7:30 a.m. and 11:15 a.m.; there are no afternoon buses. Example 2: Downtown pedestrian shoppers avoid shopping in bad weather but increase shopping during the holidays.
- *Set a geographical boundary*—The geographical boundary is local, regional, national, or international. This depends on the amount of resource you are willing to spend building a distribution network. Example 1: The bus commuters are limited to riders of the bus service stopping at the corner. Example 2: The downtown pedestrian shoppers are limited to people who shop in the surrounding four blocks of retail stores and are likely to walk past the pastry shop.

- *Identify any contextual demand-driven constraints*—Determine realistic demand population constraints in each market segment relative to its context. Example 1: The bus commuters have their choice of five 40-passenger buses a day traveling to New York City. Only a percentage of the 200 people riding the bus will buy pastries on any given day. Word of mouth on the bus about the product or service can quickly create or destroy sales. Example 2: The pastry shop is located on a city block with other retail stores. It is located two blocks from a parking garage with 150 parking slots. The downtown pedestrian shoppers will most likely park in the garage to shop downtown. Cars are parked in the garage an average of three hours. The parking garage is empty by 4 p.m.
- *Understand any regulatory market constraints*—Markets have their own sets of regulations, from requiring a license to do business to the documentation required for the collection of sales tax. Example 1: To eliminate making change, pricing is set to an exact dollar amount after sales tax. Should the state sales tax increase, the business will have to decide between taking less profit or making small change. Example 2: The pastry shop is not licensed to sell food from any outside tables.

Product Supply

Your supply chain transforms raw materials into the end products your customers want at a competitive price and competitive delivery lead time. While your supply chain network may be operated to produce many different products, focus on the supply of your highest volume product family first. A product family is a group of products, options, and accessories that are somehow related by common features or by common raw materials. A product option adds or subtracts features to or from the base product, for example, a high-power flash attachment for a camera. A product accessory is a complementary product sold to supplement the base product, for example, a carrying case for a camera. Use the following set of attributes to describe each product family:

- *Name the product family*—Give each product family a unique and descriptive name. Example: "Baked Goods" is the product family for the pastries.
- *Clearly state the product and/or service value-added*—The value-added of the product should match the customer needs of the market segment. Product example: baked fresh on-site, warm, affordable. Service example: attractive, clean seating.
- *End-customer cost meets the market segment expectation*—The product COGS before logistics costs, before distribution costs, and before margins can only be a fraction of the market expectation. Otherwise, the product solution is not viable; it must be redefined and redesigned before a supply chain network can be implemented. Example: A pastry cost of $1.75 for a pastry price of $3 works, while a pastry cost of $3.25 for a pastry price of $3 does not work.

- *Identify unusual component life cycle supply issues*—A product may be designed using high volume components from another industry to reduce costs. But such components may be near their end of life and become unavailable. Example: The entrepreneur may benefit from a one-time discount sale on butter and mistakenly costs her product based on that one-time discount.
- *Know the product's geographical boundaries*—Packaging, labeling, and regulatory requirements vary from country to country. A product developed for North America may have issues preventing its sale in Europe or Asia. Example: Depending upon the destination of each bus route, there may be ethnic preferences in pastries.
- *Identify any contextual supply-driven constraints*—Determine if the throughput of the product is somehow limited by a raw material constraint or a critical process capacity constraint. Example: Should the pastry chef leave the business, there would be no product to sell.
- *Understand any regulatory product constraints*—Regulatory compliance can impact product design in many ways, from the product surface area required for labeling to import classification and export licensing to transportation limits due to a hazardous material. Example: The pastry shop displays prominent listings of the caloric content of its baked goods and a notification of "no trans fats." The business prominently displays its Board of Health Certificate.

"Show Stoppers" in Connecting Market Demand with Product Supply

Supply chain construction is all about connecting market demand with product supply. In the pastry shop example, a single product supply is to be connected with two different market segment demands. Baked Goods is to be connected with Bus Commuters, and Baked Goods is to be connected with Pedestrian Shoppers. Each demand channel needs to be built and operated separately. You will notice that some of the demand attributes are matched directly with product attributes, while the remaining demand attributes are matched with the design and operation of the supply chain network.

- *Customer needs* (market) to match *product value-added* (product)—A mismatch here is a show stopper because the business will never achieve its intended throughput.
- *Cost expectation* (market) to match *product pricing* (product)—A mismatch here is a show stopper because the business will never achieve its intended profitability.
- *Delivery expectation* (market) to match the *network operation* (network)—The delivery expectation drives inventory investment, which largely determines the cash requirement for the business.

- *Temporal boundary* (market) to match the *network operation* (network)—The temporal boundary is reflected in such considerations as freshness, seasonality, and lost opportunity for capacity utilization.
- *Geographical boundary* (market) to match the *product design* (product) and *network design and operation* (network)—The geographical boundary is reflected in the rate of expansion of the business. It is a common mistake to attempt to supply too large of a geography with too little resource or with the wrong product. The business growth slows because of country-specific regulatory hurdles, poor delivery, poor customer service, and poor understanding of cultural preferences.
- *Demand-driven contextual constraint* (market undersized or saturated) to match *supply-driven contextual constraint* (product raw material limit or critical capacity constraint)—A mismatch here will artificially limit the maximum throughput the business can achieve.

Write a Supply Chain Construction Requirements Specification

Once company executives define a one-sentence project objective, staff the project team, and set calendar time and budgetary limits, the work of the supply chain construction project team can begin. The project team's first task is to write the Supply Chain Construction Requirements Specification (SCCRS). This greatly helps to scope the project, provide focus, and engage the project team members and provide a reference check for project results. When the requirements specification is missing, the construction project is doomed.

The Structure of the SCCRS

The SCCRS has three sections (see Table 1.3). The top section documents the construction project objective. This comes mostly from a high-level executive directive. The middle section documents the customer-driven and internally focused specifications for the network container. The customer-driven specification is the competitive price/landed cost point for the end customer that is greatly impacted by your choice of a factory and distributor. The bottom section documents the customer-driven and internally focused specifications for filling the network container with product contents. The customer-driven specification is the competitive delivery lead time that is greatly impacted by inventory placement. By the end of supply chain construction, the project team has to validate acceptable ranges for each specification in their plan A solution. Otherwise, earlier decisions must be revised with the construction details iterated to plan B.

Table 1.3 SCCRS Format

Attribute	*Description*		
Network type	1. Document the construction project objective		
Market segment			
Product family			
Project objective			
Specification	*Value*	*Dimensions*	*Validation*
Customer focused Price/landed cost	2. Build the network container		☐Accept ☐Reject
Other specifications Internally focused			
Customer focused Delivery lead time	3. Fill with product contents		☐Accept ☐Reject
Other specifications Internally focused			

Section 1 of Table 1.3 is completed for the pastry shop example, as follows:

- *Network type*—A forward supply chain.

  Are you building a forward network, a forward network with a service component, or a reverse network? Write separate requirement specifications for forward and reverse networks.
- *Market segment*—Bus commuters, grab and go, until 11:15 a.m., exact dollar amounts.

  You need to be able to articulate the market segment being served and understand the customer needs to be met. Document each delivery channel separately.
- *Product family*—Baked goods: three kinds of \$3 pastries with a \$1 lemonade drink.

  Your supply chain may deliver multiple product families. When product families manufactured by the same supply chain are matched with different market segments, write separate requirement specifications for each market segment.
- *Project objective*—"To construct a forward supply chain to deliver fresh pastries, baked on-site, to bus commuters."

  Write the project objective as a complete sentence.

How to Draw the Supply Chain Echelon Map

Writing a specification for the network container begins with a one-page Supply Chain Echelon Map. This is a rough sketch of the relationships that will be necessary to connect the material flow from the set of raw material suppliers required to manufacture the product and on through distribution to reach the intended market segment. The APICS Supply Chain Council's Supply Chain Operations Reference model, SCOR (http://www.apics.org/sites/apics-supply-chain-council), offers a set of generic terms that neatly describe these network relationships: Source, Make, Deliver, and Return. Each of these relationships is defined and described in detail in this book in Chapter 5: "Make," Chapter 6: "Source," Chapter 7: "Deliver," and Chapter 8: "Return." Returning once again to the pastry shop example, look at Figure 1.1. The entrepreneur starts her Supply Chain Echelon Map by drawing the three circles in row 1 for Source, Make, and Deliver. An echelon is an independent business organization that buys upstream and sells downstream. In row 2, she begins to name the supply chain relationships she will need for the material flow to deliver pastries to her clientele. She realizes that she will make her product at the bakery and deliver her product at the pastry shop. The bakery will need a supply base for flour, butter, and all the other ingredients in her recipes. After thinking about her supply chain a little more, the entrepreneur realizes that there are two distinct delivery channels, as shown in row 3. One delivery channel serves bus commuters at the counter, while the second delivery channel serves the

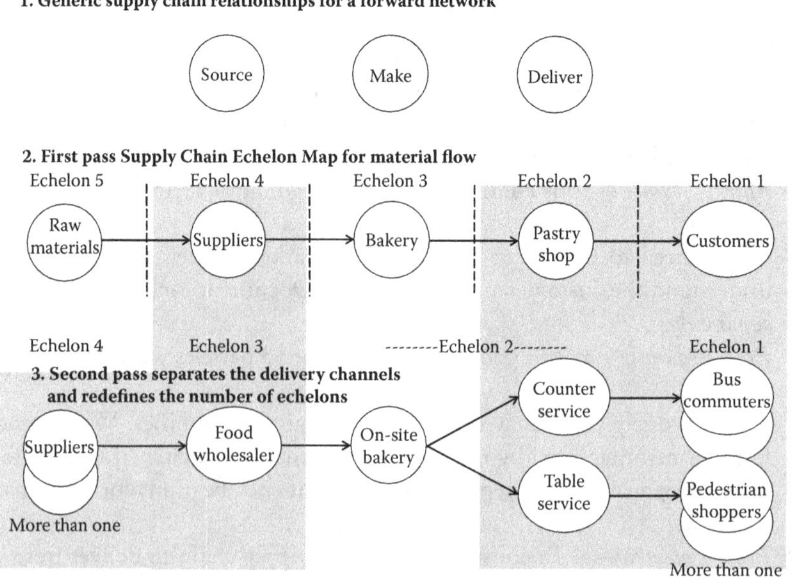

Figure 1.1 Supply Chain Echelon Map for the pastry shop and on-site bakery.

downtown pedestrian shoppers at the tables. She also thinks that while it may be a little more expensive, it will be much easier to start by buying all the ingredients from a food wholesaler, like Costco. In row 3, the on-site bakery and the pastry shop are included within echelon 2. This is because they are both in the same physical building, and the entrepreneur does not plan to separate their accounting.

In drawing your Supply Chain Echelon Map, you will want to begin with selecting a factory and a distributor because the costs associated with this pair will most likely determine whether or not you can meet your end-customer price/landed cost target. Second, determine the supply base, which is based on the set of suppliers necessary to provide raw materials and component parts to the factory for all the products you plan to make. Third, determine each delivery channel that will connect your distributor with your end customer. Figure 1.2 is a generic supply

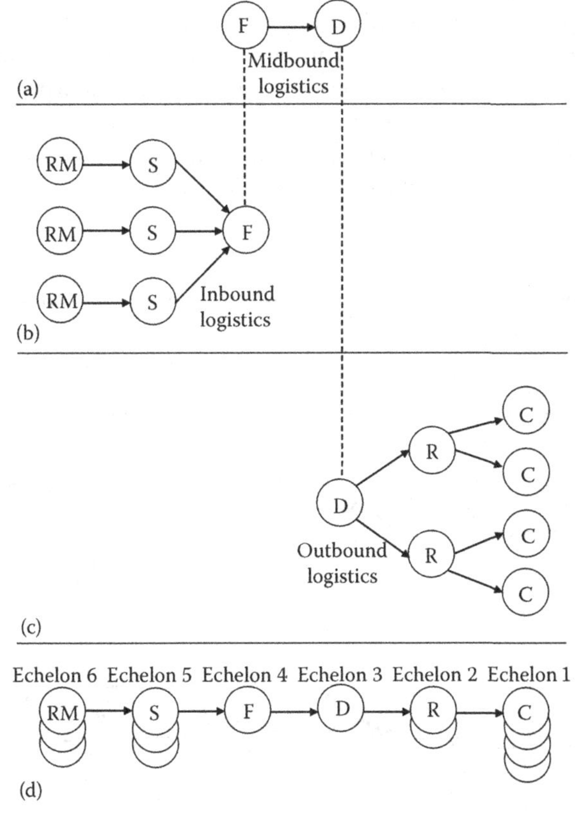

Figure 1.2 Supply Chain Echelon Map for end-to-end material flow: (a) the factory and distributor; (b) the supply base; (c) the delivery channels; (d) material flow. C = customer; D = distributor; F = factory; R = retailer; RM = raw material; S = supplier.

chain map of echelon by echelon material flow from raw materials to the end customer. The echelons are numbered, starting with the end customer as echelon 1 and numbering upstream. Notice how the upstream supply base and the downstream delivery channels may be more or less complex depending upon your requirements. Your supply chain may have a larger or smaller number of echelons.

Specifying the Network Container

The arrows on the Supply Chain Echelon Map represent material flow. The Raw Material Supplier sells downstream to the SOURCE trading partner; the SOURCE trading partner buys upstream from the Raw Material Supplier. The SOURCE trading partner sells downstream to the MAKE trading partner; the MAKE trading partner buys upstream from the SOURCE trading partner. The MAKE trading partner sells downstream to the DELIVER trading partner; the DELIVER trading partner buys upstream from the MAKE trading partner. And the DELIVER trading partner sells downstream to the Customer; the Customer buys upstream from the DELIVER trading partner. A trading partner is any independent organization buying from an upstream echelon and selling to a downstream echelon, while conducting the majority of its business within the network. In order for each of these material flows to work, there must be complete closed-loop order-to-delivery

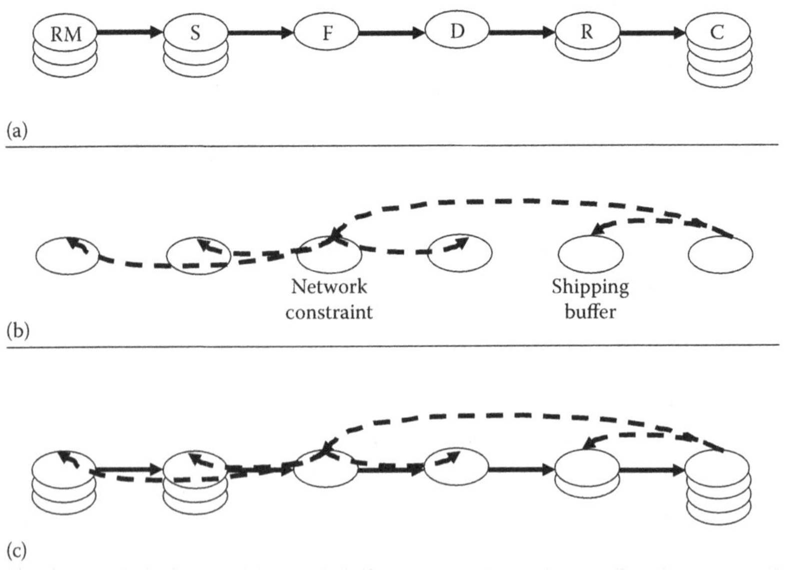

Figure 1.3 Order-to-delivery network connections: (a) material flow; (b) order information flow; (c) order-to-delivery cycles. C = customer; D = distributor; F = factory; R = retailer; RM = raw material; S = supplier.

connections all along the material flow path of the network container. Figure 1.3 shows the development of such order-to-delivery connections. Chapter 9: "Demand Planning" explains in detail why and how the customer order is communicated first to the shipping buffer and the network constraint before being rebroadcast from the network constraint to the remainder of the network trading partners.

In order for each material flow to work, there must be complete closed-loop invoice-to-cash connections all along the material flow path of the network container. Payment for each purchase is triggered when the material is received at the buyer's location, and it can be matched with the buyer's purchase order and seller's invoice. Figure 1.4 shows the development of such invoice-to-cash connections. Chapter 4: "Cash Flow" explains in detail the why and how of factory and distributor cash flows.

Working from the Supply Chain Echelon Map, the specifications for the network container include throughput, price/landed cost, and the cash-to-cash cycle. Throughput is determined from a forecast of customer demand and the minimum end-to-end network capacity. Price/landed cost is determined from the factory rates and markup, distributor rates and markup, and logistics cost factors that each add to or multiply the product's direct material cost and direct labor cost. The

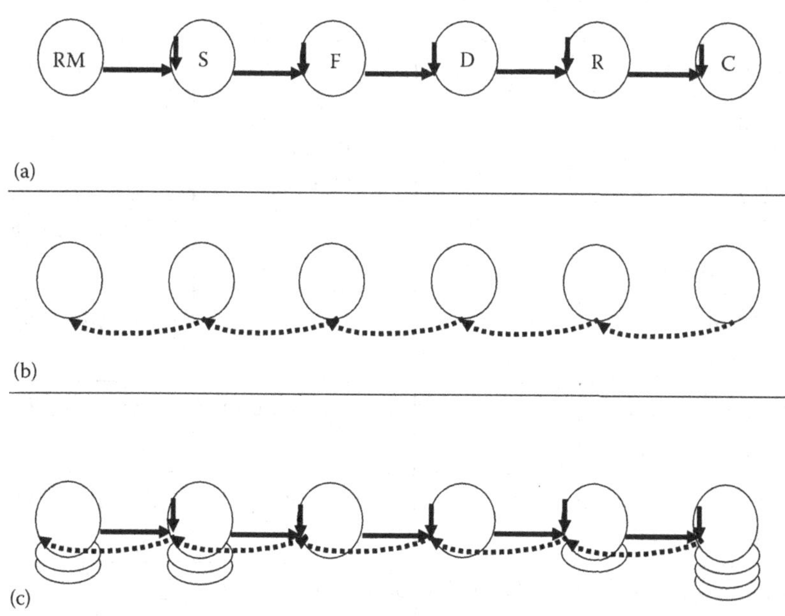

Figure 1.4 Invoice-to-cash network connections: (a) invoice information flow with material receipt triggers; (b) cash payment flow; (c) invoice-to-cash cycles. C = customer; D = distributor; F = factory; R = retailer; RM = raw material; S = supplier.

end-customer price/landed cost must fit the competitive situation within the market segment. Cash-to-cash cycles depend upon network structure and the payment terms associated with the factory and the distributor.

Table 1.4 adds the network container specification details to the middle section of the SCCRS. Chapter 11: "Performance Measures" gives a detailed explanation for each specification. Chapter 2: "The Blueprint" provides a complete detailed numerical example for a forward supply chain network, and Chapter 8: "Return" provides a complete detailed numerical example for a reverse supply chain network.

Table 1.4 SCCRS for the Network Container

Attribute	*Description*		
Network type	[*Forward network*] or [*with service component*] or [*reverse network*]		
Market segment	[*Enter*] or [*switch*] or [*existing*] or [*exit*]		
Product family	[*New*] or [*rollover*] or [*existing*] or [*obsolete*]		
Project objective	We are constructing a [*network type*] to connect this [*product family*] supply with this [*market segment*] demand.		
Specification	*Value*	*Dimensions*	*Validation*
Throughput		Dollars per month, or units per month	☐Accept ☐Reject
Factory Cash-to-cash cycle	Velocity Variability	Days +/– +/– Days	☐Accept ☐Reject
Distributor Cash-to-cash cycle	Velocity Variability	Days +/– +/– Days	☐Accept ☐Reject
Factory to distributor Price/landed cost		Dollars per unit	☐Accept ☐Reject
Distributor to store Price/landed cost		Dollars per unit	☐Accept ☐Reject
Customer focused Delivery lead time	Fill with product contents		☐Accept ☐Reject
Other specifications Internally focused			

- *Throughput*—This determines the top line revenue on your income statement.
- *Cash-to-cash cycle*—This determines the cash you need from your balance sheet to fund inventory.

Cash-to-cash velocity = Days of inventory + Days of receivables − Days of payables (1.1)

Cash-to-cash variability = Days of variance in the cash-to-cash cycle

- *Price/landed cost*—This determines price competitiveness in the market.

Buyer's Cost = Seller's price + Logistics costs (1.2)

  - Price/landed cost at the factory/distributor interface
  - Price/landed cost at the supplier/factory interface
  - Price/landed cost at the distributor/store interface

Specifying the Product Contents

Writing a specification for the product contents begins by splitting the end-to-end supply chain network in two. The upstream portion, beginning with raw materials, is called the push zone. The downstream portion ending with the end customer is called the pull zone. The two zones connect at an inventory location called the push/pull boundary (see Figure 1.5). Locating the push/pull boundary determines both the delivery lead time seen by the end customer and the operating strategy used to replenish inventory. A forecast drives inventory through the push zone into the push/pull boundary. A customer order drives inventory out of the push/pull boundary and through the pull zone.

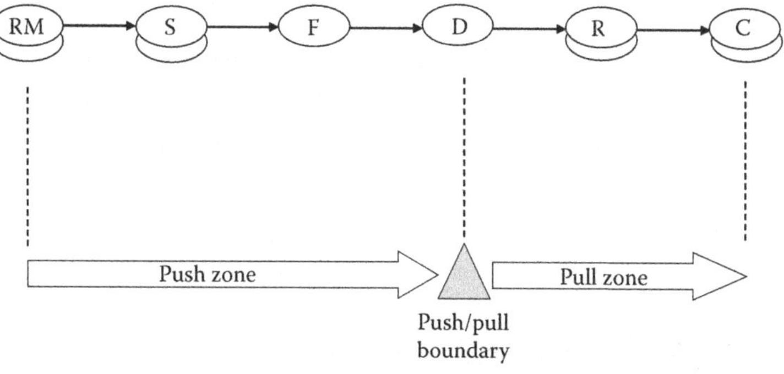

Figure 1.5 The push zone and the pull zone. C = customer; D = distributor; F = factory; R = retailer; RM = raw material; S = supplier.

Production and inventory planning and control in the push zone are accomplished through the series of tools shown in Figure 1.6. APICS, the Association for Operations Management (http://www.apics.org) certifies individuals in the use of these tools. The Demand Forecast drives the Sales & Operation Plan (S&OP). The S&OP drives the Distribution Requirements Plan (DRP). The DRP drives the Master Production Schedule (MPS). The MPS drives both the Materials Requirements Plan and the Capacity Requirement Plan. Product bills of materials (BOMs) and inventory balances are inputs used by all these tools. Chapter 9: "Demand Planning" covers how to forecast, while Chapter 10: "Inventory Management" covers planning in the push zone.

Production and inventory planning and control in the pull zone are accomplished by ensuring that the right mix of product can flow to the customer at a maximum rate of throughput. The push zone must be capable of the maximum capacity and have the maximum inventory levels preloaded before operations begin (see Figure 1.7). Inventory will turn only when demand for an item can be matched with supply. Chapter 10: "Inventory Management" covers planning in the pull zone.

Working from the push/pull boundary, the specifications for the product contents include inventory turns for the factory and the distributor, delivery lead time, the planning horizon, and return on invested capital (ROIC) for the factory and the distributor. Inventory turns are determined by the product-dependent placement and quantity of inventory held throughout the network. Delivery lead time is determined by the location of the push/pull boundary, which in turn is determined

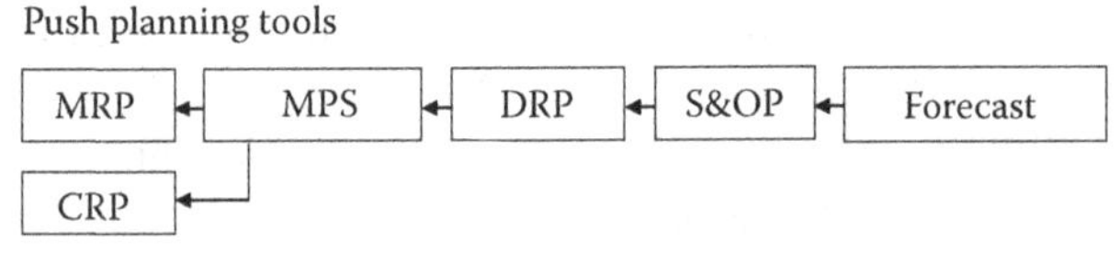

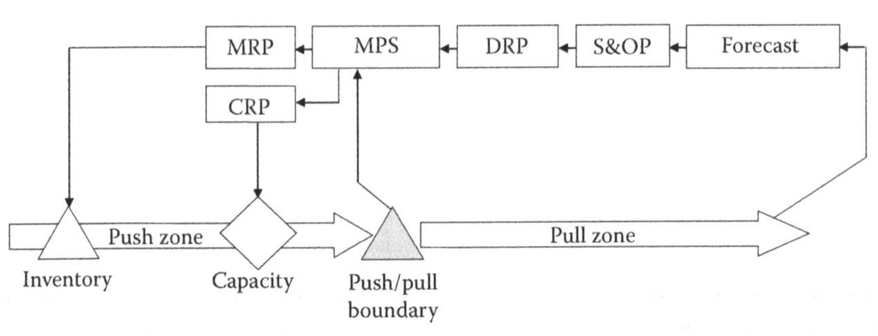

Figure 1.6 Push planning tools.

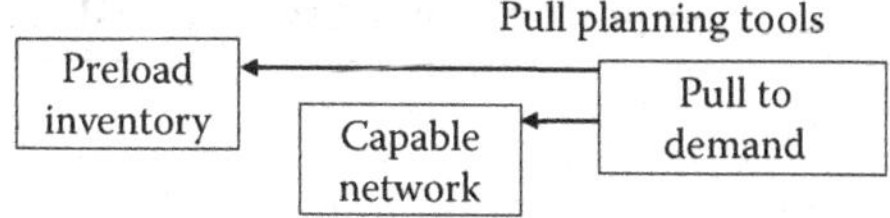

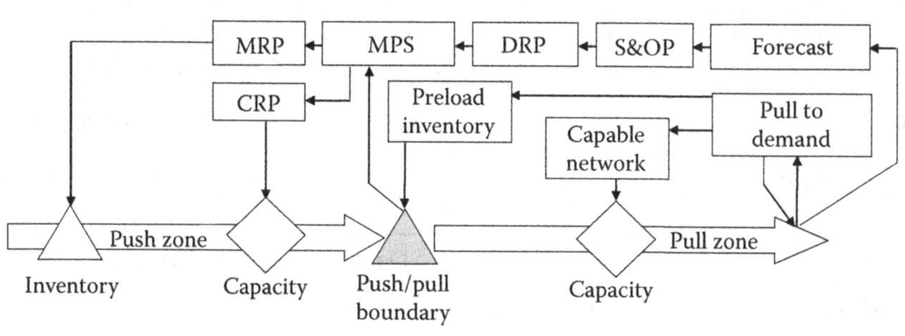

Figure 1.7 Integrated push and pull planning tools.

from the competitive situation within the market segment. The planning horizon is determined by product structure. ROIC is a calculation based, in part, on both the profit margin from the income statement and the inventory, accounts receivable, and accounts payable from the balance sheet.

Table 1.5 is the complete SCCRS. Chapter 11: "Performance Measures" gives a detailed explanation for each specification. A numerical value is assigned to each specification in the "Value" column, and you are given an opportunity to accept or reject the resulting actual supply chain performance in the "Validation" column. Chapter 2: "The Blueprint" provides a complete detailed numerical example for a forward supply chain network, and Chapter 8: "Return" provides a complete detailed numerical example for a reverse supply chain network.

- *Network inventory*—This determines the inventory investment on your balance sheet.
  - Raw material and finished goods inventory at the factory
  - Cycle stock inventory at the distributor
- *Delivery lead time*—This determines delivery competitiveness in the market.

$$\text{Vocalize from the Push/Pull Boundary} = \text{Days of Delivery Lead Time} \quad (1.3)$$

$$\text{Visualize to the Push/Pull Boundary} = \text{Days of Planning Horizon} \quad (1.4)$$

Table 1.5 Complete Supply Chain Construction Requirements Specification

Attribute	*Description*		
Network type	[*Forward network*] or [*with service component*] or [*reverse network*]		
Market segment	[*Enter*] or [*switch*] or [*existing*] or [*exit*]		
Product family	[*New*] or [*rollover*] or [*existing*] or [*obsolete*]		
Project objective	We are constructing a [*network type*] to connect this [*product family*] supply with this [*market segment*] demand.		
Specification	*Value*	*Dimensions*	*Validation*
Throughput		Dollars per month, or units per month	☐Accept ☐Reject
Factory Cash-to-cash cycle	Velocity Variability	Days +/– +/– Days	☐Accept ☐Reject
Distributor Cash-to-cash cycle	Velocity Variability	Days +/– +/– Days	☐Accept ☐Reject
Factory to distributor Price/landed cost		Dollars per unit	☐Accept ☐Reject
Distributor to store Price/landed cost		Dollars per unit	☐Accept ☐Reject
Factory Raw material (RM) and finished goods (FG) inventory		Dollars or turns	☐Accept ☐Reject
Distributor Cycle stock inventory		Dollars or turns	☐Accept ☐Reject
Delivery lead time	Vocalize Visualize	Days Days	☐Accept ☐Reject
Factory ROIC		Percent	☐Accept ☐Reject
Distributor ROIC		Percent	☐Accept ☐Reject

- *Return on invested capital (ROIC)*—This is a calculated percentage that keeps your attention focused on both the income statement and the balance sheet. Improvement in shareholder stock price for a public company generally correlates with improvement in ROIC.

$$\text{ROIC} = \frac{\$\text{After tax profit/month} \times 12 \text{ months}}{\begin{array}{c}\$\text{Inventory} + \$\text{Production capacity assets} \\ + \$\text{Accounts receivable} - \$\text{Accounts payable}\end{array}} \times 100\% \qquad (1.5)$$

Study the Blueprint before Beginning Construction

The SCCRS is often missing from the supply chain construction project. This is also the step, when missing or incomplete, that is most likely to cause the project to fail because the team objective is fuzzy. How can you build a business without having a plan for your supply chain? You will return to the SCCRS again and again to check your progress, evaluate alternative approaches, and validate/diagnose your complete supply chain solution.

The Supply Chain Construction Blueprint presented next in Chapter 2: "The Blueprint" walks you step by step through what has to be done to build the network container and fill it with product contents. It is a really good idea to read through The Blueprint, and this book, before beginning construction. The questions that The Blueprint will raise are important questions that must be resolved before your supply chain construction project can be completed. A few examples might include the following: Is your supply chain too long to achieve a competitive product price? How much inventory do you need to keep, and how will you initially pay for this investment? What are the key obstacles the project team will have to overcome? Is your supply chain project properly aligned with the critical success factors in your business? It will take more than good luck to complete a successful project.

In Summary

The primary purpose of this book is to teach those unskilled in the art how to construct a new supply chain from scratch and begin its operation successfully. The secondary purpose of this book is to teach those with some practical business experience how to successfully modify an existing supply chain and continue operations competitively. This chapter presents three key tools: the Eight-Step Approach to conduct a successful supply chain construction project, the SCCRS to document requirements, and the Supply Chain Echelon Map to diagram material flow in the network. Chapter 2: "The Blueprint" presents the Supply Chain Construction Blueprint used to build the network container and to fill it with product contents.

Chapter 2

The Blueprint—"Make It Work"

This chapter presents The Supply Chain Construction Blueprint. The Blueprint is grouped into four sections: (1) project setup, (2) construction of the network container, (3) filling the network container with product contents, and (4) start-up stabilization. The project setup ensures that the supply chain construction project has an objective, a project team, a timeline, and a budget. The supply chain construction begins with the Supply Chain Construction Requirements Specification (SCCRS). The network container is built to specification connecting the market segment with the product while meeting a competitive end-customer price/landed cost. The network container is filled to specification with product contents by transforming raw materials into end products and delivering these products while meeting a competitive delivery lead time. Trading partner cash flow and inventory turns are key parts of The Blueprint. The start-up stabilization validates intended performance levels and provides diagnostics tools to isolate and resolve any start-up issues with the new or modified supply chain. The bulk of this chapter is a step-by-step comprehensive example of the construction of a forward supply chain network. Chapter 8: "Return" presents a step-by-step comprehensive example of the construction of a reverse supply chain network.

You Don't Know What You Don't Know

They met a week later, giving Jerry, the vice president (VP) of Marketing, a little time to find out more about the market from the Computer Products Division. Alice was not present because of the demands on her expertise for the quarter end closing.

Steve, president of the Power Products Division, kicked off the meeting, "If we are going to start a new business, then we need a plan that all of us can support."

"Well, I need to know a lot more about competitive price points and the interface specifications for the new server family before my engineers can begin to design a product," offered Herb. "How long does the battery have to last? Do we need a quick charge capability? Should we protect against line distortion or just line dropout?"

Jerry replied, "My team has learned that Computer Products expects to sell 30% high power servers, 50% mid power servers, and 20% low power servers. And, the disc packs lose 65% of their rotational speed in four seconds."

George, the VP of Quality, responded, "I don't know what all that technical stuff means, but let's kick this discussion up a notch. We need to talk about a plan. I think the following analogy is appropriate here to keep this meeting on-track. When someone decides to build a new building in the city, they hire an architect to draw up a plan of the kind of building that will satisfy the client's need for function, will fit the context of the surrounding environment, and will meet the client's cost target. You remember that the folks sitting in this meeting did just that, when we decided a couple of years ago to expand the factory building on this site. After the architectural plan is drawn, a general contractor is hired to construct the building. Along the way, the architect consults with certain engineers for key design items like the steel structure. We need to think in terms of the architect, the engineer, and the general contractor."

"That's very helpful George," said Steve. "We need an architectural phase to draw up a plan. That will come from this group of functional VPs. And we need a construction phase to implement the plan. That will come from the project team that we choose to put in place. Certain specialty areas of expertise, like the battery technology that is new to us, will require engineering support and maybe even some third party consulting."

"That's exactly right!" said George.

Tom, the VP of Manufacturing, had been listening intently and offered, "You know, the output from the architect is more than just a pretty rendering of a future building. I remember that one of the key line items, when we paid the architect for this building, was The Blueprint. The general contractor used The Blueprint to build this factory in a way that met our specifications and cost target. While The Blueprint did not necessarily explain every detail of how to build our factory, it focused the knowledge and experience of the general contractor and kept him on task. After reviewing The Blueprint and asking the general contractor and architect questions in preparation for meeting with the City Municipal Planning Board, we discovered there were many things that we didn't know that we didn't know."

"Will such a blueprint help us answer the question how big is this business opportunity? How do we know if this opportunity is real before making such a large investment?" Steve asked.

George replied, "Let's talk first about how The Blueprint applies to our new business venture. I mentioned at our last meeting that we need a new supply chain to deliver the new uninterruptable power supply (UPS) products to a new base of customers. The throughput achieved through a supply chain is the revenue shown on the income statement. The right factory and distributor margins in a supply chain can make the business profitable. The inventory turns across a supply chain determine the inventory investment that must be made to sustain the business. And, the cash flow generated within a supply chain helps to fund business growth. OK, I'll stop lecturing now."

"So, The Blueprint looks at top line revenue dollars and bottom line profit?" Steve asked again. "Why isn't Alice here for this conversation?"

"Not quite so fast.... The Blueprint that I'm speaking about is a construction plan for the supply chain," replied George. "Speaking from a quality process perspective, remember you can't launch this new business without a supply chain. Our present factory doesn't build a UPS product. Our present supply chain doesn't involve distribution and retail. Our present sales force doesn't sell to Computer Product customers. And, our present customer base doesn't buy a battery backup for a power supply. We have no hope of success in this new business without building a new supply chain, in parallel with designing a new UPS product and in parallel with cultivating a new market segment. This is going to take our best minds and significant investment."

"OK. I think I get that," said Steve. "Herb, how do you see a UPS product design evolving? Jerry, what do you really know about customer demand in this new market? Tom, can our factory build this UPS?"

Herb replied, "We can leverage the power mesh design and the server interface design from our latest generation of products. I am already working on identifying a battery consultant to work with our engineers. We will probably have to shift one or two firmware designers into writing application software. My engineers are fully engaged on other projects; the big issue will be to decide which of our current projects to delay or cancel so that I can staff electrical and mechanical engineers on the UPS project."

Jerry replied, "I plan to recruit a sales manager from Computer Products. Being part of the same corporation, we can leverage recent market surveys conducted by the Computer Products Division. I'm not worried about conquering the market. We would be selling through the value-added reseller (VAR) network established by Computer Products. Steve, you know that I also have considerable wholesale and retail sales experience in my background."

Tom replied, "In a nutshell...yes, we can build it."

"George, what exactly is covered by this Supply Chain Construction Blueprint?" Tom asked.

"That's a great question. To be honest, I'm not an expert on this, but I know someone in our company who is. In layman's terms, here is how it was explained to me. The Blueprint has a couple of major sections. One section leads the project team through the sequence of tasks that builds the network container. The network container connects material flow from raw materials to end customers. You know, the supply base, the factory, the distributor, and the resellers. Another major section leads the project team through the sequence of tasks that fills the network container with the product contents. You know, the transformation of raw materials into products, inventory control, demand planning, and fulfillment."

"Sounds complicated. Is this blueprint very long? We don't have much time to go to market," said Jerry.

"As I understand it, the whole Supply Chain Construction Blueprint is about 20 steps," replied George.

"Who is this supply chain expert to whom you have been eluding?" Herb asked.

"It is Bill, our Director of Supply Chain currently on Tom's staff. He knows all about supply chains and is APICS certified in the field. Bill is published and well respected among his peers. Let me remind you that he successfully led the small team project that outsourced our sheetmetal shop last year."

"I'm not sure I can run Manufacturing without Bill," complained Tom.

"I understand how you feel." Steve ended the meeting with this directive, "It's good to know that about Bill. I want the rest of you to start thinking about who we want to assign to the UPS Project Team before we meet next time. This project will be a career opportunity for our best people."

Follow the Blueprint

Follow the Supply Chain Construction Blueprint shown below in the sequence presented. Build the network container before filling it with product contents. Complete explanations and reasons for each step in The Blueprint are found in the remaining chapters of this book. Whether you are expanding or contracting, whether you are a small or a large organization, whether you are manufacturing or service or recycling oriented, each step in the construction template has the flexibility to be adapted to your situation.

Blueprint to Construct the Network Container

The network container connects the market segment with the product's raw materials as specified in the SCCRS. The factory-to-midbound logistics-to-distributor network relationships are determined first because these decisions make or break the end-to-end price/landed cost specification. After establishing the project team in Table 2.1 steps A and B, steps 1 through 10 of the Supply Chain Construction Blueprint detail the construction task sequence. The chapter(s) listed in the right-hand column provides detailed how-to information for that step. Notice that it may be necessary to iterate from step 3 back to step 2 to meet the price/landed cost specification.

Table 2.1 The Network Container Construction Blueprint

Step	*Construction Task*	*Task Description*	*Chapter*
Follow These Steps to Set Up the Supply Chain Construction Project			
A	Set the business objective for the supply chain project.	Describe the business objective for connecting the market segment and the product.	1
B	Staff the construction project, develop the project timeline, and plan the project budget.	Formally approve project staffing. Document a project timeline and project budget.	3, 4
Follow These Steps to Construct the Network Container			
1	Write the network container portion of SCCRS.	Define the throughput, price/landed cost, and cash-to-cash velocity specifications for the forward (or reverse) network container.	1, 11
2	Use the supply chain echelon map to budget price/landed cost end-to-end echelon by echelon.	Map the supply chain echelons for material flow. Budget downstream, midstream, upstream, and logistics price/landed cost for competitive pricing and profitable margins in each echelon.	1, 3, 4
3	Start midstream with the factory through midbound logistics to the distributor (material flow).	Select a factory based on its labor rate, markup, process capability, and capacity to meet all requirements; select a distributor based on its location, inventory capability, capacity, and markup to meet all requirements.	5, 7
	If price/landed cost specification cannot be met, iterate back through step 2.		
4	Detail the upstream supply base through inbound logistics to the factory (material flow).	Build a base of suppliers to support the composite BOM. Keep direct material and inbound logistics costs within budget.	6

(*Continued*)

Table 2.1 (Continued) The Network Container Construction Blueprint

Step	*Construction Task*	*Task Description*	*Chapter*
Follow These Steps to Construct the Network Container			
5	Detail the downstream distributor through outbound logistics to the customer (material flow).	Build a delivery channel to reach the intended market segment according to customer preference. Keep price markups and outbound logistics costs within budget.	7
6	Add the service element.	Add the capability and capacity for any customer facing service element.	7
7	Connect demand broadcast information with material flow and test (information flow).	Connect customer demand to the shipping buffer and the network constraint. Rebroadcast demand in parallel from the network constraint to all other trading partners. Exercise and test every order-to-delivery loop.	7, 9
8	Connect requests for payment (information flow) with cash payments and test (cash flow).	Connect invoice information with cash payment for each networked pair of buyers and sellers. Exercise and test every invoice-to-cash loop.	4, 7
9	Detail the factory and distributor steady-state cash-to-cash cycle.	Detail the cash-to-cash cycle for the factory and for the distributor. Maximize cash velocity and minimize cash variability.	4
10	Plot a Value Circle to validate network container performance measures: throughput, cash-to-cash velocity, cash-to-cash variability, and price/landed cost.	Use the Value Circle to validate that the completed network container construction can meet the SCCRS.	11

Blueprint to Fill the Network Container with Product Contents

The network container is filled with product contents by transforming raw materials into end products as specified in the SCCRS. The push/pull boundary location and operating strategy are determined first because these decisions make or break the inventory turns specification. Table 2.2 steps 11 through 18 of the Supply Chain Construction

Table 2.2 The Product Contents Construction Blueprint

Step	*Construction Task*	*Task Description*	*Chapter*
Follow These Steps to Fill the Network Container with Product Contents			
11	Write the product contents portion of the SCCRS.	Define the inventory turns, vocalize, visualize, and ROIC specifications for product content in the forward (or reverse) network.	1, 11
12	Decide the operating strategy, locate the push/pull boundary, and identify the network constraint.	Decide the product operating strategy as build-to-stock (BTS), assemble-to-order (ATO), build-to-order (BTO), or engineer-to-order (ETO). Locate the push/pull boundary to achieve a competitive delivery lead time. Identify the network constraint.	9
13	Compile the composite BOM.	Compile the list of all unique inventory items used across all products throughout the end-to-end network. Identify every inventory location for each inventory item in its respective supply chain echelon.	6, 10
14	Forecast demand.	Forecast demand over the planning horizon. Develop supply rate and mix forecasts.	9
15	Use the supply chain echelon map to budget inventory turns echelon by echelon.	Use the supply chain echelon map for material flow to budget downstream, midstream, and upstream inventory for competitive delivery and sustainable cash flow in each echelon. Determine the lot size, reorder point, and safety stock for each inventory item at each inventory location.	1, 3, 10
	If the inventory turns specification cannot be met, iterate back through step 13.		
16	Plan and control the push zone.	Implement sales and operations planning, rough cut capacity planning, distribution requirements planning, master production scheduling, materials requirements planning, and capacity planning.	10

(*Continued*)

Table 2.2 (Continued) The Product Contents Construction Blueprint

Step	*Construction Task*	*Task Description*	*Chapter*
Follow These Steps to Fill the Network Container with Product Contents			
17	Plan and control the pull zone.	Implement pull inventory and capacity planning and control. Consider postponement.	10
18	Plot a Value Circle to validate product contents performance measures; inventory turns, vocalize (pull), visualize (push), and ROIC.	Use the Value Circle to validate that the completed product content construction can meet the SCCRS	11
Follow These Steps to Stabilize the New or Modified Supply Chain			
19	Stabilize supply chain operations and end the construction project.	Use throughput, price/landed cost, and inventory diagnostics to attain the required level of performance. Stabilize operations and cash flow by changing product features or price points and by maintaining delivery lead time or trading information for inventory.	11, 12
20	Manage supply chain risk.	Manage supply chain risk through environmental scanning and scenario planning.	12

Blueprint detail the construction task sequence. Notice that it may be necessary to iterate from step 15 back through steps 13 and 14 to meet the end-to-end inventory turns specification. Finally, Table 2.2 steps 19 and 20 are used to stabilize the new or modified supply chain start-up.

Build a Forward Supply Chain— A Comprehensive Example

The following comprehensive case study details how to complete each step of the Supply Chain Construction Blueprint to build a forward supply chain. This case study is a compilation of experiences designed to teach the application of The Blueprint. Follow each of these steps, in sequence, to build your own multiechelon, high-throughput forward supply chain. Chapter 5: "Make," Chapter 6: "Source,"

Chapter 7: "Deliver," Chapter 9: "Demand Planning," and Chapter 10: "Inventory Management" address how to construct multiechelon supply chains.

Step A: Set the Business Objective Connecting the Market Segment and Product (Chapter 1)

In step A, you set the context for the market segment and product being connected by your supply chain. The following case study is a compilation of experiences designed to demonstrate how to apply The Blueprint by focusing on a single echelon with an average throughput of one unit per day. A Ceramic Arts Studio decides to expand their website to include an Internet store. The Ceramic Arts Studio currently organizes two local shows a year for their member artists, and they have been pleased with the volume of sales that have been achieved. Based on discussions with patrons and customers, they believe there is a strong market for one-of-a-kind items priced from $85 to $300 for home decorations and personal gifts. Customers are attracted to particular artists, the colors and quality of their works, the base material and technique used to craft their works, and the one-of-a-kind nature of owning their work at a reasonable price. The market segment of people wanting to own such art from these artists extends geographically beyond the distance that local customers are willing to travel to a show. Hence the decision is to open an Internet store with shipments from a new distribution center.

After a series of planning meetings, the executive committee of the Ceramic Arts Studio decides that the store catalog will only show items in-stock at the distribution center (DC). Member artists will deliver and consign their work to the DC; they will be paid in full within 10 days of a sale. Should another sales opportunity arise, the member artists can pull their work at any time. The DC will mark up the member artist's suggested price to cover expenses and generate a small profit. Initially, the DC will be sized to inventory a set number of pieces from each member artist plus additional inventory space that will be stocked at the discretion of the Ceramic Arts Studio. The Internet store catalog software will show full-screen, high-resolution color photos of the front, back, and bottom of each piece with some indication of its relative size. Each piece will feature a written description and the member artist's professional biography. Whenever a new piece is added to the inventory, the Internet store will generate an e-mail blast to a distribution list including anyone who has previously purchased from the store. All payments will be made by PayPal, and all shipments will be handled through UPS Ground. Each piece will be shipped with a signed certificate of authenticity from the appropriate member artist. All sales will be final, and no returns will be allowed.

Step B: Staff the Construction Project, Develop the Timeline, and Plan the Budget (Chapters 3, 4)

In step B, you staff the supply chain construction project, develop the project timeline with milestones, and plan the project budget. This forward network supply chain construction project might take two people four to six months to complete. Besides the expense of staffing, the project budget would depend largely upon the necessary investment for an information system and for inventory. The executive committee of the Ceramic Arts Studio recruits two members who are experienced, retired businessmen to setup the DC and Internet store over a four-month period on a shoestring budget. The project team is authorized to spend up to $1,000 for online cataloging and shopping cart software.

Step 1: Write the Network Container SCCRS (Chapters 1, 11)

In step 1, you describe the forward supply chain network and document the top half of the SCCRS for the network container. To begin documenting the SCCRS, the Ceramic Arts Studio needs a network echelon map with an estimate of throughput volumes and a per echelon price/landed cost budget. These estimates and budgets are refined with each successive step in the Supply Chain Construction Blueprint.

The project team meets at a diner and, over coffee, sketches the Supply Chain Echelon Map on a napkin as shown in Figure 2.1. Since the supply chain Echelon Map traces out material flow, the Internet store is not shown. The Internet store is only in the path of information flow and cash flow. The echelons are numbered starting with the customer in echelon 1 and working upstream to raw materials in echelon 4. This supply chain construction project is all about organizing and implementing

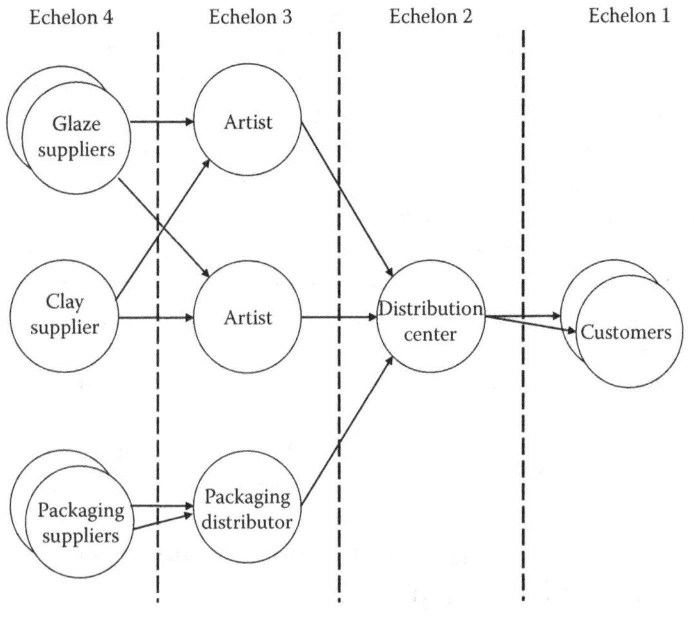

Figure 2.1 Forward supply chain echelon map.

distribution and its associated Internet store in echelon 2. The member artists in echelon 3 are the "Factories" in this supply chain. The shipping cartons and bubble wrap are to be purchased from a packaging supplies distributor, also located in echelon 3.

How to Estimate Throughput

The project team is concerned about how to finance the start-up of this supply chain construction project. Since the member artists agree to consign their work, the project avoids needing cash to buy start-up inventory. Stocking packaging materials is another matter altogether. The project team has some money to cover software for the Internet store, and the Ceramic Arts Studio already operates a website. The big concern is how to pay for a DC. Over coffee at a second meeting at the diner, the project team comes up with the idea of using a member's garage as a small DC to prove the feasibility of this endeavor.

The Ceramic Arts Studio has 21 member artists who participate regularly showing their work. The most prolific member produces two new pieces each month, while the least prolific produces two new pieces a year. They estimate their throughput to be ((1 member × 24 pieces) + (19 members × 12 pieces average) + (1 member × 2 pieces)) = 254 pieces/year, or about 21 pieces/month. Of course, their experience has shown that not every piece will sell; their supply chain may well be demand limited. On the other hand, throughput can grow with the addition of more member artists. This is an ultra-low-volume example of one shipment per day to demonstrate how to apply the Supply Chain Construction Blueprint.

How to Estimate Price/Landed Cost

When an item is sold, the DC pays the member artist's price plus nothing for midbound freight because every piece is hand delivered by the member artists. A part-time employee works at the DC each day to process orders off the website, enter new pieces into the online catalog, manage inventory, pack items, and hand off shipments to UPS. The employee's paid hours are a variable cost. When the daily items sold are low-price items, the employee works one hour a day. When the daily items sold are high-price items, the employee works two hours a day. The DC expenses include fixed costs for rent, utilities, insurance, and Internet access plus a variable cost for PayPal processing. Table 2.3 details the two extremes of the price/landed cost factors.

How to Estimate Cash-to-Cash Velocity

Velocity is the mean number of days, positive or negative, in the DC's cash-to-cash cycle. The average distributor price per unit is \$176. Suppose revenue ramps linearly from \$0 to 21 units × \$176/unit, or \$3,700 after 21 days. Customers pay through PayPal at the time of ordering, and the DC has immediate access to their payment. Member artists consign their work so the accounts payable for inventory is zero.

Table 2.3 Estimating the DC per Piece Price/Landed Cost for the Ceramic Arts Studio

	Example Lowest Price Product		*Example Highest Price Product*	
Cost Factor	*Markup Items*	*Line Total*	*Markup Items*	*Line Total*
Artist's price to the DC	$48.50		$240.00	
Midbound freight	$0.00		$0.00	
Packaging materials	$2.24		$2.24	
Authenticity certificate	$0.35		$0.35	
Total DC material		$51.09		$242.59
Part-time employee[a]	$8.80		$16.00	
Payroll taxes	$2.23		$6.05	
Total DC labor		$11.03		$22.05
Rent	$10.00		$10.00	
Total DC overhead		$10.00		$10.00
Utilities, taxes, insurance	$8.65		$8.65	
Internet access	$0.71		$0.71	
PayPal processing charge	$2.52		$9.00	
Before-tax profit[a]	$1.00		$7.00	
Total DC markup		$12.88		$25.36
Internet store catalog price		$85.00		$300.00
+Outbound freight (UPS)				
+Sales tax				

[a] Employee pay and profit are reduced when mostly lower-price items dominate.

Twenty percent of accounts payable are period expenses for rent and wages due at month end, and 80% of accounts payable are payments to the member artist due 10 days after each sale. Since all the monthly revenue in the steady state is paid by the customer before the month-end period expense has to be paid, the cash-to-cash velocity is related to paying the member artists. Step 9 below presents a detailed analysis to calculate velocity and to estimate variability.

$$\text{Cash-to-Cash Velocity} = 0 \text{ Days Inventory} + 0 \text{ Days Receivables} - 10 \text{ Days Payables} = -10 \text{ days}$$

The network container portion of the SCCRS can now be completed as shown in Table 2.4.

Table 2.4 SCCRS for the Ceramic Arts Studio Supply Chain

Attribute	*Description*		
Network type	Forward network		
Market segment	Individuals wanting to own inexpensive one-of-a-kind ceramic art hand crafted by domestic artists		
Product family	One-of-a-kind ceramic art		
Project objective	We are constructing a forward network that connects ceramic arts customers with ceramic arts studio member artists through an Internet store.		
Specification	*Value*	*Dimensions*	*Validation*
Throughput	21	Units per month	☐Accept ☐Reject
Distributor cash-to-cash cycle	Velocity –10	Days	☐Accept ☐Reject
Distributor/store price/landed cost	High: 300 Low: 85	Dollars per unit Dollars per unit	☐Accept ☐Reject
Inventory			
Delivery lead time			
Return on invested capital			

Step 2: Budget Price/Landed Cost End-to-End Echelon by Echelon (Chapters 1, 3, 4)

In step 2, you determine whether the number of supply chain echelons can yield profitable margins at the expected unit volumes. The Ceramic Arts Studio supply chain is unusual in that the expected average throughput is just one unit per day. The network container is a short four-echelon supply chain. Table 2.5 shows the

Table 2.5 The Echelon-by-Echelon Price/Cost Budget at One Shipment/Day

Price/Cost Item	*Lowest Price*	*Highest Price*	*Notes*
End customer's cost	$85.00+	$300.00+	Buyer echelon 1
Sales tax			State specific
Outbound freight			UPS distance, weight rate tariff
Distributor/Internet store price	$85.00	$300.00	Seller echelon 2
Distributor markup	$12.88	$25.36	
Distributor overhead	$10.00	$10.00	
Distributor labor	$11.03	$22.05	5 hours/week or 10 hours/week
Distributor material cost	$51.09	$242.59	Buyer echelon 2
Additional materials	$2.59	$2.59	Packaging and certificate
Midbound freight	$0.00	$0.00	Donated
Artist price	$48.50	$240.00	Seller echelon 3
Artist markup			
Artist overhead			
Artist labor			
Artist material cost			Buyer echelon 3
Inbound freight			
Supplier price			Seller echelon 4

price/landed cost budget echelon by echelon at the two price extremes. The budget is set from echelon 1 to achieve an $85 to $300 store price before shipping cost and sales tax. Note that because no physical material flows through the Internet store and because the Internet sore is not an independent organization, the Internet store does not add an echelon to the supply chain and does not add a price markup. The distributor price and the Internet store price are one in the same. To cover certain fixed costs in echelon 2, the DC has to carefully manage the hours the single employee can work each week relative to the daily prices of the pieces actually sold. Echelon 3 reflects the pricing set by the member artists. The Ceramic Arts Studio has no knowledge of the material costs, labor hours, or profit margins of the individual member artists. Echelon 4 is the going market price for molding clay, glaze, and other art supplies.

Step 3: Start Midstream with the Factory-to-Midbound Logistics-to-Distributor Material Flow (Chapters 5, 7)

In step 3, you choose the factory and distributor organizations and locations and the transportation mode for midbound logistics. In the Ceramic Arts Studio supply chain, the factories are the individual member artists. The member artists agree to hand deliver each new piece to the garage DC in person. Therefore, the member artists also provide the midbound logistics connection.

The project team discusses their requirements for the DC back at the diner over coffee. The facility must be large enough for rack space to accommodate up to 200 units. This will allow each of the 21 current member artists to consign up to five works apiece plus some room for works selected by the Ceramic Arts Studio plus some expansion for new members. There must be space to inventory a month's worth of packaging materials. When the employee is not present, the facility must be secure. The computer system running the Internet store will be located at the DC. There must be secure office space to hold the computer. There must be table space long enough to receive and unwrap artist's inventory and to wrap and ship customer orders. These musts and additional wants are shown in Table 2.6. The project team budgets $200/month for rent and sets out to locate and negotiate the use of a garage.

Step 4: Detail the Upstream Supply Base-to-Inbound Logistics-to-Factory Material Flow (Chapter 6)

In step 4, you determine supply base relationships and inbound logistics connections. The Ceramic Arts Studio supply chain has two sets of suppliers. The first set includes the art supplies, pottery clay, and glaze suppliers that each of the individual member artists uses to buy his/her raw materials. The member artists either

Table 2.6 Facility Selection Criteria for the DC

Priority	*Criteria*	*Validation*	*Value*
Must 1	Secure storage capacity	Secure cubic volume to inventory ceramics of varying shape and storage of packaging materials	Racking for 200 units and packaging
Must 2	Secure office space	Office space with the computer running the Internet store	Yes
Must 3	Throughput capacity	Table space to receive new inventory and to wrap and package inventory for shipment	One to four units/day
Must 4	Cost factors	Owner willing to rent garage for an extended time	$200/month
Want	Internet connection	Existing FiOS connection	Yes
Want	Location	Driveway access for UPS home pickup	Yes
Want	Easy access to washroom	Easy access to washroom for employee	Yes

shop themselves at art retail stores, in which case there is no inbound logistics cost, or order their raw materials online, in which case the cost of inbound logistics is added to the price. While there are many kinds of pottery clay and glazes, it is not unusual for several of the member artists to use some of the same local suppliers.

The DC uses a second set of suppliers to purchase shipping cartons, bubble wrap, labels, tapes, and other packaging materials. They decide to use the one-stop-shopping packaging distributor ULINE (www.uline.com) with two-day UPS Ground delivery lead time to the DC.

Step 5: Detail the Distributor-to-Outbound Logistics-to-Downstream Delivery Material Flow (Chapter 7)

In step 5, you determine the delivery channel relationships and outbound logistics connections. In the Ceramic Arts Studio supply chain, customer order information flows through the Internet store, payments flow through PayPal, and DC product shipments flow to the customer through UPS Ground. The DC employee manages the delivery channel by focusing on the following tasks:

- *Online catalog maintenance*—When a member artist consigns a new piece to the DC, digital photos of its front, bottom, and back have to be uploaded into the online catalog and its pricing posted. The member artist signs a certificate of authenticity to go with the work. Whenever a piece is sold, the item is removed from the online catalog.
- *Inventory management*—When a new piece is received, the DC inventory is incremented. Whenever a piece is sold, the DC inventory is decremented.
- *Order processing*—Whenever a piece is sold, the sale is confirmed back to the customer and the member artist is notified. Once processed through PayPal, the total customer payment is allocated among the DC for revenue, UPS for the outbound logistics charges, and the State for the sales tax. The customer is notified of the UPS tracking number the day the piece is shipped.
- *Shipment processing*—Whenever a piece is sold, the piece is pulled from inventory and carefully wrapped and packaged along with its certificate of authenticity signed by the artist. A UPS shipping label is printed from the UPS website. UPS is notified that a shipment is ready for pickup.

Step 6: Add Any Service Element (Chapter 7)

In step 6, you add any service that the network delivers to complement the product. Service elements often involve labor capacity, information flows, and cash flows. The Ceramic Arts Studio supply chain supports no additional customer services.

Step 7: Connect Demand Broadcast Information with Material Flow and Test (Chapters 7, 9)

In step 7, you match the information flows to replenish inventory with the material flows and test each connection. In the Ceramic Arts Studio supply chain, customers can buy only the items that are currently in inventory at the DC. Unlike most supply chains, the replenishment of the DC inventory is driven by supply rather than demand, i.e., whenever a member artist finishes a work. The member artist is told when the piece has sold, rather than when the piece is needed. On the other hand, packaging materials are stocked against future demand. Table 2.7 details each order information-to-material delivery loop in the network container echelon by echelon. Each loop should be tested during the supply chain construction project to verify that the connection is in place and working.

Table 2.7 Demand Information-to-Material Delivery Loops

Echelon 1 < > Echelon 2	
Customer < > DC	Customer orders on retail store website (information). DC accesses order from retail store website (information). DC picks and packs to customer order (material). DC ships item UPS Ground to customer (material).
Echelon 2 < > Echelon 3	
DC < > member artist(s)	Member artist brings piece to DC in person (material). Member artist consigns inventory to DC (information). DC informs member artist of sale (information).
DC < > packaging distributor	DC orders on packaging distributor website (information). Packaging distributor picks and packs to DC order (material). Packaging distributor ships items UPS Ground to DC (material).
Echelon 3 < > Echelon 4	
Member artist(s) < > pottery clay supplier	Member artist orders on pottery clay supplier website (information). Pottery clay supplier picks and packs to member artist order (material). Supplier ships items UPS Ground to member artist (material).
Member artist(s) < > glaze supplier(s)	Member artist orders on glaze supplier website (information). Glaze supplier picks and packs to artist order (material). Glaze supplier ships items UPS Ground to artist (material).

(*Continued*)

Table 2.7 (Continued) Demand Information-to-Material Delivery Loops

Echelon 3 < > Echelon 4	
Member artist(s) < > art supply supplier(s)	Member artist shops in-person at art supply store (information). Member artist hand carries items home (material).
Packaging distributor < > cardboard supplier	Packaging distributor sends order to cardboard supplier (information). Cardboard supplier fulfills packaging distributor order (material). Cardboard supplier ships items motor freight to packaging distributor (high cubic volume material).
Packaging distributor < > bubble wrap supplier	Packaging distributor sends order to bubble wrap supplier (information). Bubble wrap supplier fulfills packaging distributor order (material). Bubble wrap supplier ships items motor freight to packaging distributor (high cubic volume material).
Packaging distributor < > label + tape supplier(s)	Packaging distributor sends order to label + tape supplier (information). Label + tape supplier fulfills packaging distributor order (material). Label + tape supplier ships items UPS to packaging distributor (material).

Step 8: Connect Requests for Payment with Cash Payments and Test (Chapters 4, 7)

In step 8, you match requests for payment information with its respective cash flow and test each connection. The Ceramic Arts Studio supply chain uses three different kinds of invoice information-to-cash payment loops. First, even though sales are very low volume and may be infrequent, the DC gets its cash immediately through a customer PayPal transaction. Second, some suppliers get their cash immediately through a member artist credit card transaction. Third, other suppliers doing high volumes with the packaging distributor invoice and receive their cash payments under NET30 day terms. Table 2.8 details each invoice information-to-cash payment loop. Each loop should be tested during the supply chain construction project to verify that the connection is in place and working.

Table 2.8 Invoice Information-to-Cash Payment Loops

Echelon 1 < > Echelon 2	
Customer < > DC	Customer orders on Internet store website (information). Customer pays for order using PayPal (cash). DC accesses PayPal account balance (information). UPS requests payment (information). DC pays UPS from PayPal account (cash). DC pays sales tax from PayPal account (cash).
Echelon 2 < > Echelon 3	
DC < > member artist(s)	Member artist consigns inventory to DC (information). DC pays member artist from PayPal within 10 days of sale (cash).
DC < > packaging distributor	DC orders on packaging supplier website with credit card (payment information). DC pays credit card from PayPal within its 30-day billing cycle (cash).
Echelon 3 < > Echelon 4	
Member artist(s) < > pottery clay supplier	Member artist orders on pottery clay supplier website with credit card (payment information). Member artist pays his/her credit card within its 30-day billing cycle (cash).
Member artist(s) < > glaze supplier(s)	Member artist orders on glaze supplier website with credit card (payment information). Member artist pays his/her credit card within its 30-day billing cycle (cash).
Member artist(s) < > art supply supplier(s)	Member artist shops in-person at art supply store (information). Member artist pays his/her credit card within its 30-day billing cycle (cash).
Packaging distributor < > cardboard supplier	Cardboard supplier invoices packaging distributor (information). Packaging distributor pays cardboard supplier in NET30 days (cash).

(*Continued*)

Table 2.8 (Continued) Invoice Information-to-Cash Payment Loops

Echelon 3 < > Echelon 4	
Packaging distributor < > bubble wrap supplier	Bubble wrap supplier invoices packaging distributor (information). Packaging distributor pays bubble wrap supplier in NET30 days (cash).
Packaging distributor < > label + tape supplier(s)	Label + tape supplier invoices packaging distributor (information). Packaging distributor pays label + tape supplier in NET30 days (cash).

Step 9: Detail the Factory and Distributor Steady-State Cash-to-Cash Cycle (Chapter 4)

In step 9, you analyze the steady-state cash-to-cash cycle velocity and variability for the factory and the DC. The Ceramic Art Studio example is concerned only with the DC. Revenue is generated whenever there is a sale. As sales accumulate, the Ceramic Art Studio is responsible for collecting sales tax and forwarding this tax to the government. In this unusual supply chain, the big cash outlay for product inventory is avoided because the member artists agree to provide their works on consignment. Consignment is practical because the Internet store greatly increases the chance of member artists being able to sell their works. Consignment also ensures that the DC is paid by the customer before the DC has to pay the member artist. Member artists are individually responsible for paying personal income taxes on their earnings. At start-up, the DC will purchase a small amount of packaging materials on a credit card to be ready for the first shipments. Depending on how soon the first sale takes place, the DC may need funds to cover this material purchase.

Start-up period expense is the big cash flow issue for the Ceramic Art Studio DC. Rent, utilities, insurance, employee wage, and payroll taxes will have to be paid for one or more months before the first sale ever occurs. Since there are no guarantees that the first sale will occur any time soon after the Internet store goes live, the Ceramic Art Studio must be in a position to fund several months of period expense. Payment dates are driven by fixed billing cycles on credit cards, rent, utilities, and employee payroll. Table 2.9 details the steady-state cash-to-cash velocity and variability for the DC.

Table 2.9 DC Steady-State Cash-to-Cash Velocity and Variability

	Velocity	*Variability*	*Sell/Buy*	*Monthly Cash Flow*
1.			Consign	The member artist delivers piece to DC for sale.
2.	30 days	0 to –25 days	Buy 19%	The DC pays period expense for rent, utilities, and wages. Variability is a function of payment date vs. sales date.
3.	30 days	0 to –25 days	Buy 1%	The DC buys packaging material on credit. Variability is a function of payment date vs. sales date.
4.	0 days	0 days	Sell 100%	The customer buys a piece using PayPal.
5.	10 days	±2 days	Buy 80%	The DC pays the member artist a piece after the sale. Variability is function of sales date vs. weekend.
6.			Buy	The DC pays UPS outbound freight.
7.			Buy	The DC pays sales tax.

20% of accounts payable are due at the beginning of the month.

Revenue ramps at one sale per day for 21 working days at a projected mixed average price of $176.

80% of accounts payable track revenue by a 10-day delay.

The cash-to-cash cycle velocity for a single piece:

Days of inventory = 0 days because inventory is on consignment

Days of receivables = 0 days because revenue from PayPal purchase is immediately available

$$\text{Days of payables} = \frac{20\% \times 0 \text{ days} + 80\% \times 10 \text{ days}}{100\%} = 8 \text{ days}$$

Cash-to-cash velocity = 0 days + 0 days – 8 days = –8 days

Cash-to-cash cycle variability:

1. If the average member artist piece price drops within the 100-piece consigned inventory, then period expenses and packaging material becomes larger than 20% of accounts payable.
2. If the DC goes days between sales, then the revenue turns lumpy and may not cover the 20% accounts payable for the following month.

Cash-to-cash variability = ±10 days

Step 10: Plot a Value Circle to Validate Network Container Performance Measures (Chapter 11)

In step 10, you plot the top half of the Value Circle related to the network container, including supply chain performance for throughput, velocity, variability, and price/landed cost. You are looking to validate the Ceramic Art Studio network container construction by answering these three questions: Can your choice of network relationships maintain the required throughput? Can you operate the end-to-end network profitably? Can you predict the steady-state cash-to-cash cycle velocity for the DC and understand its probable variability? Figure 2.2 shows the Value Circle for the network container with the step 2 through step 9 specification refinements plotted against the Table 2.4 SCCRS values shown as the unit circle. The performance along each axis improves as you move toward the origin. A complete description of the Value Circle is given in Chapter 11: "Performance Measures—'Make It Work Well'."

Throughput is achievable at 21 units/month or 1 unit/day. Realistically, there will be some days with no sales and some days with multiple sales. A projected mixed average selling price of $176 per unit before shipping and sales tax results in a projected mixed average profit of $3 per unit (from Table 2.10 discussion). Cash-to-cash velocity is −8 days (favorable). Cash-to-cash variability estimated at 10 days depends on price mix changes and on the number of days without a sale.

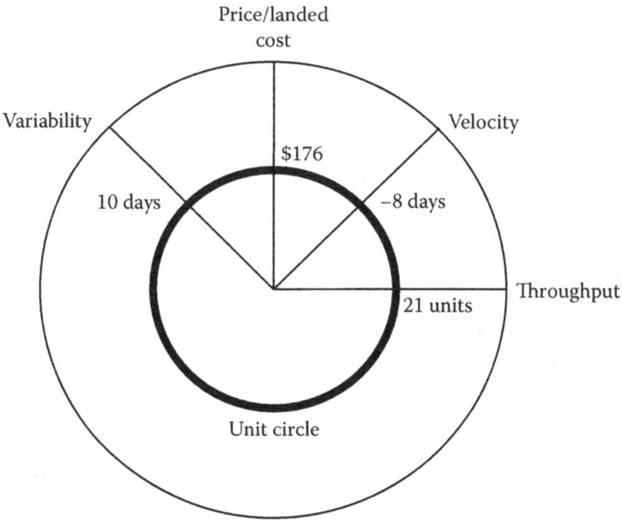

Figure 2.2 Value Circle for the Ceramic Arts Studio network container.

Step 11: Write the Product Contents SCCRS (Chapters 1, 11)

In step 11, you complete the bottom half of the SCCRS related to the product contents. Two types of inventory flow through the Ceramic Arts Studio DC. First, are the works of art created by the member artists, displayed in the Internet store catalog and sold to customers. The supply of art pieces is forecast in step 14. Second, are the indirect materials needed to package and ship the art pieces. The demand for packaging material is also forecast in step 14. A budget for end-to-end network inventory turns is determined. Normally, such inventory would drive a significant requirement for working capital; however, again, this supply chain is different because the bulk of the inventory investment is consigned by the member artists. This inventory has to be visualized through the push zone and vocalized through the pull zone. Finally, an estimate of the supply chain return on invested capital (ROIC) is made. ROIC combines aspects of the income statement and the balance sheet to show a figure of merit for the financial health of the business.

How to Estimate Inventory Value

There are six inventory locations in the Ceramic Arts Studio supply chain, as shown in Figure 2.3. Only the DC cycle stock and the member artist finished goods have relevance in the inventory valuation. This is because the member artist raw materials

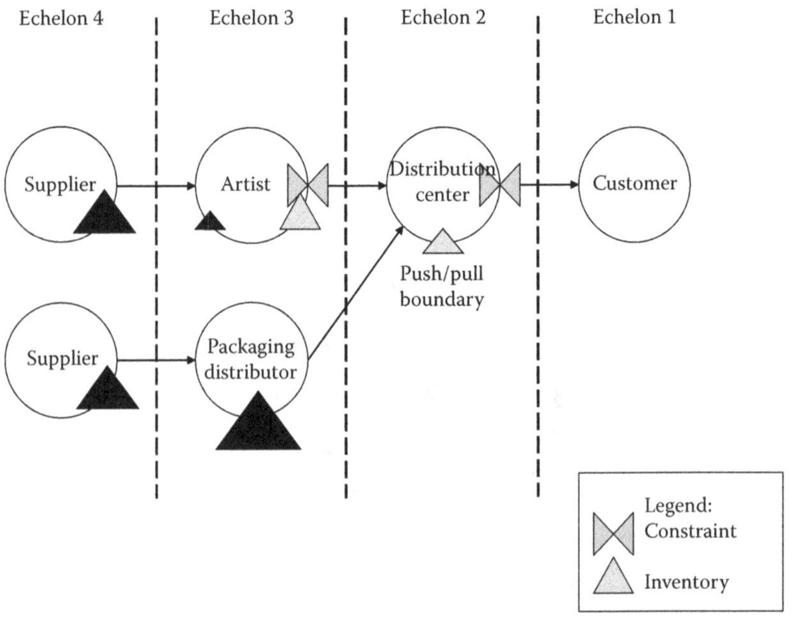

Figure 2.3 Ceramic Arts Studio forward network inventory locations.

value is very small and the other suppliers and packaging distributor inventories are very large and out of network relative to this supply chain. Cost factors from step 2 above plus lot sizes and other details from step 15 below are used to value each inventory location.

- *DC cycle stock*—The inventory held in the garage serves as both the shipping buffer and the push/pull boundary. The nonconsigned inventory is the packaging material and certificates. If 21 days of packaging material is held in inventory, then its value is (21)($2.59) = $54.
- *Member artist finished goods*—The member artists are the factories in this supply chain. As soon as a member artist completes a new work, this piece is consigned to the DC. The value of the consigned inventory is the sum of the values of each piece held at the garage. The rack space at the garage holds 200 pieces, and it is half empty at the start-up. The 100 pieces in inventory span the range of $48.50 to $240 in COGS. An estimate of the total consigned inventory value from a probable COGS distribution of 100 pieces is as follows:

(20)($48.50) + (30)($100) + (20)($140) + (20)($190) + (10)($240) = $12,970.

- *Artist raw materials*—Each member artist keeps a small supply of pottery clay, glazes, and other art supplies on-hand to be used in current and future projects. Its value is not included.
- *Artist suppliers finished goods*—The volume of material consumed by the member artists is a miniscule amount of the artist supplier's total finished goods inventory. Its value is not included.
- *Packaging distributor cycle stock*—The volume of packaging materials consumed by the DC is a miniscule amount of the packaging distributor's total cycle stock. Its value is not included.
- *Packaging suppliers finished goods*—The cardboard, bubble wrap, tape, and label suppliers each hold finished goods inventories. Its value is not included.

The total inventory value of the inventories held at the DC is $13,024.

- *Inventory turns*—$\frac{\text{21 pieces sold per month} \times 12 \text{ months}}{\text{Average of 100 pieces held in inventory}} = 2.5$ turns

How to Estimate Delivery Lead Time

Delivery lead time is the time from when the customer places an order with the Internet store until the customer receives the piece delivered from the DC. It takes one work day for the DC employee to process a new customer order from the Internet store website, pick the correct piece from inventory, and pack the piece for shipment. The DC employee is a part-time employee working Monday, Wednesday,

Table 2.10 Estimated Profitability

Price/Cost Item	*Price 1*	*Price 2*	*Price 3*	*Price 4*	*Price 5*
Distributor's price	$85.00	$138.75	$192.00	$245.75	$300.00
Distributor's profit	$1.00	$2.00	$3.00	$5.00	$7.00
Distributor's markup	$11.88	$13.13	$14.36	$16.11	$18.36
Distributor's COGS	$72.12	$123.62	$174.64	$224.64	$274.64
Distributor's overhead	$10.00	$10.00	$10.00	$10.00	$10.00
Distributor's labor (1 or 2 hours)	$11.03	$11.03	$22.05	$22.05	$22.05
Distributor's material cost	$51.09	$102.59	$142.59	$192.59	$242.59
Packaging materials	$2.59	$2.59	$2.59	$2.59	$2.59
Midbound freight	$0.00	$0.00	$0.00	$0.00	$0.00
Member artist's price	$48.50	$100.00	$140.00	$190.00	$240.00
Forecast quantity distribution	20	30	20	20	10
Projected Steady-State Monthly Average					
Revenue over 100 pieces (quantity × price)	$1,700	$4,163	$3,840	$4,915	$3,000
Estimated revenue/month	$17,618/(100 inventory/21 units/month) = $3,700/ month				
COGS over 100 pieces (quantity × COGS)	$1,442	$3,709	$3,493	$4,493	$2,746
Estimated COGS/month	$15,883/(100 inventory/21 units/month) = $3,335/ month				
Profit over 100 pieces (quantity × profit)	$20	$60	$60	$100	$70
Estimated profit/month	$310/(100 inventory/21 units/month) = $65/ month				
Artist pays over 100 pieces (quantity × artist's price)	$970	$3,000	$2,800	$3,800	$2,400

(Continued)

Table 2.10 (Continued) Estimated Profitability

Price/Cost Item	*Price 1*	*Price 2*	*Price 3*	*Price 4*	*Price 5*
Estimated artist pay/month	$12,970/(100 inventory/21 units/month) = $2,724/ month				
Payables over 100 pieces (quantity × COGS)	$1,442	$3,709	$3,493	$4,493	$2,746
Average payables	$15,883/(100 inventory/21 units/month) = $3,335				

and Friday. Transit time is determined from UPS based on the ZIP code of the customer's location. Transit time takes one additional day for local customers. Delivery lead time is the same as the vocalize time. Therefore, delivery lead time for local customers is normally three days and extends to four days over a weekend.

Visualize is the planning horizon time to push inventory to the push/pull boundary. The planning horizon is the longest time taken by a member artist to create a new piece. The Ceramic Arts Studio uses a planning horizon of six months.

How to Estimate ROIC for the DC

ROIC combines profit after taxes from the income statement with inventory, production assets, accounts receivable, and accounts payable from the balance sheet. The following steps give an approximate estimate of ROIC for the Ceramic Arts Studio DC. Table 2.10 projects a steady-state average monthly revenue and profit based on selling 100 pieces from inventory over several months with a forecast mix as shown.

The ROIC can now be calculated as follows:

1. Profit = $65/month from Table 2.10.
2. 100 pieces of inventory would be valued at $12,970, if it were not held on consignment. Adding the packaging materials brings the inventory value to $13,024.
3. Production capacity assets at the DC = $0 because there are none.
4. Accounts receivable for the Internet store = $0 because customer payments are available immediately through PayPal.
5. Accounts payable = $3,335 from Table 2.10.
6. ROIC is calculated as follows:

$$\text{ROIC} = \frac{\$\text{After tax profit/month} \times 12 \text{ months}}{\$\text{Inventory} + \$\text{Production capacity assets} + \$\text{Accounts receivable} - \$\text{Accounts payable}} \times 100\%$$

$$\text{ROIC} = \frac{\$65 \times 12}{\$13{,}024 + \$0 + \$0 - \$3{,}335} \times 100\% = 8.1\%$$

Table 2.11 SCCRS for the Ceramic Arts Studio Product Contents

Attribute	*Description*		
Network type	Forward network		
Market segment	Regional domestic individuals wanting inexpensive original ceramic art		
Product family	One-of-a-kind ceramics		
Project objective	We are constructing a forward network that connects art customers with Ceramic Arts Studio artists through an Internet store in the next four months.		
Specification	*Value*	*Dimensions*	*Evaluation*
Throughput	21	Units per month	X Accept
Distributor cash-to-cash cycle	Velocity –8 Variability ±10	Days Days	X Accept
Distributor price/ landed cost	High: 300 Low: 85	Dollars per unit Dollars per unit	X Accept
Inventory	$13,024 2.5	Dollars Turns	☐Accept ☐Reject
Delivery lead time	Vocalize 3 to 4 Visualize 180	Days based on location Days	☐Accept ☐Reject
Return on invested capital	8.1	Percent	☐Accept ☐Reject

Note: The ROIC calculation is included here for demonstration, however the ROIC percentage in this example is meaningless because the DC does not own the inventory.

The product contents portion of the SCCRS is now complete (see Table 2.11).

Step 12: Decide the Operating Strategy and Locate the Push/Pull Boundary (Chapter 9)

In step 12, you decide the operating strategy, locate the push/pull boundary inventory location, and identify the network constraint to achieve a competitive delivery lead time. The Ceramic Arts Studio supply chain is run using a Build-to-Stock operating strategy. The push/pull boundary is the cycle stock inventory held at the DC. Delivery lead time is determined from the location of the push/

pull boundary as discussed in step 11. There are two network constraints. The first is the DC single employee's ability to process and ship multiple pieces in a single day while being constrained by the number of budgeted paid hours. The second is the supply constraint of the member artists to generate new pieces for sale. In the extreme when the entire inventory is sold out, the catalog is empty and the supply chain shuts down until one of the member artists consigns a new piece.

Step 13: Compile the Composite Bills of Materials (Chapters 6, 10)

In step 13, you compile the composite bills of materials (BOM) item master and map each part number across each of its respective inventory locations. Small businesses often adopt the manufacturer's part number as their own internal part number. This is the case for the packaging materials. The member artists sign a label of authenticity at the time they consign their pieces to the DC. A flexible part numbering system is set up for the ceramic art inventory in the format "AAA-123." The first three letters are the member artist's initials. The last three digits are sequential for each new piece consigned to inventory by that member artist. Table 2.12 details where inventory items from the composite BOM are located across the Ceramic Arts Studio supply chain.

Step 14: Forecast Demand (Chapter 9)

In step 14, you forecast the demand used to push inventory into the push/pull boundary. In the Ceramic Arts Studio supply chain, both the ceramic pieces of art and the packaging material are pushed into the push/pull boundary for a customer order to pull out a shipment. Normally, packaging material would be a dependent demand calculated through the product structure from the parent product. However, the DC uses three sizes of shipping cartons to accommodate the packaging of a wide variety of shapes and sizes for the member artist's ceramics. There is no correlation between the artist or the final value of the piece and its size. Fortunately, the shipping cartons are inexpensive, and the DC overplans the most common size. Other packaging material such as bubble wrap and labels are dependent demand items with a calculated quantity.

The forecast of member artist ceramic art is really a probabilistic forecast of the availability of supply rather than the normal forecast of customer demand. While customers may want to buy more, this is a build-to-stock supply chain and the member artists are not crafting new work to order. The supply forecast is based on continuing conversations with each of the member artists about their time to completion and likely price range. The supply forecast ties into the throughput estimate from step 1: ((1 member)(24 pieces) + (19 members)(12 pieces average) +

Table 2.12 The Composite BOM

Item Part Number	*Packaging Distributor*	*Member Artist*	*DC*	*Customer*
Cardboard carton–size 1	X		X	
Cardboard carton–size 2	X		X	
Cardboard carton–size 3	X		X	
Bubble wrap	X		X	
Certificate of authenticity		X	X	X
Shipping label	X		X	
Artist 1 ceramic 1		A01-001	A01-001	A01-001
Artist 1 ceramic 2		A01-002	A01-002	A01-002
...		...	...	...
Artist 1 ceramic N		A01-00N	A01-00N	A01-00N
Artist 2 ceramic 1		A02-001	A02-001	A02-001
Artist 2 ceramic 2		A02-002	A02-002	A02-002
...		...	...	...
Artist 1 ceramic N		A02-00N	A02-00N	A02-00N
...		...	...	...
Artist N ceramic 1		A0N-001	A0N-001	A0N-001
Artist N ceramic 2		A0N-002	A0N-002	A0N-002
...		...	...	...
Artist N ceramic N		A0N-00N	A0N-00N	A0N-00N

(1 member)(2 pieces)) = 254 pieces/year, or about 21 pieces/month, and the five-part pricing structure of step 11: DC prices are set at $85, $138.75, $192, $245.75, and $300. In Table 2.13, artists 1, 2, and 3 have demonstrated track records of producing work in some, but not all, of the five price ranges. All other member artists make up the total volume for the 254 pieces per year. Keep in mind that any of the supply delivery months can slip later in time, lowering the total on-hand inventory.

Table 2.13 Forecast of Member Artist Supply Quantity per Month

Member Artist	*No./Year*	*DC Price*	*Jan.*	*Feb.*	*Mar.*	*Apr.*	*May*	*June*
Artist 1	2	$300.00		1				
Artist 2	3	$192.00	1				1	
Artist 2	9	$138.75		1	1		1	1
Artist 3	6	$138.75	1		1		1	
Artist 3	6	$85.00		1		1		1
All other artists	23	$300.00	3	3	2	3	4	2
All other artists	51	$245.75	4	4	3	5	4	4
All other artists	48	$192.00	4	3	2	4	4	5
All other artists	61	$138.75	6	5	4	4	5	5
All other artists	45	$85.00	4	4	3	4	4	3
Totals	254		23	22	16	21	24	21
Package Forecast			*Jan.*	*Feb.*	*Mar.*	*Apr.*	*May*	*June*
Carton size-1			16	16	15	16	16	16
Carton size-2			10	10	8	10	10	10
Carton size-3			6	6	5	6	6	6

Step 15: Budget Inventory Echelon by Echelon (Chapters 1, 3, 10)

In step 15, you budget inventory across the supply chain network by determining the lot size, reorder point, inventory turns, and safety stock for each inventory item at each inventory location echelon by echelon. Refer again to the inventory locations in Figure 2.3 and to the composite BOM detail in Table 2.12. In the Ceramic Arts Studio supply chain, the shipping buffer which is the customer facing inventory location, the push/pull boundary, and the DC cycle stock are all one in the same. In this supply chain, the only echelon with an inventory budget is echelon 2 for the DC.

Ordering Cost and Inventory Holding Cost Estimates

- *Ordering cost*—From Table 2.10, labor and overhead expense for the DC employee is $6,741 per year. Suppose 50% of the employee's time is devoted to processing the 254 orders for ceramic art plus processing an estimated 30 orders for packaging materials. Then the cost per order is ($6,741 × 50%/(254 orders + 30 orders)) = $11.87 per order.
- *Inventory holding cost*—From Table 2.3, rent, utilities, insurance, and taxes cost (($10.00 + $8.65) × 254 pieces) = $4,737 per year. Adding in the shipping cartons, labels, certificates, and bubble wrap, the total annual number of units becomes 254 ceramic art pieces + 254 cartons + 254 labels + 254 certificates + 4 rolls bubble wrap = 1,020 units per year. Then the inventory holding cost is ($4,737 per year/1,020 units per year) = $4.64 per unit/per item/per year.

Shipping Buffer Is Push/Pull Boundary Is Distributor Cycle Stock

- *Art piece lot size*—The member artists produce their work in lot sizes of one.
- *Shipping carton lot size* using Equation 10.9 for an economic order quantity (EOQ) is as follows:

$$\text{EOQ} = \sqrt{2\text{DS/H}} \text{ in units}$$

where

D = annual demand in units; S = the cost to place an order in dollars; H = the cost to hold one unit of inventory for one year in dollars.

D = 254 units/year; S = $11.87; H = $4.64 per unit/per item/per year

$$\text{EOQ} = \sqrt{(2)(254)(11.87)/4.64} = 36 \text{ units} = \text{distributor lot size for cartons}$$

- *Art piece reorder point*—When a piece sells, the DC employee removes the piece from the online catalog and informs the member artist of its sale. This is also the reorder point for the next piece from that member artist.
- *Shipping carton reorder point using a two-bin system*—Whenever the first 25 cartons are consumed and the second bundle is started, the DC employee orders a replacement bundle of 25 cartons. (See carton discussion below.)
- *Art piece safety stock*—This is a one-of-a-kind supply chain; there is no safety stock for the ceramic art.
- *Shipping carton safety stock using a two-bin system*—There are 100 pieces of ceramic art in inventory at any one time. All of this inventory could be ordered within a few days or none of this inventory could be ordered within six months. The Ceramic Arts Studio wants to be able to ship immediately.

However, it is constrained by the number of hours it can afford to pay the DC employee when orders bunch up. It is also constrained by the inventory investment it is willing to put into packaging materials. The DC uses a standard carton size sold in bundles of 25 with a lead time of two days. The DC decides to invest in a two-bin inventory system for each carton size. Two bundles (25 units each) of carton size 1, two bundles (25 each) of carton size 2, and two bundles (25 each) of carton size 3 are ordered and stored in the DC, for a total of 150 cartons or seven months of supply. The first 25 units are more than enough to cover the average monthly shipping volume. The distributor's lot size is close to the EOQ calculated lot size of 36. The second 25 units are safety stock. The total carton inventory investment is (50)($0.70) + (50)($0.82) + (50)($1.19) = $136.

- *Art piece inventory turns*—Throughput of 254 pieces per year divided by an average inventory of 100 pieces = 2.5 turns/year.
- *Shipping carton inventory turns*—Throughput of 254 pieces per year divided by a carton inventory of 150 cartons = 3.4 turns/year.

Step 16: Plan and Control the Push Zone (Chapter 10)

In step 16, you construct the inventory and capacity planning and control system used to push inventory into the push/pull boundary. Normally a Demand Forecast drives the Sales and Operations Plan, which drives a Master Production Schedule, which drives Materials Requirements Planning; these tools are explained in detail with examples in Chapter 10: "Inventory Management." The Ceramic Arts Studio inventory management is a little different (Table 2.14). The materials used to make the one-of-a-kind end product are managed by the individual member artists. Because of the very low shipping volume, a two-bin inventory management method is used for the packaging materials. Since the packaging distributor's minimum purchase quantities exceed the calculated lot sizes, the minimum purchase quantities must be used.

Step 17: Plan and Control the Pull Zone (Chapter 10)

In step 17, you ensure the pull zone has sufficient capacity and inventory to sustain maximized throughput.

- *Pull capacity*—The DC normally plans to ship one unit per day. There will be days when there are no orders and no shipments. The DC employee must have the paid hours to be able to ship at a peak capacity of 4 units in one day, if necessary, and 21 units for the month.
- *Pull inventory*—The one-of-a-kind inventory at the push/pull boundary is what it is. The push/pull boundary must hold a quantity of packaging materials and labels to ship a peak capacity of 4 units in one day and 21 units for the month until catalogued stock runs out.

Table 2.14 Ceramic Arts Studio Materials Management

BOM Level	*Item*	*Unit of Measure*	*Supplier*	*Planning Method*
0	Catalog item	Each	DC	Probabilistic supply forecast
..1	Ceramic art	Each	Member artist	One-of-a-kind
....2	Potters clay	Pounds	Member artist	Member artists manage their own inventories from their own suppliers
....2	Glaze 1	Pounds	Member artist	
....2	Glaze 2	Pounds	Member artist	
..1	Certificate of authenticity	Each	Member artist	
..1	Shipping carton	Each	Packaging distributor ULINE	Two-bin system Packs of 25
..1	Shipping label	Each	Packaging distributor ULINE	One-time purchase 400 labels
..1	Bubble wrap	Roll	Packaging distributor ULINE	Minimum order four rolls
..1	Sealing tape	Roll	Packaging distributor ULINE	Minimum order eight rolls
Indirect	Printer paper	Ream	Office supply Staples	Two-bin system One ream
Indirect	Black printer cartridge	Each	Office supply Staples	Two-bin system Two cartridges

Step 18: Plot a Value Circle to Validate Product Contents Performance Measures (Chapter 11)

In step 18, you plot the bottom half of the Value Circle related to the product contents. This includes supply chain performance for inventory, vocalize, visualize, and ROIC. You are looking to validate the Ceramic Arts Studio product contents construction by answering these three questions: What is the right level of product

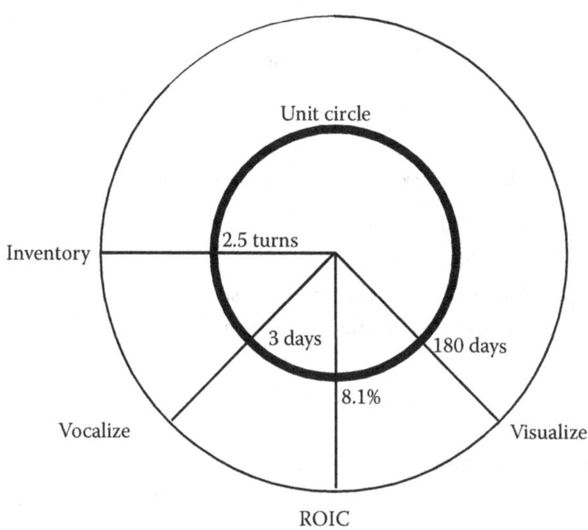

Figure 2.4 Value Circle for the Ceramic Arts Studio product contents.

inventory, and where is it located? Can you completely visualize the push and properly vocalize the pull to achieve a competitive delivery lead time? Does the profit margin from the income statement and the inventory and receivables investment from the balance sheet support a favorable investment return? Figure 2.4 shows the Value Circle for product contents with the step 12 through step 17 specification refinements plotted against the Table 2.11 SCCRS values shown as the unit circle. Each axis of the Value Circle improves moving toward the origin.

The shipping buffer and the push/pull boundary are one in the same inventory location. The push/pull boundary is operated with 2.5 inventory turns, as determined in step 15. The Internet store catalog features an average of 100 ceramic art items at any time. Vocalize is three (to four) days from the push/pull boundary depending on the customer's location and whether the piece is ordered over a weekend. Visualize is 180 days driven by six months of forecasting to cover the longest member artist's lead time. ROIC is estimated to be 8.1% in step 11. The supply chain construction for product content is now complete.

Step 19: Stabilize Supply Chain Operations and End the Construction Project (Chapters 11, 12)

In step 19, you stabilize supply chain operations until the required level of performance is reached. Then the Supply Chain Construction Project is formally ended and the project team disbanded. One big challenge with the Ceramic Art Studio supply chain is the high probability that orders will bunch up into a single day and that the DC employee will not have enough paid hours to process all the shipments. Consequently, a work schedule is set up for the employee to work two hours on Monday, two hours on Wednesday, and three hours on Friday.

Step 20: Manage Supply Chain Risk (Chapter 12)

In step 20, you assess highly probable risk scenarios that might disrupt your supply chain network. While the executive committee of the Ceramic Arts Studio can imagine many problematic external events, these are some example scenarios with a high probability of causing a business interruption.

- *Inventory theft*—The distribution employee is present at the garage only a few hours a week. The garage building and its inventory must be secured from theft, when the employee is not present.
- *Loss of the garage lease*—The owner of the garage decides not to extend the lease for personal reasons. The Ceramic Arts Studio has to move its DC operation to another location.
- *Website is hacked*—A computer hacker attacks the online catalog. The Ceramic Arts Studio does not have the expertise among its members to defend against the attack.
- *Wind damage*—During a high wind storm, a neighbor's tree falls on the garage, damaging the building and smashing some of the inventory. The property should be surveyed and the inventory insured for such a possibility.

In Summary

This chapter introduces and applies the Supply Chain Construction Blueprint to a forward supply chain network. The case study is a compilation of experiences designed to demonstrate the application of The Blueprint to a single echelon with an average throughput of one unit per day. The Blueprint documents the steps required to connect a market segment with a product. The Blueprint splits the construction project into building a network container and then filling the container with product contents. Certain steps in The Blueprint are iterative in order to meet price/landed cost budgets and inventory budgets. The iterations are (1) make it work, (2) make it work well, and (3) make it work in a flexible and risk tolerant manner.

Chapter 3

Building Relationships

Successful supply chain relationships depend on more than a carefully worded contract. Experience shows that the single biggest impediment to supply chain success is the lack of trust between parties. Trading partner relationships are formed when people decide to do business together and risk trusting each other. Often, the relationship begins between the most senior people at each company. Over time, these relationships expand to include more junior people involved in the collaborative change management that is necessary to build new supply chain network capability. This chapter describes different kinds of supply chain relationships and how to build trust across different business cultures, distance, and time zones.

Staffing the Dream Team

It was their third meeting focused on the new business venture. The quarter had ended with lousy performance, but at least now, that was history. Alice was back in the meetings.

Steve arrived a little late, having had to finish a conference call with his boss at Corporate, "Let's not do that again anytime soon! I just got my tail handed to me for such 'stellar' performance last quarter. We better make this new venture work, and work fast!"

Jerry countered with, "Yes, we can make this work. But it will take our best people and a laser-like focus on our objective."

Steve turned toward George and said, "George, you seem the most passionate and the most knowledgeable about building this new supply chain. I'm going to appoint you to be the executive champion for the Supply Chain Construction

Project Team. You will mentor them, resolve any resource issues, and be a liaison back to my staff. OK?"

"It will be my pleasure," said George. "By the way, who is on our 'Dream Team'?"

"That's what we are going to decide right now," replied Steve. "It seems to me that Bill, our director of Supply Chain, should head the Dream Team. Don't you agree, Tom?"

"What? How am I going to run all of Manufacturing with Bill gone? He could probably consult with the team, but we need him to keep the store open for our existing customers," gasped Tom.

"Yes, I know it's going to be tough for you…for all of us. We need to put our best and brightest people on this team. It's for the future of our division and the jobs of our employees. So, Bill will be the team leader. Who are other candidates for the supply chain team?"

Alice spoke next, "Cost Accounting will play a big role in all this. I would like to add Tony, my best cost analyst, to the team. Tony also has a very good relationship with our Corporate Information Technology Group that could be very useful."

"Done!" responded Steve. "Who is next?"

"Harry is the product marketing engineer on my team who has done the most research on uninterruptable power supplies (UPS) and the competition. I want him on the team," said Jerry.

"I will put John, a very seasoned hardware engineer who knows quite a lot about firmware design and instrumentation interfacing on the team," said Herb.

"Geez, do you think you can spare him with your cast of thousands in engineering?" complained Tom.

"These are all great choices. Who else?" asked Steve. "I think we need some more expertise on the business side. Tom, what about Donna in Purchasing? She seems to be doing an excellent job in supplier management."

"Oh sure! First you raid my best director. Now you take my best buyer. I know, I know, it's for the good of the company. Yes, sure, why not?" replied Tom.

"Tom, please stay a little after this meeting," said Steve. "I'd like to talk with you about how to backfill for Bill and Donna while they are assigned to this project."

"Quality is not represented yet. I'd like to see Hank, my quality director, on the team. But the team already has five members. Hank would make the sixth. It is best to have an odd number on the team so that their decisions will not become deadlocked," said George.

Steve responded, "Let's stay with five full-time team members for now: Bill, Tony, Harry, John, and Donna. If they each do a great job, I'm sure this project will go a long way toward advancing their careers. I'm sure from time to time, along the way, we will need to supplement the Supply Chain Construction Project Team with a few part-time contributors, such as Hank in Quality, to consult on specific issues. We are making good progress this morning. Now, what do we want this team to do?"

"Well, I think there are several tasks to be quickly completed once we announce the team to the division," replied George. "First, the team needs to develop a Supply Chain Construction Requirements Specification based on our business objective and the market–product connection we need to make. Then, the team needs to quickly develop a project schedule with milestones and a project budget. The schedule should be based on the Supply Chain Construction Blueprint and our business need to be done within the next 12 months. The budget should also be based on the Supply Chain Construction Blueprint and the resources that Finance believes we can support. This will probably require some additional funding from Corporate. Both the schedule and the budget will have to be approved by Steve and this staff."

"Most of the people on the team have never done this kind of scheduling or budgeting," commented Herb. "There are likely to be many missing items and financial surprises down the road."

"That's a good point," said Steve. "You know that Bill has been a project manager in his past, and Tony has assisted my staff the past couple of years in our budgeting cycle. Since George is the executive champion to the team, I'm sure he can mentor Bill and the others in preparing these plans. We need a particularly strong plan to be able to convince Corporate to give the division additional funding for this new project, especially in light of our latest performance. We will have to have a convincing plan that can achieve at least $10 million in sales the first year before Corporate will even consider funding us."

Jerry added, "Another thing to consider early on is how we can communicate our plan inside the division. This new business venture should help boost employee morale."

"We need to be careful about what and when we communicate," replied Tom. "We don't know yet whether Corporate will support the plan. We don't even know if the product will be built in this factory. I'd hate to get employees excited about jobs only to find out the jobs are going elsewhere. That might become the reality."

"Jobs will definitely be lost if our financial performance doesn't improve soon," Steve reminded everyone at the table. "What do we know about the product, so far?"

"Based on some work done by Harry, the price point will have to come in somewhere around $500 for the Product 500 UPS," said Jerry.

"A dollar per watt of protection," summarized Steve, talking in power supply terms. "However, I have been thinking about how this business is going to be fundamentally different than the power supply business. In the power supply business, our own people build products from parts procured mostly domestically, then we use our captive sales force to sell, and we ship to customers worldwide from this location. In the UPS business, we will have to decide where the product gets built. The sale will be indirect as an add-on sale to a computer server sold in the Computer Products sales channel. The product will be a coordinated shipment to a value-added reseller (VAR) before reaching the customer. This is going to involve a whole new set of supply chain relationships with the Computer Products sales channel and the VARs, just to name a few."

"Yes, and it is quite doable and pretty exciting, if you were to ask me," exclaimed Jerry.

Steve closed the meeting, "We need to get on to some other pressing business. Please get with your people to inform Bill, Tony, Harry, John, and Donna of their new assignments. George, I need a first pass schedule and budget on my desk 10 days from now. That's all for now. Tom, please hang around, I need to talk with you."

Sign Up for the Journey

There are two overarching business strategies that drive supply chains. One is the continuous and unrelenting drive to reduce costs through volume consolidation and the elimination of marginal functionality. The second is the continuous and unrelenting drive to grow throughput through generations of new products and the development of new market segments. Cost reduction goals foster single-company, vertical functional silo responses and are often win–lose. Throughput growth goals foster multicompany, horizontal, end-to-end responses and are mostly win–win. The best strategy combines throughput growth with sensible cost reduction. Supply chain management is more about this journey.

Every supply chain has four stakeholders: the owners, the customers, the suppliers, and the employees. Under a cost reduction strategy, owners and customers win, while suppliers and employees get squeezed. If a supplier is unwilling or unable to reduce its pricing, then the supply chain will eliminate that supplier in favor of some other. If a trading partner needs to slash its cost structure, what better way to achieve its goal than to reduce headcount? Or, the trading partner may decide to outsource its production to a country with a lower labor rate, which will cause job loss back home.

Under a throughput growth strategy, the supply chain network has to improve end to end. Suppliers win by retaining their network-generating revenue. As the business matures, employees learn how to be more adaptable and flexible. Employees win not through job title guarantees but rather through employment guarantees. Customers win by taking reliable, on-time delivery of value-adding products. Owners win because throughput means revenue, and revenue means earnings, and earnings mean appreciating stock value.

Whether you are building a new supply chain from scratch, enhancing an existing profitable business, recycling spent product in an environmentally responsible way, or terminating a supply chain to close up shop, the way you decide to manage relationships can make or break your business objective. You and your team need to sign up for the journey, paying close attention to human relations issues, while following the Supply Chain Construction Blueprint in this book.

Know When to Start and End a Supply Chain Construction Project

Supply chain construction projects are commissioned to improve, or to at least maintain, business performance measures. You may have built a new supply chain network and filled it with inventory, but how do you know you are getting its best performance? You may have successfully combined two supply chains when your company acquired another company; but how do you know this supply chain merger still delivers a competitive performance? A supply chain that is designed on paper and constructed by the project team needs to be validated in practice. The earlier this can be done, the lower is the business cost of having to rework the project to gain customer and management satisfaction.

Supply Chain Life Cycle Event Triggers

The start of a supply chain construction project is triggered by a life cycle event. Life cycle events occur all the time in supply chains. The most common life cycle event triggers are listed in Table 3.1. Some triggers, such as adding a new product or adding a new market segment, drive short, lightly staffed projects. Other event triggers, such as starting a new business or outsourcing a product line, drive longer, more heavily staffed projects. All too often, multiple small events pass unnoticed, and they are not acted upon until there is some crisis. Each and every life cycle event listed in Table 3.1 has the potential to trigger a new supply chain construction project.

How to Get Started…Ask These Three Questions

Once you have identified that a supply chain life cycle event trigger is eminent, you need to quickly decide how to respond. Answers to the following three key questions will start you down the right path.

1. Will any product shifts occur that require adding/subtracting suppliers and adding/subtracting inventory items at inventory locations from the supplier echelon to the push/pull boundary echelon?

   This is a small supply chain construction project starting from an existing operational supply chain. It can probably be handled by two persons working part-time for a few months. Compare the "as-is" composite bills of materials (BOM) with the "to-be" composite BOM and make the required network container and product content adjustments. Do not forget to adjust the forecast and demand information connections. Then use the Value Circle, described in Chapter 11: "Performance Measures," to validate that each performance measure is back on track, as the project is completed.

Table 3.1 Supply Chain Life Cycle Event Triggers

Start to Growth	*Mature*	*Decline to End*
Begin a supply chain		End a supply chain
Enter a market segment	Switch market segments	Exit a market segment
Add a product	Rollover a new product generation	Obsolete a product
Add a service	Rollover to a different service	End a service
Acquire a product line	Due diligence for an acquisition	Divest a product line
Implement an enterprise resource planning information system		
	Change a pricing strategy	
	New competitor enters the market	
	Substitute a trading partner	
	Outsource	
	Offshore	
	Insource	
	Reshore	

2. Will any market segment shifts occur that require expanding/reducing a delivery channel and adjusting inventory from the push/pull boundary echelon to the end-customer echelon?

   This is a small supply chain construction project starting from an existing operational supply chain. It can probably be handled by two persons working part-time for a few months. Compare delivery coverage to the "as-is" market segment with delivery coverage to the "to-be" market segment and make the required network container and product content adjustments. Do not forget to adjust the forecast and demand information connections. Then use the Value Circle, described in Chapter 11: "Performance Measures," to validate that each performance measure is back on track, as the project is completed.
3. Are more radical changes required to the network container or the product contents?

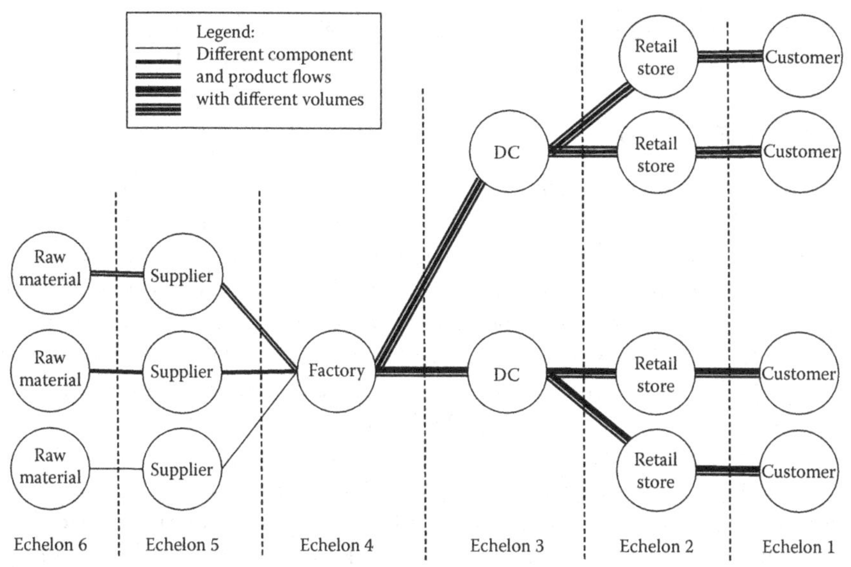

Figure 3.1 Example supply chain echelon map.

This is a large supply chain construction project. It will probably require a team with several people working full time for at least six months. This may be the start-up of a brand new supply chain. Otherwise, start by documenting the "as-is" supply chain map and performance measures. Figure 3.1 is an example Supply Chain Echelon Map. Fill in the names of the suppliers, factories, distributors, and retail stores with the cities and countries where they are currently located. This is your baseline. Now draw a second Supply Chain Echelon Map of the "to-be" supply chain, for example, the supply chain for a company to be acquired. You may decide to smash the two supply chains together, taking the best parts of each. In some cases, the extent of the changes will make the project look like building a new supply chain from the ground up. Use the Value Circle, described in Chapter 11: "Performance Measures," to validate that each performance measure is back on track, as the project is completed.

Organize the Supply Chain Construction Project

A supply chain construction project involves three sets of relationships: (1) relationships within the project team, (2) relationships among the project team members and other employees in the parent organization, and (3) relationships among the project team members and the external network trading partners. This section looks at the inner workings of the project team. Later sections in this chapter address building trust within the parent organization and with external trading partners.

Project Objective

Each supply chain construction project should have in writing a simple, highly focused objective. Avoid combining multiple objectives because this only serves to defocus the team and delay project completion. The best project objectives are just one sentence. The objective should be actionable and measurable. If the objective is too ambitious, narrow the scope. It is often better to conduct several sequential, high-impact projects than one massive and unachievable project. Check that the Supply Chain Construction Requirements Specification is consistent with the objective. Here are some examples: "Deliver product from stock to customers in the tri-state area by February 28th." "Complete the merger of the newly acquired Midwest supply chain with the current North East supply chain by the end of the third quarter." "Implement a reverse supply chain network for the product line within the European Union before May 1st." "Rationalize the product line supply base down to 150 suppliers over the next eight months." "Close the Allentown warehouse, and prepare the property for sale by August 31st."

Project Statement of Work

The project statement of work (SOW) sets the context and limits the scope of a supply chain construction project. It puts in writing what the project "is" and what the project "is not." The SOW document should be no more than one or two pages. The Project Objective, the Project SOW, and the Supply Chain Construction Requirements Specification must all be consistent. The purpose of the SOW is to prevent scope creep, which can keep even the best project team from ever completing their task. The SOW is used by the project champion executive to secure approval for the project. For example, "This five-person, 10-month project IS the North American introduction of Product Line A; this project IS NOT the introduction of Product Line A into Europe and Asia." Another example, "This seven-person, eight-month project IS the integration of the 15 products from newly acquired Company Z; this project IS NOT the redesign of the next generation of Company Z products."

Project Team

The supply chain construction project is run by a Supply Chain Construction Project Team. The project manager is most often appointed by a senior executive from one of the trading partner companies, who thereafter acts as the project champion executive. This person understands the strategic importance of supply chain management and has secured project approval from the executive team. The project champion executive must keep the enthusiasm for the project and the parent organization's trust of the team intact for the duration of the project. The project champion executive should facilitate a celebration at the successful completion of the project and ensure that each of the project team members is properly recognized and rewarded.

The project team should have an odd number of full-time core team members supplemented by some number of part-time contributors. A small company might have a three-member core team, while a large company might have a seven-member core team. Decision making and achieving forward momentum become more difficult beyond seven members. When the project team votes on alternative courses of action, the project manager breaks the deadlock.

The core team is appointed from among your best employees. This can put a burden on keeping the store open during the time it takes to complete the supply chain construction project. You may not have people in the company knowledgeable in each of these areas listed below. If this is the case, then it will be necessary to either educate an interested employee or seek outside consulting services. Core team members are not expected to do all the work in each of their respective areas, but rather to understand all the work and "connect the dots." As the volume of project-related work builds, part-time contributors will be tasked with short-term, specific jobs. Here are the suggested roles and focus for each core team member. Core teams in smaller companies may find that they have to combine role responsibilities.

- *Project champion executive*—Secures executive approval for the project, mentors the project manager, helps the team secure the necessary parent company resources, and ensures team member recognition and reward upon the completion of a successful project.
- *Project manager and logistics specialist*—Leads the team to a successful on-time, on-budget project conclusion. Focus is on cost-effective inbound, midbound, and outbound logistics solutions, warehousing requirements, and import/export regulatory compliance.
- *Information technology specialist*—Focus is on implementing changes to the information technology hardware and application software, software licensing, data file reconfiguration, and data cleansing.
- *Demand relationships specialist*—Focus is on downstream implementation of new market segmentation, new channels of distribution, demand forecasting, and customer order management.
- *Inventory management and planning specialist*—Focus is on the BOM, locating the push/pull boundary, network capacity constraints, product groupings, push planning and control, pull planning and control, and data integrity.
- *Supplier relationships specialist*—Focus is on upstream implementation of the supply base, commodity management, supplier pricing contracts, supplier order management, ISO Quality compliance, and Conflict Minerals compliance.

- *Finance and accounting specialist*—Focus is on the general ledger, new accounts receivable, new accounts payable, product cost accounting, perpetual inventory records, cash flow planning, business control, and Sarbanes-Oxley compliance.
- *Product engineering specialist*—Focus is on intellectual property protection, introduction timing, supplier requirements, inventory requirements, distribution requirements, and ISO Environmental Management compliance for new product introductions and old product obsolescence.

There is a high probability that your supply chain construction project will involve information technology consulting services. This is often the case when the project involves the deployment of a new software application. The consultant(s) should report to the project manager and participate in the team discussions, but not the team decisions. While consultants have a wealth of information to bring to the party, consultants represent technology companies or themselves and not always the best interest of the client. Always remember to ask what each new requirement is going to cost to implement and to maintain before agreeing to let a consultant implement it.

Project Timeline with Milestones

Successful projects have aggressive timelines and many intermediary milestones. Timelines are like shooting with a rubber band. If the project schedule is too easy, the rubber band is limp and nondirectional. If the project schedule is unreasonably aggressive, the rubber band is pulled past its breaking point. If the project schedule is properly aggressive, the rubber band is stretched and aimed toward the target.

Any project has three degrees of freedom: calendar time, dollars, and staffing resources. You never want to be in a situation where all three degrees of freedom are constrained. If the end date and a dollar budget are set, then you want to be able to negotiate additional staffing. If the end date and the project staffing are set, then you want to be able to negotiate additional budget.

Projects come from a set of high-level deliverables completed against a deadline. High-level deliverables are completed as a series of related lower level tasks get completed. The tasks form the basis of defining a set of milestones. For example, a prototype unit (deliverable) can be built only after a parts list is documented (milestone), after all materials are in stock (milestone), and after a workstation is outfitted (milestone). Milestones should be defined for each project team member to occur in roughly two-week intervals. When a project team member works longer than two weeks, it is too easy to spend a critical resource with no measureable result. A five-person project team on a six-month project will have 60 to 70 milestones. A milestone is a task assigned to one person with a knife edge "done/not done" measureable result. Milestones need to indicate completed tasks and not activity. For example, a meeting is an activity that consumes resources often without any measureable results. On the other hand, installing the server and successfully loading the application software, or signing a supplier pricing contract, or building the first five prototypes at the contract manufacturer are each task completions. Progress against the project timeline is measured by the number of milestones completed. Here is a simple way to develop a project timeline with milestones:

1. *Write the project objective*—The project scope and the deadline are explicit in the objective.
2. *Define the set of high-level deliverables needed to complete the project*—A supply chain network modification might require a new factory or a new delivery channel. A new product introduction might require a new pricing contract or the placement of new product inventory. An enterprise resource planning system enhancement might require hardware and software performance testing.
3. *Assign one core team member to each deliverable*—A deliverable is something physical within the expertise focus of the core team member. For example, logistics could have a deliverable of a signed competitively priced freight contract; supplier relationships could have a deliverable of a first piece delivery; and inventory management could have a deliverable of every stock keeping unit (SKU) in stock at the push/pull boundary. Assign only one person to be responsible for each deliverable.
4. *Map tasks to deliverables one by one*—Take each deliverable one at a time. Develop the sequence of tasks spaced every two weeks that connects where you are today with where you need to be to complete the deliverable (see Table 3.2). You now have one person responsible for a sequence of measurable tasks, which, when completed, will yield the deliverable.
5. *Determine the critical path*—The Critical Path Method (http://www.project-management-skills.com/critical-path-method.html) or the Program Evaluation Review Technique (http://www.netmba.com/operations/project/pert/) can be used to determine the critical path and probable time to complete a supply chain project (Figure 3.2).
6. *If the critical path calendar time comes before the deadline*—Plan to complete the project early. This gives the project team a time buffer to still complete the project on time should some unanticipated difficulty arise.
7. *If the critical path calendar time comes after the deadline*—This is the more likely scenario. First, critically review the effort and calendar time assigned to each task to ensure reasonable time estimates. Second, apply your remaining degree of freedom, such as applying extra resources or applying extra money to achieve a time compression along the critical path.
8. *Track progress weekly*—Review the successful completion of each milestone for each of the deliverables on a weekly basis. Share progress with the whole team. When a noncritical path milestone is missed, ask how this might impact the completion of any other deliverable. When a critical path

Table 3.2 Assign Team Members to Deliverables

	First Week	*Second Week*	*Third Week*	*Fourth Week*	*Fifth Week*	*Sixth Week*	*Seventh Week*
Sequence of Tasks for Team Member A to Complete Deliverable A							
Person A	Task A.1		Task A.2		Task A.3		
Deliverable A							
Sequence of Tasks for Team Member B to Complete Deliverable B							
Person B	Task B.1		Task B.2	Task B.3		Task B.4	
Deliverable B							
Sequence of Tasks for Team Member C to Complete Deliverable C							
Person C	Task C.1		Task C.2				
Deliverable C							

	Week 10	Week 11	Week 12	Week 13	Week 14	Week 15	Deadline Week 16
Person A		Task A.1	→	→	Task A.2	→	Task A.3
Deliverable A							
Person B	Task B.1	→	Task B.2	Task B.3	→	Task B.4	
Deliverable B							
Person C	Task C.1	→	Task C.2				
Deliverable C							

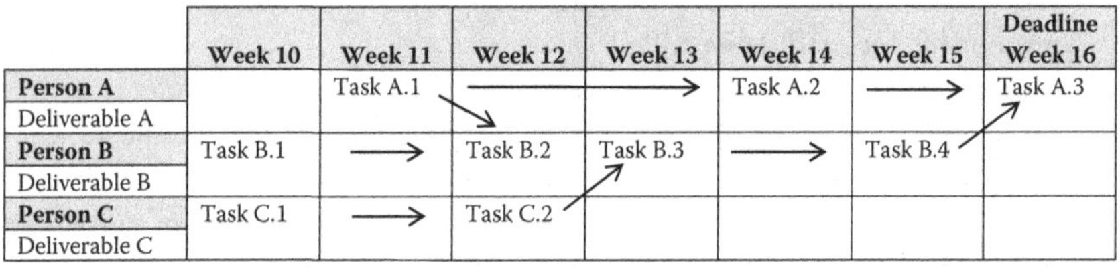

Figure 3.2 Schedule and connect task interdependencies to meet the deadline.

milestone is missed, ask how the team can recover and still make the original deadline.

9. *Allow sufficient time at the end of the project to demonstrate and validate supply chain performance*—Remember that it will take significant time, perhaps months, to prove that the results of your project really meets its intended objective.

Project Budget

Detailed information about how to budget and fund a supply chain construction project is presented in the next chapter, Chapter 4. The project manager needs to track actual expenditures against the project budget along with tracking the actual milestone completion against the project schedule. The goal of this tracking is to eliminate surprises and gauge completion. The tracking should be reviewed periodically with the entire project team and the project champion executive. If the project comes under budget pressure, then try to bring one of the other degrees of freedom to bear. For example, if the run rate of expenses is too high, perhaps the project can be conducted with leaner staffing working a longer time.

Build Strong Project Team Relationships

The project champion executive and the project manager have the added responsibility to build strong project team relationships among the core team members. Project work can be intense and frustrating, particularly when the project deadline is tight and, when in a smaller company, the core team members are also expected to maintain day-to-day operational responsibilities. Good team chemistry goes a long way toward providing motivation and satisfaction during a project.

The project champion executive needs to convince the team that the company believes in and is counting on the successful completion of their project. This needs to be repeated throughout the duration of the project. The project champion executive has a cheerleading role, whipping up excitement about the project and what it will enable the company to achieve, when it is completed. The project champion executive should facilitate core team celebrations as key intermediate goals are completed. The project team should come to know that the project champion executive will help them to knock down internal company barriers that are impeding progress.

The project manager must embody the core values of the team: respect for the individual, integrity, and trust. The project manager needs to be a bit of a strategist, able to integrate mature experience with youthful enthusiasm. A good project manager knows how to take cross-functional input from team members and others to arrive at alternative ways of accomplishing a difficult task. A good project manager embraces diversity and tolerates constructive conflict. The project manager drives the project schedule, making sure the next set of tasks are underway. The project manager should be anticipating any required change in project resources and communicating the change through the project champion executive.

Educate and Train

A supply chain network construction project is unlike any other project because its success depends so heavily on the actions of others outside your company. There are times when the external trading partners, other employees in the parent organization, and especially members of core project team can benefit from education and training. What is the difference between education and training? Education is the "why" you need to know about some aspect of supply chain construction. Education involves learning. Training is the "how" you go about doing some aspect of supply chain construction. Training involves practice.

The following are key to educating and training the supply chain construction project team, other employees in your parent company, and the trading partners in your network:

- *Common vocabulary*—The APICS Supply Chain Council's Supply Chain Operations Reference model, or SCOR, provides an industry standard for benchmarking and best practices. It is available through http://www.apics.org/sites/apics-supply-chain-council.
- *The SCOR model*—The Supply-Chain Council's Supply-Chain Operations Reference model provides an industry standard for benchmarking and best practices. It is available through http://www.supply-chain.org. Note: APICS and the Supply-Chain Council merged in 2014.
- *Principles-based education*—"How" training without "why" education is insufficient. Education is the best vehicle to learn about the end-to-end dynamics of a supply chain network and the global business processes used to operate it. The 5V Principles of Supply Chain Management developed in my earlier book, *Supply Chain Architecture: A Blueprint for Networking the Flow of Material, Information, and Cash*, provide education on throughput as a business strategy. The 5V Principles are used to make real-time, operational decisions that maximize throughput. Given a choice, you will always improve throughput by making a decision favoring higher cash-to-cash velocity and lower cash-to-cash variability. Given a choice, you will always improve throughput by making a decision favoring vocalization to pull the right mix of customer ordered inventory and visualization to push the right rate of forecasted inventory. The 5V Principles are shown:
  - *The value principle*—Every stakeholder wins when throughput is maximized.
  - *The velocity principle*—Throughput is maximized when cash-to-cash velocity is maximized by minimizing network cycle time.
  - *The variability principle*—Throughput is maximized when cash-to-cash variability is minimized by minimizing network variance.
  - *The vocalize principle*—Throughput is maximized by pulling the right inventory out of the push/pull boundary to match actual demand.
  - *The visualize principle*—Throughput is maximized by pushing the right inventory into the push/pull boundary from a supply forecast.
- *Task-focused training*—Likewise, "why" education without "how" training is insufficient. Training is the best vehicle to learn and practice narrowly focused functional tasks. Organizations such as APICS offer programs certifying member in such training.

- *Conference room pilots*—A conference room pilot is a manual walk-through of a business process. The participants follow a process flow map according to their assigned role under the direction of a moderator. The moderator directs the action along the process path, facilitates discussion and conflict resolution, and records when and where the process lacks adequate definition. This facilitates each participant being able to practice his/her role, while he/she gains an appreciation for each of the other roles. Everyone learns what information gets passed in what sequencing among the roles. Conference room pilots are usually conducted first on paper, then later using the real application software.
- *Simulation games*—Supply chain networks are complex, interrelated, and dynamic systems. It is not intuitively obvious what will happen to the customer or the owner or the supplier or the employee stakeholder when one or more variables are changed. Games, like the MIT Beer Game, provide a no-regret way to practice and learn new skills. The MIT Beer Game is available through http://supplychain.mit.edu/games/beer-game.
- *Regulatory compliance*—Supply chain management has to deal with many forms of regulatory compliance and industry standard certifications, such as import/export regulations, Customs-Trade Partnership Against Terrorism (C-TPAT) certification, ISO Quality certification, Conflict Minerals, Sarbanes-Oxley and ISO Environmental Management certification, and more. Training for specific regulations and certifications can be found on government websites; this is a fertile ground for consulting services. ISO standards are available through http://www.iso.org/iso/home/standards.htm.

Build Trust within Parent Organization Relationships

Each of the core project team members has come from a functional department within the parent organization. Each of these persons comes onto the team with personal relationships, with unique education and experience, with predispositions, and with some bias.

Wherever there are people, there are politics. The motivation for politics may be personal power, prestige, influence, wealth, or something else. When the objective of the supply chain construction project happens to align with someone's political motivation, things go well. When the objective of the supply chain construction project does not align with a person's political motivation, things can go badly. The "T" factor, trust, can creep into a person's reactions or their conversation, as in, "I don't trust you." Trust issues can occur between core team members and the parent organization at both the managerial level and the employee level. If left unaddressed, trust issues can derail a supply chain construction project.

Organization Charts and Politics

Organizational structures vary depending on a company's headcount and on its trajectory along a business life cycle. Two common organizational structures are the functional hierarchy and the matrix organization. Under a functional hierarchy, each functional area, marketing, engineering, operations, finance, etc., is a vertical silo, with direct employees reporting to supervisors, supervisors reporting to managers, managers reporting to directors, and directors reporting to vice presidents. Decision making is mostly top–down, and there are strict protocols for cross-functional communication. Under a matrix organization, the columns are functional areas, marketing, engineering, operations, etc., and the rows are product lines. Here, each product line gets a complete cross-functional team with easy cross-functional communications and mixed top–down with bottom–up decision making. A matrix organization has limited communication between product lines, and it may require "split personalities" for support functions like finance, information technology, and human resources. It is not unusual for a company to alternate from matrix to hierarchical to matrix to hierarchical over its business life cycle.

Politics is about the separation of what someone controls, what someone does not control but can influence, and what is totally out of someone's control. The object of control may be a human resource, time, budget dollars, or strategic direction. For example, if a department is forced to give up a critical person to the project or to take on incremental project work in an already overtasked environment, the department manager will not be politically supportive of the project. Sometimes, scarce budget dollars are diverted from a functional area's pet project to the supply chain construction project. Turf wars may ensue, draining energy from the project team. Project goals, resource allocations, project deadlines, and department budgets are set in fundamentally different ways in a functional hierarchy versus a matrix organization. Top–down directives versus bottom–up consensus often sets the tone for the political environment in the parent company. Try to understand from the other person's perspective what they feel is out of their control and what they are attempting to influence that may run counter to completing your supply chain construction project.

A Clash in Cultures

Every parent organization has its own culture and its own way of doing business. A technology start-up hired the best and the brightest immigrant engineers from a diversity of countries, supporting their move from green card to US citizenship status. The company culture was like a family. All of these bright people had a say in major technical product decisions. Technical alternatives were debated thoroughly, with good decisions made quickly. There were quarterly family picnics, employees went biking together at lunch, and the employees' children were welcome in the office. As the company grew in the marketplace, it was acquired for its technical expertise by a much larger company, and it moved to a new location. The new company culture was hierarchical, technically inferior, and dominated by financial considerations. Employees from the start-up now reported to the management structure of the larger company. The larger company was in the throes of implementing tight business controls to come into compliance with Sarbanes–Oxley. Employees outside a given project were discouraged from giving input on other projects. The family culture was stifled. There was no place in the new office space to store bicycles. One by one, top engineers from the start-up left for other opportunities. The acquisition to acquire technical talent resulted in a poor return on investment because of the misunderstood culture clash.

Supply chain construction projects, by their very nature, are disruptive to the status quo. The whole point of the project is to radically improve the business. Sometimes, the project team will specify a new software application or a new business process that appears counter cultural to the parent organization. Nothing is outwardly expressed, but there is passive resistance among employees. People feel they have not been involved and have not been informed; they do not own the change. People own change when they can be a party to and have input into moving from the "as-is" to the "to-be." One way to accomplish this is to have the supply chain construction project team create the "as-is" and "to-be" process maps and then facilitate town hall meetings for all the other employees. Educate the other employees about the project objective, the reasons behind the changes, and the nature of the changes. Explain to the other employees how and when they will be trained. Solicit their inputs before closing the "to-be" specification. In large company settings, outside change management and communication consultants may be attached to the project team.

Supply Chain Construction Project Communications Plan

The communications plan is an often overlooked responsibility of the supply chain construction project team. Good communications go a long way toward winning employee buy-in, blunting managerial politics, and achieving the necessary shift in business culture. Good communications help the parent organization take pride in the successful completion of the supply chain construction project.

A communications plan has two parts: content and delivery. Content comes from the project objective, the core team, and progress against the project milestones. Content covers the what, why, when, who, and how. Delivery should be repetitive and by as many means as possible. People need to hear some messages over and over again before they really "hear" it. People are attentive to different media such as meetings, bulletins, newsletters, e-mail, blogs, social media, websites, and personal testimony. The best communications plans deliver consistent messages repeatedly and regularly through several different channels. Table 3.3 shows the outline of a typical communications plan, including a blog feature where employees can respond and ask questions of the project team.

Table 3.3 Communications Plan Framework

Date	Contents	Delivery Method			
		Meeting	Newsletter	E-mail	Blog
1 Start	Commission the Team What, Why, Who, When	X	X		
2	What, Why, Progress			X	X
3	What, Progress, When			X	X
4	Overcoming Obstacles	X			X
…					
N	What, Progress, When			X	X
N + 1 End	Review the Results Celebrate Success!	X	X		

Develop Network Relationships

The Supply-Chain Council has taken the analysis of a network down to the process level within their hierarchical SCOR model. At level 1, the SCOR model uses process types PLAN, SOURCE, MAKE, DELIVER, RETURN, and ENABLE to describe a supply chain network. From there, network processes are refined into ever more detail through level 2 process categories, level 3 process elements, and level 4 activities. The SCOR model was developed to be able to compare networks across industries to identify and benchmark best practices. This book uses the level 1 SOURCE, MAKE, DELIVER, and RETURN terminology to position relationships within the network.

The set of required supply chain relationships begins with an understanding of the nature of your supply chain. Is your supply chain a forward network that builds and delivers for-revenue products to a market segment? Does your supply chain include a service component that creates and delivers one-time or recurring for-revenue services to a market segment? Or is your supply chain a reverse network that collects products from a market segment to be repaired, remanufactured, or recycled for a profit? Some businesses have simple supply chain networks, while other businesses have complex supply chain networks. When the business needs both a forward and a reverse network, the project team is well advised to execute two separate supply chain construction projects. In such a case, there should be two sets of Supply Chain Construction Requirement Specifications with two separate project timelines and two separate project budgets.

Understanding Network Vocabulary

Before going too much further, you need a working vocabulary to be able to read The Blueprint correctly. You need to understand whether the construction is progressing upstream toward the seller or downstream toward the buyer. You need to understand whether the context applies to a single, specific trading partner or to the entire end-to-end network. This book uses the following vocabulary to orient you to the correct supply chain context:

- *Supply chain node*—This is any self-contained organization within a supply chain. Examples of nodes include suppliers, contract manufacturers, factories, distributors, postponement centers, service providers, VARs, retail stores, customers, accumulators, separators, remanufacturers, recyclers, and more.
- *Supply chain arc*—This is any connection between two nodes. Arcs include logistics connections carrying materials, information technology connections carrying information, and financial connections carrying cash.
- *Trading partner*—A trading partner is any independent organization buying from an upstream echelon and selling to a downstream echelon, while conducting the majority of its business within the network.
- *Upstream*—This is the location of the seller. Cash flows upstream to the seller.
- *Midstream*—This is the connection between the factory and the distributor.
- *Downstream*—This is the location of the buyer. Material flows downstream to the buyer.
- *Echelon*—An echelon is an independent business organization that buys upstream and sells downstream.
- *Series*—Nodes that chain together from left to right are in series. For example, a supplier feeding a factory feeding a distributor feeding a retail store feeding a customer are all in series.
- *Parallel*—Nodes that stack top to bottom within the same echelon are in parallel. For example, three suppliers each feeding the same factory are in parallel.

Forward Network Relationships

The forward network examples in this book are focused on discrete manufacturing. The most basic forward network consists of a raw material supply, suppliers to SOURCE components, a factory to MAKE the product, a distributor to DELIVER the product, and many customers. From here, forward network construction may be made more complex for different purposes as shown in Figure 3.3. Product BOM complexity may cause additional breadth and depth to be added upstream of the factory. A proliferation of different demand channels may cause additional

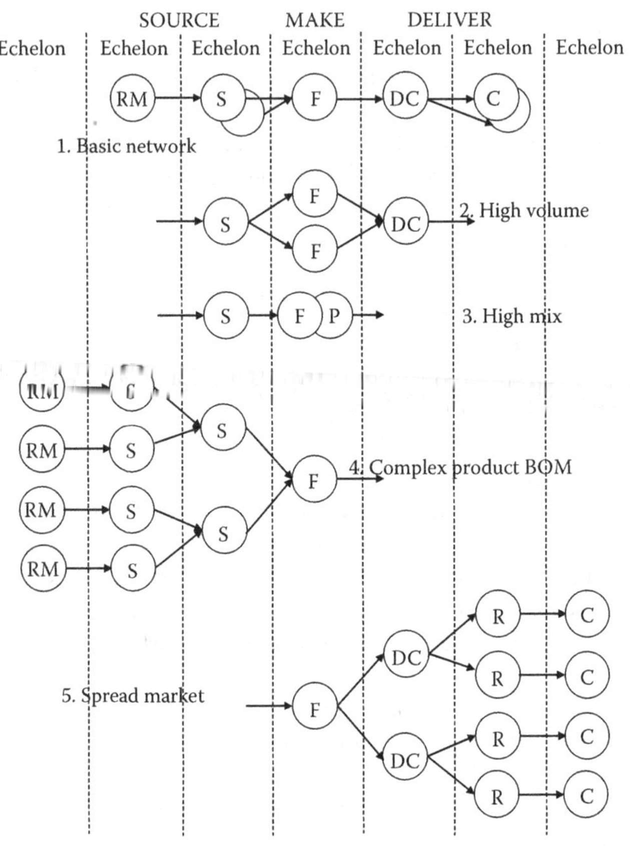

Figure 3.3 Supply chain echelon maps of forward networks for different purposes. C = customer; DC = distribution center; F = factory; P = postponement; R = retailer; RM = raw materials; S = supplier.

breadth and depth to be added downstream from the factory. Each column in the network map indicates an additional echelon in the supply chain.

- *For high volume*—Parallel independent factories may be used to multiply the network throughput capacity. For example, the apparel industry faces at least four short-duration fashion seasons a year, yet it has to deliver a high volume of the latest fashion to all of its retail stores.
- *For high mix*—High mix can be achieved by combining a factory and postponement center together in the same building. For example, a window manufacturer postpones the installation of specialty hinge and latching hardware for its custom window manufacturing in the same production space.

- *A deep supply base for a complex product*—Products with multi-level BOMs listing hundreds of components from dozens of suppliers require several upstream echelons in their supply base. For example, an electronics manufacturer building a spectrum analyzer might have 15 to 20 levels in the product BOM. Suppliers closest to the factory are often named "Tier One" suppliers and given the role of managing each of the upstream suppliers that feed into them.
- *Parallel delivery channels to reach a complex market*—Market segments spanning large geographical areas containing populations in the millions require extensive networks with multiple parallel distribution centers (DCs) and large numbers of retail stores. For example, fast-moving consumer goods businesses such as a grocery might employ 20–50 DCs and 5,000–10,000 retail stores.

Service Network Relationships

Revenue-generating services typically provide highly skilled labor and/or access to customized information to the customer in exchange for a cash payment. Service networks are usually customer facing and include relationships that provide:

- *One-time service revenue*—For example, installation or training service.
- *Recurring subscription service revenue*—For example, a website data service.
- *Repair and equipment maintenance*—For example, preventative maintenance of engines and pumps.

Reverse Network Relationships

The basic reverse network accumulates returned products, called "cores," modifies the core through remanufacture or value-subtracting processes, and redistributes the result to an aftermarket and/or through environmental stewardship. The reverse network configurations detailed throughout this book are shown in Figure 3.4. The basic network changes depending on the purpose of the supply chain being repair, remanufacture, or recycling. Each column in the network map indicates an additional echelon in the supply chain.

Examples of for-revenue reverse networks include the following:

- *Send–repair–return*—Product repair and/or calibration. For example, a business that repairs and calibrates digital voltmeters, frequency generators, and other electronic test equipment.
- *Collect–remanufacture–resell*—Product remanufacturing for an aftermarket segment. For example, a business that refurbishes engine parts for motorcycles.
- *Collect–disassemble and separate–recycle*—Spent and/or defective product accumulation, disassembly, and recycling. For example, a business that collects obsolete personal computers, disassembles them, and recycles the plastic, aluminum, copper printed circuit boards, and glass displays.

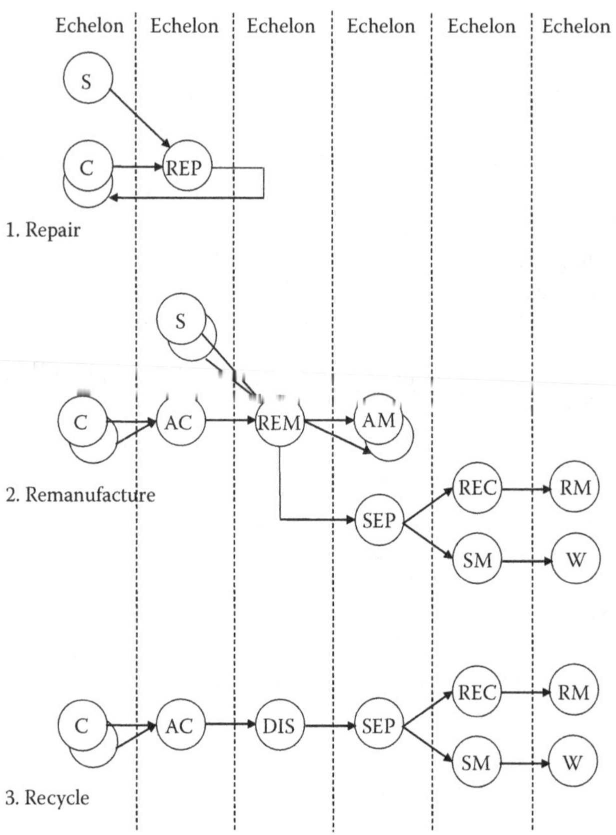

Figure 3.4 Supply chain echelon maps of reverse networks for different purposes. AC = accumulator; AM = aftermarket customer; C = customer; DIS = disassembler; REC = recycler; REM = remanufacture; REP = repair; RM = raw materials; S = supplier; SEP = separator; SM = smelter; W = waste.

Build Trust with External Relationships

There are time, distance, and cultural differences between the relationship of the project team with its parent organization and the relationship of the project team with its other trading partners. The people within external trading partner organizations are not as readily available. You cannot just walk down the hall to be face to face with the other person. When you pick up your phone or type at your keyboard, you may have to wait half a day for the other person to come online. When you layer on top of time and distance the high probability of cultural differences and language barriers, there is no wonder trading partner communications and trust are so difficult.

Trading Partner Communications

The first weekly teleconference between the factory in New Jersey and the supplier in Germany was held on March 19. New Jersey initiated the call at 11:00 a.m., which was 4:00 p.m. in Germany. The same teleconference was held on March 26. On April 2, New Jersey initiated the call at 11:00 a.m., but the phone rang and rang and rang in Germany. Finally, the night guard at the supplier responded saying it was after 5:00 p.m. and the company had gone home for the evening. Daylight savings time in Europe changes later than in the United States.

It is easy to misinterpret international communications and to miss international deadlines, as the following suggests:

- *English to metric dimensions*—Length 45 inches is 1,143 millimeters; date March 6, 2014 is 6.3.14; weight 265 pounds is 120.4 kilograms.
- *Currency conversions*—$2,000.00USD is equivalent to 1,545.60 Euros. Currency conversion is dynamic, with exchange rates constantly changing.
- *Language*—Local language dialects and idioms sometimes cloud the meaning of spoken and written language.
- *E-mail*—Write one question per e-mail, and ask for an acknowledgment. When there are several questions, send several e-mails, each with a different subject line.
- *Holidays*—Holidays in multicultural countries like Malaysia include Vesak Day, Hari Raya Puasa, National Day, Hari Raya Haji, Deepavali, and many others.
- *Regional vacation times*—Many countries in Europe take the whole month of July for vacation; Chinese New Year runs nearly two weeks. Factories are closed during these periods.
- *World time zones*—Local time relative to Greenwich Mean Time. When you are doing business globally, it is important to organize your day around the windows of time you will be able to speak with folks in Europe and with folks in Asia.

Bridging Cultural Differences

It is difficult to earn someone's trust if you have never met face to face and have never experienced their culture. Relationships with strategic trading partners, such as contract manufacturers and distributors, often start from a personal relationship between two senior executives who have met sometime in the past and have shared some experience. This mutual respect relationship is bound by their personal relationship and a sense of shared business values. In their global travels, they have probably visited and sampled each other's cultures. But as the relationship is shifted to underlings, the new faces have neither the personal bounds nor the cultural appreciation held by their executive. There may be no budget allocation to travel to a foreign site. Still, there are several important steps that can be taken to bridge the cultural gap.

- Always be polite and respectful.
- Give the other party a face-saving "out" when they do not know or cannot answer.
- Do what you say you will do in the timeframe promised.
- Ask for an acknowledgment on each communication that restates the question.
- Wherever possible, include photos with textual instructions.
- When documents are translated, employ a "round-trip" translation; compare the reverse translation with the original document.
- Develop a second independent information path to confirm what you are hearing from the first path.
- Picture books from your area of the United States make good presents.
- Look up reference books on their country in the children's section of a public library. Such books cover food, dress, customs, and a language lesson in a few pages with lots of pictures.
- At the end of each teleconference or video conference, spend a few minutes on the phone or video link learning about their culture.
- If at all possible, travel to share a meal face to face at their location.
- Learn a few words in their language.

A global manufacturing company deployed several international procurement organizations (IPOs) to countries having strategic sources of supply. One such IPO team consisting of a buyer, a materials engineer, and a logistician was in Singapore to facilitate understanding local laws, customs, and logistics infrastructure for material moving from Malaysia, Thailand, Vietnam, and Singapore to the United States. When a division of the company asked a certain contract manufacturer in Malaysia if a product shipment had been made, the answer came back as "yes." But the IPO had visited the contract manufacturer just the day before and had learned of a production hold. Furthermore, the IPO had not yet received copies of the ocean freight manifest from the forwarder. In fact, the product had not left the factory. In the Asian culture, "yes" means that your question was heard but not necessarily that the answer to your question is yes. The parallel information path from the IPO was invaluable in setting the right expectations for the real delivery date into the United States.

Some Common Causes of Mistrust

Certain issues will absolutely trigger a lack of trust from your trading partner, whether they are international or domestic. The first is concerned with the probability of getting paid. Perhaps, the buyer and seller found each other through an Internet search. When the two parties have never met face to face and have never done business together, the buyer usually questions the quality and delivery of the goods and the seller usually questions the amount and receipt of the payment. The buyer requests samples or a supplier visit. The seller requests prepayment or a letter of credit. A letter of credit places the full payment with a third-party bank until the product delivery is confirmed. It is important to separate what the seller and buyer control versus what is out of control of the seller and buyer. Sometimes, a lack of trust gets built on an issue that is out of the control of both the seller and buyer; this is unfortunate. For example, neither party controls inflation or currency exchange rates or fuel surcharges or import quotas or duties or extreme weather conditions.

A second lack of trust trigger is the way you and the trading partner handle intellectual property. Much of the time, it is your intellectual property that the trading partner pledges to not steal. Sometimes, it is the intellectual property owned by the trading partner that you pledge to not steal. Intellectual property is normally covered first by a nondisclosure agreement (NDA) and later by a pricing contract. The NDA specifies that neither the signatory nor any of their employees will leak the information. Patents become problematic because they can be researched through public websites. For this reason, some very valuable inventions and trade secrets are never patented or registered. Engineering conversations with salespeople and production line visits by suppliers have been known to divulge trade secrets. Sensitive information is best kept on a strictly need-to-know basis. Some Asian countries set the expectation that if you want to do business with them, it will cost you in the transfer of some significant intellectual property. The ultimate goal for that country is to be able to replicate what you can do at a much lower cost, thereby becoming your competitor.

A third lack of trust trigger comes from delivery channel conflict. Channel conflict can occur when the same product is offered through two different delivery channels at two different prices. For example, the same product might be sold through a self-service website where there is no sales commission and sold through a sales representative who is paid a commission. Disintermediation refers to a supply chain with a multiechelon delivery channel attempting to eliminate one of its intermediary distribution echelons to improve profitability. This causes a lack of trust within the delivery channel and an unwillingness to freely share customer and ordering information.

Finally, and unfortunately, a trusting relationship can be disrupted when one of the parties is promoted, changes employers, or dies. Since trust is normally between individuals who represent their organizations, it can be very difficult for a new person to earn the trust of the remaining partner. This is where it is helpful to have at least a memorandum of understanding (MOU) drafted between the original parties. The MOU documents the reason and basic benefit for the relationship, but it can never replace the personal trust factor.

Pricing Contracts

A pricing contract is a common form of a contractual relationship with a trading partner. A pricing contract is an agreement from the seller to provide a minimum quantity of specific product(s) at a guaranteed price to the buyer over a fixed time period. The seller uses the pricing contract as the basis of buying raw materials and component parts at volume discounts from their supply base. The buyer uses the pricing contract to lock in pricing over an extended period. Some think that a pricing contract trumps cultural differences and mistrust. Nothing could be further from the truth. Where strong cultural differences exist, you may never achieve a written contract. Where trust issues exist, you will spend a great deal of resources attempting to terminate a written contract.

Two common forms of the pricing contract are the annual volume agreement, also called a blanket agreement, and the long-term agreement (LTA). Annual volume agreements are used for high-value items, when you have sustained a high-volume business. Annual volume agreements are written to cover one year between renewals. Purchase orders are released as needed and linked to the blanket agreement. LTAs are used when your product depends upon a sole sourced technology. The LTA is usually written to cover three or more years between renewals. The LTA locks in pricing and serves to maintain your allocation of the supplier's inventory regardless of market forces and/or interruptions to the supplier's supply chain. Because of the amount of resources it takes to write, negotiate, and maintain contractual agreements, many companies limit their contracts to sole-source and single-source suppliers and to their strategic commodities.

Here are the main paragraphs found in pricing agreements:

- *Contract parties*—This is the name and contact information for the seller and the buyer.
- *Contract purpose*—The contract guarantees pricing and allocates product for the buyer; the contract guarantees volume and allocates strategic market access for the seller.
- *Nonexclusive*—The parties reserve the right to do business related to the same set of products with other third parties not named in the contract.
- *Signatures*—This is the signature of an executive in each organization having the agency to make this contract.
- *Appendices with price, volume, products, product revision*—The details of price and volume by item number are usually placed in an appendix to facilitate changing the product details without changing the legal body of the contract.
- *Licensing*—The seller is licensed by the buyer to produce a product design owned by the buyer. It is common LTA practice for the product design documentation to be held in escrow with a third party as insurance against a contractual default.

- *Forecasts and planning*—This is the frequency and planning horizon for updated demand information given to the seller by the buyer.
- *Provision for product revision*—These are additional costs for the seller to process a product revision.
- *Provision for custom tooling*—These are additional costs for the seller to provide custom tooling.
- *Warranty*—This is the period of time the seller warranties material and workmanship. Ninety days and one year are both common warranty periods.
- *Terms of payment*—Use the Unified Commercial Code for domestic agreements and INCOTERMS for international agreements.
- *Performance measures*—These are specific key performance indicators directly related to the contract.

Terms regarding the length of the agreement include the following:

- *Starting date and ending date*—This is the period of time the contract is in force.
- *Evergreen clause*—If the business arrangement has gone well, this extends the contract with the same provisions for another period without a contract negotiation. It requires the signatures of both parties.
- *Termination due to seller's lack of performance*—Early contract termination is driven by the seller's lack of delivery or quality performance.
- *Provision for inventory allocation*—The seller specifies how limited product will be allocated against this agreement.
- *Provision for residual inventory*—The buyer must take receipt of and make payment for any product volume that has not been consumed by the end of the contract period.

Terms regarding legal issues that should be written and reviewed by legal counsel include the following:

- *Intellectual property*—This is legal protection of the intellectual properties of both parties.
- *Confidential information*—Both parties agree to respect certain kinds of confidential information.
- *Governing law*—This is the name of the state and country whose governing law holds precedence.
- *Conflict resolution and arbitration*—The buyer and seller agree to third-party arbitration rather than a jury trial for any conflict they cannot resolve between themselves.
- *Entire agreement*—The document constitutes the entire agreement.
- *Supersedes*—The document takes the place of any earlier agreement between the parties.

- *Indemnification*—Each party agrees to not hold the other party liable for unrelated actions.
- *Severability*—If some part of the contract is determined to be illegal, the remaining parts of the contract are still in force.
- *Force majeure*—Unprecedented events, acts of God, extreme weather, riot, and civil discontent, etc., do not constitute a lack of performance.
- *Compliance with the law*—The seller agrees to comply with all labor and employment laws.
- *Executed in counterparts*—Identical copies of the pricing contract can be signed in parallel by the parties, and then swapped for the matching signature.

In Summary

This chapter explains how to build trusting relationships. To be effective, members of the project team need to trust their project manager and project champion executive. In turn, in spite of the politics, the project team has to gain the trust of the functional departments within their parent organization. Mutual respect and trust must be built across the different cultures, geographical distance, and time zones that can separate the SOURCE, MAKE, DELIVER, and RETURN trading partner relationships that make up a supply chain network. A contractual agreement will never replace a trusting relationship. Finally, this chapter details supply chain echelon maps for both forward and reverse supply chain networks.

Chapter 4

Cash Flow

This chapter focuses on cash flow. It explains why cash flow is so important to a business and how to accelerate it. Building high-velocity cash flow is one key to constructing a great supply chain. Cash flow begins with setting the right pricing, echelon by echelon, across the supply chain network. Product pricing leads to revenue on the income statement, which in turn leads to margin, and ultimately, to net profit, which generates cash. Cash is consumed operationally by inventory, accounts receivable, and other things as recorded on the balance sheet. The cash flow statement records changes to cash flow from operations, from investing, and from financing. This chapter also details how to budget for financing the supply chain construction project. By the end of this chapter, you will understand how cash flows into and out of the balance sheet, how cash is replenished from income statement profit, how changes to cash are tracked on the cash flow statement, and how to estimate extra cash needs for your supply chain construction project.

A Dollar Wise and $10 Million Foolish

"I really don't see how we can even get started on this project. We know nothing about the product," said Donna, the buyer assigned to the Supply Chain Construction Team. Donna had been amazed that she was asked to join such an auspicious team. Her personality was to be very direct, and she knew how to get purchasing done with a bit of a "take no prisoners" attitude.

"Actually, we have a couple of key pieces of information about the product even at this early date in the project," said Bill, the program manager. Bill had been chosen to lead the team through the Supply Chain Construction Blueprint because of his supply chain knowledge. "We know, for instance, that the target price is $500 for the Product 500 model, or 'a dollar a watt.' Maybe Harry can tell us more?"

Harry was the third member of the new team. As a product marketing engineer, he had been working under Jerry's direction for the past two months to understand the VAR landscape and to gather information about the competition. Harry replied, "We want to market an uninterruptable power supply (UPS) product family that maps into the new family of midrange servers from the Computer Products Division. We think the middle UPS product, the Product 500 model, will have the highest volume. This should be our flagship model."

Harry continued, "Several competitors have UPS models at about a $500 price point; of course, they don't have the feature set that ours will have. From our power supply experience with costs across a product family, it is very likely that the Product 250 model will be priced a little more than a dollar per watt, while the Product 1000 model will be priced a little less than a dollar per watt."

Since Harry was talking about cost, Tony's attention perked up, "Yes, that's right. We have seen that kind of trend again and again across our power supply product families because of the fixed material costs involved. By the way, what is a VAR?" Tony worked for Alice in Finance and had been helping Bill put together a budget for the supply chain construction project.

Harry replied, "A value-added reseller (VAR) is a systems integrator who takes delivery of the individual computer system components, assembles, and programs the system, then delivers and installs the system at the customer's location all at once."

"You said that we know a couple of things?" Donna asked.

Bill replied, "Yes, in the past two weeks, Engineering has roughed out a block diagram for the UPS product and has estimated the material cost of the main components. John, how does that look?"

John was the fifth member of the team. He was quiet and thoughtful, and he would become intimate with every detail of the UPS product design. John said, "Right, building on our experience designing families of power supplies, there are certain things that we know. For example, the package design will use a common front and rear frame, with the depth of the package growing as the power level increases to accommodate a larger number of battery cells. The same basic battery cell will be used in each product, but the number of cells will vary. The control board and basic circuit can be identical across the family. The battery to line voltage power inverter is similar to our switching power supplies, but some of the transformers and capacitors will have to change across power levels."

"What about material costs?" Bill asked again.

"Engineering is estimating $180 in direct material for the Product 500 model UPS, but that is likely to go up a few dollars by the time the design is completed," replied John.

Tony was busy punching numbers into his calculator. He then said, "If we use a ratio of 50% direct material to cost of goods sold (COGS) and a ratio of 75% COGS to selling price, then $180 in direct material gives us a $480 selling price. We're good to go!"

"Not so fast," said Bill. "You are forgetting one very key factor. We manufacture and distribute our power supplies today direct from this location to worldwide customers. But we are going to sell our UPS product family through VARs. According to Jerry, these VARs expect to purchase our product at a 30% discount."

"Oh," said Tony, in a deflated voice.

Bill continued, "You have the calculator Tony. What is 50% direct material to COGS and 75% COGS to VAR price and 70% VAR price to selling price on $180 of direct material?"

"$686. We're screwed," said Tony quietly.

Donna suggested, "If the volume exceeds some breakpoint, maybe we can get a price discount on material purchases. What volume are we talking about anyway? Do you have a forecast, Harry?"

Harry replied, "We still have a lot of work to do with the sales guys and the VARs before we can get to a good forecast."

"How do we construct a supply chain if we don't know the unit volume?" asked Donna again.

"Harry, as a top priority from this team, you need to find out the forecast for the new server family from your contacts at Computer Products. Every server will need a UPS, right?" asked Bill.

Harry responded, "Well, no. There will be a connect rate because some servers will go into installations that already have emergency generators and battery backup. I'll see what I can find out."

"We can estimate volume from one assumption for now. This is suspect because it is based on a management wish rather than a demand forecast. I'm talking about Steve's statement that Corporate will not support any new business that does not achieve at least $10 million in sales in its first year. Clearly, this is not based on any market research. But how many UPS units is that, Tony?" asked Bill.

Tony punched more numbers into his calculator, "20,000 units at $500/unit equals $10 million in revenue. If the business ramps linearly from 0 to 20,000 units in 12 months, then the run rate at the end of the first year is 3,333 units per month. If the business starts faster, the run rate drops toward an average of 20,000 units divided by 12 months, or 1,667 units per month."

"To answer your question, Donna, start with a working assumption for purchasing of an annual throughput of 20,000 units at a run rate of, say, 2,500 units per month. But when Harry gets the real server forecast, don't be surprised if that number is much smaller," said Bill.

"That's a higher volume than normal! I can work with that," replied Donna.

Bill continued, "There is one more thing we need to estimate while we are roughing out parameters for the new business. We need to estimate how much cash the Power Products Division will need to fund the start-up. There are two major cash investments: accounts receivable and inventory."

"Why do we need cash for accounts receivable? Don't customers pay for their purchases?" asked John.

"That's a good question, and the answer is that most customer accounts are NET30 days, meaning we give 30 days of credit before payment is due. I'm sure the VARs, as our customers, will get NET30 day terms," replied Bill.

"At a run rate of 2,500 units per month and a VAR price of $350 per unit, that's $875,000 for 30 days of accounts receivable," calculated Tony before being asked.

"Inventory investment is harder to figure until we develop a planning cycle and how much safety stock we might need. But, as a guestimate, suppose we can turn inventory every three months, or four times per year, and that the inventory profile looks like a sawtooth repeating every three months. And suppose we are able to get the product COGS down to $262 per unit. Then the average inventory would be (one half) times (2,500 units per month) times (three months) times ($262 per unit) or, looking to Tony, $982,500," continued Bill.

"Almost a million dollars… That's a pile of cash!" whistled Tony.

"Yes, and that cash stays always invested in inventory. That is because when last month's inventory is paid for from customer orders, we have to turn right around and reinvest that cash to buy new inventory for next month's shipments," lectured Bill.

"Ouch," exclaimed John.

"OK, let me summarize where we stand at the start of our supply chain construction project. We need to deliver a family of three different UPS products through the Computer Products VAR channel. The flagship model is the Product 500 UPS; it needs to sell to the VAR for $350 to sell to the end customer for $500. Engineering's first estimate of direct material cost is about $180. This does not fit into our current pricing model. A guestimate of unit volume is a first year throughput of 20,000 units with a run rate of 2,500 units per month by the 12th month. Harry has the action item to get a real forecast. Finally, Corporate will have to invest about $1,857,500 in accounts receivable and inventory during the first year of start-up. That's it, see you next week."

Get a Handle on the Balance

Think about your personal checking account. This is your operating cash. Cash payments in the form of checks are made for things that you buy—food, housing, clothing, transportation, etc.—from your upstream suppliers. Cash receipts in the form of deposits are made from things that you sell—hours of employment, shares of an investment, etc.—to your downstream customers. The following relationships hold from period to period:

$$\text{Ending cash} = \text{Starting cash} + \text{Cash receipts} - \text{Cash payments} \tag{4.1}$$

$$\text{Starting cash to the next period} = \text{Ending cash from the last period} \tag{4.2}$$

Your current checking account balance determines the total amount of cash you have to spend. You cannot spend more than the cash you have on-hand unless you increase your checking account balance by taking out a bank loan, borrowing against a credit card, or convincing a friend to "invest" in some project you are doing. The bank loan and the credit card debt must be paid back in full with interest within a stipulated timeframe. The bank and the credit card company can force you into personal bankruptcy if you cannot make the payments. The friend expects some return on his or her investment in the not too distant future, but he or she may not have much leverage if you just spend the money. The friend is better off to expect some kind of collateral or "ownership" in the project as leverage against a return on investment.

When cash flows freely in and out of your checking account, the cash flow is said to be liquid. Liquidity is a key property of cash flow for any business. When cash is constrained either going into your account or coming out of your account, the cash flow is said to be illiquid. This means that you cannot buy and sell freely. This can quickly become a big obstacle to your business. Complete illiquidity is a common cause of business failure.

Balance Sheet Basics

While it is assumed that many people understand a balance sheet, experience teaches that this is not the case. A balance sheet records assets, liabilities, and net worth at a point in time. This is usually at the start and again at the end of an accounting period, for example, at the start and at the end of a calendar month. The balance sheet shows assets on the left side. Liabilities and net worth are shown on the right side. Assets and liabilities come in two flavors, current and long-term. A current asset or current liability is relevant for less than one year. A long-term asset, also called a fixed asset, and a long-term liability, also called long-term debt, is relevant for more than one year. A balance sheet is always in balance; therefore, total assets must equal total liabilities plus total net worth. Table 4.1 shows the accounts are included on most balance sheets.

$$\$\text{Total assets} = \$\text{Total liabilities} + \$\text{Total net worth} \tag{4.3}$$

$$(\$\text{Current assets} + \$\text{Fixed assets}) = (\$\text{Current liabilities} + \$\text{Long-term debt}) + \$\text{Net worth} \tag{4.4}$$

- *Current assets: cash*—Money available to the business to buy things.
- *Current assets: accounts receivable*—Money customers owe the business for product shipped.
- *Current assets: inventory*—The dollar value of raw material, work-in-process, and finished goods owned by the business.
- *Long-term assets: fixed assets*—The dollar value of land, plant, and equipment owned by the business.

Table 4.1 Example Year-End Balance Sheet

Balance Sheet *Company Name* *Dec. 31, 20YY*			
Assets		*Liabilities*	
Cash +Accounts receivable +Inventory	$350,000 $610,000 $1,285,000	Accrued expenses payable +Accounts payable +Accrued income taxes payable	$210,000 $395,000 $91,500
Total current assets	$2,245,000	Total current liabilities	$696,500
Fixed assets −Accumulated depreciation	$2,000,000 −$175,000	Long-term debt	$2,448,500
		Total liabilities	$3,145,000
Total asset book value	$1,825,000		
		Net Worth	
		Paid-in capital +Retained earnings	$800,000 $125,000
		Total net worth	$925,000
Total assets	$4,070,000	Total liabilities + Net worth	$4,070,000

- *Long-term assets: accumulated depreciation*—A reduction in the value of assets over time as a result of wear and tear.
- *Long-term assets: asset book value*—The sum of fixed assets minus accumulated depreciation.
- *Total assets: total assets*—The sum of total current assets plus total asset book value.
- *Current liabilities: accrued expenses payable*—Accumulated, noninventory expenses owed but not yet paid.
- *Current liabilities: accounts payable*—Money the business owes suppliers for materials received.
- *Current liabilities: accrued income taxes payable*—Accumulated income tax payments due but not yet paid.
- *Long-term liability: long-term debt*—Loans to finance the business that run for more than one year.
- *Total liabilities*—The sum of total current liabilities plus long-term debt.

- *Net worth: paid-in capital*—Money given to the business in exchange for fractional ownership of the business.
- *Net worth: retained earnings*—The accumulation of a portion of net profit kept for reinvestment in the business.
- *Net worth: net worth*—The sum of paid-in capital plus retained earnings.

Four of these balance sheet accounts play a key role in supply chain cash-to-cash cycles. These accounts are cash, accounts receivable, accounts payable, and inventory.

Cash In on the Cash-to-Cash Cycle

Supply chain networks consist of a series of interlocking echelons that flow material downstream while flowing cash upstream. Each trading partner in a supply chain buys from other organizations in upstream echelons and sells to other organization in downstream echelons. In this way, material flows downstream, while cash flows upstream. The cash-to-cash cycle time is the number of days difference between when the trading partner has to pay the upstream seller (supplier), the average time inventory is held, and when the trading partner gets paid by the downstream buyer (customer). This cash-to-cash cycle may be positive or negative.

- When a trading partner gets paid by its customer before having to pay its supplier, the cash-to-cash cycle is negative. This is because the downstream buyer's cash is used to pay the upstream seller.
- When a trading partner has to pay its supplier before getting paid by its customer, the cash-to-cash cycle is positive. This is because the trading partner has to finance some number of days of cash to pay the seller.

Common Forms of Orders, Deliveries, and Payments

Ordering, delivering, and cash payment take many forms, as shown in Table 4.2. Different market segments tend to have different combinations of preferences. In a retail store scenario, the customer comes to the store to shop, brings the product up to the cash register, and pays the cashier with cash, a debit card, or a credit card. In an industrial purchase scenario, a buyer places a purchase order against the company's credit limit, later accepts a less-than-truckload delivery, and finally approves the payment of the invoice for an Automated Clearing House (ACH) wire transfer. In an Internet shopping scenario, the customer goes online to view an electronic catalog, places his or her order into an electronic shopping cart, pays for the order with a credit card, and waits for next day delivery of the product from UPS or FedEx.

Table 4.2 Common Forms of Orders, Deliveries, and Payments

Flow	*Format*
Orders	Purchase orders Catalog phone order or mail order Fax order Electronic data interchange (EDI) In-person shopping Internet catalog and shopping cart
Order acknowledgment	E-mail Electronic data interchange (EDI)
Delivery	Third-party logistics, including airfreight, rail freight and ocean freight packaged in cartons, pallets, less-than-truckload (LTL), truck load (TL), less-than-container load (LCL), container load (CL) Customer pickup Small-parcel deliveries like UPS, FedEx, USPS, DHL
Delivery acknowledgment	Advance shipping notice (ASN) UPS, FedEx, USPS, DHL tracking websites Proof of delivery
Payment	Cash payment Debit cards Credit cards and procurement cards PayPal Automated Clearing House (ACH) electronic wire transfers Electronic data interchange (EDI) Invoice and check Letters of credit (LOC)
Payment acknowledgment	Online bank statement Account alerts Electronic data interchange (EDI)

In each of these scenarios, in the case of a product return, a warranty claim, or a product recall, the seller must be prepared to reverse the set of transactions with the buyer. In such a case, the buyer usually initiates the reversal by asking the seller for a return authorization; this is the order. The seller instructs the buyer on how to package and ship the returned or defective product; this is the delivery. The seller than decides to either refund the payment, issue a credit for a future purchase, or replace the initial product with a replacement; this is the cash.

Every trading partner's supply chain operation in every echelon can be broken down into four parts: the supply side order-to-delivery-to-cash (ODC) cycle, the trading partner's operations that turn inventory, the trading partner's operations that fund cash, and the demand side ODC cycle.

Supply Side ODC Cycle

Each trading partner establishes a supply side order-to-delivery-to-cash (ODC_{Supply}) cycle with each and every upstream organization that sells to them. ODC_{Supply} cycles apply to both inventory and noninventory purchases depending on the purpose of the organization. ODC_{Supply} cycles may be repetitive, occasional and on-demand, or one-time transactions. Ordering and acknowledgment, delivery and acknowledgment, and payment and acknowledgment may take any of the forms shown in Table 4.2. A basic information set including such items as contact names, e-mail addresses, physical addresses, phone numbers, account numbers, etc., is required to define an ODC_{Supply} cycle between the seller and the buyer.

When the ODC_{Supply} cycle spans a large geographical area, there are time zone conversion considerations. Information, material, and cash moving from east to west will gain time according to the time zone differences between the origin and destination. On the other hand, information, material, and cash moving from west to east will lose time according to the time zone differences between the origin and destination. In every case, there will be matchups; if the order gains time, then the material delivery will lose the equivalent time. If the invoice loses time, then the cash payment will gain equivalent time. Several Internet websites, such as http://www.timeanddate.com/worldclock/, provide times for world cities and time zone conversion charts.

There are four kinds of ODC_{Supply} cycles: reoccurring inventory purchases, one-time inventory purchases, reoccurring noninventory purchases, and one-time noninventory purchases. Reoccurring inventory and noninventory purchases mean that it is worth the effort to establish an efficient ODC cycle because it will be exercised again and again. One-time purchase cycles, while they may be for large dollars or may involve high risk, will probably never be exercised again.

Operations That Turn Inventory

Trading partners and nominal trading partners hold one or more kinds of inventory and need to turn this inventory to continue operations. Inventory is said to turn when its quantity is completely consumed and has to be replenished.

- *Supplier and factory operations*—Suppliers, factories, fabricators, contract manufacturers, and original equipment manufacturers (OEM) turn raw material inventory first into work-in-process inventory and then into finished goods inventory through some transformational, value-adding manufacturing process.
- *Postponement center operations*—Postponement and fulfillment centers turn cycle stock inventory into finished goods inventory through some transformational, value-adding postponement process that completes the product.
- *Distributor and store operations*—Distributors, warehouses, wholesalers, retail stores, and accumulators turn their cycle stock inventory through some nontransformational, value-neutral distribution process.
- *Service operations*—Service bureaus and service centers may not carry inventory. Repair facilities turn cycle stock inventory through some nontransformational, value-neutral service operation.
- *Logistics operations*—Third-party logistics companies, forwarders, carriers, or customs hold inbound, midbound, and outbound in-transit inventory. Such in-transit inventory is turned through some nontransformational, value-neutral logistics process.
- *Remanufacturing and recycling operations*—Remanufacturers, recyclers, disassemblers, and smelters turn core inventory into work-in-process inventory into raw material inventory through some transformational, value-subtracting reverse process.

Operations That Fund Cash Flow

Trading partners and other organizations tied to the network hold one or more kinds of cash and need to fund more cash flow to continue operations.

- *Fund cash flow from current accounts receivable*—As customers pay for products and services, their payments are added to your cash flow that pays for your purchases.
- *Fund cash flow from an open line of credit*—You establish an open, revolving line of credit with your bank. This may or may not involve collateral such as inventory. When your current accounts payable exceed available cash flow, you can dip into this line of credit to make your payments. You must pay interest on any outstanding balance until you are able to pay back the principle.

- *Fund cash flow from a procurement card*—This is a business credit card used for limited kinds of purchases such as small inventory items, expendable supplies, and certain noninventory purchases. Procurement cards are a type of credit used for convenience and for small dollar purchases that are not worth the processing costs of a purchase order. You must pay interest on any outstanding balance until you are able to pay back the principle.
- *Fund cash flow from long-term debt*—This is a business loan used to fund the cash flow to make large purchases such as plant, equipment, inventory, and accounts receivable. The loan often involves some kind of collateral such as the bank holding title to a building or a machine tool or inventory. The loan carries monthly interest payments, with the principle being paid back either in installments or as a balloon payment at the end.
- *Fund cash flow from additional paid-in capital*—You may decide to raise additional capital to fund cash flow by selling additional shares of stock in your company. Such a sale dilutes the stock holdings of other investors and may result in another party, such as a venture capitalist, taking ownership of your business.
- *Fund cash flow from factoring*—This is a last resort measure. Factoring means that you sell your accounts receivable to a third party for immediate cash. However, the third party may only pay out 80% of the value of your receivables. In essence, you are trading 20% of your revenue to gain immediate liquidity.

Demand Side ODC Cycle

Each trading partner establishes a demand side order-to-delivery-to-cash (ODC_{Demand}) cycle with each and every downstream organization that buys from them. ODC_{Demand} cycles apply to both inventory and noninventory purchases depending on the purpose of the organization. ODC_{Demand} cycles may be repetitive, occasional and on-demand, or one-time transactions. Ordering and acknowledgment, delivery and acknowledgment, and payment and acknowledgment may take any of the forms shown in Table 4.2. A basic information set including such items as contact names, e-mail addresses, physical addresses, phone numbers, account numbers, etc., is required to define an ODC_{Demand} cycle between the seller and the buyer.

When the ODC_{Demand} cycle spans a large geographical area, there are time zone conversion considerations. Information, material, and cash moving from east to west will gain time according to the time zone differences between the origin and destination. On the other hand, information, material, and cash moving from west to east will lose time according to the time zone differences between the origin and destination. In every case, there will be matchups; if the order gains time, then the material delivery will lose the equivalent time. If the invoice loses time, then the cash payment will gain equivalent time. Several Internet websites, such as http://www.timeanddate.com/worldclock/, provide times for world cities and time zone conversion charts.

There are three kinds of ODC_{Demand} cycles: irregular sales, periodic sales, and subscription sales. An irregular sale means that the sale may occur just one time, or that the customer, or customer location, or product, or shipping method changes each time. Something about the ODC_{Demand} cycle is in constant flux. With a periodic sale, you are delivering the same product to the same customer location on a regular basis. Subscription sales occur for certain types of service revenue on a repetitive, often monthly, basis. Periodic sales and subscription sales exercise the exact same ODC cycle again and again.

Cash-to-Cash Cycle

A trading partner's cash-to-cash cycle begins with the strategic operating decision of whether to run the business as build-to-stock (BTS), build-to-order (BTO), assemble-to-order (ATO), or as engineer-to-order (ETO). These operating strategies are covered in Chapter 9: "Demand Planning." In a BTS business, the upstream seller (supplier) gets paid before the downstream buyer (customer) pays; this results in a positive cash-to-cash cycle. An ODC_{Supply} cycle is followed by an operation that turns raw material inventory into finished goods inventory, which is followed by an ODC_{Demand} cycle.

$$\begin{aligned}\text{Days of cash-to-cash cycle} &= \text{Days inventory outstanding} \\ &+ \text{Days sales outstanding} - \text{Days payable outstanding}\end{aligned} \tag{4.5}$$

$$\$COGS = \$Material + \$Labor + \$Overhead \tag{4.6}$$

$$\begin{aligned}\text{Days inventory outstanding} &= (\$Inventory_{Start} + \$Inventory_{End}) \\ &\times 365 \text{ days}/(2 \times \text{Annual COGS})\end{aligned} \tag{4.7}$$

$$\begin{aligned}\text{Days sales outstanding} &= (\$AR_{Start} + \$AR_{End}) \\ &\times 365 \text{ days}/(2 \times \$\text{Annual revenue})\end{aligned} \tag{4.8}$$

$$\begin{aligned}\text{Days payable outstanding} &= (\$AP_{Start} + \$AP_{End}) \\ &\times 365 \text{ days}/(2 \times \$\text{Annual COGS})\end{aligned} \tag{4.9}$$

In a BTO business, the downstream buyer (customer) pays before the upstream seller (supplier) has to be paid; this results in a negative cash-to-cash cycle. An ODC_{Demand} cycle is followed by an ODC_{Supply} cycle, which is followed by an operation that turns raw material inventory into finished goods inventory.

The decision on whether to operate with a BTS, BTO, ATO, or ETO strategy is based on the competitive delivery lead time you want to achieve. Delivery lead time is determined by the location of the push/pull boundary and is covered in detail in

Chapter 9: "Demand Planning." Many businesses run a combination of BTS for some products and BTO for other products. This means that individual products run both positive and negative cash-to-cash cycles.

Example Cash-to-Cash Cycle

The ODC_{Supply} cycle pertains to the organization buying upstream. The ODC_{Demand} cycle pertains to the organization selling downstream. Figure 4.1 shows an example factory BTS scenario. In this example, ODC_{Supply} is 56 days, while ODC_{Demand} is 32 days. Twenty-five days after receiving the factory's raw material order, the supplier ships the raw material and issues an invoice to the factory with NET30 day terms. Two days later, the factory receives the raw material. The factory takes 10 days to build the product and put it into finished goods inventory. After an average holding time of 10 days, the factory receives a customer order and takes one day to make the shipment. The factory ships the product from finished goods inventory and invoices the customer with NET30 day terms. In this example, the average cash-to-cash cycle is a positive 23 days, while the delivery lead time seen by the customer is 5 days.

Notice that in such a BTS scenario, the inventory holding time variability of ±5 days directly impacts the cash-to-cash cycle time by ±5 days. But as long as the product is in stock, the inventory holding time variability makes no difference in the delivery lead time.

The following three actions exacerbate positive cash-to-cash cycles and should be avoided, where possible.

- *Prepaying for materials*—Sellers will sometimes force small buyers or first-time buyers to prepay.

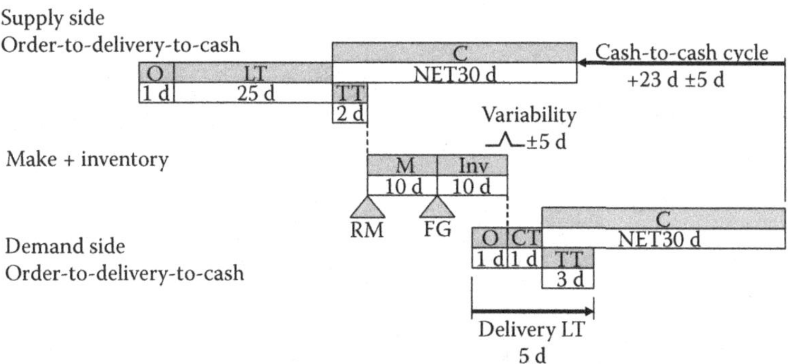

Figure 4.1 Factory BTS cash-to-cash cycle. C = cash; CT = cycle time; d = days; FG = finished goods inventory; Inv = inventory; LT = lead time; M = make; O = order; RM = raw materials inventory; TT = transit time.

- *Building excessive finished goods inventory*—The longer a product sits in finished goods, the more positive its cash-to-cash cycle.
- *Selling on credit*—Offering your customers credit lengthens a positive cash-to-cash cycle. Selling on credit and letting customers buy with a credit card are not the same. Selling on credit is bad for cash flow because it means you agree to invoice for a purchase and to wait 30 days or more for your payment. Letting customers buy with a credit card is good because you receive payment almost immediately.

Cash Gets Tied to Inventory…Forever

It is important to understand the interaction of cash and inventory through one complete build and ship cycle, as illustrated in Figure 4.2. For the purpose of this explanation, only the direct material cost will be considered, accounts receivable will equal only the direct material in a product, and the balance sheet will remain out of balance with a net $100 in assets.

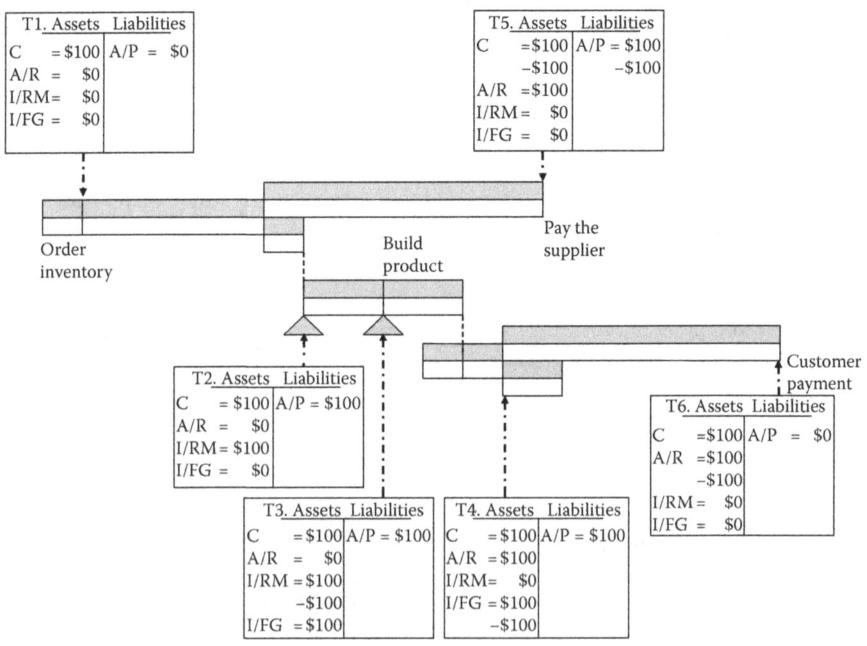

Figure 4.2 Balance sheet transactions during the cash-to-cash cycle. A/P = accounts payable; A/R = accounts receivable; C = cash; I/FG = finished goods; I/RM = raw materials; T = time.

- At time T1, the factory places an order for raw material. The balance sheet shows $100 cash (asset), no accounts receivable, no inventory, and no accounts payable.
- At time T2, the factory receives the raw material from its supplier. The balance sheet shows $100 cash (asset), +$100 in raw material inventory (asset), and +$100 in accounts payable (liability).
- At time T3, the factory converts raw material inventory into finished goods inventory. The balance sheet shows $100 cash (asset), raw material inventory (asset) netted out to $0, +$100 in finished goods inventory (asset), and $100 in accounts payable (liability).
- At time T4, the factory ships product from finished goods inventory to a customer. The balance sheet shows $100 cash (asset), +$100 in accounts receivable (asset), finished goods inventory (asset) netted out to $0, and $100 in accounts payable (liability).
- At time T5, the factory pays its accounts payable to the supplier. The balance sheet shows cash (asset) netted out to $0, $100 accounts receivable (asset), and accounts payable (liability) netted out to $0.
- At time T6, the factory receives payment from its customer. The balance sheet shows accounts receivable (asset) netted out to $0 and +$100 in cash (asset). This is exactly where we started, ready to invest $100 cash in the next round of inventory purchases.

At each time in this example build and ship cycle, the balance sheet remains out of balance with a net $100 in assets. On the next build cycle, the $100 of cash just recovered from the sale of the first product will be spent to buy raw materials to build product for the next build cycle. This cycle of buying inventory, then replenishing cash from the product sale; buying inventory, then replenishing cash from the product sale; buying inventory, then replenishing cash from the product sale goes on and on. As the inventory turns over and over, a certain amount of cash remains locked up in the inventory, as described in Chapter 10: "Inventory Management."

Let the Velocity and Variability Principles Guide Construction

ODC cycles have to be constructed between every relevant pair of sellers and buyers in a supply chain network. Upstream, the pairs that are relevant are determined by the product bill of materials (BOM) as discussed in Chapter 6: "Source." Downstream, the pairs that are relevant are determined by the market segment delivery channels as discussed in Chapter 7: "Delivery." Some ODC cycles may only be exercised once, for example, for a one-time customer or for a one-time supplier. However, you should construct your ODC cycles to be exercised efficiently again and again.

Velocity Principle

The *velocity principle* states that throughput is maximized when the cash-to-cash cycle velocity is maximized by minimizing cycle time.

To build a supply chain link that works, you need to connect ordering information between the selling and buying organizations, flow material downstream from the selling to the buying organization, and flow cash upstream from the buying to the selling organization. Figure 4.3 shows the construction of two common forms of ODC cycles. The right half or downstream side of the figure shows a seller/buyer interface using an Internet-based product catalog and shopping cart with payments by credit card. The left half or upstream side of the figure shows a seller/buyer interface using purchase orders and invoice attachments to e-mail.

To make an ODC cycle efficient, you want to apply the velocity principle. Cycle time may include order processing cycle time, purchasing lead time, manufacturing cycle time, distribution cycle time, transit time, customs clearance time, queue time, inspection time, and payment processing cycle time. Once a process map has been drawn, here are ways to improve its velocity:

- Eliminate unnecessary steps.
- Convert serial processing into parallel processing.

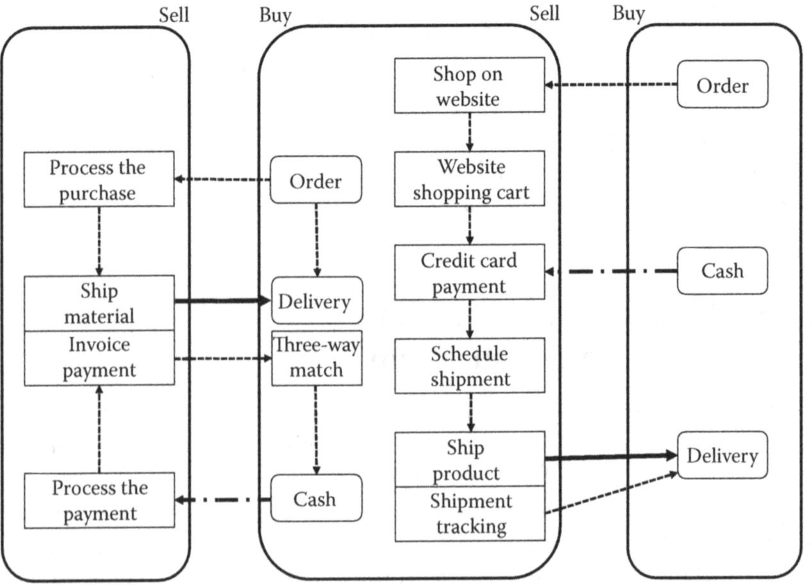

Figure 4.3 Two common forms of ODC cycles.

- Automate steps.
- Adjust capacity to minimize queue time.

The following are ways to make each ODC cycle process step risk tolerant:

- Train personnel on the process step.
- Assign backup responsibilities.
- Provide a redundant communications path.
- Exercise an acknowledgment message for each and every transaction.
- Define a cash flow funding escalation procedure.
- Require prenotification for a late shipment.

Variability Principle

The *variability principle* states that throughput is maximized when the cash-to-cash cycle variability is minimized by minimizing cycle time variance.

To make the ODC cycle predictable, you want to apply the variability principle. This means you want to identify variability in any of the ODC cycle process steps and eliminate it. Variance in logistics transit times due to traffic patterns, variance in process cycle times due to differing levels of employee training, and variance in accepting a customer order due to credit checking are common examples of the root cause of process variability.

Once a process flow map has been drawn, expected variances can be documented for each step. Do the following to minimize the overall ODC cycle variability:

- List the process step variability in descending order from the largest to the smallest.
- Find the root cause of the variability.
- Work to either eliminate or minimize the largest variability.
- Work to eliminate or minimize the second largest variability, etc.

Combining Variability in Parallel and Series

Suppose the variability in a process step can be modeled by a normal distribution with a mean (M) and a standard deviation (SD). When two process steps, each with a normally distributed variance, are combined in parallel, the combined process mean is the larger of the individual means and the combined process standard deviation is the larger of the individual standard deviations.

$$\begin{gathered}\text{Process } M_1,\ SD_1 \text{ in parallel with Process } M_2,\ SD_2\\ \text{yields Parallel Process } \max(M_1, M_2),\ \max(SD_1, SD_2)\end{gathered} \tag{4.10}$$

For example, a factory waiting to receive two parts each from a different supplier, one with a lead time of 20 ± 2 days and the other with a lead time of 10 ± 3 days, should expect a combined wait of 20 ± 3 days. Here, 20 days is the maximum of the 10 and 20 days means and ±3 days is the maximum of the ±3 and ±2 days standard deviations.

When two process steps, each with a normally distributed variance, are combined in series, the combined process mean is the sum of the individual means and the combined process standard deviation is the root-mean-squared (RMS) of the individual standard deviations. RMS is the square root of the average of the squared values. Note that if one standard deviation is much larger than the others, then it will dominate the combined standard deviation.

$$\text{Process } M_1, SD_1 \text{ in series with Process } M_2, SD_2$$
$$\text{yields Series Process sum}(M_1, M_2), \text{RMS}(SD_1, SD_2) \tag{4.11}$$

where

$$\text{RMS} = \sqrt{\frac{(SD_1 \times SD_1 + SD_2 \times SD_2 + \ldots + SD_n \times SD_n)}{n}} \tag{4.12}$$

For example, a logistics leg involves an ocean freight transit time of 24 ± 3 days and a customs clearance time of 1 ± 1 day. The total expected logistics time is 25 days ± square root of ((3 × 3 + 1 × 1)/2), or 25 ± 2.24 days. Here, the 25 days is the sum of 24 days plus 1 day and the ±2.24 days is the calculated RMS value of the ±3 and ±1 day standard deviations.

Bigger and Slower...A Story of Misguided Business Controls

A small business with 35 employees had just two employees in operations, one in planning and one in purchasing. While the engineering department selected vendors, the purchasing guy created and approved all purchase orders for this small business. The downside was that this practice violated good business controls. The upside was that the cycle time from identifying a need for material to placing an order was very fast; it was usually completed within three days.

The small business was bought out by a larger firm with 100 employees. This larger firm was top heavy with financial expertise but lacked manufacturing experience and was in the midst of creating Sarbanes-Oxley compliance standards. The purchasing process was improved by adding a purchase requisition to the purchase order. The buyer was authorized to create the purchase requisition, but accounts payable created the purchase order. A signoff authorization of purchasing dollar limits was established based on job titles in the organizational hierarchy. Regular high dollar production inventory purchases now required the buyer's signature, two finance signatures, and the general manager's signature. The general manager traveled four days out of five. The purchase order required two additional signatures by financial vice presidents. The new, improved process, while providing good business controls, added two weeks on the front end of the ODC cycle. The buyer was never sure when the purchase order was being sent to the vendor. Inventory lot sizes grew to cover variability in the signoff time. And the company tied up precious cash flow to fund the invisible two weeks of non-value-added inventory investment. Both the velocity principle and the variability principle had been ignored.

Build an Information Backbone

Businesses today use a wide range of information technologies, from simple Excel spreadsheets run on a laptop computer to customized, mobile software applications run on iPads to per-use enterprise resource planning (ERP) rentals run on the cloud with third-party servers. Information technology (IT) can be intoxicating. Enormous amounts of precious time, money, and human resource can be poured into solving the IT puzzle for your business. This book takes a different track. This book focuses on helping you understand how the pieces fit together and how the data have to flow to ensure that the system requirements to run your supply chain information backbone are covered.

Every Business Has Two "Inventories"

Every business has to manage two kinds of "inventories." One is the material flow into and out of your physical inventory, while the other is the cash flow into and out of your cash inventory. Both kinds of inventory behave the same way.

$$\text{Ending material} = \text{Starting material} + \text{Receipts} - \text{Issues} \tag{4.13}$$

$$\text{Ending cash} = \text{Starting cash} + \text{Deposits} - \text{Withdrawals} \tag{4.14}$$

The business needs to keep perpetual inventory records on both material and cash. The word *perpetual* means a continuous, running balance in real-time. A perpetual inventory for cash is easy. This is your checkbook. You can go online and see the most up-to-date account balance along with each and every deposit and withdrawal transaction you have ever made. A perpetual inventory for material is harder. This is because there are hundreds or maybe thousands of part numbers, each with multiple physical locations. A perpetual inventory is the application of Equation 4.13 to each part number in each physical location within the supply chain network kept up-to-date in real time. This is difficult to achieve, especially for small businesses.

Elements of the Information Backbone

The information backbone for your business begins with financial data. Financial data recorded in a general ledger, accounts receivable ledger, accounts payable ledger, and cash journal provide the means by which the balance sheet, the income statement, and the cash flow statement are generated.

One way to conceptualize your information backbone is to think of an accounting system base tied to both a perpetual material inventory and a perpetual cash inventory. Then, customer relationship management (CRM) spans between product inventory and accounts receivable cash to satisfy demand. And supplier relationship management (SRM) spans between parts inventory and accounts payable cash to provide supply. Supply chain management lies across the top; this system component coordinates and integrates across the supply chain network to match supply and demand. Key performance indicators (KPIs) measure network performance (see Figure 4.4).

The detail behind the revenue resides in the CRM and order management modules of the IT system. CRM is the repository for basic network relationship information about the customer, including organizational structure, names, titles, addresses, e-mails, phone numbers, social media connections, last contact, last face-to-face contact, customer satisfaction rating, product preferences, market segment served, business volumes, and more. CRM should be used to manage the frequency of customer contact and to maintain an up-to-date list of all open and resolved issues with each customer.

Order management captures product configurations ordered, quotes, pricing agreements, credit checking, ship to locations, shipment logistics instructions, delivery schedules, promise dates, acknowledgments, bill to addresses, ordering

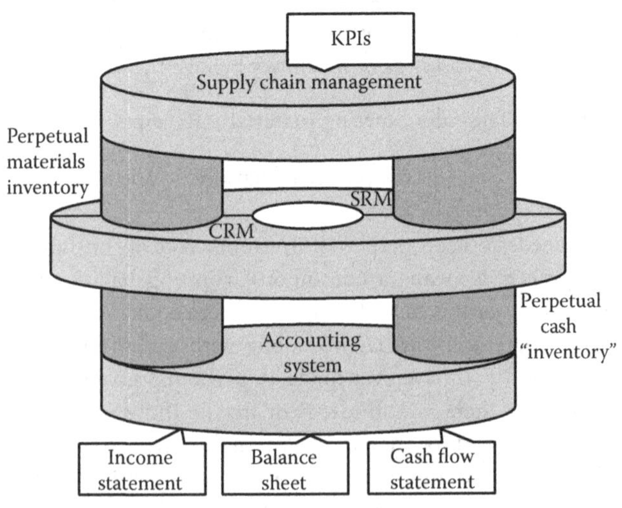

Figure 4.4 Components of a supply chain network information system.

history, etc. Order management tracks and updates the changing status of each sale from probable forecast to order backlog to shipment to invoice paid. Orders open in order management are still active and may require some action, such as completing a shipment or sending an invoice.

Profit from the Margin

Think about your personal budget. You total up each source of income, such as wages, bonus, commission, tips, etc. You total up each class of expense, such as food, mortgage or rent, utilities, transportation, medical premiums, insurance, taxes, etc. The difference in your total income minus your total expense is your margin. This margin may be invested for something bigger and better or saved to be spent on something in the future. If you conclude that you have no margin, then you have not covered your expenses. You will have to somehow increase income or decrease expense. Or you can spend your savings until it is depleted. Or you can try to borrow, which will put you into personal debt.

Your budget covers some period of time, for example, one year split into 12 months. A budget is a reminder that certain expenses have to be paid monthly or quarterly or annually. A budget is used to time certain large purchases, when you have enough savings to smooth out your cash flow. A budget is used to project how long it will take to accumulate enough savings to pay back an earlier loan. If there is a good margin, you can quickly pay back the loan. If there is no margin, you will never pay back the loan.

Income Statement Basics

The income statement is like your personal budget. An income statement records period income, period expenses, and period profit/loss margins. The income statement stretches across the timeframe between the balance sheet at the start of the period and the balance sheet at the end of the period. The line items shown in Table 4.3 are included in most income statements. Notice the progression from gross revenue to net revenue to gross margin to operating margin to net profit.

- *Gross product revenue*—Income from product sales.
- *Gross service revenue*—Subscription income for reoccurring services and non-subscription income for one-time services.
- *Discounts*—Revenue adjustments for reduced pricing for customer contracts and volume purchases.
- *Returns*—Revenue adjustments and credits for product returns.
- *Net revenue*—Gross revenue adjusted for service revenue, discounts, and returns. Note: net revenue is used as the 100% denominator in calculating other line items percentages.

Table 4.3 Example Income Statement for January

Income Statement *Company Name* *For the Month of January 20YY*				
Line Item	*Amount*		*Percent*	
Gross product revenue		$8,400,000		104.0%
Gross service revenue		$2,000,000		
Discounts	$300,000		3.0%	
Returns	$100,000		1.0%	
Net revenue		$10,000,000		100.0%
COGS	$6,650,000		66.5%	
Gross margin		$3,350,000		33.5%
SG&A	$2,385,000		23.8%	
Depreciation	$15,000		0.2%	
Operating profit		$950,000		9.5%
Interest expense	$200,000		2.0%	
Profit before taxes		$750,000		7.5%
Income tax	$250,000		2.5%	
Net profit		$500,000		5.0%

- *Cost of goods sold (COGS)*—Period expense for the inventory direct material, inbound logistics, direct labor, and overhead in the value-added transformation of product shipped within that period.
- *Gross margin*—Net revenue minus COGS.
- *Selling, general, and administrative expense (SG&A)*—Period expense for non-inventory material, indirect labor, and overhead needed for the nontransformational processes necessary to run the business.
- *Depreciation expense*—Reduction in the value of assets over time as a result of wear and tear.
- *Operating profit*—Gross margin minus SG&A minus depreciation.
- *Interest expense*—Period interest payment on outstanding debt.
- *Profit before taxes*—Operating profit minus interest expense. Profit before taxes is the numerator of the equation for return on invested capital.

- *Income tax*—Period expense for income tax, which is normally accumulated and paid quarterly.
- *Net profit*—Operating profit minus interest expense minus income tax.

Top Line Revenue for Forward Supply Chain Networks

Revenue streams are groups of customers buying the same types of products or services. When the product offering and markets served are large, products are usually grouped together in product families, with market segments grouped by geography or application focus. For example, a manufacturer of test equipment might group their products into analyzers, calibrators, counters, data loggers, etc. This manufacturer might segment its business by North America, Europe, Japan, Asia Pacific, and the rest of the world (ROW). Revenue from a sale is calculated as follows:

$$\text{\$Gross revenue} = \text{\$Price/Unit} \times \text{Unit volume and} \tag{4.15}$$

$$\begin{aligned}\text{\$Net revenue} &= ((\text{\$Price/Unit} - \text{\$Discount/Unit}) \\ &\quad \times (\text{Unit volume} - \text{Unit returns})) - \text{\$Credit.}\end{aligned} \tag{4.16}$$

For example, suppose a product has a retail price of \$20. A customer with a preexisting credit of \$300 buys 100 units at a 10% volume discount but returns 5 units within 10 days. The gross revenue is \$20/unit × 100 units, or \$2,000. But the net revenue is ((\$20/unit × 90%) × (100 units − 5 units) − \$300), or \$1,410.

Revenue for a group of products is the sum of the individual product revenues over the same time period.

$$\text{Total \$Net revenue} = \sum_{i=1 \text{ to } n} (\text{\$Net revenue for product}_i) \tag{4.17}$$

$$\text{\$Gross margin} = \text{\$Net revenue} - \text{\$COGS} \tag{4.18}$$

Top Line Revenue for Reverse Supply Chain Networks

When an organization is part of a reverse supply chain network in the RETURN echelons, their income statement looks like one shown in Table 4.4. Warranty repair organizations perform nontransformational, value-neutral work. If the returned product cannot be repaired, it is replaced with a new product. Remanufacturing organizations provide transformational, value-added work. The remanufactured product is sold into an aftermarket at a reduced price. Recycling organizations

Table 4.4 Typical Income Statements for Reverse Supply Chain Organizations

Line Item	*Warranty Repair*	*Remanufacture*	*Recycle*
Income			
Repair revenue	$9		
Aftermarket revenue		$8	
Recycle recovery			$6
Service contracts	$2		
Total income	$11	$0	$6
Expense			
COGS	$4	$1	
Freight and duty	$1	$1	$1
Warranty expense	$1		
Replacement parts		$1	
Operating expense	$1	$1	$2
Administrative	$1	$1	$1
Taxes	$1	$1	$1
Total expense	$9	$6	$5
Net profit	$2	$2	$1

perform transformational, value-subtracting work. Value-subtracting work means products and/or assemblies are converted into components and/or raw materials destroying their product structure. Chapter 8: "Return" presents a complete and detailed blueprint for a reverse supply chain construction project.

Price Based on Cost

While finance is focused on cash flow and dollars, operations is focused on throughput in terms of unit volume. Units and dollars come together as revenue. Units are a function of inventory management, while dollars are a function of pricing. Product pricing is the first step in forecasting revenue and planning for cash replenishment.

There are two fundamentally different ways to set the price on your product or service: value-based pricing and cost-based pricing. Value-based pricing is a top–down method that depends on the buyer sensing that your product has been positioned as offering some unique value-added feature unlike any other from a competitor. Value-based pricing is mostly used for the first product in a new product class for a new market segment, for example, the first Apple iPad or the first Intel microprocessor chip. Cost-based pricing is much more common. Cost-based pricing is a bottom–up method that depends on the seller understanding real product volumes. Value-based pricing is usually replaced with cost-based pricing once competitive products are joined to the market.

Cost-Based Pricing

Cost-based pricing is a markup on the COGS. Markup comes from the ratio of COGS to net revenue on the income statement; markup is the amount by which the cost of a product is increased to derive its selling price.

$$\%\text{COGS} = \frac{\$\text{COGS} \times 100\%}{\$\text{Net revenue}} \tag{4.19}$$

$$\$\text{Price} \geq \frac{\$\text{COGS} \times 100\%}{\%\text{COGS}} \tag{4.20}$$

For example, a factory has an annual revenue of $1,000,000 and annual COGS of $650,000. The factory needs to price a new product with COGS equal to $520. To maintain a %COGS at 65% as calculated from Equation 4.19, the factory price for the new product must greater than $800 as calculated from Equation 4.20. A more complete discussion of factory pricing is presented in Chapter 5: “Make.”

%COGS and %Markup are related as shown in the following equation. If you know one, you can compute the other. For example, 42.9% margin is derived from 70.0% COGS by Equation 4.21, and 80.0% COGS is derived from 25.0% margin by Equation 4.22.

$$\%\text{Markup} = \frac{(100\% - \%\text{COGS})}{\%\text{COGS}} \times 100\% \quad 42.9\% = \frac{(100\% - 70.0\%)}{70.0\%} \times 100\% \tag{4.21}$$

$$\%\text{COGS} = \frac{100\%}{(\%\text{Markup} + 100\%)} \times 100\% \quad 80.0\% = \frac{100\%}{(25.0\% + 100\%)} \times 100\% \tag{4.22}$$

For example, a distributor runs a markup of 30%. The factory wants the distributor to offer a new product that has a distributor COGS of \$150. From Equation 4.22, the distributor's %COGS is 76.9%. To maintain the distributor's income statement ratios, from Equation 4.20, the distributor's price for the new product should be at least \$195. A more complete discussion of a distributor pricing model is presented in Chapter 7: "Deliver."

Volume Assumption in Cost-Based Pricing

The cost for a single item is the sum of a fixed cost element plus a variable cost element. A fixed cost remains the same independent of unit volume. A variable cost is proportional to and decreases with an increase in unit volume. The total cost for a product consisting of many items is the sum of the individual costs for each item and, therefore, the sum of the individual fixed costs plus the sum of the individual variable costs.

$$\text{Cost} = \text{Fixed cost} + \text{Variable cost} \tag{4.23}$$

$$\text{Total cost} = \text{Cost}_1 + \text{Cost}_2 + \ldots + \text{Cost}_N \tag{4.24}$$

For N items

$$\begin{aligned}\text{Total cost} = {} & (\text{Fixed cost}_1 + \text{Fixed cost}_2 + \ldots + \text{Fixed cost}_N) \\ & + (\text{Variable cost}_1 + \text{Variable cost}_2 + \ldots + \text{Variable cost}_N)\end{aligned} \tag{4.25}$$

Cost versus volume is often nonlinear and discontinuous. This is because as volume grows, material purchases can be consolidated into a larger spend. As volume grows, labor purchases move down the learning curve, becoming more efficient. As volume grows, different more efficient processes become economical within manufacturing, distribution, and logistics. Pricing sheets are often tables expressed as Price_1 for quantities from 1 to 10, Price_2 for quantities from 11 to 25, Price_3 for quantities from 26 to 100, etc., or perhaps price quotes with breakpoints at 500/1,000/2,000/5,000/10,000 units.

Many new products achieve their mature volumes later and lower than was originally forecasted. A common mistake when estimating price is to use the mature volume for a new product with no history of demand. This puts you immediately behind the curve because your initial purchases of raw materials and component parts will be for smaller quantities at much higher prices. If, on the other hand, you sign a contract to guarantee that you will purchase a high total quantity over a 12-month period, then you are stuck when you cannot sell the product in that quantity. You will be contractually obligated to accept delivery and pay for the total quantity after the 12th month.

Budgeting Price/Landed Cost across the Supply Chain Network

The end customer's product cost is a "landed cost." Landed cost accumulates all the COGS and markups plus inbound freight, midbound freight, and outbound freight throughout the supply chain network from raw materials to the end customer. Consider the cost structure of the traditional supply to factory to distributor to demand network connection shown in Figure 4.5. This is the factory income statement nested inside the distributor income statement.

At the interface between supply chain echelons, the upstream organization is selling at a price to a downstream organization that is buying at a landed cost. Moving across an echelon, the inbound landed cost becomes an outbound price determined by the organization's COGS and markup. The longer the supply chain network, the greater is the number of echelon markups and the higher is the landed cost to the end customer. Table 4.5 shows an example echelon-by-echelon budget of price/landed cost across a supply chain network. In this typical example, $25 of direct material grows to a product landed cost of $95.17 for the end customer. When the total number of echelons can be reduced, the landed cost to the

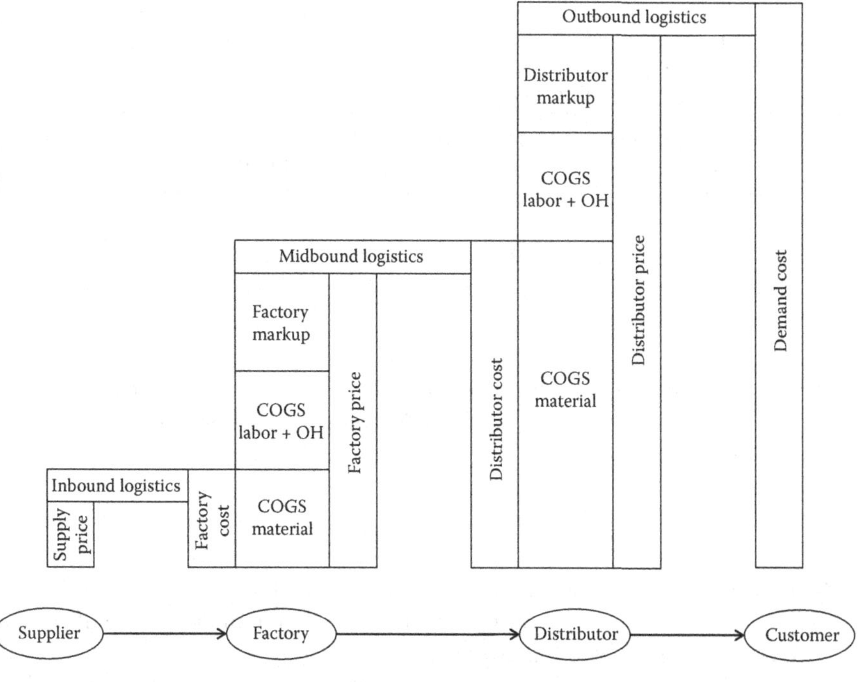

Figure 4.5 Nested factory and distributor income statements.

Table 4.5 Example Echelon-by-Echelon Price/Landed Cost Budget

Echelon	*Line Item*	*Price/Landed Cost*	*Budget*
1	Demand landed cost to the end customer	Landed cost	$95.17
	Outbound logistics + (duty)		$0.85
2	Distributor price	Price	$94.32
2	Distributor markup at 35%		$24.45
2	Distributor COGS at 74.1%		$69.87
2	Distributor product cost	Landed cost	$64.34
	Midbound logistics + (duty) + (cross docking)		$2.15
3	Factory price	Price	$62.19
3	Factory markup at 42.3%		$18.49
3	Factory COGS at 70%		$43.70
3	Factory material cost	Landed cost	$26.35
	Inbound logistics + (duty)		$1.35
4	Supply price of direct materials in the BOM	Price	$25.00

end customer can be reduced. When the supplier's price for the direct materials required by a product BOM can be reduced, the product's landed cost to the end customer can be greatly reduced.

- *Demand landed cost*—The landed cost to the end customer, or store, is the distributor price plus the cost of outbound logistics from the distributor to the end customer or store.

$$\$\text{Demand landed cost} = \$\text{Distributor price} + \$\text{Outbound logistics} \quad (4.26)$$

- *Distributor price*—The distributor price is a function of the distributor labor rate, the distributor overhead, and the distributor markup. COGS is the leverage point for distributor pricing.

$$\$\text{Distributor price} = \$\text{Distributor COGS} \times (1 + \%\text{Distributor markup}) \quad (4.27)$$

- *Distributor COGS*—The distributor COGS is the distributor's product cost plus the warehouse labor and overhead to deliver the product.

$$\begin{aligned}\$\text{Distributor COGS} &= \$\text{Distributor product cost} \\ &+ \$\text{DC Labor} + \$\text{DC Overhead}\end{aligned} \tag{4.28}$$

- *Distributor product cost*—The landed cost to the distributor is the factory price plus the cost of midbound logistics plus potentially cross-docking charges from the factory to the local distributor. Cross-docking charges can occur when one DC in a distribution network passes the product through to another DC within the same distribution network.

$$\begin{aligned}\$\text{Distributor product cost} &= \$\text{Factory price} \\ &+ \$\text{Midbound logistics} + \$\text{Cross-docking}\end{aligned} \tag{4.29}$$

- *Factory price*—The factory price is a function of the factory labor rate, factory overhead, and the factory markup. COGS is the leverage point for factory pricing.

$$\$\text{Factory price} = \$\text{Factory COGS} \times (1 + \%\text{Factory markup}) \tag{4.30}$$

- *Factory COGS*—The Factory COGS is the factory's direct material cost plus the direct labor and overhead to make the product.

$$\begin{aligned}\$\text{Factory COGS} &= \$\text{Factory material cost} \\ &+ \$\text{Factory labor} + \$\text{Factory overhead}\end{aligned} \tag{4.31}$$

- *Factory material cost*—The landed cost to the factory is the summation of the supply prices plus the cost of inbound logistics from each supplier to the factory.

$$\$\text{Factory material cost} = \sum (\$\text{Supply price} + \$\text{Inbound logistics}) \tag{4.32}$$

- *Supply price*—The price of raw materials or components from the supplier is a function of the cost of the raw materials, the supplier labor rate, and the supplier markup.

Price/landed cost is a line item on the requirements specification and an axis on the Value Circle. The price/landed cost will be different depending on the echelon context of the Value Circle, i.e., factory or distributor. Logistics costs include freight cost and duty cost when the shipment is international. Freight costs are driven primarily by weight, cube, distance traveled, and the mode of transportation. Cross-docking is the direct flow of material from receipt to shipping bypassing storage and issuing. In complex distribution networks, freight may enter the network at one distribution center (DC) and be cross-docked across other DCs until it reaches the DC delivering to the intended local market. Warehousing costs are usually included in the overhead line items in factory COGS and in distributor COGS. Warehousing costs are driven primarily by the footprint and cube of the inventory and by the length of time the inventory is stored.

The One Dollar Product

To do the best possible job pricing a product, you want to be able to estimate both the maximum cost and a reasonable quantity for your product. Dollar Tree, Inc., provides a great illustration of how to do this. Dollar Tree, Inc., is a chain of wholly owned discount variety retail stores backed by a distribution network that sells every item to its customers for \$1. The sale is \$1 per unit regardless of the item or quantity purchased. The beauty of this example is that the \$1 price eliminates the issue of price mix from the equation. Suppose you decided to respond to a request for a quotation from a Dollar Tree, Inc. purchasing agent looking for new items to freshen up their offerings. You would need to know something about the Dollar Tree, Inc. supply chain, the maximum price you could charge, and the probable quantity you would have to supply. Some simple ratios provide the answer.

The US Securities and Exchange Commission Form 10-K is a free, public document showing the annual report of any company traded on the stock exchange. It contains the income statement, balance sheet, cash flow statement, financial ratios, a description of the business, risk factors, corporate governance, majority stock ownership, and much more. Dollar Tree, Inc., is a well-established company operating 4,600 stores across 48 states in 2013. Its average store was about 8,000 square feet and carried some 6,200 different items each priced at \$1. Its net revenue was \$7.4 billion in 2013 with a %COGS of 64%, a %SG&A of 23.5%, and a percentage net profit of 8%. Its inventory turned an average of 4.3 times during the year. The Form 10-K lists the location and square footage of its nine DCs and the geographical distribution of its stores state by state.

To be considered, your product cost and production capacity would have to conform to the Dollar Tree, Inc., requirements (http://www.dollartreeinfo.com/vendor-partners/). First, your maximum price could be determined as follows from the income statement:

$$\begin{aligned}\$1.00 \text{ Revenue} \times 64\% \text{ COGS} &= \$0.64 \text{ Landed cost into Dollar Tree distribution} \\ &= \text{Your factory price} + \text{Midbound logistics costs}\end{aligned} \tag{4.33}$$

The required production capacity could be estimated as follows:

$$\text{Annual quality} = \frac{\text{Dollars of annual revenue}}{(\#\text{Stock keeping units [SKUs] at \$1})} \tag{4.34}$$

$7.4 billion annual revenue/6,200 SKUs at $1 each
= 1,200,000 Units per year

and

$$\text{Quantity per SKU per store per week} = \frac{\text{Dollars of annual revenue}}{(\#\text{Store} \times (52\ \text{weeks/year}) \times (\#\text{SKUs at \$1}))} \tag{4.35}$$

$7.4 billion annual revenue/4,600 Stores
= $1.6 million revenue per store per year

$1.6 million revenue per store per year/52 Weeks per year
= $30,800 Revenue per store per week

$30,800 Revenue per store per week/6,200 SKUs at $1
= 5 Units per SKU per store per week

You would have to deliver 1.2 million units of your product at a distributor product cost of less than 64 cents each. Since the inventory turns about four times a year, deliveries would be 300,000 units every three months. Such pricing, quantity, and delivery probably involve an offshore factory in Asia with an ocean freight connection into California. You would have to determine how many containers would be required to hold 300,000 units of product and how much the shipping cost would be for these containers. Suppose the midbound freight and duty was 12 cents per unit, then the maximum factory price for your product would be 52 cents each.

Forecast Cash Replenishment

Cash replenishment is a key consideration in growing a business. The cash initially secured through the combination of short-term loans, long-term debt, and equity funding has to be repaid for the business to be viable over the long haul. As a business grows, it consumes even more cash to finance more inventory, more receivables, and more fixed assets. This requires good maintainable margins. Such margins come from delivering products and services of great value, segmenting the market properly to generate continuing demand, and pricing products competitively. Planning for cash replenishment is the third step in moving from product pricing to revenue forecasting to planning cash replenishment.

Working Capital and Fixed Capital

Working capital is an uneven cash flow used to pay for inventory, wages, period expenses, credit sales, and seasonal fluctuations. Working capital is raised, invested in the business, paid back through product sales, and reinvested for the next sales cycle. Any growth in days of inventory/or days of accounts receivable credits requires growth in working capital. Working capital is liquidated by turning inventory and by turning accounts receivable credits. Working capital is considered to be short-term, i.e., less than a year.

Fixed capital is the long-term investment in land, buildings, machinery, and other durable fixed assets. Fixed capital meets multiyear needs. Once invested, fixed capital is often hard to liquidate.

Start with Accounts Receivable and Accounts Payable

Consider a typical timeframe based on your cash-to-cash cycle time as discussed earlier in this chapter. Suppose your cash-to-cash cycle averages a positive 30 days; this means you need to finance 30 days of cash flow. The question is, how do you forecast your day-to-day cash needs? And, at the current margin, how long will it take to pay it back? The answer to these questions begins with a detailed understanding of accounts receivable and accounts payable.

Table 4.6 is a summary of the weekly accounts receivable for month *N*. There are shipments to four customers: Johnson, Williamson, Tyler, and Brooking. Clearly, your actual accounts receivable ledger would have many more entries with the

Table 4.6 Accounts Receivable for Example Month *N* Shipment Revenue

Customer Revenue Account	*Receivable*	*Shipment*	*Receivable Due*
Johnson	$150	Month *N*–week 1	Month *N*+1–week 1
Williamson	$75	Month *N*–week 2	Month *N*+1–week 2
Tyler	$200	Month *N*–week 3	Month *N*+1–week 3
Brooking	$325	Month *N*–week 4	Month *N*+1–week 4
Total month *N* receivables	$750		

details of each product type, quantity, and price per shipment. While the invoice goes out at the time of the shipment, each customer has NET30 day terms. This means the customer has four weeks until payment is due. This also means that none of these four payments will arrive during month *N*, although sometimes customers can be incentivized through price discounts and other means to make an early payment. In Table 4.6, the total $750 revenue for shipments completed within the month does not get paid until the following month.

Table 4.7 is a summary of all the accounts payable due to be paid within month *N*. Some of these payments are obligations initiated in previous months, maybe month *N*–1 or month *N*–2, and some of these payments are for expenses incurred within the current month *N*. The payment detail is broken down by week for inventory materials, payroll, interest on debt, and other expenses. Clearly, your accounts payable ledger would have many more entries with all the details of exactly what was purchased and organized according to a full charter of accounts. In Table 4.7, a total of $712 needs to be paid this month.

Table 4.7 Accounts Payable for Example Month *N* Expenses

Expense Account	*Payable*	*Payment Due*
Inventory material	$120	Month *N*–week 1
Inventory material	$45	Month *N*–week 2
Inventory material	$35	Month *N*–week 3
Inventory material	$100	Month *N*–week 4
Payroll	$36	Month *N*–week 2
Payroll taxes and benefits	$14	Month *N*–week 2
Payroll	$36	Month *N*–week 4
Payroll taxes and benefits	$14	Month *N*–week 4
Interest on debt	$15	Month *N*–week 4
Other expenses	$66	Month *N*–week 1
Other expenses	$72	Month *N*–week 2
Other expenses	$81	Month *N*–week 3
Other expenses	$78	Month *N*–week 4
Total month *N* payables	$712	

How to Construct the Cash Forecast

A cash forecast is used to determine your immediate cash requirements over the short-term so that your cash balance never goes negative. The accounts receivable and accounts payable ledgers can now be combined into a cash forecast paying strict attention to the relative timing of each amount. This is done using the very simple, but very powerful, cash forecast matrix shown in Table 4.8. The table columns cover the number of weeks, and sometimes even days, at least equal to the worst-case cash-to-cash cycle time. The table rows are starting cash, +receipts, –payments, and ending cash. Within each column, the ending cash equals the starting cash plus any receipts minus any payments, from Equation 4.1. The starting cash in the next column equals the ending cash from the previous column, from Equation 4.2.

The starting cash in the first week is set equal to \$0. Each of the four weekly receipts is entered into their corresponding month *N*+1 weeks; the receipts total the \$750 in accounts receivable. The payments are subtotaled by week and then each of the four weekly payments is entered into its corresponding month *N* week; the payments total the \$712 in accounts payable. When the cash forecast is complete and the calculations refreshed, observe the following:

- With the starting cash in the first week set equal to 0, the most negative ending cash number in the table, <\$712> in this example, is the peak dollar value that must be financed to keep the operation running. Since none of the revenue associated with month *N* was received in month *N*, the peak cash to be financed happens to equal the month *N* payments total. However, if any of month *N* revenue had been received within the month, the peak cash to be financed would be reduced.
- The ending cash number at the end of the cash-to-cash cycle, \$38 in this example, is generated by the net profit. If exactly the same monthly cycle were repeated without any change in monthly revenue, it will take \$712

Table 4.8 Cash Forecast

	Month N				*Month N+1*			
	Week 1	*Week 2*	*Week 3*	*Week 4*	*Week 1*	*Week 2*	*Week 3*	*Week 4*
Starting cash	\$0	<\$186>	<\$353>	<\$469>	<\$712>	<\$562>	<\$487>	<\$287>
+Receipts					\$150	\$75	\$200	\$325
–Payments	<\$186>	<\$167>	<\$116>	<\$243>				
Ending cash	<\$186>	<\$353>	<\$469>	<\$712>	<\$562>	<\$487>	<\$287>	\$38

divided by $38 or 18.7 months to repay the starting cash position. It will take much stronger margins and a much larger cash infusion to grow the business quickly.

- When the starting cash in the first week has a carryover from the previous month, the peak cash that needs to be financed will adjust. For example, if the starting cash is set to $100, then in this example, the peak cash to be financed drops to $612. The cash margin generated by the end of the second month will equal the starting cash plus the net profit margin, or $100 + $38.
- Net cash flow is not the same as net profit. Net cash flow depends on both the starting cash position and on the length of the cash-to-cash cycle relative to the one month timing of an income statement.

Budget Cash for the Supply Chain Construction Project

There is significant cost to any supply chain construction project. This cost is in the key staff who are redirected to work on the project team, in the calendar time it takes to see the resulting benefit of the project, and in the cash flow to cover project expenses and asset investment.

The Supply Chain Construction Project Budget

The supply chain construction project budget is built from a subset of the income statement and balance sheet line items. The expenses in this budget reflect the incremental spending to assemble a project team, build the network, and begin delivery of products and services.

1. *Finance wages and salary*—People are the most important resource in any business. It is important that you and your staff get paid a reasonable wage on a regular basis during the project. Holding back pay until a start-up is profitable or investing the entrepreneur's salary as part of the start-up funding is a false economy that will cause morale problems later.
2. *Finance payroll taxes*—You are legally required to pay the payroll taxes on your employees. In the United States, this includes federal income tax withholding, state income tax withholding, and FICA taxes for social security and Medicare.
3. *Finance employee benefits*—This is an area that can become quite expensive, especially for medical insurance, and requires careful research and planning. While you must comply with employment law, the number of benefits and the dollar value of each type of benefit will be a function of your business philosophy and the size and profitability of the business.

4. *Finance office space rent and utilities expenses*—Rent for office space and utilities, including water, gas, electricity, a cleaning service, fire and security monitoring, insurance, etc., are monthly expensed items.
5. *Finance travel expenses*—While travel expense is considered to be discretionary and can easily spiral out of control, developing relationships to start a new business or to modify an existing supply chain network requires significant face-to-face time with other parties.
6. *Finance plant and equipment*—The cost of plant and equipment will depend on whether you intend to be a virtual company, partner with an existing company, or collaborate with a group of companies. Do you expect to rent, lease, or own a building, office furniture, vehicles, production equipment, inventory storage space, and/or material handling equipment?
7. *Finance IT*—Every business needs telephone systems or cell phones, Internet access, workstations, or personal computers, or tablets for each employee, plus computer systems for production and inventory planning and control, accounting systems, etc. There may be additional software licensing fees, equipment maintenance contracts, and consulting fees. Information system purchases are a mix of expensed and capitalized items. The balance sheet shows the capitalized fixed asset portion often covered by long-term debt, while the expensed portion is covered by monthly cash outlays on the income statement.
8. *Finance inventory*—You will have to finance the cost of inventory through accounts payable to support planned throughput plus buffer inventory and safety stocks throughout the supply chain network.
9. *Finance accounts receivable credit*—When you sell a product on credit, you have to finance some number of days of accounts receivable until the customer makes the payment.
10. *Finance marketing/sales collateral expenses*—To develop demand for the business, you will have to tell potential customers about your product and develop marketing strategies to penetrate new markets. This might include sales brochures, catalogs, websites, trade shows, etc. These are accrued expenses.
11. *Finance business fees and income taxes*—The structure of fees and taxes depends upon the geographical location of the business and potentially upon tax incentives for new business start-ups. These topics are outside the scope of this book.
12. *Finance termination expenses*—There may be one-time expenses for employee severance packages, the final dispositioning of obsolete inventory, breaking leases on buildings, etc.
13. *Finance legal review*—There may be legal fees to write and review contractual agreements.

A Virtual Enterprise Plans Its Start-Up Cash Flow

A small team of experienced people decide to start a new virtual business. By "virtual," they mean to leverage manufacturing and distribution facilities operated by other organizations so that they do not have to make large initial investments for plant and equipment. The team figures they can add value and control the supply chain network because they own an innovative product design, and they have a vision of how to sell that solution into a new market segment. The team has written a business plan and has attracted investors willing to fund their start-up. One reason investors are willing to invest is the match of product value to market segment need just makes sense; it is easy to explain and to understand.

A second reason the investors are willing to invest is that the team's business plan includes the supply chain construction project budget shown in Table 4.9. The investors realize that the team has the management maturity to detail their cash needs through the first 12 months of their business plan. The supply chain construction project budget is organized as follows. The columns on the spreadsheet represent months and extend 12 months into the future. The rows on the spreadsheet are segmented into three groups. The first group of rows details the basic team employee expenses for wages, payroll taxes, benefits, and rented office space. These expenses will have to be paid regardless of the outcome of the project. The second group of rows details specific investments for travel to form the virtual relationships, for unique tooling and equipment to be added to a third party's plant, and for an IT solution to run the network. These investments are necessary to build the supply chain network. The third group of rows details investments for product inventory, accounts receivable, and marketing and sales collateral. These investments are necessary to begin delivery of the product through the new or modified supply chain. The numbers at the beginning of each row refer to the expense categories described above.

The time fences that segment the columns in Table 4.9 are less obvious. Team wages extend throughout the whole 12 months of the project. The team plans to take three months to build the network. They plan to take an additional four months for material purchasing lead time and manufacturing cycle time to build a finished goods inventory of product. The team expects sales revenue generated in the second half of the year to be profitable by the 12th month of the project. The team also developed a worst-case budget for its investors, with network construction taking five months, filling the network with product inventory taking six months, initial sales taking six months, and first profit by the 18th month.

The fourth group of rows is the cash flow projection. The team plans to ask for an initial investment of $400,000. This investment would support a team of four people, each being paid about $42,000 for the first year, plus inventory investment beginning in month 4, production equipment in month 6, and account receivable credit beginning in month 8. With a $400,000 initial investment, the best-case ending cash flow bottoms out at $39,000. This leaves a cash cushion that is too small to support the worst-case 18-month project. Should the ending cash flow go negative, the team will have to ask for additional funding. Revenue will have to grow quickly in the second year to generate a reasonable return on investment for the investors.

Table 4.9 Example Start-Up Supply Chain Construction Project Budget (Figures in 1,000s)

	Build the Network			*Build Product Inventory*				*Build Revenue*				
Month	*1*	*2*	*3*	*4*	*5*	*6*	*7*	*8*	*9*	*10*	*11*	*12*
Assemble the team												
1. Salary	$14	$14	$14	$14	$14	$14	$14	$14	$14	$14	$14	$14
2./3. Payroll tax + benefits	$4	$4	$4	$4	$4	$4	$4	$4	$4	$4	$4	$4
4. Offices	$7	$7	$7	$7	$7	$7	$7	$7	$7	$7	$7	$7
Build the network												
5. Travel	$1	$3	$3	$3	$3	$3	$3	$1	$1	$2	$1	$1
6. Equipment						$43	$15					
7. Info tech			$14		$2			$2			$2	
Begin product/service delivery												
8. Inventory				$14	$14	$14	$35	$35	$42	$42	$50	$50
9. A/R credit								$12	$12	$12	$17	$17
10. Marketing						$4	$4	$4	$4	$4	$4	$4
Totals	$26	$28	$42	$42	$44	$89	$82	$79	$84	$84	$99	$97
Cash flow projection												
Month	*1*	*2*	*3*	*4*	*5*	*6*	*7*	*8*	*9*	*10*	*11*	*12*
Starting cash	$400	$374	$346	$304	$262	$218	$129	$47	$39	$40	$40	$40
+Receipts								$71	$85	$85	$99	$99
–Payments	($26)	($28)	($42)	($42)	($44)	($89)	($82)	($79)	($84)	($85)	($99)	($97)
Ending cash	$374	$346	$304	$262	$218	$129	$47	$39	$40	$40	$40	$42

An Existing Business Upgrades Its Supply Chain

A small business has grown through acquisitions and is in desperate need of reinventing its supply chain. Senior management decides to consolidate DCs and factories, keeping its suppliers and retail stores intact. Engineering work has already been done to convert the product and part numbering schemes from the acquired businesses to the parent company's methodology. Now, an experienced five-person task force is assigned the job of implementing the supply chain upgrade. The task force decides to combine all production into the largest of two existing factories, while terminating business with the smaller factory. A $30K welding machine will have to be purchased; it has a 14-week lead time. The larger factory will have to prove that it can meet the cost and quality targets for each product currently made by the smaller factory. The task force decides to contract with a new third-party logistics (3PL) company to manage the distribution and warehousing for all its products. This means existing inventory must be pulled out of the existing distribution network and moved to new warehouse locations. This upgrade requires significant data rerouting and report reformatting within the IT system. Senior management has agreed to spend $15K to upgrade the information system. The task force is challenged to both complete the upgrade within six calendar months and make the upgrade transparent to customers. Since continuity of supply is a must, the new network and inventory must be in place before the old network and inventory can be turned off.

This supply chain construction project involves a high degree of negotiation to choose a new 3PL distributor, to exit the existing distribution network, and to end production at the smaller factory. Negotiation means staffing, travel, communications, and legal review expense. The project involves data integration and redirection; these mean staffing and IT expense. The project involves building and testing some new assembly processes at the larger factory, including a new welding process. This means staffing, communications, travel, and equipment expense. The project involves repositioning existing inventory to new locations, redirecting supplier shipments to the larger factory, and redirecting shipments from new warehouse locations to the existing set of retail stores. This means staffing, communications, inventory, and logistics expenses. Table 4.10 shows the first steps in preparing a supply chain construction project budget for a transitional project. The columns represent each month in the project. Although senior management wants this project wrapped up in six months, there are a lot of moving parts and difficult negotiations. Such a project could easily drag on for the better part of a year. The rows are grouped around five tasks: (1) assembling the team, (2) building the new network, (3) exiting the old network, (4) beginning product delivery from the new network, and (5) ending product delivery from the old network. The bullet points for each task group are reminders of the most significant deliverables. The "x's" in each row indicate the expected monthly timing for that expense. The project budget is completed by dollarizing each of the "x's".

When modifying a supply chain, you have to plan your cash flow from the current "as-is" state until the time that you can achieve the "to-be" state. Table 4.10 covers the "as-is" state by the row groups "exit the old network" and "end product delivery from the old network." Table 4.10 coves the "to-be" state by the row groups "build the new network" and "begin product delivery from the new network." Six to eight months is a reasonable planning period unless you know of critical process tooling or long lead time materials that will take longer. Revenue will fall off during the transition, and funding must be provided to keep the business going until the "to-be" revenue meets and exceeds the "as-is" revenue. The ending cash must never be allowed to go negative.

Table 4.10 Example Transitional Supply Chain Construction Project Budget (Figures in 1,000s)

Month	*1*	*2*	*3*	*4*	*5*	*6*
Assemble the team Five people assigned to the project for six to eight months.						
1. Salary	x	x	x	x	x	x
2./3. Payroll taxes + benefits	x	x	x	x	x	x
4. Office space + utilities	x	x	x	x	x	x
Build the new network • Consolidate factories; add a $30K welding machine. • Use new 3PL relationship to manage distribution. • Invest $15K to upgrade the information system.						
5. Travel	x	x	x	x	x	x
6. Process equipment				$30	x	
7. Info technology	x	$9	$6	x	x	x
13. Legal review expense			x	x		
Exit the old network • Exit the smaller factory. • End the current warehouse relationships. • Move inventory to the 3PL.						
5. Travel	x	x			x	x
12. Termination expense						x
13. Legal review expense		x				x
Begin product delivery from the new network Expect an initial drop in revenue.						
8. Inventory			x	x	x	x
14. Logistics expense			x	x	x	x
9. A/R credit						x
10. Marketing expense				x	x	x

(Continued)

Table 4.10 (Continued) Example Transitional Supply Chain Construction Project Budget (Figures in 1,000s)

Month	*1*	*2*	*3*	*4*	*5*	*6*
End product delivery from the old network						
Continuity of supply is a "must."						
8. Recycle inventory				x	x	x
12. Termination expense						x
Totals						
Cash flow projection						
Starting cash						
+Cash receipts						
–Cash payments						
Ending cash	$>0	$>0	$>0	$>0	$>0	$>0

Fund the Construction Project

You will need to have a financial plan prepared for the cost of either starting up a new supply chain when starting a new business, or the cost of modifying an existing supply chain as the business changes. You will need to estimate the total amount of funding required, to know the source of these funds, and to forecast how quickly business profits can pay back the funding. This is a critical period for any business, as you will have to balance the use of any profit between growing the business and paying off debt. A cash flow shortage can bring your business to its knees. Financing poured into a business that does not turn a profit within a reasonable timeframe will turn away future investments.

Cash Flow Statement Basics

The cash flow statement shows the sources and uses of cash in your business over a long period such as a fiscal year. The cash flow statement is part of a company's financial records along with its balance sheet and income statement. The cash flow statement shows the sources and uses of cash separated into three components: operations, investments, and financing. The net change in cash flow may be positive or negative, meaning that your total cash has increased or decreased over the period. Line items in the cash flow statement, such as net earnings and depreciation, are adjusted to reflect only real cash balances without future credits. Table 4.11 shows an example statement.

Table 4.11 Example Annual Cash Flow Statement (Figures in 1,000s)

Cash Flow Statement *Company Name* *For the Fiscal Year Ended Dec. 31, 20YY*	
Cash flow from operations	
Net earnings (adjusted for credits)	$2,900
Period depreciation (this is not a cash flow)	$175
Cash in from operations	
Decrease in inventory	$0
Decrease in accounts receivable	$0
Increase in accounts payable	$155
Cash out from operations	
Increase in inventory	<$270>
Increase in accounts receivable	<$150>
Decrease in accounts payable	$0
Cash flow from investing	
Cash in from investing	
Divest an old asset (such as building and equipment)	$0
Cash out from investing	
Purchase a new asset (such as building and equipment)	<$940>
Cash flow from financing	
Cash in from financing	
Secure a new loan	$100
Sell additional shares of stock	$0

(*Continued*)

Table 4.11 (Continued) Example Annual Cash Flow Statement (Figures in 1,000s)

Cash Flow Statement *Company Name* *For the Fiscal Year Ended Dec. 31, 20YY*	
Cash out from financing	
Pay dividend to shareholders	$0
Pay interest to bond holders	$0
Make balloon payment on debt	$0
Net cash flow for fiscal year ended Dec. 31, 20YY	$1,970

- *Cash flow from net earnings*—Real cash in and cash out from net profit/loss adjusted for future credits. Depreciation is always added back because it is not a real cash flow.
- *Cash flow from operations*—Real cash in and cash out from operational changes during the period to inventory, accounts receivable and accounts payable.
- *Cash flow from investing*—Real cash in and cash out from investments over the period.
- *Cash flow from financing*—Real cash in and cash out from financing over the period.

The cash out to fund your supply chain construction project impacts net cash flow during the calendar period of the project. If the current cash balance and projected net cash flow are insufficient to cover the planned cash budget for your project, then additional financing will be required.

Equity and Debt Financing

A supply chain construction project is initially funded from the liability and net worth side of the balance sheet. At the start-up of a company, paid-in capital plus long-term debt determines the total amount that can be spent. Once a company operates, the paid-in capital and long-term debt are offset by assets, current or fixed. To make more funds available for supply chain construction, increases in paid-in capital or long-term debt are required. Paid-in capital implies the transfer of partial ownership of the business in exchange for the expectation of an investment return on company stock. This is equity financing. Long-term debt implies a financial loan to be paid back with monthly interest either in monthly installments or with a balloon payment at the end of the loan period. This is debt financing.

- If the business start-up cannot generate a competitive return, then the venture capitalist and/or other investors will withdraw their support in search of a better return on investment.
- If the need for funding becomes dire, then the entrepreneur may find that he or she no longer owns the company because a majority of the ownership has been sold in exchange for an infusion of cash.
- If the business start-up defaults on its monthly debt payment or on the balloon payment at the end of the loan, the business will face bankruptcy.

You must understand the parameters for the minimum and maximum rate of growth that your business can sustain. When starting a new supply chain network from scratch, you have to plan your cash flow from the time of investor funding until the time that the revenue generated from the sale of your products and services becomes self-sustaining. The investor cash flow will start from a fixed amount and will be spent until it is depleted. The revenue generated from product sales will start at zero and will hopefully grow to a large number. If the business cannot sustain its immediate cash flow requirements, then it has the following alternatives in descending order of desirability:

- Secure a revolving line of credit at a high interest rate to handle peak cash demands.
- Refinance its debt at a lower interest rate, if market conditions allow.
- Secure additional long-term debt, putting the business farther behind in its ability to pay off its debt.
- Raise additional paid-in capital by selling more stock. This dilutes the company ownership of previous shareholders and can tip the majority ownership to someone outside the company.
- Shrink its business footprint with layoffs and the sale of assets.
- Factor its accounts receivable and inventory with a third party.
- Enter bankruptcy proceedings.

In Summary

This chapter explains how cash flows into and out of the balance sheet, how cash is replenished from income statement profit, how changes to cash are tracked on the cash flow statement, and how to estimate extra cash needs for your supply chain construction project. The cash-to-cash cycle is defined for trading partners buying upstream and selling downstream. The velocity and variability principles are used to determine how to accelerate the cash-to-cash cycle velocity and minimize its variance. The chapter looks at margin from an income statement perspective. Product pricing must be high enough to generate a profit margin yet low enough to be competitive in the market. The timing of accounts receivable from income statement revenue and the timing of accounts payable from income statement expenses are translated into a cash flow projection. This answers questions of how much cash is needed to run the business and how long it will take to replenish the initial cash investment. The cash flow statement documents the sources of cash from operations, from investing, and from financing. Finally, the chapter describes how to budget cash for a supply chain construction project.

Chapter 5

Make

Whether you are in the business of making a product yourself or contracting production out to a domestic contract manufacturer (CM) or outsourcing production to another country, the supply chain construction guidelines in this chapter are relevant. The factory for a supply chain network can be located almost anywhere. But the factory organization and geographical location selected to manufacture the product are critical to achieving your price/landed cost, product flexibility, and delivery reliability goals. On the one hand, a factory located close to the market may have a noncompetitive labor rate. On the other hand, a factory located in a distant land to be close to raw materials (RMs), cheap labor, or cheap energy may be noncompetitive in international logistics costs and flexibility. Information regarding the bill of materials (BOM), product configurations, forecasts, planning, supplier purchases, invoicing, and customer shipments must flow seamlessly among the trading partners. In this chapter, you learn how to select a factory to best fit your supply chain needs.

Connecting the Dots

Bill stood at the whiteboard and drew three circles in a row. He labeled them "SOURCE," "MAKE," and "DELIVER." On the line connecting MAKE and DELIVER, he wrote "value-added reseller (VAR) product cost = $350." On the line connecting SOURCE and MAKE, he wrote "material landed cost = $180."

"This is our current supply chain echelon map. Remember, it is always the seller's price and the buyer's cost," he said. "Tony, would you please brief the team on the refined cost model that you and I discussed? Use the whiteboard, and write it all down."

Tony walked to the whiteboard, "This is the cost model we are going to use for this project. The factory material cost is the supplier material price plus inbound freight cost. The factory labor cost is the labor hours to build the uninterruptable power supply (UPS) times the factory labor rate in dollars per hour. The factory overhead is a multiple of the factory labor cost. The factory cost of goods sold (COGS) is the sum of material plus labor plus overhead. The factory selling price is factory COGS times one plus the %factory markup. The %factory markup is determined from income statement ratios. The VAR product cost is the factory selling price plus the midbound logistics cost. That's it."

"Gee, that sounds really simple," kidded Donna.

"OK. Maybe an example will help," admitted Tony. "Suppose the factory has a labor rate of $24/hour, a factory overhead of 200%, and a factory markup of 43%. The 43% gives us a 70% COGS-to-revenue ratio. Then for a UPS product design with $180 in material cost and 1.5 hours of labor content, the factory selling price would be calculated like this. Material cost is $180. Labor cost is 1.5 hours times $24/hour, or $36. Overhead at 200% is two times $36, or $72. COGS is $180 plus $36 plus $72, or $288. The factory selling price with a 43% markup is $288 times 1.43, or $412."

"That doesn't work. You are already over the $350 VAR cost," said Harry.

"Oh, you noticed?" said Bill. "This is the first key supply chain decision point for this team. The example numbers Tony used are real numbers for our factory. The example says that unless Engineering can refine the design and significantly cut material cost and labor hours, we cannot manufacture the UPS product in our factory here."

Everyone on the team fell silent.

"What about inbound and midbound freight?" asked Donna, finally after studying Tony's numbers.

"You can use 6% of material as a starting estimate for inbound freight. That adds $180 times 6% times 1.43, or $15.44, to the factory selling price," said Bill.

"…And midbound freight?" This was a subject Donna wanted to learn more about.

"It only gets worse," replied Bill. "It depends on where the factory is located. A UPS is heavy and bulky because of its batteries. Motor freight can be used domestically. But if we decided to manufacture out of the country, in China for example, then we would probably use ocean freight to the west coast and motor freight across the country."

"How do we decide where to manufacture?" asked John. "China is new to us."

"That's a great question!" replied Bill. "When the labor content is the most significant part of COGS, there are other countries in the world that have much cheaper labor rates than we do. When the material content is the most significant part of COGS, you can only go back into the design and simplify or cost reduce the BOM."

"What do you mean?" asked John.

Bill continued, "Let's look at a couple of scenarios. Suppose we could find a factory in China where the labor rate is $2/hour, overhead remains 200% and factory markup remains 43%. Then forgetting logistics costs for the moment, material is $180. Labor is $3. Overhead is $6. COGS is now $189. The factory selling price is $189 times 1.43, or $270. Or, suppose Engineering could pull $50 out of material cost with everything else remaining the same. Then material is $130. Labor is $36. Overhead is $72. COGS is $238. The factory selling price is $238 times 1.43, or $340."

"So, if we could take out some material cost, then we could manufacture here?" asked Harry.

"That would be great. I know the folks in our plant would be happy to hear that. Maybe with the higher volumes, Purchasing can get some good material discounts," said Donna wistfully.

"I don't want to burst anyone's bubble, but there is a second supply chain decision point we need to discuss. But first, a question to Harry…how many VARs does Computer Products sell through?" asked Bill.

"I would have to find out the exact number, but it's probably in the range of 100 to 150 VARs," replied Harry.

"Right. Would we really expect the midbound logistics for 2,500 heavy, bulky UPS products per month from China to 100 different VAR locations to be economical with predictable delivery lead times? No, I don't think so. Who can tell me the implication of midbound logistics from a distant factory?" Just then, a light bulb went off in Harry's mind. "We are going to need to add a distribution center (DC) between the factory and the VARs," he said quietly.

"Yes. And when that happens, we add another echelon into our supply chain," said Bill.

Harry replied, "There will be another markup factor. Now we have a factory markup, a distributor markup, and a VAR markup. Let's see, working backwards…$500 customer cost times 70% for a VAR markup times 70% for a distributor markup times 70% for a factory markup leaves just $172 for factory COGS. This is less than our current material cost alone. Maybe the VAR and distributor factors will only amount to 75% each. That would give us a factory COGS of $197."

"The costs are a little more complicated. The distributor has warehouse labor and overhead just like the factory before any markup. We want to at least distribute from our own division for revenue recognition. Suppose the distribution labor is 0.15 hours. Then working forward the distributor's price becomes the $270 Chinese factory price plus $3.60 for labor plus $7.20 for overhead for a distributor COGS of $281 here in the United States. This gives a distributor price of $373 using a 33% markup," said Tony.

"…Plus the $15 for inbound freight," said Bill. "The freight connection between the factory and the distributor is called midbound freight. It's time in our discussion to estimate a number for midbound freight. Today, a 40 TEU ocean freight container, which is 40 twenty foot equivalent units (TEU), from Hong Kong to Oakland, California, costs about $2,400. It can hold 40 pallets double stacked. While it will depend on the final pack out dimensions of our UPS product, suppose that each pallet can hold 24 units. Then 24 units per pallet times 40 pallets per container would yield 960 UPS products in one container. $2,400 in ocean freight costs divided by 960 products equals $2.50 midbound logistics cost per product. We would need to add motor freight costs on both sides of the ocean freight connection. One motor freight leg is from the factory to the port of origin and the second motor freight leg is from the port of destination to the distributor. This is a complete guess, but say, the total motor freight adds $8, then the total midbound logistics cost is $10.50 plus duty."

"So what are we looking for in a factory?" asked Donna.

"In this scenario, the addition of a distributor forces us to license our product design to a CM. The CM we choose must have high-quality electronics manufacturing experience, a labor rate less than one tenth of ours, and a capacity to build at least 2,500 units per month. I'll speak with George to see if he has any advice. We can use the Internet to search for candidates," said Bill.

"I sure don't like the idea of building our product somewhere else," said Donna.

Stepping back to the whiteboard, Bill acknowledged their feelings and said, "It's a tough business decision. We have batted around a lot of numbers with many different assumptions. Let me summarize what I will be telling the vice presidents. The team needs to construct a six-echelon supply chain network: echelon 6, raw material, feeds echelon 5, an international supply base, which feeds echelon 4, a foreign CM, which feeds echelon 3, our site as distributor, which feeds echelon 2, domestic VARs, which feeds echelon 1, domestic customers. On a per-unit cost basis for this to work, the material cost is $130, inbound freight is $15, the factory labor hours are 1.5 hours, the factory labor rate is $2/hour, the factory overhead is 200%, the factory COGS is 70% of factory price, midbound freight is $10.50, distributor hours are 0.15 hours, distributor labor is $24/hour, distributor overhead is 200%, and the distributor COGS is 70% of distributor price and we will add $3 for outbound freight and use a VAR COGS at 70% of the VAR price for a product price of $498. Engineering has to reduce material cost by $50 and license the product design. Operations has to select a CM and expand on-site distribution here. Marketing has to get the Computer Products server forecast and negotiate a favorable discount with each VAR."

Summary: material landed cost = $145; factory price = $220; distributor price = $345; VAR price = $498.

Know What Your Customer Values

Before supply chain networks, there were factories. These factories considered themselves to be self-sufficient. They had complete functional structures with management, sales and marketing, engineering, quality, finance and accounting, information systems, production, materials, purchasing, facilities, and human resources. They invented products; they built products; they sold products. Factory competed against factory. They thought they were the masters of their own destiny.

In today's world, there are supply chain networks. Supply chains compete against supply chains. The factory is but one echelon within a supply chain network. The factory may be a division of a multinational corporation, an independent third party, or an incomplete functional structure dependent upon other functions owned by other organizations within the network. You need to understand the subtle differences.

This Customer Valued Flexibility

The Power Supply Division was a very successful $100 million division of a multinational corporation. The power supply factory was self-contained and totally focused on power products; in fact, it was the only factory in the corporation making these products. It accumulated customer orders from a captive field sales force selling a wide variety of products made across all the divisions in the corporation. It shipped factory direct from its east coast plant to end customers worldwide. The power supply factory organization included significant hardware and firmware design engineering resources and a captive fabrication shop that built custom power magnetic components.

The fastest growing market segment for the Power Supply Division was European cell phone original equipment manufacturers (OEMs). This was during the time of rapid expansion in cell phone manufacturing capacity. The life cycle time for next-generation handsets had shrunk from several years to less than a year. New OEM customer automation had to be built to accommodate the miniaturization of each new handset generation. Each new handset production line was an opportunity for the power supply factory to win a new OEM customer automation sale. Yet, over time, it had become apparent that winning a sale at one manufacturing site of one of the competing cell phone parent companies did not guarantee winning the sale at another manufacturing site for the same cell phone parent company. The power supply factory was winning orders by being more flexible than its competitors. Once the next-generation handset design was made known, engineers from the power supply factory would travel to the OEM customer site to accelerate the design and implementation of customizations on its own product. These customizations increased handset throughput, which gave the OEM customer a big advantage.

At about the same time, the huge parent company of the Power Supply Division split into two smaller, independent companies. When the dust settled, the new parent company found it necessary to expand its international manufacturing presence to continue selling into certain world markets. The new operating strategy called for outsourcing the production of power supplies to Southeast Asia. Temporary staff was hired to form sending and receiving teams responsible for the details of the product transfer. Additional cash was invested in building buffer inventory to ensure a continuity of supply for customers. The transition plan was both aggressive and well executed.

The power supplies were slated to be outsourced to a lower-cost factory in Penang, Malaysia, that was previously owned and operated by the new parent company. This factory was a highly automated electronics component manufacturer. Its workforce was highly skilled in loading and unloading silicon diffusion furnaces, in wafer cutting, in die attach, in lead bonding, and in operating chip encapsulation equipment. But this Malaysian workforce knew little about mechanical assembly, chassis wiring, final test, or custom fabrication of ferrite core magnetics. While the labor rate was much lower, the assembly times were longer until the newly trained workforce moved down the learning curve. Management at the new factory did not see any need to incur the expense of flying its engineers to Europe for new product customization meetings. Where the domestic factory had shipped product 3,900 miles by airfreight to meet tight competitive deadlines, the Penang factory shipped product 12,600 miles by ocean freight to save cost, thereby missing critical deadlines. In the end, even though the product was technically superior, this cultural misunderstanding of the need for manufacturing flexibility and rapid response lost the cell phone handset business to the competition.

That Customer Valued Capability

A seven-person start-up technology company had leveraged its ideas into a viable $5 million business by creating a virtual supply chain network. The founders did not own anything other than a very clear sense of the market, some hardware patents, and a deep understanding of the technology cost drivers. Not wanting to turn over ownership of their fledgling company to venture capitalist, the founders struggled to finance their cash flow with personal debt. They managed to grow their presence in the marketplace by wedding, then divorcing, a series of partner companies who each provided new cash infusions against the potential for high growth.

To the outside world, the virtual supply chain architecture gave the little company the appearance of a much larger footprint. The core of the business, held by the founders, was rooted in intellectual property and great salesmanship. The founders had managed to secure a series of win–win relationships with other organizations to outsource functional pieces that the technology start-up was missing. The commercialization of their latest technology held great promise for huge revenue and profits for all the parties. A relationship with a local electronics CM was one such key relationship. Over seven years, throughput grew to $4 million/year in hardware sales, which was half of the local CM's total revenue. The local CM both built the base products and kitted the products with a wide range of accessories that the local CM either built or purchased. The business was highly volatile in both the rate of base product shipments and the mix of specific product accessory kitting. The local CM managed its workforce and its inventory to accommodate this shipment volatility at a minimal cost to its now largest customer.

When the technology company had grown to 35 employees, a revenue run rate of $12 million, and the founders had grown tired of living hand to mouth, the business and intellectual property was sold to a $100 million company. The new owner had existing relationships with other CMs. The new owner was anxious to consolidate production and showcase its manufacturing prowess. But in performing its due diligence while acquiring the technology company, the new owner failed to understand the magnitude and sales implications of being able to make and deliver such a volatile product mix. The new owner's preferred electronics manufacturing services (EMS) organization built 20 times the volumes of a few products. This EMS was not attracted to the low volume of $4 million/year in incremental sales spread over a mix of dozens of kitted accessories. The EMS reluctantly agreed to "give it a go" as a favor to the new owner, but at a barely competitive product price. Each time the EMS had to adjust its workforce or expand its inventory, the new owner received surprise invoices from the EMS. The low-volume, high-mix manufacturing plus the requirement to act as the distributor just did not fit the EMS's focus on high volume, low mix. The resulting cost and delivery performance was disappointing.

Understand What Makes a Good Factory

As you shop around for a factory organization to meet your supply chain network needs, you will meet willing people and come across business solutions that may seem to fit. But just what makes an organization a factory rather than a distributor or supplier or service bureau or recycler? Consider the basic process flow that you need to manufacture your product, the types of product information flow that is unique to manufacturing, and the internal organizational structure needed to support manufacturing.

Manufacturing Transformational Process Flow

Component parts flow into the input of your factory and finished product flows out of the output of your factory. In between, the manufacture of your product requires some kind of value-added transformation. This transformation may be accomplished by direct labor, by production equipment, or by a combination of direct labor and production equipment. Transformation examples might include the mechanical assembly of parts in an electronics work cell, the robotic welding of a car chassis on an automotive production line, or the overhead crane-assisted wing attachment to an airframe in an aircraft production hanger.

You need to know the set of production processes your product requires. You do not want to load your product production requirements into a factory that has no manufacturing experience or production equipment to do your job. A factory with an electric arc welding competency with metals is not going to be able to ultrasonically weld plastics. The production equipment is different and the base materials are different. In another example, a factory that currently builds complex wiring harnesses for off-road vehicles and military customers would probably be a good fit for making other kinds of high-reliability cable assemblies for construction equipment operated in harsh environments.

Think of manufacturing simply as a series of transformational process steps. There may be one, two, or a dozen different transformations in series and in parallel until a complete product comes out the other end. The following actions need to be organized for each separate manufacturing process:

- *Identify and count*—Each of the input component parts and materials needs to be identified and counted. This is often facilitated by the supplier's lot sizing, packaging, marking, bar coding, and radio frequency identification (RF ID) tagging.
- *Move and stage*—Sets of input component parts and materials have to be moved from receiving or the warehouse or the output of the last process to the input of the next process. Staging could mean placing parts on gravity-fed rollers, arranging parts in bins around a work cell, dumping parts into vibrating hoppers, or threading parts into magazine feeders.
- *Value-added transformation*—The direct laborers, with the aid of production equipment, MAKE one kind of transformation over and over until a complete set of parts and materials has received this particular transformation. These transformations ultimately produce the end product.
- *Types of manufacturing inventory*—The type of inventory found in manufacturing varies along the transformational steps of the process.
  - *Raw material inventory (RM)*—The lower-level items specified in the product BOM that are required to make the product. RM is valued at the price of the material.
  - *Vendor-managed inventory (VMI)*—Small items, such as hardware fasteners, managed and delivered directly to factory floor locations by the supplier. VMI inventory is owned by the supplier until it is consumed by the factory. Accounts are settled once a month.
  - *Quarantined inventory*—RM found to have a specification discrepancy or a defect that is waiting for a settlement between the factory and the supplier.
  - *Customer-owned inventory*—Special RMs purchased and owned by the customer for a specific factory job like a new product pilot. The inventory is transferred to the factory when the RM is consumed.
  - *Work-in-process inventory (WIP)*—Inventory found in fabrication and assembly areas of the factory. This inventory is issued and received against a work order. It is valued as material plus labor plus overhead. The details of WIP are generally not addressed in this book merely to simplify the discussion of accounting for costs while converting from RM to FG inventory.

- *FG inventory*—Finished product inventory ready for shipment. FG is valued at material plus labor plus overhead, or COGS.
- *Consigned inventory*—Finished goods physically located offsite, such as for spares or customer demonstrations, which are still owned by the factory.

■ *Pack and move*—The output subassembly or product is collected and either protected for movement by being loaded into totes or packaged and palletized for shipment. The output is then either moved to the input of the next transformation work center or moved to the shipping area.

Each of these actions is repeated as a set for each manufacturing process until the product is completed (see Figure 5.1). Each process has a capacity that is dependent on material yield, the number of dedicated machines and machine hours, and the number of trained direct laborers and direct labor hours. The application of Lean Manufacturing principles works to minimize or eliminate the non-value-added aspects of identifying, counting, moving, staging, and packing, leaving only purely valued-added processes.

While a given process can often accommodate a broad range of products, profitable factories usually focus their attention on a particular industry segment, such as automotive, textiles, etc. This is because the investment in material handling and process tooling is tailored to fit specific size parts built from specific RMs. While the same six-axis robot programmed to weld on an automotive assembly line could be programmed to load and unload a plastic injection molding machine, it would simply not make much sense. The materials are steel versus plastic; their weights and densities vary considerably. The product sizes are huge versus tiny. The welding torch, the vision system, and the articulation patterns are different. Moreover, the economics of capital investment in robotic technology versus manual labor hours saved are vastly different.

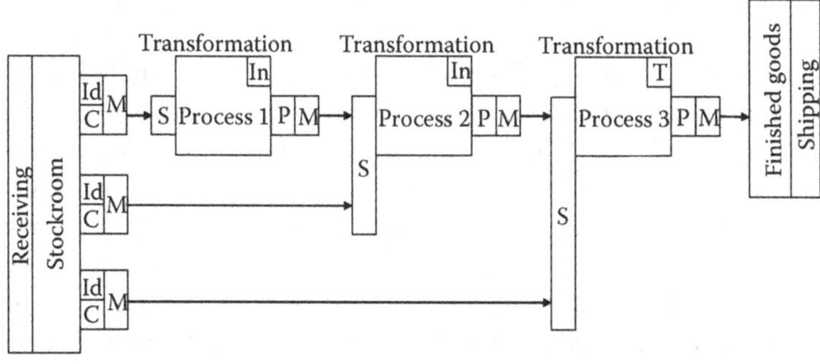

Figure 5.1 A manufacturing transformational process model. C = count; Id = identify; In = inspect; M = move; P = pack; S = stage; T = test.

Manufacturing Documentation Requirements

Whether you decide to build a product yourself or contract with a factory to have the product built to your specification, manufacturing requires this minimum set of technical and operational documentation:

- *Nondisclosure agreement (NDA): Keeping secrets secret*—The exchange of the product and process technical information required to make the product often begins with an NDA. This legal document assures both parties that the other party will not divulge specified areas of intellectual property and/or trade secrets for a specified period of time, usual three to five years.
- *BOM: The material to build the product*—The BOM consists of an item master and a product structure. The item master is the list of unique component parts and RMs with their approved suppliers that the factory's purchasing department must buy from the upstream supply base. The product structure describes the parent-to-child relationship for each component part and RM, including the quantity used per relationship.
- *Process sheets: The labor and machine instructions to build the product*—These engineering documents are specific to each type of transformational process. A mechanical assembly operation uses assembly drawings, a surface mount reflow soldering operation uses temperature profiles and carrier speeds, a robotic spot welder uses weld maps, etc.
- *Routing file: The process sequence to build the product*—This document describes the sequence of steps to transform a set of parts into a completed product. The routing file specifies which work center will perform each process step and usually gives the standard time expected to complete the work. This routing is a key input into identifying the capacity constraint on the shop floor. Sometimes, when a particular work center is over capacity, an alternative or secondary routing is used to break the constraint.
- *Test and inspection criteria: The method of validating the product*—Each and every product must be tested and inspected before being packaged for shipment. In today's high-quality production environment, the product is continuously checked within the current process step before being passed on to the next process step in its routing. This minimizes rework and maximizes yield. When the product is complete, it is normal to test and validate the performance of specific key parameters against a test and inspection criteria. Statistical process control is used to identify when a particular product fails.
- *Document revisions: Knowing the product is being built to the latest change*—Each of the different documents described above may be revised at any time. It is often a nightmare for the factory to keep current with product and process engineering design changes. You must keep a highly disciplined filing scheme for updating, tracking, and confirming that all production documentation is current.

- *Pricing agreements: Product pricing*—This is a contractual business document that guarantees a product price for a specified volume of production over a specified timeframe, such as one year. Contracts usually include much more such as the maximum inventory the factory will carry for the customer; typical delivery lead time and added costs for handling engineering change.

Manufacturing Organizational Structure

The organizational structure for a manufacturer flows from Figure 5.1 above and from the cash-to-cash concepts described in Chapter 4: "Cash Flow." Each of the functional requirements listed in the bullets below needs to be addressed. In small factories, some functions are missing altogether. In medium-size factories, some employees wear multiple hats. In larger factories, each function is a different individual. It is important that you assess the internal organization of a factory before deciding to do business with them.

The following functional areas implement the factory's order-to-delivery-to-$\text{cash}_{\text{Supply}}$ cycle:

- *Forecasting*—Forecasts the rate and mix of products to be manufactured.
- *Planning*—Schedules the shop floor based on the forecast and current order backlog. Generates the master production schedule input into materials requirements planning (MRP) and capacity requirements planning (CRP).
- *Purchasing*—Manages the purchase orders that are one output of MRP to order RMs and component parts from the supply base. Performs supplier relationship management tasks. Matches supplier invoices against inventory receipts and purchase orders (order information: factory to supplier) (invoice information: supplier to factory).
- *Receiving and incoming inspection*—Receives RMs and component parts from suppliers against open purchase orders (material: supplier to factory).
- *Accounts payable*—Manages the cash flow to pay supplier and logistics invoices (cash: factory to supplier).

The following functional areas implement the factory's value-added transformation:

- *Manufacturing engineering*—Validates customer product documentation and creates factory process documentation. Inputs BOM information into MRP and routing file information into CRP.
- *Stockroom and material handling*—Stores received RMs and component parts. Identifies, counts, and issues RMs and component parts to manufacturing.
- *Shop floor control*—Manages the sequencing of work orders, another output from MRP, that are used to order the production of specific quantities and types of product.

- *Transformational value-adding process*—Basic manufacturing process that inputs direct labor and direct material and transforms it to output an assembly or a complete end product. It is related both to a specific transformation operation, i.e., welding, assembly, or mixing, etc., and to a generic product type, such as automotive, electronics, or pharmaceutical, etc.

The following functional areas implement the factory's order-to-delivery-to-cash$_{\text{Demand}}$ cycle:

- *Sales and marketing*—Develops the market; quotes and sells the product to the customer.
- *Order processing*—Manages the customer's order from booking through shipment. Keeps the customer advised of the shipping date (order information: distributor to factory).
- *Accounts receivable and credit management*—Approves customer order booking based on the customer's open credit. Manages the invoicing and cash flows from the customer payment (invoice information: factory to distributor) (cash: distributor to factory).
- *Shipping and freight management*—Identifies, counts, and packages final product for shipment to customers. Schedules pickup for midbound logistics (material: factory to distributor).
- *Export control*—Performs regulatory documentation and export compliance tasks for international shipments.

The following functional areas provide infrastructure and support within a factory organization:

- *Finance and cost accounting*—Maintains the general ledger, performs margin analysis of product pricing, values inventory on the balance sheet, and provides management reporting including income statements, balance sheets, and cash flow statements. Advises general management.
- *Human resources*—Hires and trains both direct and indirect labor. Manages payroll. Manages employee benefits. Manages employee evaluation process.
- *Quality*—Establishes a company-wide philosophy of quality, validates material compliance to specification, validates process compliance to specification, trains and audits for International Organization for Standardization (ISO) certification compliance. Samples product performance to specification.
- *Information technology*—Installs, upgrades, and maintains the information technology systems used throughout the factory. Maintains software licensing. Provides application training. Formulates disaster recovery plans.
- *Facilities*—Maintains the physical building, the production equipment, and the grounds. This usually includes specialty work such as estimating, mechanical, plumbing, electrical, heating ventilation and air conditioning (HVAC), and site security.

- *General management*—Consists of the C-level officers, i.e., chief executive officer, chief financial officer, chief technology officer, and chief operating officer, responsible for business strategy, market development, product development, financial return, organizational structure, sustainability strategy, supply chain strategy, risk management strategy, regulatory compliance and more.
- *Consultants*—In addition, there may be any number of specialized consultants on-call such as legal attorneys and patent attorneys.

Select the Best Factory

One key topic of this chapter is learning how to make a good factory selection to meet your Supply Chain Construction Requirements Specification. And if your organization is the factory, then this section describes how to best position your organization to gain additional business. When you speak with a factory representative or search Internet sites such as www.alibaba.com, there is an overwhelming amount of detail to consider. You need a clear road map through the maze and haze.

A Case of Misguided Assumptions

A three-person team was tasked with selecting a new contract manufacturer (CM) for a growing electronics business with the objective of getting the lowest product cost. Business revenue was currently $14 million and was projected to grow to $50 million within two years, mostly through acquisitions. The team's approach was to (1) establish decision criteria, (2) compile a list of possible candidates, (3) reduce the list through phone interviews and Internet research, (4) schedule face-to-face visits with the top three contenders, (5) issue a request for quote (RFQ), (6) evaluate the written response, (7) make a selection, and (8) lock in the decision with a contract.

The candidate pool grew to 25 entries, including the current manufacturer, a couple of regional manufacturers, a manufacturer in Mexico, two in China, three multinational electronics manufacturing services (EMS) companies, and a manufacturer suggested by senior management. After some analysis, it became apparent that the candidate pool could be grouped into three tiers. Each tier was based on the relative revenue of the manufacturer, the geographical footprint of the manufacturer, and the degree of manufacturing engineering support (see Table 5.1). A regional CM had only one factory. A national plus EMS typically had one or two domestic factories plus a relationship with a factory in another country. A global EMS had multiple factories around the world with the ability to quickly shift production from one country to another.

The selection team gravitated toward the tier 1 EMS but later discovered that their entry-level COGS volume of $8 million was unattractive to any tier 1 EMS. The EMS would not accept the promise of large future orders from such a small customer. In addition, the high product mix drove low inventory turns and high support costs, which was also unattractive to any tier 1 EMS. The tier 1 EMS response was a "no bid" from

Table 5.1 Manufacturer Classification

	Regional Footprint	*National Plus Footprint*	*Global Footprint*
Process and product engineering support			Tier 1 EMS ($1–>$3 billion revenue)
Process engineering support		Tier 2 EMS ($100–>$300 million revenue)	
No engineering support	Tier 3 CM ($10–>$30 million revenue)		

one company and a price higher than they were currently paying from another company. The selection team then began to focus on the tier 2 EMS. The top runner was a company that had a relationship with one of the senior executives from a previous employment. This tier 2 EMS was located a thousand miles away in another time zone. It slowly became apparent that this tier 2 EMS had a pricing model consisting of a fixed menu with many cost adders. While the pricing for the base product appeared to be competitive, building product options was extra, holding inventory was extra, process support was extra, and engineering change orders were extra. The bottom line was that pricing from this tier 2 EMS was not competitive when the required high product mix and distribution capabilities were added in.

The selection team next considered the incredibly low labor rates found in China. But the effort to develop a relationship with a Chinese factory with which there was no previous relationship could be monumental. The hidden expense of international travel, potential theft of intellectual property, inventory locked into 8,000 miles of ocean freight logistics, the lack of fulfillment flexibility, potential quality issues with full containers of product, the supply chain risk, the trends in labor rates and currency exchange, and the necessity of committing the company's best people to a long-term project was unpalatable to senior management.

Eventually, the selection team got around to asking the question, "Just what will we gain over our current CM at this point in our company's growth?" The tradeoffs were clear. On the one hand, the current CM could not offer engineering support and would eventually run out of capacity. On the other hand, the current CM offered competitive pricing and amazing flexibility in light of the product mix requirements. The current CM knew the product and the customers they served. The selection team decided to recommend investing more with the current CM to develop some specific process engineering capability and to postpone talks with any tier 2 EMS until their COGS volume exceeded $20 million.

Factory Selection Decision Criteria

The following decision criterion in Table 5.2 enables you to quickly eliminate possible factory choices that do not fit in order to spend your time evaluating criterion that are more difficult to determine. This is to be a relationship, like a marriage, that you will want to continue for a long time. The "must" criteria are normally documented in the Supply Chain Construction Requirements Specification. If a factory candidate does not satisfy all the "musts," then do not waste any more time with that candidate. Evaluating pricing is hard; it will take a great deal of your time. The "want" criteria will be satisfied, to a greater or lesser degree, depending on the candidate. While it is easy to add more "wants," you can make a good decision with just this set. Execute an NDA with each candidate factory before sharing information.

Table 5.2 Factory Selection Criteria

Priority	*Criteria*	*Validation*	*Numerical Value*
Must 1	Requirements specification: transformation capability	1. The right process capability? 2. The right commodity expertise?	
Must 2	Requirements specification: throughput capacity	1. Your percentage of their throughput? 2. Any constraints to doubling growth?	Less than 20% to 35%
Must 3	Requirements specification: price/landed cost at volume	1. Driven by labor rate? 2. Driven by %overhead? 3. Driven by %factory markup? 4. Driven by midbound logistics?	$Landed cost
Must 4	Product quality	1. Evidence of quality philosophy? 2. ISO certification? 3. Workforce turnover?	%Failure rate
Want	Factory management team	1. Financial track record? 2. Cultural compatibility? 3. Risk management experience?	

(*Continued*)

Table 5.2 (Continued) Factory Selection Criteria

Priority	*Criteria*	*Validation*	*Numerical Value*
Want	Flexibility	1. Can respond easily to mix change? 2. Can respond easily to rate change?	
Want	Engineering support	1. Process engineering? 2. Product engineering? 3. Sustainability engineering?	
Want	Information systems	1. Information completeness? 2. Ease of interfacing? 3. Internal IT staff support?	
Want	Inventory management	1. Perpetual inventory accounting? 2. Measured inventory accuracy?	
Want	Sustainability	1. Has computed its carbon footprint? 2. Product made from sustainable material? 3. Environmentally responsible packaging? 4. Environmentally responsible recycling?	

Compare Factory Price/Landed Costs for Distribution

The price/landed cost model for factory pricing plus midbound logistics cost seen by the DC is built around the factory's income statement. A unit volume assumption must be stated. Here are the factors that go into this model:

- *Direct material dollars*—Direct material costs are based on the sum of the BOM supply prices including inbound freight cost. Inbound freight can be estimated as 6% of the direct material cost. From Equation 4.32, $Factory material cost = ∑($Supply price + $Inbound logistics).
- *Direct labor hours*—The direct labor hours are hours required to manufacture the product.
- *Direct labor rate*—Labor rate is expressed in dollars per hour and is country specific. A single labor rate may be given which is a blended rate of workers

with different skills. For example, an electronics technician makes a higher wage than an electronics assembler. Five assemblers each making \$18/hours working with one technician making \$26/hour would result in a blended rate of \$19.33/hour: ((5)(\$18) + (1)(\$26))/(5 + 1) = \$19.33.

- *%Overhead multiplier*—Overhead is calculated by multiplying the total direct labor dollars by this percentage. Two hundred percent is a good starting estimate for factories without automation. Four hundred percent is a good starting estimate for factories with automation. The higher percentage for automation is driven by higher salaries for the supporting engineering staff and by the depreciation on capitalized production equipment included in the overhead.
- *\$Factory COGS*—The \$Factory COGS is calculated using Equation 4.6:

$$\text{\$Factory COGS} = \text{\$Direct material} + (\text{Labor hours}) \times (\text{\$/Hour labor rate}) \times (1 + \text{\%Overhead multiplier}).$$

$$\begin{aligned}\text{For example: Factory \$COGS} &= \$25.00 + (0.5\text{ hours}) \times (\$22.00/\text{hour}) \times (1 + 200\%)\\ &= \$25.00 + (0.5\text{ hours} \times \$22.00/\text{hour}) \times 3\\ &= \$58\end{aligned}$$

- *%Factory markup*—This is a percentage that reflects all the other factors besides COGS, when the factory is making its desired profit.

$$\text{\%Markup} = \frac{(100\% - \text{\%COGS})}{\text{\%COGS}} \times 100\%$$

For example: If the desired %COGS for the factory is 70%, then

$$\text{\%Factory markup} = \frac{(1 - 0.70)}{0.70} \times 100\% = 42.9\%$$

- *\$Factory price*—This is the price the factory will charge to build this product at the specified direct material content, labor hour content, and unit volume. From Equation 4.30, the \$Factory price is

$$\text{\$Factory price} = \text{\$Factory COGS} \times (1 + \text{\%Factory markup}).$$

For example: \$Factory price = \$58 × (1 + 0.429) = \$82.88

Table 5.3 Factory Pricing Comparison Model (per Unit)

Cost	*Reference*	*Multiplier_A*	*Factory_A*	*Multiplier_B*	*Factory_B*
Quoted for 1,000 units of Product Z					
Direct material (includes inbound freight)	$25.00 costed BOM	$DM × 1.00	$25.00	$DM × 1.00	$25.00
+Direct labor	0.5 hours timed bill of labor	$22.00/hour labor rate	$11.00	$1.80/hour labor rate	$0.90
+Overhead multiplier	Estimated percentage (higher with more automation)	$DL × 2.00	$22.00	$DL × 2.00	$1.80
Factory COGS subtotal			$58.00		$27.70
+Factory markup	Converts COGS to profitable revenue	COGS × 0.429	$24.88	COGS × 0.333	$9.22
Total factory price			$82.88		$36.92
+Midbound freight	Total weight cubic volume	Motor freight 20 miles	$4.96	Ocean + motor 8,400 miles	$2.26
+Cross-dock	Pass thru another DC	Not applicable	$0.00	Not applicable	$0.00
+Midbound duty	Not applicable domestically		$0.00	7.2% × price import duty	$2.57
Distributor's landed cost			$87.84		$41.75

- *$Distributor product cost*—Equation 4.29 is used to determine $Distributor product cost:

$$\text{\$Distributor product cost} = \text{\$Factory price} + \text{\$Midbound logistics} + \text{\$Cross-docking.}$$

Table 5.3 uses the above cost-based model to compare the per-unit landed cost to the distributor for the same product's quoted price from competing domestic and international factories. This can be easily formulated into an Excel spreadsheet. Domestic factory A quotes $22.00/hour labor, 200% overhead, and 43% factory markup. Factory A is 20 miles from the DC by truck. International factory B quotes $1.80/hour labor, 200% overhead, and 33% factory markup. Factory B is 8,400 miles from the DC by ocean freight plus motor freight without cross-docking, and the product has a 7.2% import duty. The factory B price is US dollar (USD) denominated; this means the product is sold and bought in USD and not in a foreign currency.

Figure 5.2 emphasizes that the landed cost difference between competing factory choices is often dominated by the factory labor rate and the mode of transportation. Both the factory labor rate and the mode of transportation are driven by the country where the factory is located relative to the domestic market location. A factory located in China relative to the United States might have one tenth the labor rate but would require either four weeks of inventory transit time by ocean freight with the corresponding cash investment in inventory or very expensive airfreight logistics. Many other factors would need to be considered, such as payment by a letter of credit (LOC), the reduction in flexibility, and the increased risk of a quality defect permeating an entire container load (CL) of product.

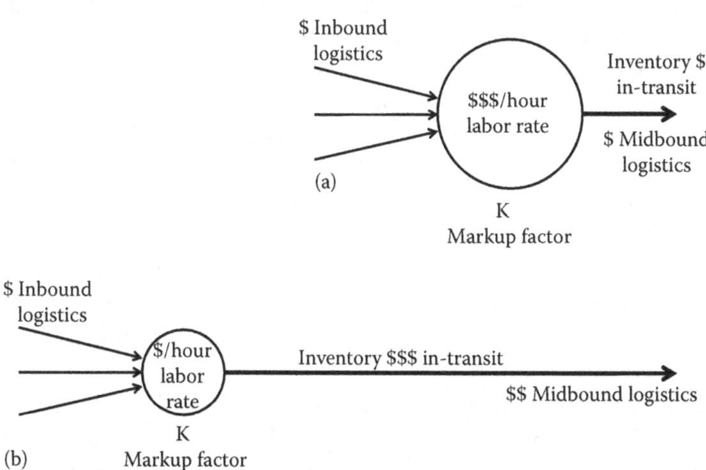

Figure 5.2 (a) Factory choice A versus (b) factory choice B.

Prepare the RFQ

Once you have selected a short list of potential candidate factories, you will send an request for quotation (RFQ), and if at all possible, visit each candidate factory. The RFQ should fairly represent the manufacturing scenario you intend to buy. The RFQ should ensure that the pricing response from each candidate factory is directly comparable. There is no greater management time sink than when multiple RFQ responses come back with different pricing models under different assumptions shown in different formats.

Describe Your Business Scenario

Once the list of potential factories has been winnowed down to three or four top candidates, you will have to share certain information with each of them to make a final decision. Here is a way to describe your business scenario:

- *Exercise an NDA*—Insist on a signed NDA with each potential factory before sharing detailed information about your business. This is particularly important if you are a small start-up business with intellectual property to protect.
- *Describe each product with a color photo, BOM, assembly drawing, and routing file*—This explains the complexity of the purchasing and the process sequencing needed to build your product.
- *Provide the total direct material cost and total direct labor hours for each product*—This is needed to calculate COGS and factory pricing and helps to put returned RFQs on an equal footing.
- *List the expected range of volumes product by product*—This describes the required range of quantity rate and mix. It is needed by the candidate to estimate the percentage of total capacity required and the opportunity for volume purchasing.
- *List the factory ship-to destinations and expected mode of transportation*—This describes the degree of flexibility the candidate has in lot sizing and packaging product for shipment.
- *List any special requirements that may invoke cost adders*—The candidate needs to know such things as sole-source suppliers for key components, special pricing arrangements that can be extended to the candidate, custom processes that will be provided to the candidate, inventory holding requirements, regulatory compliance requirements, factory certification maintenance requirements, etc.
- *Describe a typical order-to-delivery-to-cash$_{Demand}$ cycle*—This tells the candidates how they will receive orders to be shipped and how they can expect to be paid.
- *Specify the expected information technology interface*—Describe how you want to communicate supply chain information with the candidate and the frequency of this exchange.

- *Provide a contact name, phone, and e-mail*—This is the contact person should the candidate seek additional information to answer questions during the quoting process.

Specify the RFQ Response Format

Spend time to describe exactly how you want the candidate factories to respond and save yourself countless hours in follow-up phone calls, e-mails, and visits. You must be able to make an apples-to-apples comparison across the top three candidates. Of course, it goes without saying, that having signed NDAs, neither you nor any of your employees can divulge the pricing information returned from factory A with any representative of factory B.

- *Set a deadline for the return*—Allow two to three weeks for candidate factories to process the RFQ.
- *Validate their receipt of the document and their intention to respond*—Confirm their receipt of the RFQ and that they understand the deadline.
- *Return contact*—Specify the person's name, title, surface address, and e-mail where the RFQ response is to be sent.
- *Specify the model*—The expected response should fit the landed cost model described in this book. You need to learn the labor rate, overhead multiplier, and factory markup the candidate factory used to compute their product pricing. Include a statement that the quote will not be considered unless all the requested information is provided.
- *Volume breakpoints*—Indicate the range of volumes you want quoted, as in 200, 500, and 1,000.
- *Include a sample formatted response*—The sample response (see Table 5.4) shows the format of the information you expect to receive.

Evaluate First Samples

The manner in which the newly selected factory handles its first samples is critical to building trust in a newly formed relationship. The comments to follow about first samples also apply to newly selected parts suppliers. This is where the rubber meets the road. Can the seller deliver the goods? Can the buyer deliver the cash?

- Has the factory or supplier identified missing information on the product or part specification drawing before starting to build the item?
- What payment schedule does the factory or supplier demand before starting to build the item? Is there a full payment required with the product sight unseen, or an letter of credit (LOC), or payment to cover the long lead time material or payment to cover just the custom material?

Table 5.4 Sample Response Expected from This RFQ

Given Items	*Provided in the RFQ*		*Expected Response*	
Product to be quoted (name)	Product A			
Product volume (units)	Quoted at 1,000 units			
Direct material (dollars)	$25.00			
Direct labor (hours)	0.5 hours			
Response Items			*Example*	*Actual*
Direct labor rate (dollars per hour)			$22.00/hour	
Overhead multiplier (percent)			200%	
Factory markup (percent)			43%	
Factory price (dollars)			$82.94[a]	
Volume Price Breaks	*200 Units*	*500 Units*	*1,000 Units*	*2,000 Units*
Factory price (dollars)				

[a] $82.94 = ($25.00 + (0.5 hour × $22.00/hour) × (1 + 200%)) × (1 + 43%).

- How does the factory or supplier build its first small quantity when delivery for some of the material is inside its lead time?
- Does the factory or supplier require a customer signoff on first samples before starting volume production?
- How does the factory or supplier label the revision on the physical product or part?
- Will the factory or supplier use exactly the same materials and processes to build the first samples as it will use to build volume production? Or have the first samples been subcontracted to another party?
- If there are quality issues during production, will the factory or supplier communicate them to the customer?
- Will the factory or supplier continue to produce lot after lot of production in exactly the same manner as the first samples without implementing an unapproved "cost reduction?"
- What are the cycle times to make payment? To deliver the first sample? To evaluate the first sample? To correct any material or process issues? To deliver first production perhaps including weeks of ocean freight? To compare the first production product against the first sample?

Optimize Midbound Logistics Costs

Midbound logistics connect the factory with the distributor. While midbound logistics may involve motor freight, rail freight, ocean freight, air freight, or intermodal, one characteristic of a midbound logistics shipment is that it repeatedly involves a large quantity, high cubic volume of a few stock keeping units (SKUs). Midbound logistics is often your opportunity to ship full container loads (CL) rather than less than container loads (LCL). The predictability of midbound freight makes it an easy place to optimize shipping costs. Design your midbound product packaging carefully and choose your mode of transportation wisely. Chapter 6: "Source" covers inbound logistics and import regulatory considerations, while Chapter 7: "Deliver" covers outbound logistics and export regulatory considerations.

Three Rules for Palletization

Wood and plastic pallets have standard English footprints of 48 inches × 40 inches in the United States and metric 1,200 millimeters × 1,000 millimeters in the European Union. One inch equals 25.4 millimeters. Pallet footprints are much less standardized throughout Asia, although one of the dimensions is usually a metric 1,200 millimeters. Wood pallets are typically 5 inches high and weighs 50 pounds; 2.204 pounds equals 1 kilogram. Some distributors specify plastic or specially treated wood pallets because of the environmental concern of beetles and other insects being transported internationally then causing infestations in certain varieties of trees.

A unit load is a palletized stack of product cartons. The number of cartons in the stack is the number of cartons per layer times the number of layers. Keep the following three rules in mind when palletizing your unit load:

- *The unit load must not overhang the pallet footprint.*
  - Design your carton dimensions such that a layer of product takes advantage of the full pallet footprint, the width times the length, but does not extend over either dimension. This is because the pallet should protect the product carton from being crushed by forklift moves during loading and unloading. Most modern pallets provide four-way entry, meaning a forklift can approach from any side.
  - For example: A product carton measures 8″ wide × 12″ deep × 7″ high. Flip the carton around, checking how every dimension best divides into the pallet footprint. In this case, 8″ divides five times evenly into 40″ and 12″ divides four times evenly into 48″. Therefore, one layer would hold 5 cartons × 4 cartons = 20 cartons and have a layer height of 7″.
- *A double-stacked unit load must clear the container's doorjamb.*
  - This is the height restriction that determines how many layers of cartons can be stacked on a single pallet. Consider that the door opening height

on a standard 40-foot container is 7 feet 6 inches (or 2,286 millimeters). The double-stacked pallet height must be less than 90 inches in order to load and unload through the container door using a forklift. This means the total layer height for one pallet must be less than 38.5″ to give clearance to 2× unit load height plus 2× pallet height of 5″ plus travel clearance for the forklift's fork. Otherwise, you will pay a hidden cost to unstack and restack your product. The stability of the palletized layers is ensured by interleaving the carton stacking and by adding corner guards to the four vertical corners then shrink wrapping or banding the entire unit load.

  – Continuing the example: The 7″ layer height divides into 38.5″ five times. Therefore, each pallet would hold 20 cartons per layer × 5 layers, for a total of 100 cartons. A sixth layer would make the stack too tall.

- *The unit load should weigh less than 1,000 pounds (or 454 kilograms).*
  – The total number of products on the pallet times their individual weight including carton weight plus the 50 pounds (or 22.7 kilograms) for the pallet should total less than 1,000 pounds (or 454 kilograms). This is for safety in pallet handling and lifting in the warehouse. Note that for dense products, total weight may be more restrictive to the number of product layers per unit load than total height.
  – Completing the example: If the empty carton weighs 1 pound and the wooden pallets weigh 50 pounds, then for 100 products per pallet, the product weight must be less than (1,000 pounds – 150 pounds)/100 products = 8.5 pounds/product (or 3.86 kilograms/product).

Containers come in two lengths: 20 foot, the TEU (Twenty-foot Equivalent Unit) and 40 foot, the FEU (Forty-foot Equivalent Unit). While there are several container formats including standard, high cube, and refrigerated, one TEU can generally hold 20 pallets double stacked, and one FEU can generally hold 40 pallets double stacked. Containers have tare weight, which is the unloaded weight of the box. Containers also have a maximum weight restriction. Therefore, the total weight of the number of unit loads the container holds must be less than the maximum weight minus the tare weight.

Cost Drivers versus Transportation Mode

Once you know the number of pallets, their total weight and total cubic volume, the point of origin, and the point of destination, you are ready to obtain midbound logistics pricing. Common carriers quote their transportation cost structures in rate tariffs that are tables of cost versus distance traveled, weight and/or cube, and the type of freight. Motor freight is the most convenient. Airfreight is the most expensive. Ocean freight takes the most time. Rail freight can be subject to high variability. Be on the lookout for possible intermodal combinations that can service your origin to destination; intermodal freight can provide faster transit time at an intermediary cost.

- *Motor freight less than truckload (LTL)*—LTL motor freight is quoted by freight class in dollars per hundred weight ($/cwt) for distance traveled. Fuel surcharges apply. The National Motor Freight Traffic Association defines 18 freight classes in terms of weight, length and height, density, ease of handling, value, and carrier liability. The lower the freight class, the lower is the freight cost. LTL freight may be consolidated by freight forwarders into full truckloads by combining freight pickups from other customers.

  For example: A 340 pound shipment quoted at $22.85/cwt from origin to destination in freight class 110 is priced at (340/100) × $22.85 = $77.69, where "hundred weight" means dividing the actual weight by 100 and multiplying by the listed tariff rate.
- *Rail freight less than container load (LCL)*—LCL rail freight is quoted in $/kg V/M, which is dollars per kilogram dimensional weight for an origin–destination pair. See the explanation of V/M below under airfreight. Fuel surcharges apply. LCL rail freight may be consolidated by a freight forwarder into full CL rail freight by combining freight from other customers. Rail freight is cost effective for high-cubic-volume and/or heavy-weight loads. Rail freight can have transit time variability because of the transit time through switching yards and the number of crew changeovers. Intermodal rail freight sometimes has the advantage of being able to bypass road congestion in heavily populated areas.
- *Ocean freight container load (CL)*—CL ocean freight is quoted in $/kg V/M, which is dollars per kilogram dimensional weight port-to-port. See the explanation of V/M below under airfreight. Fuel surcharges and harbor maintenance fees apply. The more you can fit into the container, the cheaper the per-unit transportation cost. Be aware that some ocean freight carriers steam at reduced speed to manage their fuel costs; this extends transit time.
- *Airfreight*—Airfreight is quoted in $/kg V/M, which is dollars per kilogram dimensional weight origin to destination. Fuel surcharges apply. Under dimensional weight, the airline uses a density equivalence factor to convert cubic volume into an equivalent weight. The quoted $/kg is applied to both the weight and to the equivalent weight. The larger of the two numbers is the transportation cost. Airfreight is often four or five times more expensive than the other modes, and it does not have the capacity to move as much freight.

  For example: The airfreight for a unit load of 48″ wide × 40″ deep × 55″ high weighing 150 pounds is quoted at $5.15/kg V/M. The airfreight shipment's actual weight is 150 pounds. The airfreight shipment's dimensional weight is calculated from the cubic volume in inches and the airline's density equivalence factor of 166 cubic inches per pound. The 48″ w × 40″ d × 55″ h dimensions equal 105,600 cubic inches of volume, which converts to a dimensional weight of 636 pounds when divided by the 166 conversion factor. The airline will charge the larger of the two weights, or 636 pounds. Using the conversion factor of 2.2 pounds per kilogram, the metric-based pricing of $5.15/kg converts to English-based pricing of $2.34/pound. This air shipment will cost ($2.34/pound) × (636 pounds) = $1,488.

- *Fuel surcharge*—Common carriers add a fuel surcharge to every mode of transportation. This is a cost adder, which is usually calculated as a percentage of the underlying transportation cost.
- *Packaging materials*—Be sure to include the costs for labels, shipping cartons, filler material, plastic floaters, pallets, corner guards, shrink wrap, and banding straps. These are indirect material costs.
- *Logistics documentation*—There are bill of lading and commercial invoice documentation requirements for each mode of transportation. If the midbound logistics connection involves the factory exporting and the distributor importing, then the shipment becomes an international shipment requiring additional documentation. Remember that if the product has to be returned to the factory for any reason, then the distributor is exporting and the factory is importing. The product requires a Harmonized Tariff Schedule (HTS) classification for import, a schedule B classification for export, and an Export Control Classification Number (ECCN) for exports. The factory and the distributor must comply with import regulations and export regulations according to the laws of the respective origin and destination countries. These topics are covered in Chapter 6: "Source" and Chapter 7: "Deliver."
- *Transportation to/from the port and cross-docking*—Short motor freight legs will be used to move freight from its origin to a port, rail head, or airport and to move freight from a port, rail head, or airport to its destination. In addition, cross-docking charges can occur when one DC in a distribution network passes the freight through to another DC within the same distribution network. For example, when a factory in China delivers by ocean freight to a distributor in New York, one routing could be from the factory to motor freight to port of Hong Kong to ocean freight to port of Oakland, California, to motor freight to distributor cross-dock to motor freight to distributor cross-dock to motor freight to distributor to UPS to the customer.
- *Import duty and value-added tax (VAT)*—For international shipments, depending on origin and destination countries, there may be duty and VAT costs. Duty is based on the HTS classification the factory assigns to the product. Where applicable, both duty and VAT are calculated as percentages of the commercial invoice value of the product being transported.

Transportation Fuel Efficiency

Besides cost and transit time, fuel efficiency is a hidden cost and risk tradeoff in the selection of your logistics transportation mode. Higher fuel efficiency means less dependence on the price of oil and a smaller carbon footprint generated while moving freight. Ocean freight is considered to be the most efficient and cleanest form of transportation; it is used as the point of reference. The number of British Thermal Units (BTUs) per ton-mile is used to compare freight movement made by other modes of transportation against the same freight movement theoretically made by ocean freight. This is a relative comparison method and not an absolute measure where a smaller number is a better number.

- *Ocean freight*—This is the mode of transportation with the lowest BTU per ton-mile.
- *Rail freight*—The US Department of Energy estimates that the BTU per ton-mile for rail freight runs about 1.3 times the BTU per ton-mile for ocean freight.
- *Motor freight*—The US Department of Energy estimates that the BTU per ton-mile for motor freight runs about 15 times the BTU per ton-mile for ocean freight.
- *Airfreight*—The US Department of Energy estimates that the BTU per ton-mile for airfreight runs about 44 times the BTU per ton-mile for ocean freight.

Suppose you are considering an offshore factory in Hong Kong delivering half of the products to a DC in Oakland and half of the products to a second DC in Chicago versus a domestic factory in Atlanta delivering the same products split to the same two DCs. Under alternative 1, the total product weight is shipped from Hong Kong to Oakland, and then half of the weight is forwarded to Chicago by rail. Under alternative 2, half the product weight is shipped to Chicago and half of the product weight is shipped to Oakland. Table 5.5 uses the relative fuel efficiency

Table 5.5 Midbound Logistics Relative Fuel Efficiency Example

From	*To*	*Mode*	*Tons*	*Mileage*	*Relative BTU/ Ton-Mile*	
Alternative 1						
Hong Kong	Oakland	Ocean	4 tons	×6,906 miles	×1.0	27,624
Oakland	Chicago	Rail	2 tons	×2,126 miles	×1.3	5,528
Total						33,152
Alternative 2						
Atlanta	Chicago	Truck	2 tons	×717 miles	×15	21,510
Atlanta	Oakland	Truck	2 tons	×2,460 miles	×15	73,800
Total						95,310

method to show that the less weight shipping from Hong Kong means the generation of a smaller carbon footprint.

Beware the Hidden Costs of Offshore Manufacturing

Manufacturing in a country with a $2.50–$4.00/hour labor rate can look very attractive when your domestic rate is $25–$40/hour. But your final landed cost will be much higher than one tenth of your current cost. Start by asking the question, "Is this product direct material intensive or direct labor intensive?" If your product cost is dominated by material, then even if the labor content went to zero, your product cost would mostly reflect the material cost. If you have significant labor content, then consider the following investments and risks carefully.

Making the Investment

The following lists key investments you will have to make:

- *Committing the company's best people to a long-term project*—This is the planning time, travel time, and telecom and video conferencing time of your best employees dedicated to making the relationship work. If your business is small, you may not have the critical mass of employee resources both to keep the store open and to conduct a distant project.
- *The expense of international travel*—This is the airfare, ground transportation, hotels, meals, telecommunications, and visas for foreign travel. Flights booked at the last minute and extended stays, both without and with family members, can become cost prohibitive.
- *Buffer inventory investment*—You will have to build a buffer inventory ahead of making the transition to ensure continuity of supply for your customers.
- *In-transit inventory investment*—In a new relationship, you will have to pay for production inventory upfront, probably with an LOC. Once the product ships, it may sit in a container on the ocean for 18 to 32 days.
- *The logistics costs of shipping start-up inventory*—You will have to pay for extra packaging materials and many small deliveries of start-up inventory components.
- *The product and testing costs for quality sampling*—You will want to conduct periodic destructive testing of product samples to track and ensure that quality production methods are being followed.
- *The cost of production tooling and product models*—These are start-up costs that are sometimes unexpected. The new manufacturer may not have that custom tooling that your current manufacturer has; if you decide to share it between factories, you risk continuity of supply during the interim. You may have to pay a duty assist on tooling provided to the new factory.

Managing the Risk

The following lists key risks you will have to manage:

- *Continuity of supply*—Expect critical component parts to get lost. Expect the start-up of new production processes to take longer than was scheduled.
- *Cultural incompatibility*—You may find over time that the exotic combination of language translation, time differences, vast distances to be traveled, and dramatically different cultures become incompatible with your business needs.
- *Potential theft of intellectual property*—Some countries have very different legal systems and weak protection of intellectual property. The expectation of some foreign governments is that you will give away some technical knowledge as the ante to manufacture your product in their country.
- *Confiscated property risk*—In some unstable countries, there may be a risk that the government will decide to seize your property. Doing business in these countries should be avoided.
- *Accelerated quality issues*—Direct labor turnover is high as employees jump to another employer for the highest going wage. Poor workmanship can lead to product quality issues discovered by customers that may lead to the discovery of full CLs of defective product.
- *A lack of fulfillment flexibility*—It becomes very difficult to quickly change the rate and mix of production or the product delivery point over 8,000 miles of separation and 12 hours of time zone difference.
- *Labor rate trends*—As the standard of living improves in a low-cost country and a middle class develops, the country's labor rate rises.
- *Trends in the price of oil*—Certain RM costs and fuel surcharge costs track world changes in the price of oil.
- *The negotiation of new trade treaties change some import duty classifications each year*—If your cost structure is based on an import duty exemption that gets reversed, your profitability margin is lost.
- *Currency exchange rate*—It is best to buy and sell in USD-denominated amounts. You cannot predict how an exchange rate might change in the future. Sophisticated currency exchange hedging strategies are outside the context of this book.
- *Internet blockage*—The exchange of supply chain operational information regarding forecasts, orders, shipments, invoices, and cash payments depend upon open Internet connections among trading partners. Where country governments decide to block and censure the Internet, this can cause disruption to the flow of operational data.

A Case of Chinese Manufactured Cables

A domestic factory produced expensive, labor-intensive wiring harnesses in a secondary operation to the production of their main product. As the product line expanded the number of product configurations it supported, the mix of wiring harness grew. The product line soon required six different medium- to low-volume harnesses, with the most expensive harness costing $127. Supply chain management decided to investigate the possibility of a lower cost solution.

With the rapid product expansion, engineering never had the time to go back and consolidate and simplify this commodity. Therefore, the first step was to compare the BOMs and wiring diagrams of each of the six current harnesses against one another. The result was the realization that all six harnesses had the same connector on the near end, could be the same overall length, number of conductors, and wire gauge, but had a different set of connectors on the far end. This conclusion presented the possibility of a postponement solution. The total mix volume could be combined for a low-cost manufacturer to build and test a generic wiring harness consisting of the total harness length with the near end connector attached and wired. Then, a low-cost postponement operation could be added within distribution to complete and test the wiring harness on the far end to the customer's order.

The supply chain management team set about developing a list of potential CMs at home and abroad. At that time, the domestic factory paid $28.15 for direct material and $22.00/hour for the one hour of direct labor. The team considered a factory in Nogales, Mexico, with a $6.00/hour labor rate; a factory in Shenzhen, China, with a $1.75/hour labor rate; and a factory in Chennai, India, with a $1.30/hour labor rate. A cost model was developed that accounted for direct material including inbound logistics, direct labor, labor rate, a percentage overhead multiplier, percentage factory markup, and midbound logistics. Each candidate CM was sent an RFQ. The cost model showed a total domestic cost of $127, a landed cost from Mexico of $76, a landed cost from China of $50, and a landed cost from India of $68. Even though India had a lower labor rate than China, India was more expensive for this commodity because of the logistics cost for the large-cubic-volume, heavy harnesses. While the Chinese labor rate was only 8% of the domestic labor rate, the landed wiring harness cost was only reduced to 39% of the current domestic cost.

The Chinese factory was awarded the work with RMB-denominated pricing. The Chinese factory produced high-quality harnesses with reliable deliveries. Product pricing to the end customer was reduced, reflecting the fact that COGS for the wiring harness had been reduced by $77 ($127 – $50), or 60%. The price reduction made outsourcing a one-way decision. With the overall reduced product pricing, the product line could never go back to manufacturing the wiring harness domestically and still be competitive in the market. However, the future remains to be seen. Labor rates in China are increasing as the standard of living rises; the cost of copper wire is increasing; ocean freight container shipping costs are increasing; the exchange rate of Chinese RMB currency to the USD is weakening. Table 5.6 shows the multiyear trend for each of these cost drivers along with their impact on the $50 wiring harness. Notice that while the %overhead multiplier and %factory markup multiply the impact, the fact that each cost delta is but a percentage of the whole landed cost tends to dampen the impact. When each cost driver trends in

Table 5.6 Cost Driver Multiyear Trends

Cost Driver	*Item*	*Direction*	*Change*	*Multipliers*	*Impact*
Material	Copper prices	Increase +5%	From: $14.00 To: $14.70	×Factory markup	+2.1%
Labor	Labor rate	Increase +14%	From: $1.75/hour To: $2.00/hour	×Overhead multiplier ×Factory markup	+1.7%
Ocean freight	Fuel surcharge	Increase +8.6%	From: 38.1% To: 46.7%	Logistics is a fraction of landed cost	+2.2%
Exchange rate	RMB to USD	Increase +8.5%	From: 6.664 to 1 To: 6.141 to 1	RMB denominated Factory price	+8.5%
Multiyear cumulative impact on landed cost					+14.5%

the same direction, the impact becomes cumulative. The +14.5% cumulative cost increase erodes a full quarter of the savings gained by manufacturing the wiring harness in China. If the deal could have been negotiated as a USD-denominated purchase, then the RMB-to-USD exchange rate risk could have been eliminated.

In Summary

This chapter shows how to select a factory that fits your Supply Chain Construction Requirements Specification. The characteristics that differentiate a factory relationship from other kinds of supply chain relationships are discussed. A factory selection criterion with musts and wants is presented. A model to evaluate landed cost taking into account material cost, inbound logistics, labor cost, the percentage overhead multiplier, percentage factory markup, and midbound logistics is developed. The details of midbound logistics are discussed for each mode of transportation. Finally, the challenges of preparing and evaluating candidate factory responses to an RFQ along with the hidden challenges of using an offshore factory are revealed.

Chapter 6

Source

The numbers of suppliers, the structure of the supply base, and the range of material commodities to be purchased are all determined by the product bill of materials (BOM). Consequently, the construction of the network container requires knowledge of its likely product contents. This chapter begins with a brief description of a practical part numbering scheme, then explains the workings of the product BOM. The chapter explains how to organize purchasing around commodity management. The chapter describes how to perform supplier selection to meet a direct material budget. Last, since inbound logistics is an important cost factor in material sourcing, the chapter discusses inbound logistics cost drivers and import regulatory considerations.

When You Care Enough to Source the Very Best

George, the Supply Chain Construction Team's executive champion, explained to Bill, the Supply Chain Construction Team project manager, that Steve, the chief executive officer (CEO), and Tom, the vice president of Manufacturing, had a line on a potential contract manufacturer. In Corporate review meetings that Steve had attended with the CEO of Computer Products, Steve had learned that Computer Products was buying high-power, low-cost switching power supplies from a company named Astec. Astec was headquartered in Hong Kong with an Australian CEO and had a low-cost manufacturing site in Kuantan, Malaysia. Steve and Tom had contacted Astec management some six months before to explore their interest in licensing the manufacture of power supplies designed by Power Products.

Now, Bill and Tom were on a United Airlines flight to Singapore with a planned visit to the factory in Kuantan and a supplier visit to an aluminum extruder in

Penang, Malaysia. Tom was relaxing, listening to music using headphones. Bill broke the silence, "This is pretty exotic traveling halfway around the world. I've never been to Asia before."

Tom peeled off his headphones, "Better get used to it. If we go with these guys, you will get to do this repeatedly. Now, tell me our arrangements again."

"Around noon tomorrow, we take a short flight from Singapore to Kuantan. We're staying at the Kuantan Hyatt," replied Bill. "We are meeting with Safdar, the Astec operations manager, and Renu, an Astec engineering manager, who is flying up from Hong Kong. There will also be some folks from our company there. Corporate has established an international procurement operation, or IPO, in Singapore. Grace, a buyer, and Chee Beng, a materials engineer, from the IPO will meet us at the plant. They are both Chinese but apparently speak English very well."

"What's an IPO?" asked Tom.

Bill replied, "An IPO brings together materials engineering, purchasing, and logistics expertise to solve sourcing issues and to monitor parts quality. Since these folks are based in Singapore, they can be at the factory the next day. They can confirm the status of product leaving the plant and sailing from Singapore."

"What's the agenda?"

"This trip is to kick the tires. You know…introduce Power Products, meet the senior staff, walk the production process, review material procedures, get a handle on their product quality, due diligence stuff," said Bill. "Our company and Astec have already signed a nondisclosure agreement. It's OK to discuss most business-related topics."

"You really think it's going to take three days to do this? I need to get back home for some family obligations with my daughter. Maybe we can cut this short and book an earlier return flight," said Tom.

Bill rolled his eyes, "What? You're already talking about going home, and we haven't even arrived? Don't forget, we also have a flight to Penang Island after this to visit the extruder Fuji Sash on the Penang mainland. And, based on the pushup we went through to book our United Airlines tickets, you know that the flights over the next couple of days are oversold. We're in the midst of holiday travel."

"Yeah, I know," sighed Tom. "Why am I going to Fuji Sash anyway? Maybe you could do that yourself?"

"There are a couple of reasons. First, if we go with a contract manufacturer in Asia, then it makes good cost and control sense for the supply base to be close to the factory in Asia. Second, Engineering wants to use extruded aluminum for the uninterruptable power supply (UPS) front and rear frames. These are large parts that would cost too much to ship from the United States. Third, we are not sure their extrusion process can hold the tolerances we need. We are fortunate that Chee Beng can accompany our visit to the extruder to access his capability. All of this impacts manufacturing volumes back home," replied Bill.

"I have a lot of budgeting work that Steve needs from me. I may have to stay at the Hyatt one day while you visit the plant," announced Tom. Then he pulled on his headphones.

They checked in and out of the Le Meridian Hotel near Changi Airport and then took a short hop on Dragon Air to Kuantan, arriving midafternoon. After immigration, baggage claim, and customs, they looked for the taxi stand and found an Indian driver who spoke English. Their jet lag was starting to kick in, but Safdar and Renu were picking them up for dinner. "What time are we meeting in the lobby?" asked Tom.

"Six p.m. I'm going to set my alarm so I don't sleep though our appointment," replied Bill.

The Hyatt was under construction, with considerable hammering and drilling noise. The Hyatt front desk did not have a reservation for Bill, but they were willing to upgrade for additional cost. Bill was indignant, "Look, my reservation was made days ago. I've traveled halfway around the world to meet with Astec, and now you don't have a room?"

At the mention of Astec, the largest employer in Kuantan, Bill's room reservation was suddenly found and at the reduced corporate rate. "Yes sir. We're very sorry for this inconvenience, sir," said the desk clerk.

Safdar, a short, sturdy-looking Malay gentleman, and Renu, a tall swarthy Indian, met the two Americans in the lobby a little after 6 p.m. After greetings, the first negotiation was where to go for dinner. They settled on a seafood restaurant that Safdar knew as common ground to start the visit.

The conversation was lighthearted during dinner, with Bill and Tom mostly learning about the local Malaysian culture.

When Bill returned to his room exhausted after dinner, he was startled to find a bright orange object on the floor plugged into the wall and buzzing away. Bill dialed the front desk and said, "There's something buzzing in my room that you need to come and take away right now!"

"Yes sir. You want to keep that. It is a piezoelectric device that keeps the mosquitoes out of your room," replied the desk clerk.

Bill awoke the next morning refreshed and without any mosquito bites. After breakfast, he and Tom took a taxi to the plant, where the Astec reception desk made them feel quite welcome. Their names were even listed on the notice board as VIPs from the United States!

Safdar greeted them in the lobby and then led them into a small conference room to meet six members of his factory staff. The room was quite crowded with Renu, Chee Beng, and Grace bringing the total attendance to 12 people. Tom gave a pitch on Power Products and explained the purpose of the visit. Safdar gave a pitch on Astec Kuantan, welcoming the start of a mutually beneficial business relationship. After that, it was decided to break into small groups to address specific topics with a summary meeting to include everyone at the end of the day.

Chee Beng and Grace went off to conduct other purchasing issues the Computer Products Group had with Astec.

By midafternoon, Bill was deep into his meetings. "As Tom said during his introduction, we are looking for the right contract manufacturer to be licensed to produce our design for a family of UPS products. These must be produced at a very low cost with a very high quality. Your company comes recommended as the electronics manufacturer who can do this. While we see a lot of commonality of materials across the family of UPS products, some parts are single sourced and not necessarily from Asia. You will have to manage these single sourced suppliers."

"Wouldn't your Engineering be able to assist managing the single source suppliers?" asked Renu.

"I think it comes down to the specific issue," said Bill. "If, for example, there is a supply allocation issue, then I would expect Astec Purchasing clout to be able to resolve it. On the other hand, if there is a quality issue with the root cause being the way the component is used in the circuit, then certainly our Engineering would get involved."

"Yes, and also the IPO has certain expertise that can help in such effort," added Grace.

Renu responded, "That sounds reasonable. Astec buys high volumes of many kinds of electronics components from preferred suppliers in Asia and also from Europe. Our quality is exceptional. We are ISO certified. We will have you spend time with our director of quality tomorrow."

"That's great. Now, while I'm here, I would like to walk your process from the receipt of raw materials through finished goods shipping," said Bill. "And I would like to see your quality control on the manufacturing floor."

They started the plant tour in a secondary building serving as the receiving warehouse. The building had a packed dirt floor and partial outside walls. There was no air-conditioning or humidity control. Very expensive components were locked in a full enclosed room. Continuing to the production floor, Bill noticed that the line workers were all female, while the technicians and the production manager were all male. Different color shirts designated the hierarchy, and communication paths were restricted according to cultural norms. This was unlike anything Bill had ever experienced in the United States.

Start with Part Numbering

Many businesses have a hierarchy of product offerings. Systems are at the top of the hierarchy. A system is a set of products. A computer system might have a display, a keyboard, a computer, various cables, and software, where each product in the system has its own product number. Products are next in the hierarchy. Products often come in families and may have options and accessories. A computer display might come with optional 21-, 19-, or 17-inch diagonal screens. The same display might be offered with an accessory wall mount. Component parts are the next level down in the hierarchy. Component parts are internal to the product, and they are often grouped by commodity type. The display product is built from components, including a stand (aluminum), a case (plastic), a display (display), a power supply (power supply), an electronics board (printed circuit assembly), connectors (electromechanical), and more. Raw materials form the base of the hierarchy. Raw materials might include copper, aluminum, steel, plastic, gold, etc.

A Simple Part Number Scheme

A part number is assigned to each unique item, be it a system, product, accessory, option, part, or raw material. Part numbers are also assigned to engineering documentation that describes product manufacture, product tooling, and to software and firmware source code and object code.

Part numbers should be short and human friendly. Part numbers generally should not have a lot of intelligence built into them. In the following four example part numbering approaches, the last approach is preferred:

- *Computer-generated schemes, such as 0010000000075621892*—Some computer applications generate long sequential numbers that are not human friendly. It is far too easy to mistake the correct number of zeroes.
- *Intelligent ordering schemes, such as 23-444Y-529-6-1447*—Some businesses with many product configurations build intelligence into their ordering numbers by hyphenating option groupings. This scheme requires a program called a "configurator" to decode the ordering number and to check that product combinations are technically compatible.
- *Reuse the manufacturer's part number*—Smaller companies often reuse the manufacturer's part number as their own. The disadvantages are that different manufacturers have different part number formats and that not every item can be covered in this manner.
- *A practical, human-friendly part numbering scheme, such as 025-224*—This six-digit scheme works very well for businesses with a few thousand parts numbers. The six digits in two groups of three are easy to remember. The first three digits are used to specify a broad system, product, commodity, or raw material group within the hierarchy. The second three digits are assigned sequentially without any specific intelligence. For example, if 325- is the category for electrical switches, then 325-001 as a double-pole, single-throw, 2-amp, 110-volt slide switch might be followed by 325-002 as a single-pole, single-throw, 5-amp, 220-volt toggle, switch, which might be followed by 325-003 as a single-pole, single-throw, momentary, 5-amp, 110-volt push button switch. Engineering maintains a part number log used to assign the next sequential part number and an item value sort document used to identify if a specific part is in the item master.

Stock Keeping Units Are Different

Stock keeping unit (SKU) numbers are assigned to an organization's billable products and services within the downstream delivery channels of a supply chain. SKU numbers differ from the item part numbers found in the midstream and upstream supply base in three ways. First, an SKU can be used to indicate different packaging for the same product. For example, a case of 12 and a case of 6 of the same product are two unique SKUs. Second, an SKU can be assigned to a billable service. Third, an SKU can be assigned to a nonphysical billable product, such as a warranty agreement or an hour of repair.

Translate the BOM into Requirements for a Supply Base

Every item must be given a part number and a description. If that exact item is in use in the supply chain, then it is merely a question of looking up the part number and description and copying it exactly into the BOM for the next new product. Companies maintain an item value sort to make the lookup process very efficient. If the item has never been used before in any other product, then a new part number and a new description are assigned. It is a good idea to establish commodity categories of items beforehand. The new item is first matched with its correct commodity grouping then gets assigned the next sequential part number.

BOM: Item Master File

A BOM is normally created as the product is crafted or invented. The product idea might start from a sketch, a block diagram, a cost estimate, or a parts list of significant materials. Next, a complete list of all the materials is created. Third, the parts list is completed and reorganized into a BOM having two parts: an item master and a product structure. The item master is a listing, in part number order, of each and every unique item with its attributes. The item master is a key file in your information technology backbone and includes the following minimum set of attributes:

- *Item number*—Unique part number for this item.
- *Item description*—Unique short text title for this item.
- *Commodity group*—Assigns the item to a particular commodity group.
- *Cross-reference to a manufacturer's part number*—Useful when dealing with a fully specified industry standard part.
- Engineering details
  - *Documentation part number*—Part number(s) for part manufacturing process documentation.

  - *Revision*—The latest engineering revision for this item; the first release is revision A.
  - *Programming documentation*—Part number for programming source code and object code.
- *Unit of measure*—The measure used to count this part, such as each, pound, roll, etc.
- *Lowest BOM level*—The lowest level in any BOM product structure where this item is found.
- *Unit cost*—Last purchased cost based on the lot size quantity. The definition of this term depends on the accounting system used by the business. Also used to assign inventory value for this item.
- *Lead time*—Number of days from order to delivery.
- *Purchased or manufactured*—Specifies if this item is purchased or manufactured.
- *Preferred supplier*—Primary source for this item.
- *Approved secondary supplier*—Secondary or backup source for this item.
- Shipping details
  - *Lot size*—Normal quantity ordered at one time.
  - *Packaged weight*—Shipping weight per lot size.
  - *Packaged cubic volume*—Dimensions and cubic volume per lot size.
- *Payment terms*—Specifies if this item is purchased prepaid, by letter of credit, or on credit.
- *International sourcing terms (INCOTERMs)*—Internationally recognized sourcing terms covering the transfer of title, which party pays the logistics costs, and which party holds the risk for insurance.
- Import/export details
  - *Harmonized tariff schedule (HTS)*—Import duty classification number.
  - *Schedule B*—Export duty classification number.
  - *Export control classification number (ECCN)*—ECCN from the commercial control list (CCL) of exported items requiring an export license.
  - *Country of origin*—Country where the item is manufactured according to import/export rules of origin.
- *Warranty period*—The manufacturer's warranty period for this item, as in 90 days or one year.

When an existing product without a BOM is introduced into the supply chain, maybe through the acquisition of a small company by a larger company, then a BOM must be created from scratch. The product is broken down into its component parts by disassembling and reverse engineering a physical sample. Digital color photos are taken during each step of the disassembly. Each item is matched to the current parts value sort. When no match can be found, a new part number is assigned. The incremental set of new part numbers is then added to the item master, and the incremental set of new structure relationships is added to the product structure file.

BOM: Product Structure File

The product structure is a key file in the information technology backbone, and it includes the following minimum set of attributes:

- *BOM level*—The structural hierarchy from complete products at level 0 to raw materials at level *N*.
- *Parent item number*—The upper level part number.
- *Parent item description*—Short text description of the parent item.
- *Child item number*—The lower-level part number.
- *Child item description*—Short text description of the child item.
- *Quantity per*—The number of child parts required to make one parent part.
- *Unit of measure*—The measure used to count this part, such as each, pound, roll, etc.
- *Revision*—The latest engineering revision for this BOM. The first release is revision A.

Each row in the product structure file is a single parent–child relationship. Therefore, if a parent item is built from quantities of five different children items, then there are five rows in its product structure file. The BOM level is normally printed in an indented fashion, with each lower structure level indenting farther to the right. The product structure file is read from top to bottom. Child items are indented to the right of their parent item until the indentation reverses to the left. For example, suppose the BOM level from top to bottom reads .1, ..2, …3, …3, …3, …3, ..2, then the four level 3 children are used to make the upper level 2 parent, and both the upper level 2 child and the lower level 2 child in this example are used to make the top level 1 parent.

Table 6.1 is an example BOM broken down into its item master in Table 6.2 and product structure in Table 6.3. It is often the case that companies forget to put the shipping carton and shipping labels on the product BOM. This means that certain costs are missed in accounting and that purchasing is unaware that it needs to order shipping cartons and labels. While the lead time to purchase cardboard cartons is usually only a few days, the lead time to print a specialty label can be several weeks.

In Table 6.2, the preferred supplier column from the item master file defines the set of supplier relationships that need to be established to complete the network container during supply chain construction. In this example, there are order-to-delivery-to-cash connections between the factory and Echo Molding, between the factory and Jet Pro, between the factory and Avery, between the factory and Cushman, between the factory and Ace Hardware, and between the factory and other suppliers. Every effort should be made during product development to minimize both the total number of items and the total number of suppliers.

Table 6.1 Example Multilevel BOM

Level	*Part Number*	*Description*	*Qty Per*	*Unit of Measure*	*Supplier*	*More...*
0	510-012	Packaged product	1	Each		Make
.1	500-012	Product	1	Each		Make
..2	003-001	Top cover	1	Each	Echo Molding	Buy
..2	003-002	Bottom cover	1	Each	Echo Molding	Buy
..2	021-001	Subassembly A	1	Each		Make
...3	More...	More...	More...		More...	Buy
...3	021-023	Subassembly D	1	Each		Make
....4	More...	More...	More...		More...	Buy
..2	199-035	6-32 Screw	8	Each	Ace Hardware	Buy
..2	007-001	Decal	2	Each	Jet Pro	Buy
.1	120-005	Shipping carton	1	Each	Cushman	Buy
.1	007-002	Shipping label	1	Each	Avery	Buy

In Table 6.3 the rows of the product structure file are sorted in order first by BOM level, second by the parent item number, and third by the child part number.

The BOM is used to map the supply chain network relationships from the factory within the MAKE echelon(s) upstream to the supply base in the SOURCE echelon(s). If the factory or any of the suppliers build or assemble more than one level of the BOM, then there will not be a one-to-one relationship between BOM levels and network echelons. The number of unique suppliers listed on the item master is the number of unique suppliers in your supply base. However, since any one supplier may source more than one item, the product structure file may show material flow connections between the supplier and more than one downstream organization. Such connections may also span more than one echelon.

Composite BOM Item Master

To construct a full supply base and properly plan inventory, it is necessary to have a complete picture of all the items that will fill the network container. The composite

Table 6.2 Example Item Master File

Part Number	*Description*	*Unit of Measure*	*Cost*	*Preferred Supplier*	*Lead Time*
003-001	Top cover	Each		Echo Molding	
003-002	Bottom cover	Each		Echo Molding	
007-001	Decal	Each		Jet Pro	
007-002	Shipping label	Each		Avery	
021-001	Subassembly A	Each		The Factory	
021-023	Subassembly B	Each		The Factory	
120-005	Shipping carton	Each		Cushman	
199-035	6-32 Screw	Each		Ace Hardware	
500-012	Product	Each		The Factory	
510-012	Packaged product	Each		The Factory	
More...	More...			More...	

BOM item master provides this picture. The composite BOM item master is a complete listing of every unique item used anywhere throughout the supply chain. It is generated by comparing and accumulating the items from every individual product BOM into a list of nonrepeating unique items in the network composite BOM.

Start by considering which product sets are being offered to which market segments; there is more about this topic in Chapter 7: "Demand Planning." A product set represents each entry in the product catalog for a given market segment. A product set might include systems, products, product options, accessories, and services. Product sets may overlap several market segments. Once the catalog of product sets is determined, then explode the list of the individual systems, products, options, accessories, and services that make up the product set. For example: Table 6.4 shows a product set consisting of product A, product B, accessory 1, accessory 2, and an installation service.

The composite BOM item master, with an example shown in Table 6.5, is created using the following steps. Entries include system and product numbers. Items should include both part numbers and SKUs requiring physical inventory locations within the network container. Entries are recorded at their highest level in the product structure.

1. Sort each multilevel BOM first by level, then by item number. Note that the product structure information is lost with this sorting scheme.

Table 6.3 Example Product Structure File

BOM Level	*Parent*	*Parent Description*	*Child*	*Child Description*	*Qty Per*	*Unit of Measure*
0	510-012	Packaged product	007-002	Shipping label	1	Each
0	510-012	Packaged product	120-005	Shipping carton	1	Each
0	510-012	Packaged product	500-012	Product	1	Each
.1	500-012	Product	003-001	Top cover	1	Each
.1	500-012	Product	003-002	Bottom cover	1	Each
.1	500-012	Product	007-001	Decal	1	Each
.1	500-012	Product	021-001	Subassembly A	1	Each
.1	500-012	Product	199-035	6-32 screw	8	Each
..2	021-001	Subassembly A	021-023	Subassembly D	1	Each
..2	021-001	Subassembly A	More...	More...		
...3	021-023	Subassembly D	More...	More...		

2. Start with the multilevel BOM for the first product and create a list of unique item numbers, working from the highest structure level to the lowest structure level. Where the same item number is repeated on multiple structure levels, include that item number only once.
3. Continue to the multilevel BOM for the second product and create its list of unique item numbers, working from the highest structure level to the lowest structure level. Where the same item number is repeated on multiple structure levels, include that item number only once.
4. Place the lists for the first and second products side by side. Work down the unique item number list for the first product top to bottom. Add to the first list any new item numbers from the second list, while ignoring any item numbers, which are common to both lists.
5. Repeat steps 3 and 4 for each product in the catalog until all the unique part numbers from every product BOM have been combined.
6. Indicate which factory or supplier is the source for each item. "->F" to the right of an item indicates the factory as its source. "->S_N" to the right of an item indicates supplier *N* as its source.

Table 6.4 Example Product Catalog

Market	Market Segment Y			Market Segment Z	
Product catalog	Catalog Y			Catalog Z	
Product set	Product set 1	Product set 2	Product set 3	Product set 4	Product set 5
System					
Product	1× Product A	1× Product A	1× Product B		
Product option					
Accessory		1× Accessory1		1× Accessory1	2× Accessory2
Service		1× Installation	1× Installation		

Mapping the BOM to a Supply Base

For the supply chain network to be complete, there must be a supplier or a factory for every part number and a factory or a distributor for every SKU in the composite BOM item master. There will also be at least two physical inventory locations, an origin and a destination, for every item number in the composite BOM item master, as explained in Chapter 10: "Inventory Management." Use the following steps, demonstrated in Figure 6.1, to map your supply base.

1. Place the factory in the midstream echelon of a supply chain echelon map. List each product item at the output of the factory. The product item number may continue downstream through the delivery channel, or the product number may become one or more SKUs, if the product is packaged and sold in different ways.
2. Identify each subassembly item made within the factory. Because the factory may build more than one BOM level of a product, there is not a one-to-one correspondence between BOM levels and echelon numbers.
3. Identify each item that gets delivered to the factory regardless of its BOM level. Group these items by the name of their suppliers. Add each supplier to the supply chain echelon map one echelon upstream from the factory. When the same supplier sources to more than one echelon, place that supplier one echelon upstream from the lowest BOM level it sources.

Table 6.5 Generating the Composite BOM Item Master

First BOM	*Second BOM*	*Third BOM*	*...Nth BOM*	
0Product A	0Product B	0Accessory1	0Accessory2	
..1Carton F	..1Carton F	..1Carton G	..1Carton G	
..1Assembly S	..1Assembly S	..1Assembly H	..1Assembly H	
....2Part C	....2Part H	....2Part J	....2Part J	
....2Part D	....2Part J	....2Subassy N	....2Subassy O	
......3RawMat I	....2Subassy K	......3Part P	......3Part P	
..1Part E	......3Part L	......3Part Q	......3Part R	
	..1Part T			
First Product	*Second Product*	*Third Product*	*...Nth Product*	*Composite BOM Item Master*
0Product A				0Product A->Factory
	0Product B			0Product B->Factory
		0Accessory1		0Accessory1 ->Factory
			0Accessory2	0Accessory2 ->Factory
..1Part E				..1Part E->Supplier2
..1Carton F	..1Carton F			..1Carton F->Supplier1
		..1Carton G	..1Carton G	..1Carton G->Supplier1
..1Assembly S	..1Assembly S			..1Assembly S->Factory
		..1Assembly H	..1Assembly H	..1Assembly H->Factory

(*Continued*)

Table 6.5 (Continued) Generating the Composite BOM Item Master

First Product	*Second Product*	*Third Product*	*...Nth Product*	*Composite BOM Item Master*
	..1Part T			..1Part T->Supplier3
....2Part C				....2Part C->Supplier4
....2Part D				....2Part D->Supplier2
	....2Part H			....2Part H->Supplier5
	....2 Part J	....2 Part J	....2 Part J	....2Part J->Supplier6
	....2Subassy K			....2Subassem K->Factory
		....2Subassy N		....2Subassem N->Factory
			....2Subassy O	....2Subassem O->Factory
......3RawMat I				......3RawMatl ->Supplier7
	........3Part L			......3Part L->Supplier8
		.......3Part P	........3Part P	......3Part P->Supplier9
		.......3Part Q		......3Part Q->Supplier9
			........3Part R	......3Part R->Supplier10

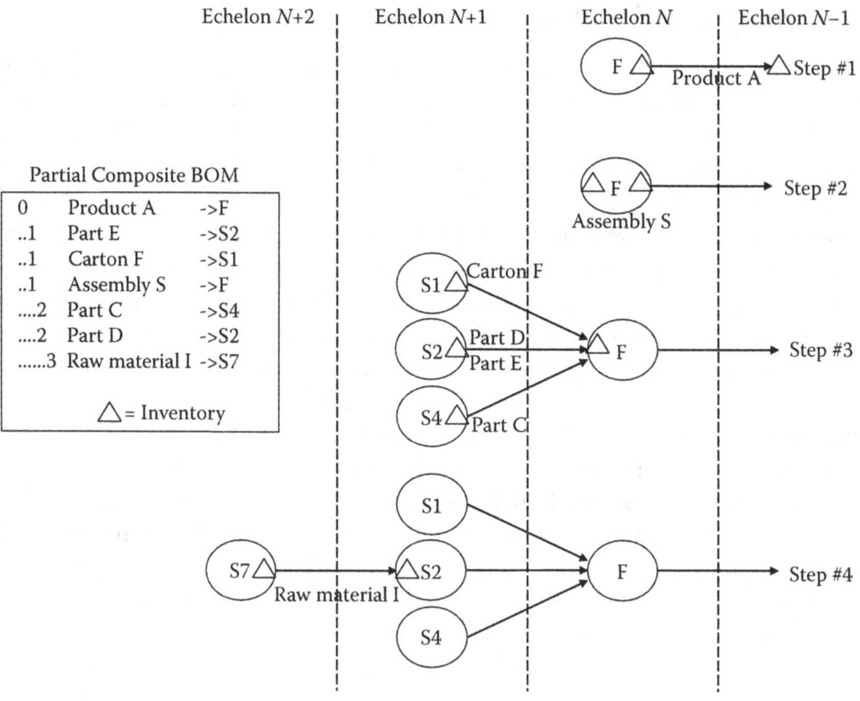

Figure 6.1 Steps to map the BOM to a supply base.

4. Review each supplier one at a time. Identify and group raw material items that get delivered to this supplier. Add the raw material supplier to the supply chain echelon map one echelon upstream from the supplier that it sources.

Practice Commodity Management

The practice of commodity management is a good way to rationalize and maintain an appropriate number of suppliers in your supply base and to control the purchasing spend. Commodity management groups parts made from the same raw material together. For example, sheet metal parts are grouped together, plastic parts are grouped together, passive electronic parts are grouped together, or electronic memory devices are grouped together. Then purchasing selects just two or three suppliers to cover the range of items within the commodity category. This builds volume with a few suppliers, reduces the investment in custom tooling, and gives the buyer leverage in price negotiations.

Unmanaged and Out of Control

Otherwise, here is what happens. Every new product generation used a different type of hardware fastener from Phillips head to Pozi drive to Torx head and from English to Metric, some in steel and some in stainless steel. Engineering management had allowed the mechanical design team to switch fastener systems willy-nilly. When the new purchasing manager took over the department, he was shocked to discover that manufacturing depended on 112 suppliers for 239 hardware fastener part numbers. The cost of the hardware fasteners was miniscule in comparison with the total material cost of the product. However, even if one fastener part number was out of stock, it could delay shipments and revenue worth hundreds of thousands of dollars. While it was economically infeasible to devote engineering time to redesign older products to consolidate fastener requirements, there was still much that purchasing could accomplish. The 239 part numbers were grouped according to common industry usage and relative volume within the business. Purchasing found a high-quality hardware distributor in Brooklyn, New York, who was able to cover 65% of all requirements and provide a high level of quality control. This consolidated 42 of the original suppliers into one distributor. The consolidated purchase volume resulted in a 3% reduction in cost.

How to Group Suppliers and Commodities

Suppliers come in three flavors: sole source, single source, and multiple sources. A sole source supplier is the only organization in the world that can supply a particular item; this is for reasons of sole access to a precious material, a secret production process, or undisclosed intellectual property. A single source supplier is one of several that can supply the particular item, but you have chosen to work only with this supplier for your own business reasons. Multiple sources means that several suppliers are capable of supplying the item, and you can use any of them.

Once the composite BOM item master is created, you can begin to group items by commodity type and target the number of suppliers required to construct your supply base. Items, in general, fall into three classes.

- First are the standard, off-the-shelf parts purchased from a parts distributor's catalog. There are usually multiple source suppliers who can provide standard parts at competitive prices. It is often the case for small accounts that you will be forced to purchase from a supply distribution network and not from the supplier directly.
- Second are custom fabricated parts. Here, the buyer provides a customized parts drawing to a supplier with a standard process. For example, a sheet metal supplier offers standard processes to shear, punch, fold, and anodize aluminum sheet metal; the buyer provides the design drawings to make the

Table 6.6 Example Purchasing Landscape

	Commodity 1 Strategic Impact	*Commodity 2 Highest Dollar Spend*	*Commodity 3 Second Highest Dollar Spend*	...	*All Other*
Standard off the shelf		Supplier B distributor	Supplier E Supplier F distributor		Supplier H Supplier I Supplier J
Custom fabricated		Supplier C Supplier D			Supplier K
Proprietary sole sourced	Supplier A		Supplier G		

aluminum sheet into a custom bracket. There are usually several single source suppliers who can provide fabrication services over a range of prices.

- Third are proprietary, sole sourced parts. These are often the one or two parts that set the price/performance point for your product.

You want to split your composite BOM item master into 6 to 12 commodity groupings (see Table 6.6). This will focus your purchasing resources in the right direction without becoming unwieldy. The exact list of commodities depends upon the type of product delivered through your supply chain network. Select commodities based on their strategic impact and cost impact.

Five Triggers for Reviewing the Supply Base and Commodity Groupings

Here are five optimal times in the life cycle of a business that should trigger a review of the supply base and commodity groupings managed by purchasing:

1. *Building a new supply chain from scratch*—This is the best time to rationalize the supply base and select the right group of commodities from which to manage direct material costs.
2. *Expanding an existing product line with next generation products*—Next-generation products often drive a business into a new technology, requiring additional suppliers and replacing one commodity group with another more strategic group.

3. *Acquiring and merging two companies*—In the crush to build and deliver acquired products, companies often lose the opportunity to consolidate suppliers and commodity groups. This exercise is a tradeoff among committing engineering resources to design out certain parts, keeping operations in inventory to "keep the store open," and committing purchasing resources to rationalize supply.
4. *Divesting or outsourcing product lines*—Here, the issue becomes identifying certain suppliers that straddle the product line being kept and the product line being divested. If the remaining parts cannot be moved to the set of preferred suppliers, then the reduction in parts volume will cause parts prices to increase.
5. *Obsoleting and discontinuing an old product*—This event perpetrates the long tail of inactive suppliers and no turn inventory kept just in case for warranty support.

Determine a Material Budget before Shopping for Suppliers

It is very important for you to know how much can be spent on direct materials before you go shopping for a supply base. Direct material purchases need to be a zero-sum game against a total material budget. If you are surprised by a higher-than-expected cost within one commodity group, then you will have to compensate by cutting the cost within a second commodity group. The following paragraphs discuss common types of pricing agreements and how to determine a direct material budget.

Types of Pricing Agreements

The single biggest factor in winning a pricing concession is your ability to increase the volume awarded to the supplier. Product line rationalization to reduce the total number of commodities and unique part numbers along with supply base rationalization to reduce the total number of suppliers is the best means of increasing volume. The type of pricing agreement you have with each supplier in the supply base depends upon the frequency of purchase, the volume of the purchase, and the type of supplier, i.e., multiple source, single source, or sole source.

- *One-time Internet catalog or Internet auction buy*—The commodity is purchased at the current catalog price or spot price. This is sometimes done inside normal lead time at the start-up of a new product or when there is the crisis of an inventory shortage. There is no room for price negotiation. There is no relationship with the supplier. There is often the risk that the inventory item with the broker is a counterfeit. Never buy unsealed or resealed cartons, and trace the lot code/date code back to the original producer. Since this is a one-time buy, you usually have to pay upfront.

- *Infrequent purchase order*—This often occurs with low-turn, inexpensive parts bought from established multiple source suppliers. The purchase order is the contract. While there is some relationship, there is usually not enough volume to warrant any price discount.
- *Market basket pricing*—You can sometimes gain a volume advantage by sourcing multiple part numbers through one supplier or supplier's distributor. This provides an opportunity to negotiate market basket pricing based on the total volume across all the part numbers. Market basket pricing means that some items will have better pricing than the competition would, while other items will have worse pricing than the competition would; but the total spend will be less that if each item had been purchased separately.
- *Annual pricing contract*—Here, a formal agreement is reached with a preferred supplier to provide a discounted price as long as you purchase and take receipt of a certain annual volume by a certain deadline. Purchase orders are then released against this annual agreement, which is often called a blanket agreement.
- *Long-term agreement (LTA)*—You will want to have multiyear LTAs with any sole sourced suppliers that provide the key technology commodities for your business. This relationship agreement protects your source of supply, even when volumes are low during the early sales of a new product start-up. Such agreements include legal nondisclosure provisions to protect intellectual property, including patents and trade secrets. A small customer must bring something strategic to the table for the supplier to consider signing an LTA.
- *Additional costs*—Suppliers often tack on additional costs, some which may be unexpected. There are one-time setup costs, tooling costs, costs to subcontract part of the process, documentation costs, costs to implement revisions, and inventory holding costs. These must all be taken into consideration when comparing "apples-to-apples" pricing between competing suppliers.

How to Determine an Affordable Budget for Direct Materials

Consider again the seller's price to buyer's landed cost implications of the "connecting the dots" storyline at the beginning of Chapter 5: "Make." The price of direct material from the supplier gets added to by logistics and factory labor, then multiplied by factory and distribution markups until the list price to the end customer is quite large. The best way to control escalating product list prices is to know your budget for direct materials before you start lining up a supply base. Table 6.7 calculates backward from the $500 target customer landed cost to the affordable total material budget.

Table 6.7 Calculating the Direct Material Budget from the Product Price

Per Unit	*Pricing*	*Deliver Spend*	*Make Spend*	*Source Spend*
Target customer landed cost	$500			
Outbound logistics$_2$	<$2>	$2		
VAR price	$498			
VAR markup	<$150>	$150		
Outbound logistics$_1$	<$3>	$3		
Distributor price	$345			
Distributor markup	<$104>	$104		
Distributor labor + Overhead	<$11>	$11		
Midbound logistics	<$10>		$10	
Factory price	$220			
Factory markup	<$66>		$66	
Factory labor + Overhead	<$9>		$9	
Material landed cost	$145			
Inbound logistics	<$15>			$15
Total material budget	$130			$130

How to Make Direct Material Landed Costs Fit Competitive Customer Pricing

Table 6.7 illustrates that the drivers of the end customer's landed cost include direct material dollars, direct labor hours, factory labor rate, factory overhead, factory markup, distribution labor rate, distribution overhead, distribution markup, and all forms of logistics. Logistics costs are driven by the transportation mode, the weight and cubic volume of the freight, and by duty on international shipments. You will often find that the computed budget for direct materials does not come close to achieving the market pricing you need to be competitive. At this point, you need to rethink how the network container and its product contents are constructed. The following list of the key cost driver leverage points can help you achieve your direct material budget.

- Reduce total direct material dollars
  - *Redesign the product*—Rework the product. Focus its purpose and take out extraneous features. Specify different, cheaper materials. Consider

alternative technologies that provide the same functionality. Reduce the total number of components.
  - *Increase and consolidate purchase volume with suppliers*—Reduce the total number of suppliers providing the most expensive parts. Purchase multiple part numbers from the same supplier. Develop a supply base of preferred suppliers.
  - *Contract for longer period*—If you are sure the product will be viable in the market for several years, negotiate a pricing agreement covering two years.
  - *Eliminate quality yield problems*—Eliminate the need to buy extra quantities of a material because of an unaddressed quality yield problem.
- Reduce total direct labor hours
  - *Ensure that product prototypes emulate the final product*—Be wary of situations where a prototype manufacturing process is different from the volume manufacturing process.
  - *Redesign the product*—Rework the product to require less direct labor. Reduce the number of hardware fasteners inserted by hand. Reduce the number of times the product has to be reoriented during assembly. Reduce the number of times and the distance the product has to be moved. Simplify part identification. Simplify product packaging.
  - *Automate*—Eliminate labor through automation. Invest in tooling that eliminates labor variability.
  - *Increase volumes of fewer products*—Keep the upstream product assembly generic and high volume. Push product mix changes to the end of the line downstream. Move quickly down the learning curve.
- Reduce supply chain length
  - *Upstream supply base*—Reduce the total number of upstream echelons as each echelon introduces its own markup. Deal directly with the supplier on expensive items and avoid the added cost and additional echelon of a supply distribution network.
  - *Downstream delivery channels*—Reduce the total number of downstream echelons, as each echelon introduces its own markup. Where geography, delivery lead time, and product mix allow, go directly to the end customer and avoid the added cost of layered distribution.
- Reduce supply chain breadth
  - *Rationalize the supply base*—Operate with fewer suppliers, each sourcing more items.
  - *Rationalize distribution*—Operate with fewer distribution centers, each covering a greater geographical area.
  - *Break a very complex supply chain into two simpler supply chains*—Focus to simplify.
- Reduce trading partner markups
  - *Outsource manufacturing to a country with a lower labor rate*—When the product or a subassembly has significant labor content, seek a country of

manufacture with a lower labor rate. Redesign the product to reduce its labor content.
  - *Identify hidden quality issues that inflate trading partner markups*—Material yield factors, process quality, and employee training issues that go unaddressed drive higher-than-necessary markups.
  - *Seek manufacturing locations offering tax incentives*—Eliminate or reduce taxes from the markup by building the product in a location offering tax incentives.
  - *Partition the BOM to postpone within distribution*—Focus the factory on building higher volumes of fewer generic products by shifting the mix component into distribution.
- Reduce total logistics costs
  - *Partition the BOM to minimize duty*—Import incomplete product assemblies duty free.
  - *Locate manufacturing in a free trade zone (FTZ)*—Use manufacturing in FTZs to import and export duty free and to take advantage of reduced labor rates.
  - *Duty drawback*—Apply for duty drawback credits on items that are imported into then exported out of a country that charges duty on that item.
  - *Shorten the logistics path*—Select noncritical suppliers that are closest to the factory or distributor.
  - *Package product to decrease weight and cubic volume*—Minimize the weight and cubic volume of the packaging materials themselves. Drive empty space and underused footprint out of palletization and containerization.
  - *Design lower-cost product packaging*—Consider alternative packaging materials and methods to ship the product. Reuse packaging materials.
  - *Trade off longer transit times for lower freight costs*—Shift from higher-cost motor freight to lower cost rail or ocean freight at the expense of a longer transit time.

Select the Best Supplier

You are now ready to search for and select the best suppliers to construct your supply base. From this chapter, you know the commodities needed and what you can afford to pay. From Chapter 10: "Inventory Management," you know the quantities needed and the lead time you can afford to wait to receive inventory. The Internet provides many catalogs of potential suppliers. Three examples of numerous websites from which to start your search are http://www.alibaba.com for factories and suppliers, http://www.digikey.com for electronic components, and http://www.mcmaster.com for industrial components.

Supplier Selection

The following decision criterion, Table 6.8, enables you to quickly eliminate supplier candidates that do not fit your Supply Chain Construction Requirements Specification. The "must" criteria are knockout criteria. Your initial search can be based on just the three "must" criteria for commodity capability, landed cost considering the supplier's location, and throughput capacity based on the number of employees. If all three "musts" cannot be satisfied, then move on to another supplier candidate. Each "want" criterion will be satisfied, to a greater or lesser degree, depending on the candidate. While it is easy to add more "wants," you can make a good decision with just this set. Execute a nondisclosure agreement with each candidate supplier before sharing information.

Supply Base Rationalization

You use Table 6.8 to choose a supplier when you have none. But sometimes, you need to work in the opposite direction to consolidate the supply base when you have too many. This is called supply base rationalization. It is best carried out one

Table 6.8 Supplier Selection Criteria

Priority	*Criterion*	*Validation*
Must 1	Commodity technology and process capability	1. The right technology? 2. The right commodity process expertise?
First Choice: Off-The-Shelf Multiple Suppliers	*Second Choice: Custom Preferred Supplier*	*Third Choice: Proprietary Sole Sourced*
Must 2	Landed cost at volume (dollars)	1. Driven by labor rate? 2. Driven by raw material costs? 3. Driven by inbound logistics and import duty rate due to plant location?
Must 3	Throughput capacity	1. Company size based on number of employees. 2. Ideally, your demand should be >5% and <35% of the supplier's throughput.

(*Continued*)

Table 6.8 (Continued) Supplier Selection Criteria

Priority	*Criterion*	*Validation*
Want	Part quality (demonstrated failure rate)	1. Evidence of a quality philosophy? 2. ISO process certification? 3. Workforce turnover?
Want	Delivery lead time (days)	Select the best supplier, not just the first one that can deliver in time for first production.
Want	Delivery reliability	1. Delivery lead time variability? 2. Responsiveness to new mix and rate requirements?
Want	Information systems	1. Information completeness? 2. Ease of interfacing? 3. Perpetual inventory accounting?
Want	Financial stability	Perform due diligence that the supplier is financially viable and able to carry its debt for the foreseeable future.
Want	Engineering support	1. Process engineering? 2. Who owns the process tooling? 3. Sustainability considerations?
Want	Prototyping capability	1. Lead time for prototyping? 2. Cost for prototyping? 3. Are prototypes built using the production process?
Want	Workforce management	Perform due diligence that the supplier is law abiding and nondiscriminatory in its workforce management.
Want	Environmental stewardship and sustainability	1. Perform due diligence that the supplier does not have an environmental risk exposure for violation of clean air, clean water, or toxic chemical dumping. 2. Has computed its carbon footprint? 3. Product made from sustainable materials?

commodity at a time starting from your highest spend and/or most strategic commodities. The approach answers the question, "Can you achieve a lower total landed cost for this commodity by using fewer suppliers?"

Follow these steps to rationalize your supply base:

1. Choose a commodity that is either very significant across all the items contained in the composite BOM relative to COGS or very significant to revenue should there be a shortage of supply.
2. Document your baseline. List each supplier for the commodity, its factory and distribution geographical locations, every item you buy from the supplier, and how much you spend in total with the supplier.
3. The new total landed cost you will pay for each item depends upon the following:
   a. The current price at the current volume purchased.
   b. Minus any price discount due to a larger total volume across several items to be purchased from the same supplier.
   c. Plus any price premium to be paid to access a specific production capability.
   d. Plus any stranded inventory cost. In the process of rationalizing the supply base, you may decide to walk away from some inventory. Stranded inventory is inventory that you own that has no future demand.
   e. Plus the difference in freight cost between your current inbound logistics path and your future inbound logistics path.
4. Identify candidate suppliers, either ones you already use or new ones, which are process and capacity capable of sourcing more of the whole set of commodity items than they are currently doing. You may have added suppliers in the past for good reasons because of part pricing, or growth in the number of products you offer, or because of a business merger. Now you are catching up.
5. Consider shifting item sourcing to a different supplier when that supplier is capable of sourcing a greater piece of the whole commodity.
6. When you have a plan that covers every item in the commodity while using a significantly smaller number of suppliers, negotiate item pricing to confirm your total landed cost.
7. If your negotiated total landed cost across the whole commodity will result in a better than 10% total landed cost reduction, then pull the trigger and implement your plan.

Optimize Inbound Logistics Costs

Inbound logistics connects raw material and part suppliers with contract manufacturers and factories. While inbound logistics may involve motor freight, rail freight, ocean freight, or air freight shipping either domestically or internationally, one characteristic of inbound logistics is that it is a relatively fixed, sometimes infrequent, network delivering many items in small quantities and small cubic volumes.

And, there may be a few items that require special logistics considerations for high weight, high volume, refrigerated handling, or hazardous materials handling. Additional import duty classification and regulatory considerations come into play when you are importing raw materials and other items from a supplier located in another country.

Without careful inventory planning, inbound freight can degenerate into high levels of expensive expediting. Taking control of your inbound expediting can eliminate most of your inbound logistics cost surprises. Additionally, many freight cost tracking systems report well after the fact, making it impossible to correct bad situations in real time. Chapter 5: "Make" covers palletization, containerization, mode of transportation, and midbound logistics considerations, while Chapter 7: "Deliver" covers outbound logistics and export regulatory considerations.

Domestic Inbound Logistics

While the basics of transportation pricing versus the mode of transportation are discussed in Chapter 5: "Make," inbound logistics has the following specific considerations.

- *Small-parcel and document deliveries by UPS, FedEx, US Postal Service*—These small-parcel service accounts have negotiable rates based on the total volume of business conducted. It is sometimes possible to consolidate freight volume among multiple divisions of the same company to achieve lower rates. UPS and FedEx deliver and pick up once each working day. They each provide special computer terminals to enter shipment descriptions and destination information that will print shipping labels at your location. They all offer international delivery services. There is a wealth of information about shipping rates, packaging requirements, and point-to-point transit times on their respective websites: http://www.ups.com, http://www.fedex.com, and http://www.usps.com.
- *Local supplier self-deliveries*—Some local suppliers, such as corrugated carton suppliers, are willing to make deliveries using their own transportation. This is because their commodity occupies a large volume on their production floor, and they want to move it out quickly.
- *Less-than-truckload (LTL)*—LTL shipments are expensive and are arranged through a freight forwarder. If possible, consolidate the freight on such a shipment with other local businesses to get full truckload pricing.
- *The bread man*—The bread man is a vendor-managed inventory (VMI) supplier who manages and delivers inventory to a specific location on your production floor. This is consigned inventory that you buy as it gets consumed. The logistics cost for a VMI arrangement is built into the part pricing.
- *Milk runs*—Sometimes, a number of suppliers in the supply base are geographically close to the factory. A milk run is the contracting of a local trucking company to swing by each supplier, perhaps once a week, to deliver the mixed inventory back to your factory.

- *Special handling commodities*—Certain types of commodities require special handling, such as refrigerated freight or radioactive isotopes or corrosive hazardous materials. There are airfreight restrictions on concentrated packaging of lithium batteries. It is imperative that you know and adhere to the transportation regulations for such shipments. Your freight forwarder can put you in touch with the most up-to-date regulatory requirements.
- *Receiving and warehousing*—Be prepared to receive the cubic volume and handle the weight of all inbound shipments. Refusing delivery and double handling freight adds hidden costs and potentially will cause missed shipments to your customer. Occasionally you will need additional space to quarantine defective material awaiting disposition from the supplier. Finance needs a three-way match to pay the supplier's invoice. The three-way match consists of the buyer's purchase order, the seller's invoice, and physical proof of delivery from the buyer's receiving dock. The part number, description, quantity, and supplier must all match. Receiving needs to verify all inventory receipts reliably and timely. Should you run out of space to store inbound freight, you will have to scramble to set up a secondary warehouse and/or secure temporary trailers in the parking lot.

International Inbound Logistics and Importing

When the inbound logistics connection involves the seller (supplier) exporting and the buyer (factory) importing, then the shipment involves international logistics. Remember that if the product has to be returned for any reason, then the buyer (factory) is exporting and the seller (supplier) is importing. The seller and buyer must comply with import regulations according to the laws of their respective countries. Import regulations define duty on every kind of merchandise and specify country-specific trade quotas, trade embargoes, and antidumping and countervailing laws that work to level the playing field against illegal international price fixing.

The International Chamber of Commerce, http://www.iccwbo.org, provides access to internationally recognized purchasing terms and conditions (INCOTERMS), explanations of how to use letters of credit and arbitration services. The US International Trade Commission website, http://www.usitc.gov, publishes the harmonized tariff schedule (HTS). The US Customs and Border Protection website, http://www.cpb.gov, provides a wealth of information on international trade compliance. While Chapter 7: "Deliver" discusses export compliance, here are the key considerations for import compliance:

- *Commercial invoice*—This is a document signed by the seller or their agent providing the following kinds of information: port of entry; names of the buyer and seller; if consigned, names of shipper and receiver; description of the merchandise; number of packages, package weights and measures; purchase price of each item and its currency; charges upon the merchandise, such as freight, insurance, and commissions; allowed rebates and drawbacks; country of origin; and more.

- *Duty assist*—The buyer provides the seller with dies, molds, tooling, artwork, or engineering work used in the production of each unit sold by the seller. Duty applies to the value of this assist and is paid upon the first shipment.
- *HTS classification*—Imported goods are subject to duty or duty-free entry according to their classification under the harmonized tariff schedule (HTS). This is a 10-digit code expressed as xxxx.yy.zzzz, which is determined from the HTS by the manufacturer, sometimes with help from a customs broker. The tariff schedule is divided into chapters, which separate merchandise into broad categories for classification.
- *Duty drawback*—This is a refund of duties paid on imported merchandise used to manufacture items that are subsequently exported back to the same country. For example, cables manufactured in the United States are exported to Mexico, where they are attached to a printed circuited assembly and the assembly is imported back into the United States. Duty drawback eliminates the double payment of duty on the cables. Duty drawback is documentation intensive, and it takes time to be refunded.
- *Advance manifest rules*—The United States has set time limits on the application of an advanced manifest to Customs before an inbound import shipment can be accepted. These advance manifest rules are transportation mode specific, as follows: 1 hour before arrival for motor freight, 2 hours before arrival for rail freight, 4 hours before wheels up for airfreight, and 24 hours before landing for ocean freight.
- *Rules of origin*—Rules of origin are complex and generally require the assistance of a customs broker. A preferential rule of origin means the merchandise classification is covered under one or more bilateral or multilateral trade agreements such as the Generalized System of Preferences, the North American Free Trade Agreement, etc. Rules of origin specify how to determine the local content required substantiating the country of origin and the conditions under which a "tariff shift" to a lower duty rate may be possible through a "substantial transformation" of the item.
- *Foreign trade zone (FTZ)*—This is a geographic area where goods may be imported, handled, manufactured, or reconfigured and reexported without paying duty. This privilege is granted because organizations agree to hire employees from the host country to staff their FTZ operations. Duty is paid for any product sold to the host country from the FTZ.
- *Country of origin certification*—The supplier or factory provides country of origin certification to validate preferential duty treatment.
- *Country of origin marking*—This marking is a legible, indelible, and permanent indication of the country of origin placed on each item. Subsequent packaging labels from the carton to the master carton to the pallet to the container must be consistent in the country of origin marking and documentation.

- *Liquidation*—This is the Customs acceptance of the classification and valuation of an import with payment of any duties.
- *Customs power of attorney for the importer of record*—This is the Customs broker given legal authority by the importer to represent the importer to Customs.

There are several common business risks associated with import compliance. First, at the time of liquidation, the importer of record can be challenged by Customs to substantiate the HTS classification. Second, one must not fail to recognize and pay any duty assists. Third, it is a good idea to classify all items on the composite BOM item master, as you never know when an item will be sourced as an import through an alternative supplier.

Outsourcing the Supply Base: A Case Study

In the face of stiffening competition and an eroding order picture, the product line made a decision to close a captive Metal Fab Shop and outsource all its metal parts. The organization's core competencies had evolved well beyond metal fabrication. The organization needed increased flexibility with overhead expenses to retain its leadership position in the marketplace. Management established the seemingly impossible goal of terminating all shop activity within six months to be able to lease the 16,000 square feet of physical space to an unrelated third party within eight months. At the time, 36 employees were working split between two shifts using 75 metal-forming machines to fabricate 1,270 part numbers all for internal product manufacturing consumption.

An important distinction was made between the short-term objectives and the medium-term objective. Priorities were established to focus on continuity of supply and piece part quality in the short-term and to focus on achieving equivalent piece part prices in the medium term. While the very short timeframe for outsourcing drove the project team to make decisions in a timely fashion, management knew it would have to absorb transitional costs in the form of higher piece part prices and inventory investment.

[Author's note: This project occurred at about the midpoint of the author's professional life, while he was a purchasing manager. It occurred at a time before the Supply Chain Construction Requirements Specification existed, before the Supply Chain Construction Blueprint existed, and before the Value Circle existed. As you will learn, the end results of this project were mixed.]

Defining the Metal Fab Shop Outsourcing Project

The 1,270 parts consisted of sheet aluminum or a sheet steel bracket and chassis parts, vinyl-clad aluminum covers, painted and silk screened front panels, and extruded aluminum heat sink parts. A segmentation matrix was made of all the part numbers into "A," "B," "C," and support life categories (see Figure 6.2). "A" parts turned once a month, "B" parts turned once a quarter, and "C" parts turned

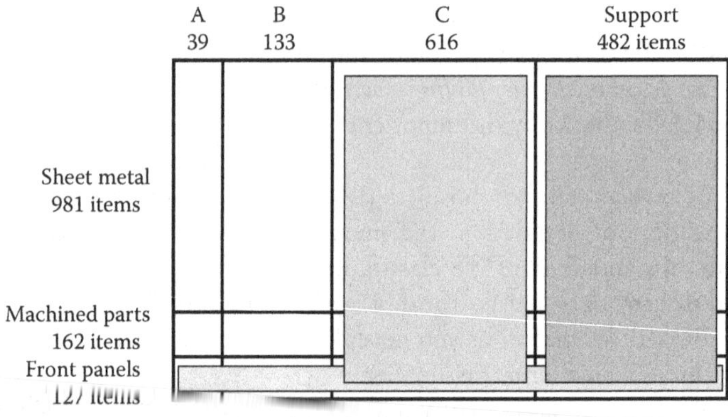

Figure 6.2 Break the supply base problem into a set of smaller problems.

once a year. Of the total 1,270 part numbers, 482 were classified as support life parts; it was decided to deal with this group of parts on an as-needed basis. It was also decided to build a one-year inventory of the 616 "C" part numbers while the Metal Fab Shop was still intact. This reduced the size of the project and bought time to focus resources on the critical "A" and "B" parts; it also meant that "C" part production could occur while all specialized tooling was still in place.

As the word got out that the Metal Fab Shop was closing, local suppliers came forward with offers to take over the business. It quickly became clear that a strategy and supplier selection decision criteria were needed. The "musts" became continuity of supply and piece part quality. The "wants" became the following:

- Achieve external supplier piece part pricing equivalent to the internal Metal Fab Shop transfer cost.
- Minimize the total number of suppliers added to the supply base.
- Receive both prototypes and production parts from the same supplier using the same processes.
- Transfer part design information and design for manufacturability (DFM) feedback electronically.
- Favor geographically local suppliers to maximize communications and minimize freight costs.
- Optimize for the least total cost of outsourcing.

Identifying Potential Suppliers

A list of potential suppliers was compiled from a variety of sources, including current subcontractors, new business contacts including those who had offered their services, references from other divisions of the corporation, and local suppliers listed in the Thomas Register. With some research, the candidate supplier list was segmented into groups by business revenue and fabrication processes offered. In many cases, candidate suppliers did not offer both sheet metal fabrication and machined part capabilities. Negotiations started with larger businesses that offered a full range of capabilities with the hope that one such supplier could do it all.

A Supplier Day was held in which the business opportunity was described. Senior managers from several suppliers were invited to spend a day at the plant learning about requirements, viewing the processes in operation, and inspecting the metal-forming equipment. Each was requested to prepare a formal request for quotation (RFQ) on the "A" and "B" parts, and each was told that the metal-forming machinery was also available for sale. Each contender was given a small representative set of sample parts and a complete set of shop drawings. They were asked to prepare their most aggressive offer along with documentation of their set of assumptions. They were told the custom tooling would be made available to the supplier winning the bid. During the two weeks following Supplier Day, the Metal Fab Shop manager, a buyer, and a metals engineer toured the complete facilities of each top contender. These day-long meetings followed the format of a supplier qualification audit. The team looked for key differences among the candidate suppliers and answered detailed questions about the RFQ. The team articulated the decision criteria often to stress the expectation of continuity of supply and piece part quality within a win–win relationship. The candidate suppliers complained that the RFQ deadline did not allow anywhere near enough time to estimate pricing from hundreds of shop drawings. The team patiently replied that the project timing was aggressive and that this opportunity was unlike any other they might have in the near future.

An Outsourcing Strategy Evolves

The original plan was to outsource the business to one of the large suppliers who could meet all of the diverse needs. The team soon realized that the local companies that had been approached were optimized for either sheet metal fabrication or machined parts fabrication, but not both. The outsourcing strategy had to evolve into one of managing a small number of suppliers split by process capability, as shown in Figure 6.3. The sourcing for sheet metal parts became a decision of whether or not to keep some competition between preferred suppliers A and C to motivate each into continuous improvement and price reduction. If supplier C would not come down in price within a year, then a third competitor, supplier E, would be brought into the supply base. The part numbers were split evenly between suppliers A and C, with front panels and covers all assigned to supplier C, which had stronger painting and finishing processes. The preferred sourcing for machined parts boiled down to a decision between a vertically integrated extruder/fabricator, supplier B, and a custom extrusion house, supplier D. The vertically integrated fabricator would have to subcontract certain secondary assembly operations. The custom house depended on other extruders for their raw materials supply. Supplier D could be brought on-line later, if supplier B did not work out.

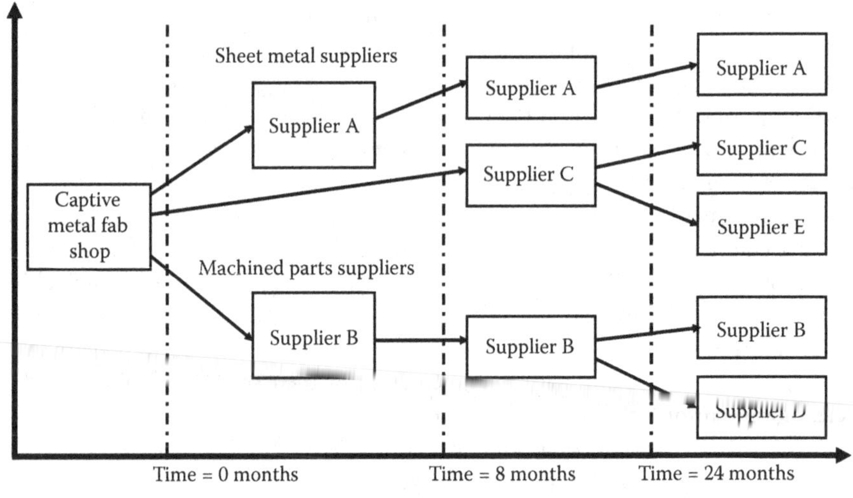

Figure 6.3 A supply base strategy.

The team then set about formalizing each new relationship with a set of annual volume agreements. The first contracts were for a one-year period. Each contract set an agreed-upon price for a specific range of part numbers but emphasized continuity of supply and an aggressive quality performance measurement. The contract was worded to make it easy to both add new part numbers and to roll the contract into a longer term relationship, once each supplier had demonstrated sustained performance. In return, the team agreed to purchase 100% of the specified part numbers from that single supplier and to share their process expertise for building each part.

Part Transfer Process

Each part number was outsourced using the same 10-step transfer process detailed below. These transfers required considerable coordination between the new supplier and mechanical engineering and between purchasing and the new supplier's order processing and scheduling. Part transfers were prioritized based on the inventory needed to achieve production schedules. The supplier prioritized the initial production of each part based on the availability of tooling and machine capacity. In some cases, the same custom tooling was simultaneously required for start-up production at the receiving supplier and for the buffer inventory production of "C" parts back in the sending Metal Fab Shop. A few complicated transportation schedules were required to shuttle one-of-a-kind tools back and forth between organizations.

1. Review the part specification drawing; change to the next revision for new supplier production.
2. Agree to a lot size for the new supplier.

3. Transfer the fastener hardware inventory to the new supplier.
4. Transfer, or if necessary share, custom tooling.
5. Change the drop shipment address for raw sheet stock to the new supplier.
6. Implement the routing file at the new supplier.
7. Keep one original part as a "golden sample" for dimensional checks.
8. Teach part inspection to the new supplier during the first production run.
9. Optimize part packaging for transit.
10. Consume all old inventories with the last revision first.

Human Costs

While the team was successful in meeting its objective of closing the Metal Fab Shop operation on time without any continuity of supply issues, there were many serious personnel issues. When the second shift operation was terminated, a few people transferred to the first shift and lost their shift premium. When all Metal Fab Shop production activity was halted after six months, four employees were absorbed into other site opportunities, two employees stayed on to assist in the disposal of the machinery, and the rest were laid off. The company provided retraining resources, outplacement assistance, and an attractive severance package including COBRA transitional healthcare. Several people took advantage of the incentive payout to go back to school and/or to move their families to other parts of the country. A few employees found employment opportunities with the new suppliers. But for many months after the layoffs, the morale of the whole plant was low as employees who remained experienced close friends leaving the business.

It took two full calendar years to work through the volume of transfers associated with the "C" parts. This time fully occupied some of the company's best purchasing and mechanical engineering people, forgoing other business opportunities. Untold hours were spent working out the details of drop shipping raw materials, transferring specialty hardware inventories, and adapting customized tooling fixtures to the new supplier's machinery. Communications with the new suppliers across some distance forced a higher level of formality with DFM feedback for new part design. No longer could a design engineer walk down to the hall to the Metal Fab Shop and talk face to face with the punch press operator about a new part design concept.

Piece Part Quality

Defect rates on every type of metal part increased, while the new suppliers learned the necessary process controls. For some part numbers, the initial lots ran 35 times higher in parts per million defects than the closing rates of the internal Metal Fab Shop. Cosmetic defects, sliver problems with the vinyl-clad aluminum, and metal flaking with the heat sink extrusions caused very high initial levels of inspection and rework. Missing holes, holes not tapped, and burring were the next order of quality problem. A third set of problems were related to missing hardware; this was finally brought under control after hardware counters were installed on certain insertion machines.

These quality issues were addressed through the transfer of process technology and the application of continuous process improvement. Each preferred supplier already had in place a mature quality system. Immediate feedback was provided to the new suppliers on problems as they were found, and example defective parts were returned for their review. Problems were classified and charted. The team looked for repeating offenders on sequential work orders of the same part number so that the supplier's employees could receive additional training. To their credit, the new suppliers reorganized and simplified their process steps, tuned their performance measures, and retrained all their employees.

Piece Part Cost

The first round of contracts gave priority to continuity of supply and allowed each new supplier some leeway in piece part pricing. Contract pricing negotiations had been built around certain benchmark part numbers, with average prices for the remaining volume of part numbers extrapolated by spreadsheet from these benchmarks. It was recognized that the candidate suppliers had not been given adequate time to review and quote on the thousand individual specification control drawings. During the first contract cycle, as the new suppliers gained experience fabricating the parts, it became obvious that the pricing was noncompetitive. While the volume weighted average price had looked reasonable, pricing on some specific part numbers ran 55% higher than the transfer cost standards from the internal Metal Fab Shop. This situation was remedied during the second round of contract negotiations. The supplier D and supplier E strategies never had to be deployed.

Tradeoffs of Warehouse Space, Inventory Investment, and Freight Expense

The internal Metal Fab Shop operated its own warehouse. Scheduling and part inspection were done by Metal Fab Shop employees. Small lots of metal parts finished goods were issued daily from the warehouse to the final product assembly; there was no incremental freight cost for this material handling.

The team had to address many obvious issues. When first switched to outsourcing, the final product assembly was overwhelmed by the cubic volume of metal parts shipped from the new suppliers. The lot sizes received each day were much greater than had been dealt with internally. An overflow area was set up to accommodate the dozen skids of metal parts arriving daily. The first covers were so well wrapped in protective plastic that it took two materials handlers six hours to unwrap just 100 parts. Electrical incoming inspectors had to be trained on reading mechanical drawings and on operating precision measuring equipment to check metric dimensioning. While the scheduling workload disappeared, the purchasing, cost accounting, incoming inspection, and materials handling workloads exploded. And inbound freight costs went up dramatically. These were all unintended consequences.

Sale of the Metal-Forming Machinery and Environmental Expense

The internal Metal Fab Shop had been well equipped with 75 capital assets including two Strippit NC punch presses, Pacific brakes and presses of different tonnage, an auto loading Muzak machining center, and an automated chromate line. It was essential to maximize the return on the sale of these assets to reduce the fixed portion of the overhead. One of the shop supervisors and one buyer were tasked with selling this machinery. Their objective was to maximize sales and to have all the machinery physically removed.

Only a few of the machines had been bought by the suppliers who had been awarded the business. The buyer had had considerable experience buying raw material in sheet form and was very familiar with certain distributors and machinery brokers who might be interested in the equipment. He compiled a list of potential buyers and set up individual appointments for each party to inspect the equipment and its associated tooling. Terms included that the facilities staff would disconnect each machine at an agreed-to date, that there was a firm deadline for the removal of the machine, that specified tooling would be included in the bid, that payment would be upon receipt in the form of a cashier's check, and that the equipment buyer was responsible for scheduling and paying to rig the machinery out of the building.

The metal-forming machinery was in excellent repair, and it brought handsome prices. One exception was the automated chromate line. While the process line was ultimately sold, there were considerable environmental expenses to be paid for cleaning and proper parts disposal and for the refurbishing of the area to meet the specification of the new tenant.

In Summary

This chapter explains how to construct the upstream supply base. It begins with a discussion of part numbers, the BOM, and the composite BOM item master. The composite BOM item master is used to identify the set of suppliers necessary to operate the supply chain. Next, commodity part groupings and types of pricing agreements are discussed. This leads to developing a budget for direct material and the types of leverage points that can be used to manage the ratio of the supplier's direct material price/landed cost to the price/landed cost seen by the end customer. A supplier selection criterion is presented. Finally, there is a discussion of inbound logistics and import regulatory compliance. The chapter ends with a detailed case study of a supply base outsourcing project.

Chapter 7

Deliver

Distributors are found throughout the supply chain network. There may be raw material distributors, supply distributors, factory distributors, market channel distributors, and even country trading companies that provide distribution access into a country, like Japan. It is important to know with whom you are really dealing for each supply chain network relationship. The further removed you become from the actual producer of raw material, parts, or product, the more expensive the product price becomes for your customer. Buy your materials directly from their source, if you can, and use distributors to provide access to the market segments you choose to serve.

A distributor is different from a warehouse. A warehouse is a large room that holds inventory, while a distributor combines a warehouse with an organization that buys and sells, material handling equipment, an information system, and relationships with logistics service providers. Distributors should be geographically close to the markets they serve or have an economical logistics solution to next-day delivery. For this reason, distributors are often arranged in networks to cover larger geographical areas. In this chapter, you learn how to select a distribution organization to best fit the market segments and product demands of your business.

Where in the World Has My Product Gone?

Today, the Supply Chain Construction Project Team was focused on brainstorming the changes that would have to be made to the Power Products Division distribution center. The team realized how important it was for the division to remain a supply chain trading partner; otherwise, there would be no direct revenue recognition for all their efforts. Since it looked like the division would not manufacture the uninterruptable power supply (UPS) product, being the distribution center (DC) for North America was the next best thing.

"Let's begin by looking at the Supply Chain Construction Blueprint and brainstorming what needs to change," said Bill, the Supply Chain Construction Team project manager.

"First of all, 2,500 units per month and hopefully more is a large volume for our facility," said Tony from Finance. "We might have to expand the warehouse or rent additional space. That will take some money for construction and some time to secure the building permits."

"At least there will be opportunity to expand the number of our employees working in Order Processing and Shipping," offered Donna, the buyer. "They will also need training."

"What delivery lead time are we quoting the value-added resellers (VARs)?" asked Harry from Product Marketing. "Also, we will need to develop a database for all the VAR contact information."

"We might have to re-line the employee parking lot so that tractor trailers hauling containers have room to access any of our docks and to turn around. We will need our forklift to load and unload containers. We might want to get a second employee trained and licensed on the forklift," said Donna.

"This is a great list!" said Bill. "What else?"

"From an engineering perspective, I'm concerned that we might have to charge the UPS batteries before shipment. They have a discharge rate. If the UPS leaves Astec fully charged, takes a month to arrive here, and sits in inventory another couple of weeks or a month, then the customer will receive a discharged battery," said John.

"Does that mean the warranty clock starts a couple of months before a customer purchase?" asked Harry.

"That's a difficult question to answer," said Tony. "Should we charge the batteries here? How much are we paying Astec to charge the batteries?"

"Since this is a brainstorming session, it is not appropriate to answer these questions now. And, I do have all your questions captured on the list," said Bill. "What else?"

"How will we place orders with Astec? Does the international procurement operation (IPO) get involved with ordering? If not, how does the IPO know when we are expecting a shipment? Will Astec send us an advance shipping notice (ASN)? Are we buying UPS product in US dollars or Malaysian ringgits? What about currency exchange rate fluctuation?" responded Donna in a burst of questions.

"Slow down! I'm writing as fast as I can," said Bill.

"Likewise, on the customer side, how does a VAR place an order with us? What level of credit does each VAR get? Will this increase accounts receivable beyond what was estimated? How do we acknowledge a shipment? How do we provide the VAR with UPS tracking information?" asked Harry.

"And I have one," said Bill. "How does product get to New York City from Malaysia?"

The midbound logistics connection from the factory to the DC was complicated. Astec would arrange motor freight for the 7-hour, 225-mile trip from Kuantan to a freight forwarder at the Port of Jurong in Singapore. The forwarder would complete the required documentation, load the container, arrange export clearance, and get the container booked and loaded on a container ship bound for Oakland, California. The 8,500-mile sailing would take 22 to 24 days. Once the container was offloaded, cleared through Customs, and its duty charges liquidated, another freight forwarder would arrange for the container to be driven 4.5 days over the remaining 2,900 miles across the United States to New York City. This intermodal approach was cheaper and faster than going through the Panama Canal to the Atlantic Ocean and up the East coast. The container would be unloaded at the DC and the empty container picked up according to a schedule. Otherwise, additional charges called demurrage would have to be paid to hold the empty container beyond its scheduled pickup.

When Bill was in Kuantan, Grace from the IPO had mentioned that her colleague, Wu Soo, the IPO logistics coordinator, worked closely with logistics experts at Corporate. Bill decided to call and introduce himself to Susan Cooke, the corporate modal manager for ocean freight.

Bill got Susan on the phone. "Hello, Bill. Yes, I handle ocean freight contracts for the corporation worldwide. Yes, I work with Wu Soo in Singapore all the time."

"I'm new at this, and I need your advice in choosing a shipping line to move product from Singapore to California then over-the-road to New York City, please." said Bill.

"OK. I can point you in the right direction. You don't work directly with a shipping line because your volume is tiny. Instead, you will work through a global logistics company to do your documentation, freight forwarding, carrier coordination, and Customs clearance. Take a look at Kuehne + Nagel; they provide competitive rates for our company," said Susan. "Also, and this is very important, please contact Jill Thomas in Corporate Customs. She can assist you in getting your product properly classified for import duty and export licensing."

Over the next couple of months, Bill and the team made countless e-mails and phone calls constructing new network connections for the Power Products Division Distribution Center.

They were finally ready to do a pilot run to bring the first product into the DC. The pilot run was too small to be transported by ocean freight, and besides, it would take much too long. Instead, two pallet loads of products, 56 units in total, would be flown from the factory to the DC to be received into inventory. The units would have to packed and labeled in a specific way, as the airlines had strict rules about transportation of batteries. As Kuehne + Nagel was arranging their ocean freight, the flights were also arranged through Kuehne + Nagel, but with a different division. The pilot run inventory would undergo inspections for packaging degradation by Receiving, product inspections by Quality, and rigorous product performance testing by Engineering before Astec Production would be authorized to start volume production.

Bill explained to the team, "Astec will have the pilot run units to Singapore on the 12th. They are being flown from Singapore (SIN) through Los Angeles (LAX) to New York City (JFK) on a freighter aircraft and should arrive on the 14th."

"How will we know when they arrive?" asked Donna. "When we start getting full container loads of products at our receiving dock, we had better be ready in the warehouse to put away 40 pallets with 28 units per pallet, or 1,120 units!"

Bill replied, "First, the IPO will send an e-mail when the units leave Malaysia. Singapore is 12 hours ahead of us; we should get plenty of warning. Second, Kuehne + Nagel, our freight forwarder, will send an advance shipping notice (ASN) with an estimated time of arrival."

But when nothing had arrived by the afternoon of the 15th, Bill contacted Kuehne + Nagel. "You say your freight is coming in through LAX from Singapore (SIN)?" the forwarder asked. "That's not what the air waybill says. It says your freight went to Seoul, Korea (SEL), on Cathay Pacific Airlines, then to O'Hare (ORD) in Chicago on Korean Airlines, and then it's coming into Newark (EWR) on United Airlines. It should be delivered tomorrow, the 16th, as long as there are no issues clearing Customs."

"Apparently, you are confused about 'New York' at Kennedy versus 'New York' at Newark," replied Bill. "Are there cartage, i.e., trucking, arrangements to bring the pallets from the correct area airport to the plant?"

"Oh yes. We have that covered," said the forwarder, and he confirmed the "deliver to" address.

Know the Nature of Market Demand

In each echelon of a supply chain network, at each interface between organizations, the upstream organization is selling at a price, while the downstream organization is buying at a landed cost. When the majority of one organization's selling and another organization's buying stays within the network, the seller and the buyer are trading partners. The in-network supply chain ultimately connects downstream with the intended market segment. The out-of-network branches at the echelon interfaces may connect with other market demands that are not part of the supply chain network under construction. Trading partners depend on the in-network throughput that the others provide to stay financially viable. Revenue flowing out of network at any echelon does not contribute to network throughput. Chapter 9: "Demand Planning" covers forecasting and revenue planning techniques for the in-network throughput.

Market Segmentation

The central idea of market segmentation is that every customer within a given segment is thought to act in a homogeneous way. Each customer in the segment accepts the same product pricing for the same product value. Each customer in the segment prefers to order the same way, i.e., online, through a salesperson, by phone, or in-person. Each customer in the segment prefers to take delivery the same way, i.e., door-to-door delivery, overnight delivery, or customer pickup. Each customer in the segment prefers to pay for purchases the same way, i.e., cash, check, credit/debit card, Automated Clearing House electronic funds transfer, or electronic data interchange (EDI). And each customer in the segment prefers warranty policy and product return processing the same way.

The people in a market segment do not have to be in the same geography, although they prefer their own local language, their own local time zone, and their own local currency. Selling products worldwide adds real complexity to supply chain construction. Local laws, local value-added taxes, duties, subtle differences in infrastructure, cultural differences, language differences in product labeling requirements, and vast differences in distance and time zones are just some of the causes of this complexity. Some global companies manage this complexity by establishing separate regional distribution networks for North America, South America, Europe, Japan, and Asia. Even within a region, it is sometimes beneficial to maintain country-focused distribution.

Consumer Goods Demand Patterns versus Industrial Products Demand Patterns

Consumer goods and industrial goods have fundamental differences in the way product value, product mix, and the calendar time to make the sale are approached. At the extreme ends of the spectrum, contrast a consumer walking into a convenience store and making an impulse buy versus a board of directors voting to approve a million dollar capital equipment purchase that has been in the works for six months. Demand for fast moving consumer goods (FMCG) drives high product volume that is in stock, while full line industrial catalogs offer high product mix that is yet to be built. Chapter 9: "Demand Planning" addresses how to adapt your supply chain to the type of product contents flowing through your network container.

The following demand patterns are typical for consumer goods:

- *FMCG*—Daily replenishment of what was taken off the shelf.
- *Seasonal apparel*—Four to six complete fashion cycle per changeovers per year.
- *Grocery*—High mix with weekly, holiday, religious holiday, and school calendar seasonality.
- *High volume mass customization products*—Every product, every configuration, all the time.

- *Fast turn cell phone hardware*—One-time build that covers the entire product life cycle.
- *Next-generation product introductions*—Careful pricing and timing that clears last generations product out of the delivery channel making way for the next generation.
- *Cell phone subscription service*—Monthly reoccurring service fee for each handset.

The following demand patterns are typical for industrial products:

- *One-time projects*—Project management against a fixed demand quantity.
- *High-value, capitalized products*—Long lead time with board of directors approving the purchase.
- *Highly customized products*—Sufficient lead time to engineer-to-order.
- *High-mix industrial products*—Full catalog offering with products completed through postponement.
- *High-mix, high-volume products*—Combines all the risks of high mix with high volume.
- *Appliance installation service*—A one-time service call scheduled at the time of purchase.
- *Refurbished equipment for aftermarkets*—Aftermarket demand limited by the supply probability of core returns and probability of reusable parts.

Use Customer Preferences to Define Delivery Channels

How did you first hear about a product? Where did you go to learn about this product? How did you decide if the product offers enough value to buy one? Where did you shop for the product? Maybe you heard from a friend or business acquaintance; maybe you used an Internet website or social media or a product catalog to learn more; maybe you have a particular problem that this product seems to solve. What is your preference? The next set of issues revolves around the question "where do you go to get the product?" The product's price, delivery, quality, and service support must each align with your expectations, or there will be no purchase. How did you pay for your purchase? Again, what is your preference? The delivery channel definition provides answers to all these questions.

Delivery Channel Descriptions

A delivery channel is the customer facing downstream portion of a supply chain network that ultimately connects with the factory. Many supply chain networks support several delivery channels simultaneously depending on how their product is sold to the end customer (see Figure 7.1). The delivery channel processes customer order information upstream, delivers product inventory downstream,

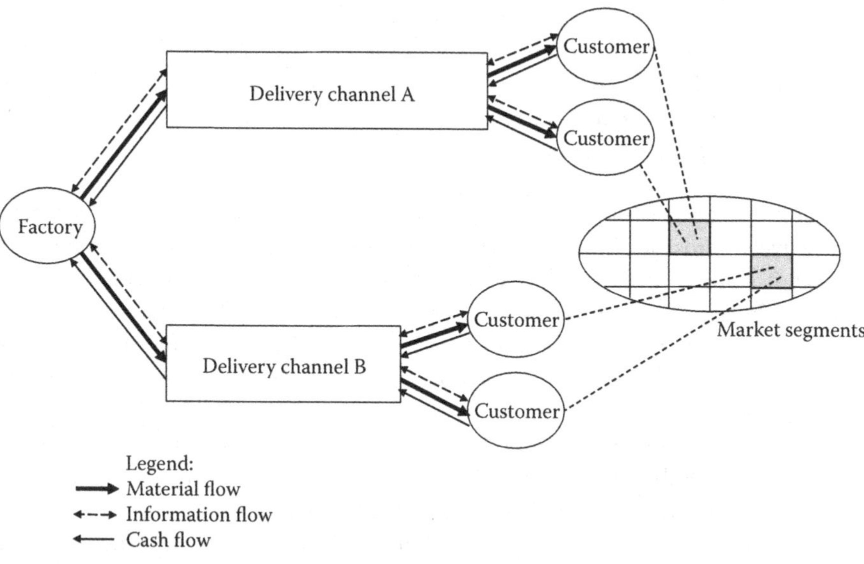

Figure 7.1 Customer facing delivery channels.

processes customer payment information downstream, and delivers cash payments upstream.

The number of delivery channel echelons on the supply chain echelon map depends upon the number of independent organizations that serially touch the physical product delivery. Internet service providers hosting Internet store websites; credit card processing service providers like VISA, Master Card, and American Express; and outbound logistics service providers like UPS and FedEx do not add echelons to a supply chain network. This is because the revenue generated by these service providers, acting as extensions of the material, information, and cash flows of the other trading partners, does not contribute directly to network throughput. Here are some examples of different length delivery channels.

- *Zero echelon*—The factory and the DC are in the same building and part of the same company. The factory's finished goods pass through the DC to be shipped directly to end customers anywhere in the world.
- *One echelon*—A VAR, a postponement center, or a regional factory distributor stands between the factory and the end customer.
- *Two echelons*—A wholesale distributor and a retail store stand between the factory and the end customer. Customers come to the retail store to pick up their product; there is no outbound logistics.
- *Three echelons*—A country trading company, a wholesale distributor, and a retail store; or a factory-owned DC, a wholesale distributor, and a retail store stand between the factory and the end customer.

- *Global coverage*—High-volume, high-mix global coverage is achieved either by a single factory feeding regional DCs within North America, South America, Europe, Asia, and Japan or by separate and independent supply chains with their own factories and distributors established within North America, South America, Europe, Asia, and Japan.

Omni-channel retailing means that the customer is able to execute a purchase and delivery across multiple channels. The customer might research the product at a retail store, buy the product online, take delivery at a local warehouse, and expect to be able to return the product to a service center. The order-to-delivery-to-cash cycles have to complete across channels, not within the same channel. This becomes a huge push-up for information technology (IT) to transparently share and interconnect across channels.

There are also upstream supply delivery channels. Some raw material suppliers operate wholly owned DCs. This puts an additional echelon between the suppliers and its source of raw materials. Some parts suppliers operate wholly owned DCs. Again, this puts an additional echelon between the factory and its supplier. And some complex product industries, like automotive, organize their supply base into a hierarchy of supplier echelons with the echelon closest to the factory, called a tier 1 supplier. The tier 1 supplier acts as an assembler and distributor of product components from the supply base one or more echelons upstream. This is done to simplify planning and control at the factory on products with thousands of parts.

Fewer Delivery Channel Echelons Drive Lower Product Landed Cost

The distribution organization and geographical location selected to deliver the product are critical to achieving reliable delivery lead time at a competitive product landed cost. When a DC is located close to the market, delivery lead time is excellent. Factory-to-DC midbound logistics costs and DC-to-customer outbound logistics costs roll up into product landed cost. When the market spans broad geographies or multiple continents, there needs to be multiple DCs. Different product configurations, options, and accessories add complexity. Next-day delivery from remote DCs requires expensive airfreight and expedited small-parcel transportation. The order-to-delivery-to-$\text{cash}_{\text{Demand}}$ cycle depends on order configurations, delivery instructions, and invoicing information flowing seamlessly with the customer.

The breadth and length of your delivery channel depend on several factors. Delivery channel breadth means the sheer number of customer locations your supply chain network has to reach. Breadth encompasses both volume and geography. As the geographical footprint spreads from a local market to a regional market to a national market to a global market, you encounter complex tradeoffs between the expense of adding another echelon of distribution and the expense of next-day outbound logistics to maintain competitive delivery lead times. The length of a delivery channel is determined by the number of echelons between the end customer and the factory (see Table 7.1).

- The decision to add a store echelon depends on your customers' preference to be able to shop seeing physical product samples and to walk away with their merchandise versus shopping from a catalog or website and waiting for next-day or two-day home delivery.
- The decision on the number of middle echelons of distributors depends upon the tradeoffs of increasing volume and product mix, increasing the pricing for a less competitive end-customer landed cost, and increasing the network inventory investment versus decreasing transit time for a more competitive delivery lead time. Referring again to Table 7.1, as the delivery channel length grows, the landed cost to the end customer increases. This is due to increasing numbers of echelon markups and logistics connection costs. However, the distance from the inventory to the customer is shorter.
- The decision to add a trading company echelon may be dictated by the country whose market you are trying to penetrate, for example, Japan.

How to Specify a Delivery Channel

Information flow, material flow, and cash flow connections for each delivery channel must be made through some number of echelons to connect the downstream customer with the upstream factory. The demand side information flow includes not only ordering and invoicing information but also some method for the customer to learn of and shop for the product. Table 7.2 provides delivery channel preference options for the ways the customer and the factory get connected with the delivery channel.

Delivery channels are specified for construction by customer connection preferences, the number of echelons connecting the customer with the factory, and the factory connections. Here are construction specifications for two typical delivery channels:

- A commercial product sold through an Internet store with next-day delivery
  - Customer preference from Table 7.1—CS6, CO7, CD1, CP5
  - Network container—echelon 1: customer with surface address and Internet access; echelon 2: distributor with FedEx outbound; echelon 3: factory with motor freight midbound
  - Factory connection from Table 7.1—FS5, FO8, FD1, FP10
- An industrial product sold through a factory representative with two-week delivery
  - Customer preference from Table 7.1—CS4, CO2, CD3, CP9

Table 7.1 Longer Delivery Channels, Higher Customer Landed Costs

<table>
<tr><td colspan="3" rowspan="2"></td><td>Echelon 2</td><td>Echelon 1</td></tr>
<tr><td>Factory + DC</td><td>Customer</td></tr>
<tr><td colspan="5">Customer $Landed Cost = Factory $Price + Outbound $Logistics</td></tr>
<tr><td colspan="2" rowspan="2"></td><td>Echelon 3</td><td>Echelon 2</td><td>Echelon 1</td></tr>
<tr><td>Factory</td><td>Distributor</td><td>Customer</td></tr>
<tr><td colspan="5">Customer $Landed Cost = Distributor $Price + Outbound $Logistics
Distributor $Price = (DC $Landed Cost + DC $Labor + DC $Overhead) × (1 + %DC Markup)
DC $Landed Cost = Factory $Price + Midbound $Logistics</td></tr>
<tr><td rowspan="2"></td><td>Echelon 4</td><td>Echelon 3</td><td>Echelon 2</td><td>Echelon 1</td></tr>
<tr><td>Factory</td><td>Wholesale</td><td>Retail</td><td>Customer</td></tr>
<tr><td colspan="5">Customer $Landed Cost = Retail Store $Price + $0 for Customer Pickup
Retail Store $Price = Retail Store $Landed Cost × (1 + %Retail Store Markup)
Retail Store $Landed Cost = Wholesale Distributor $Price + Outbound $Logistics
Wholesale Distributor $Price = (DC $Landed Cost + DC $Labor + DC $Overhead) × (1 + %DC Markup)
DC $Landed Cost = Factory $Price + Midbound $Logistics</td></tr>
<tr><td>Echelon 5</td><td>Echelon 4</td><td>Echelon 3</td><td>Echelon 2</td><td>Echelon 1</td></tr>
<tr><td>Factory</td><td>Trading Company</td><td>Distributor</td><td>Store</td><td>Customer</td></tr>
<tr><td colspan="5">Customer $Landed Cost = Store $Price + $0 for Customer Pickup
Store $Price = Store $Landed Cost × (1 + %Store Markup)
Store $Landed Cost = Distributor $Price + Outbound $Logistics
Distributor $Price = (DC $Landed Cost + DC $Labor + DC $Overhead) × (1 + %DC Markup)
DC $Landed Cost = Trading Company $Price + Midbound₂ $Logistics
Trading Company $Price = Trading Company $Landed Cost × (1 + %Trading Company Markup)
Trading Company $Landed Cost = Factory $Price + Midbound₁ $Logistics</td></tr>
</table>

Table 7.2 Delivery Channel Preference Options

Factory Side	*Shopping Options (Information Flow)*	*Customer Side*
FS1	Forecast	CS1
FS2	For sale product	CS2
FS3	Physical sample	CS3
FS4	Data sheet	CS4
FS5	Catalog	CS5
FS6	Website	CS6
FS7	Rating service recommendation	CS7
FS8	Word of mouth	CS8
Factory Side	*Ordering Options (Information Flow)*	*Customer Side*
FO1	Order in person at the store's cash register	CO1
FO2	Order in person through a salesperson	CO2
FO3	Order by phone	CO3
FO4	Order by smart phone	CO4
FO5	Order by e-mail purchase order	CO5
FO6	Order by fax	CO6
FO7	Order online through the website shopping cart	CO7
FO8	Order by e-mail purchase order	CO8
FO9	Order by electronic data interchange (EDI)	CO9
FO10	Order by *kanban*	CO10
FO11	Customized order (checked through configurator software)	CO11
FO12	Change order	CO12

(*Continued*)

Table 7.2 (Continued) Delivery Channel Preference Options

Factory Side	*Delivery Options (Material Flow)*	*Customer Side*
FD1	Midbound/outbound logistics	CD1
FD2	Customer pickup	CD2
FD3	Postponement	CD3
FD4	Product return	CD4
Factory Side	*Payment Options (Information/Cash Flow)*	*Customer Side*
FP1	Pay cash at cash register	CP1
FP2	Partial payment at cash register with discount coupon	CP2
FP3	Pay debit card/credit card at cash register	CP3
FP4	Pay procurement card at cash register	CP4
FP5	Pay debit card/credit card on a website	CP5
FP6	Pay with PayPal on a website	CP6
FP7	Partial payment on a website with discount code	CP7
FP8	Pay procurement card on a website	CP8
FP9	Mail Invoice Pay By Check	CP9
FP10	Mail invoice pay by Automated Clearing House (ACH) wire transfer	CP10
FP11	Email invoice pay by check	CP11
FP12	Email invoice pay by ACH wire transfer	CP12
FP13	EDI invoice pay by EDI wire transfer	CP13
FP14	Return Credit	CP14

- Network container—echelon 1: industrial customer; echelon 2: distributor with UPS outbound; echelon 3: postponement center with UPS outbound; echelon 4: factory with less-than-truckload (LTL) outbound
- Factory connection from Table 7.1—FS4, FO8, FD3, FP12

At what point do you need to add a new delivery channel? If an additional payment option is being added, say adding payment by PayPal to payment by credit card, then you will not construct a new delivery channel. If you were adding an echelon of distributors to reach both North America and the European Union, or if the market segment demanded much lower cost with much faster delivery, then you would define and construct a new delivery channel. Beware, too many uncoordinated delivery channels can foster channel conflict and artificially restrict your growth in sales.

Understand What Makes a Good Distributor

As you shop around for a distributor to meet your supply chain needs, you will come across many alternatives that may seem to fit. But just what makes an organization a distributor rather than a factory or a supplier or a service bureau or a recycler? Consider the basic purpose and process flow that you need to distribute your product, the types of information that are unique to distribution, and the internal organizational structure needed to support distribution.

Basic Distribution Capabilities

The distributor that you choose should have each of the following capabilities. A well-designed distributor flows inventory quickly and accurately through its warehouse, paying attention to minimize the distance each item has to travel.

- *Break bulk*—The capability of segregating incoming freight to store as multiple stock-keeping unit (SKU) inventories.
- *Cross-dock*—The capability of moving pallets from receiving directly to shipping without intermediate storage or reconfiguration of the pallet.
- *Warehouse*—The capability to store inventory in cartons and/or pallets in racking and/or on the floor.
- *Postpone*—The capability of modifying product functionality before shipment to match a customer order.
- *Consolidate*—The capability of combining multiple SKU inventories for a single outbound shipment.

DC Process and Inventory Flow

Unlike manufacturing, a distributor does not provide transformational value-added unless postponement is involved. Instead, a distributor provides value through consistent, reliable fulfillment service within a specific market segment bounded by a specific geography. Consistent, reliable fulfillment service comes from keeping inventory turning on high-volume SKUs, from coordinating the delivery of multiple SKUs to the same customer location, and from storing the right level of safety stock on high-mix SKUs.

Inventory turns and moves may be at the item or SKU level, the carton level, the pallet level, the drum level, or the container level. On the inbound side, pallets may be broken down into cartons containing one item for inventory or mixed items. Inventory may be stocked by item, by carton, by pallet, or by drum. When broken down to the item level, its packaging materials such as plastic and cardboard must be detrashed. Sometimes, the product is returned from a customer; its disposition determines whether to repackage and restock the item or to scrap it. On the outbound side, items, cartons, and drums are picked, counted, packaged, and labeled for shipment as a single SKU or mixed SKU freight. Entire pallet loads, called unit loads, can be cross-docked without having ever been stored. Sometimes, freight has to be inspected per the customer's request before it can be released for shipment.

Inventory can be received as either a shipment from a domestic source or an import from a foreign source, where the source is responsible for the import classification. The DC is responsible for import customs compliance and is usually responsible for paying inbound freight. Inventory can be issued to either a domestic shipment or an export shipment to a foreign customer. The DC is responsible for export licensing and export customs compliance, while the DC's customer is usually responsible for paying the outbound freight.

Figure 7.2, and the list following, highlight the many different processes found within a DC. Whether you are selecting a distributor organization or setting up a satellite warehouse, you should ensure that process documentation and employee training exist and are followed for each of these processes.

- *Receive new inventory*—Inbound freight is unloaded from trucks, counted, checked against purchase orders, and entered into the inventory management system often using bar code or radio frequency identification (RF-ID) tagging. The serial numbers of container seals are recorded when opened.

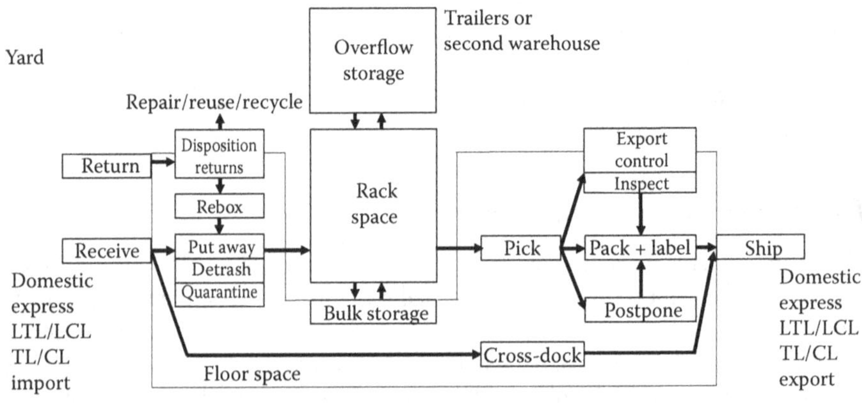

Figure 7.2 DC process and inventory flow.

- *Trigger accounts payable payment*—A three-way match among an item and count confirmation of the inventory receipt, the purchase order, and the seller's invoice triggers payment for the inventory.
- *Break bulk*—Cartons are unstacked from pallets. Individual boxes are removed from cartons.
- *Detrash*—Empty pallets are gathered up and stored. Cardboard is gathered up and taken to a compactor. Plastic is gathered up and separated by type for recycling. Paper is recycled.
- *Inbound inspection*—Inventory designated for inspection is opened and checked against its technical specification, then resealed. Careful records are kept, as this is often done using a sampling plan.
- *Quarantine*—Inventory found to have a quality problem is segmented and held in quarantine until such a problem can be resolved with the seller.
- *Cross-dock*—Inventory, once received, is moved directly to shipping without being stocked.
- *Receive a return*—Sometimes, the inbound freight is a return. It is checked against a return material authorization and counted.
- *Disposition a return*—The condition of the return is determined to be new and unused, new and used, damaged and repairable, or scrap. The inventory count is entered into the inventory management system, and the physical items are processed according to their disposition.
- *Tamper-proof labeling*—The removal of a tamper-proof label from an "unused" return proves that the product is in fact "used."
- *Rebox*—Returned and reusable inventory may need to be reboxed before resale as used product.
- *Relabel*—Reboxed returns and new inventory received with damaged labeling are relabeled.
- *Location assignment*—Inventory locations can be fixed or randomly assigned by the inventory management system. Under fixed assignment, the same item number is always stocked at the same location and any overflow goes into a bulk storage location. Under random assignment, the item goes into the next open location; sometimes, the same item number is split across several locations.
- *Put away*—Inventory is assigned a floor or a rack location. It is physically moved to that location, and an inventory count of the item is incremented in the inventory management system at the assigned location.
- *Cycle count*—A specific inventory location is physically counted. The count is compared with the inventory record. If the count is off, the inventory processing is investigated to determine the defect.
- *Pick*—The inventory management system generates a list of items, stocking locations, and counts. The picker goes to each location in sequence and gathers the quantity of inventory on the pick list. The entire picked inventory is then moved to the packing area. Inventory counts at each location

are decremented on the inventory management system, when the item is picked.

  - *Zone picking*—One employee is responsible for all the picking within a group of stocking locations. This reduces the defect rate of wrong locations and wrong item numbers.
  - *Batch picking*—Multiple quantities of the same item are picked for multiple orders at the same time to minimize repeat visits to the same stocking location. Batch picking makes direct labor more effective in smaller warehouses.
  - *Wave picking*—Uniform volumes of items are picked for multiple orders and then collated at a later point in the process. Wave picking balances the direct labor effort and distance traveled; it is usually only found in larger warehouse operations having the necessary information systems.
  - *Pick-to-light*—Warehouse racking is outfitted with a light system that indicates the next location to be picked. The pick location is confirmed by pushing a button, which causes the next pick location to light. Pick-to-light requires a capital equipment investment.
  - *Pick-to-voice*—Warehouse employees wear a headset and are directed to the next item and location to be picked through a wireless connection with a central computer, which translates instructions into the employee's native language. Voice picking systems support simultaneous languages to fit the warehouse workforce at a reasonable cost.

- *Stock rotation*—Inventory is picked from the oldest location and from the oldest date code. Cartons are physically rearranged to place the oldest inventory next in line on the rack to be picked.
- *Postpone*—The picked inventory is a partially assembled product. Postponement completes the product assembly, software loading, test, and/or labeling only after a customer order is released.
- *Pack and label*—The picked inventory is boxed, put into master cartons, and/or palletized according to the requirements on the customer order. Each box, carton, master carton, and/or pallet is properly labeled and bar coded or RF-ID tagged.
- *Shrink wrap and label*—Pallets are shrink wrapped in plastic to stabilize the load and add some protection from the weather. Shipping labels are secured and visible on the outside of the shrink wrap.
- *Sort*—Master cartons and palletized unit loads are sorted by their destination zip codes and carrier.
- *Inspect outbound*—Sometimes, customers require the inventory to be inspected before their shipment can be released. This happens with government orders and with exports to certain foreign countries. The freight cannot be scheduled for pickup until an inspector comes to the DC and signs.

- *Export control*—The outbound shipment must have proper export documentation, proper export licensing, and proper checks against the denied parties list before the shipment can be released.
- *Seal*—The door of a full container load or a full truck load is sealed with a serialized, tamper-proof seal.
- *Ship*—Outbound freight is loaded onto a truck; however, the mode of transportation may change a short distance later. An advance shipping notice (ASN) is sent to the buyer. An invoice is sent to the buyer. The distributor's revenue is incremented.
- *Trigger accounts receivable payment*—A shipment triggers an invoice to the buyer for a payment.

DC Physical Layout Considerations

DCs of all shapes and sizes share many physical aspects in common. Visit the warehouse and ask to inspect the facilities and to walk their processes before committing to a relationship. Look for the following in your assessment of a distributor's physical layout (see Figure 7.3). Keep in mind that dry goods storage will be different from refrigerated storage, which will be different from hazardous materials storage.

- *Yard*—The DC is sited on a property having a yard large enough for tractor-trailers to turn around.

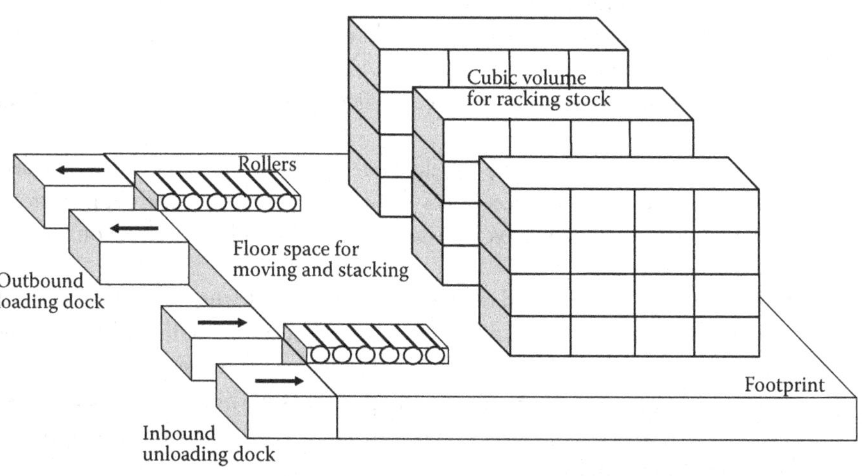

Figure 7.3 DC footprint and cubic volume.

- *Yard security*—The yard is secured with a fence, a camera, and either a gate or a guard to prevent tampering or theft of overflow inventory kept in trailers or theft from other vehicles in the yard.
- *Security cameras and motion detectors*—The DC operates a security system inside and outside.
- *Unloading/loading dock*—Preferably, there are multiple separate docks for unloading and for loading.
- *Dock floodlights*—Dock floodlights are secondary lighting used to illuminate the inside of a trailer during unloading/loading.
- *Dock bumpers*—These are heavy rubber cushions used to prevent backing vehicles from damaging the loading dock.
- *Dock leveler*—This device adjusts a ramp from the level of the truck bed to the level of the warehouse floor, making forklift and pallet jack operations safe.
- *Dock seals and strip curtains*—Dock seals provide a seal with the sides and top of the trailer during inclement weather. Strip curtains help to maintain a controlled warehouse temperature.
- *Compactor*—This device crushes and compacts cardboard into a smaller volume for recycling.
- *Rollers*—Rollers facilitate the movement of cartons from dock areas to/from staging areas. Rollers are beneficial when used properly but can cause problems when inventory is allowed to be stored indefinitely on the rollers.
- *High-speed sortation*—DCs with multiple docks assign certain carriers to unload and load at designated docks. High-speed sortation systems are motorized rollers with sensor-activated switches that automatically accumulate cartons onto a series of sidings that feed each dock.
- *Scales*—Scales are used to weigh rather than count certain types of commodities and/or small parts.
- *Pallet jack*—This is a hand-operated device used for moving loaded pallets on a level floor.
- *Scanning guns*—These are handheld laser devices that can read bar-coded information at some distance. Some devices decrement the current pick from inventory and receive the next picking location through a wireless connection with a central computer.
- *Forklift truck*—A motorized device for moving and lifting loaded pallets.
- *Narrow-aisle, high-reach forklifts*—Some warehouses are built with especially flat floors and a wire grid embedded in the cement. Narrow-aisle forklifts are driven by the guided wire, allowing high speeds within very narrow aisles. The perfectly flat floors allow the fork to safely reach their loads at extreme heights without tipping.
- *Forklift battery charging station*—Forklifts are powered either by storage batteries or propane. Forklift batteries are typically charged overnight. Safety around the charging station is a key concern.

- *Pallet wrap machine*—This device spins a loaded pallet while shrink wrap is applied for protection.
- *Inventory storage space*—Inventory storage space is organized differently for high-volume, high-cube, and high-mix items as follows:
  - *Picking face*—These are the optimal stock locations for the most direct, easiest access where the highest-volume SKUs are stored.
  - *Floor space foot print*—This is the square footage available inside the DC for break bulk, staging, consolidation, packing, and the floor storage of pallets.
  - *Rack space cubic volume*—This is the cubic volume available inside the DC for carton and pallet storage. Racking determines the maximum pallet storage capacity of the DC. The height of the ceiling, the flatness of the floor, the width of the aisles, and the building's temperature and humidity controls especially toward the top of the racks are all part of a warehouse specification.
  - *Bulk storage*—Large quantities of an item are split between bulk storage locations in the back or up high versus a small quantity of the same item stored at the picking face in the front and down low.
  - *Overflow storage*—When the number of pallets to be stored exceeds the warehouse capacity, there must be some provision for a temporary overflow. This could be empty, rented trailers in the parking lot or access to a satellite warehouse a few miles away.
  - *Inventory for recycling*—This includes defective or spent inventory held for environmentally responsible recycling.
- *Storage organized for specialized inventory*—Some warehouses must accommodate mixed types of inventory and have separate storage facilities for the following:
  - *Dry goods storage*—This is a common type of warehouse with floor space and racking.
  - *Returns storage*—This is inventory that has been returned awaiting disposition or refurbishment.
  - *Refrigerated storage*—Cold chain inventory requires specialized controlled, refrigerated temperatures. This may be one freezer room or the whole facility.
  - *High-security storage*—High-value inventory such as pharmaceuticals and certain electronics and gold requires completely enclosed, protected, monitored, and alarmed storage.
  - *HAZMAT Storage*—Corrosive chemicals, certain types of batteries, radioactive material, etc., that are classified as hazardous materials (HAZMAT) require specialized storage areas and handling procedures compliant with their appropriate regulations.
- *Lighting*—DCs usually have very large footprints and very high ceilings. Running proper lighting economically can be a challenge. One solution is

high-intensity lights activated by motion sensors. Whenever a section of the warehouse is not being accessed, it is kept dark.

- *Sprinklers*—Inventory insurance consideration drives the need for sprinklers and a fire detection system installed throughout the warehouse.
- *Physical security*—Inventory insurance and customer requirements drive the need for locks, gates, motion detectors, cameras, and other security monitoring and alarm systems in the warehouse.
- *Employee and visitor entrance security*—Only employees and those authorized to enter the building should be allowed access to the warehouse and its inventory.
- *Employee and driver facilities*—Such facilities include lockers, a lunch room, vending machines, and toilets to be used by both employees and truck drivers. There should be physical security preventing nonemployee truck drivers from access inside the warehouse.
- *Office space*—A small portion of the building will be dedicated to office space. This office space should keep out the noise from warehouse operations and protect employees from high-speed forklift maneuvering.
- *Warehouse management system (WMS)*—This is the information system used to receive inventory, issue inventory, generate batch picks and/or wave picks, and print shipping labels. Picking lists may take the form of paper, cards, tags, or wireless instructions sent to scanning guns.

A Liability Case from a Missed Inventory Rotation

Modern inventory management systems randomly assign the next inventory receipt to any open rack location. This means a given item can be stored at one location today and in a different location tomorrow. In addition, when the received inventory quantity exceeds the capacity of a single rack location, the inventory is split among two or more locations.

A contract manufacturer makes a weatherproof electronics module where a microprocessor soldered to a printed circuit assembly is enclosed within a two-piece custom plastic case. The top and bottom halves of this plastic case are ultrasonically welded together to seal the enclosure. Once the case is welded, it cannot be opened without irreparable damage to the case and other internal components. The microprocessor operates from firmware that is frequently updated by engineering. These firmware updates need to have the module open for access to the microprocessor's memory. A label on the outside of the enclosure indicates the current firmware revision. The contract manufacturer is also the distributor for the product line.

Six months ago, the forecast for modules was overstated, causing some 800 modules to be held in finished goods inventory. Four months ago, customers reported a serious application issue in the field. Customer service working with engineering traced the problem back to a firmware bug in the microprocessor's program. Customers were upset, and they threatened to abandon the product line.

A fix was quickly made and implemented for new production. The company paid to replace the defective units in the field; the module replacement took nine weeks to complete. And the company paid to have the contract manufacturer cut open the cases of every unit in stock, reprogram the microprocessor, replace other destroyed parts, retest, weld, and relabel the finished goods inventory.

Two days ago, a customer doing a new installation reported a field failure with the same symptoms as before. After detailed checking, the contract manufacturer admitted finding that 33 defective modules had been discovered comingled in finished goods inventory after all the updates had been completed. The contract manufacturer had failed to institute a robust stock rotation program that included split batches and multiple stocking locations. The contract manufacturer was found liable for all of the company's expenses to rectify the latest issue; however, significant customer goodwill was lost along the way, and the company's image was tarnished.

A Case of Non-Value-Added Distribution

A start-up technology company required a specialty sensor for its application. Engineering researched all commercially available sensors for the performance required and cost they could afford. When they finally located a part they could use, they were forced into dealing with a regional distributor at the going price of $81 for 50–100 pieces. The start-up company had no track record, little demand volume, and, consequently, no clout with the supplier. The regional distributor collected and forwarded the orders to the supplier's distributor, forwarded the prepackaged product from the supplier's distributor to the customer, and handled customer invoicing. This four-echelon delivery channel, supplier to supplier's distributor to regional distributor to the technology company (the supplier's customer), had an eight-week lead time.

As time went on, the application gained market share, and demand for the sensors approached 1,000 units per month. Engineering had some new requirements for the sensor, and purchasing thought it was time to try and deal directly with the supplier's distributor. When the regional distributor was approached to set up a meeting with the supplier, the technology company was stonewalled into meeting with the supplier's distributor instead. The supplier's distributor was primarily an automotive parts distributor; it packaged and labeled parts for its customers. The technology company learned that it had become a major account for the sensor, and a case was successfully made for a volume discount at 1,000 units with a $64 price. But the request for the sensor supplier to ship the product directly to the technology company was denied.

Then, unfortunately, the sensor developed a quality problem in the field. The regional distributor and the supplier's distributor were both engaged, but neither had anything to offer in the way of technical support. Management at the technology company pushed and pushed, until finally, contact was made directly with the sensor supplier. Engineering at the sensor supplier had been considering a lower-cost sensor redesign for the nonautomotive market that would also solve the quality issue. The supplier's distributor had no interest in distributing the nonautomotive design. A deal was cut directly between the technology company and the sensor supplier for the direct shipment of the new sensor design at a 1,000 unit price of $52. The sensor delivery lead time dropped to three weeks.

While the regional distributor and the supplier's distributor added lead time, network inventory, and price markups, these organizations never added any value. The longer supply chain also exacerbated the total number of defective sensors in the network. This case is not to say that distribution adds no value. Rather, the case is meant to demonstrate that you need to be able to articulate where and how each distribution echelon adds value.

DC Organizational Structure

Much of the organizational structure found in a distributor is similar to that found in a manufacturer. However, there are some differences. Look for the following functions being performed. In small distributor organizations, some functions may be performed by a single person. In larger distributor organizations, some functions may be centralized back at a headquarters location.

The following functional areas implement the distributor's order-to-delivery-to-cash$_{\text{Supply}}$ cycle:

- *Forecasting*—Forecasts product demand and warehouse capacity.
- *Planning*—Generates the distribution requirements plan (DRP), workforce capacity requirements, rack space capacity requirements, and packaging material usage. Plans inventory safety stock levels.
- *Purchasing*—Manages the purchase orders for finished goods inventory and accessory components from the factory. Manages the factory relationship. Matches factory invoices against inventory receipts and purchase orders (order information flow: distributor to factory or supplier) (invoice information flow: factory or supplier to distributor).
- *Direct labor to receive, material handle, and put away*—Unloads trucks. Receives finished goods and accessory components from the factory against open purchase orders. Unpacks and moves inventory to its stocking location (material flow: factory or supplier to distributor).
- *Accounts payable*—Manages the cash flow to pay factory invoices (cash flow: distributor to factory or supplier).

The following distributor functional area adds value to the product:

- *Postpone*—Product assembly is completed, a product is customized, software is loaded, and/or documentation is printed on-demand within the DC to match a customer order.

The following functional areas implement the distributor's order-to-delivery-to-cash$_{\text{Demand}}$ cycle:

- *Inside sales and marketing*—Develops the market; quotes and sells the product to the customer.
- *Account management*—Manages long-term customer relationships and contract negotiations.
- *Order processing*—Manages the customer's order from booking through shipment. Keeps the customer advised of the shipping date (order information flow: customer to distributor).
- *Accounts receivable and credit management*—Approves customer order booking based on the customer's open credit. Manages the invoicing and cash flow from customer payment (invoice information flow: distributor to customer) (cash flow: customer to distributor).
- *Traffic*—Schedules the most efficient time windows for carriers and third-party logistics to access loading and unloading docks.
- *Direct labor to pick, material handle, pack, and ship*—Locates the item at its stocking location, material handles to packaging, and shipping. Loads product onto trucks for movement to customers (material flow: distributor to customer).
- *Export control*—Performs regulatory documentation and export compliance tasks for international shipments.

The following distributor functional areas provide infrastructure and support:

- *Finance and accounting*—Maintains the general ledger, performs margin analysis of product pricing on the income statement, values inventory on the balance sheet, and provides management reporting including monthly income statements, balance sheets, and cash flows. Advises general management.
- *Human resources*—Hires and trains both direct and indirect labor. Manages employee benefits.
- *Quality*—Establishes a company-wide philosophy of quality, validates material compliance to specification, validates process compliance to specification, trains, and audits for International Organization for Standardization (ISO) certification.
- *IT*—Installs and maintains each of the IT systems used for distribution, such as warehouse management systems (WMS) and transportation management systems (TMS). Interfaces with third-party logistics services provided applications for tendering freight including FedEx, UPS, and Customs.
- *Facilities*—Maintains and secures the physical building, equipment, and yard.
- *General management*—Consists of the C-level officers, chief executive officer, chief financial officer, chief technology officer, chief operating officer,

etc., responsible for business strategy, market development, organizational development, sustainability strategy, supply chain strategy, risk management, regulatory compliance, etc.
- *Consultants*—In addition, consultants may be on call for product packaging, warehouse layout, sustainability, and alternative logistics.

Embrace Specialized IT

Effective inventory management systems are critical to distribution. The specialized application of information technology (IT) is evident everywhere, from basic stockroom management to advanced omni channel distribution. The following highlights the IT benefits of managing complexity, ensuring accuracy, reducing logistics-related cost, and providing security.

Any warehouse with hourly receipts and issues, hundreds of stocking locations, and thousands of SKUs with lot numbers, serial numbers, expiration dates, and revision codes is complex indeed. Software algorithms determine the next stocking location based on open rack space and the shortest distance traveled from receiving to shipping. Programs continuously locate inventory that has been split and moved to multiple locations. Inventory serialization can be tracked downstream to a customer and location. Inventory lot codes can be traced upstream to a particular supplier and raw material source. The inventory for each stocked item is rotated and cycle counted, while a perpetual inventory balance is maintained on the system.

- *Track downstream*—The visibility and ability to validate when an item has reached its destination through the use of technologies such as bar code, quick response (QR) tags, serial numbers, and global positioning satellite (GPS).
- *Trace upstream*—The visibility and ability to determine the origin of an item through the use of batch numbers, serial numbers, date/time stamps, and RF-ID tags should product defects, spoilage, contamination, or counterfeiting become an issue.

An important element of customer service is distribution picking accuracy. When a customer receives the wrong item, the wrong item count, or a missed item, the root cause is usually traced back to the picking process. Modern IT has developed several tools for this application. Part identification has gone from reading a paper label to scanning a bar code to sensing an RF-ID tag. While paper and bar coding each has a very limited number of characters to describe the part, an RF-ID tag is a pointer to a computer file of unlimited length. RF-ID tags used in the pharmaceutical industry capture the complete and unique supply chain path from origin to destination for each bottle of pills. In this way, pharmaceutical companies can identify and thwart a counterfeit product whenever there is an attempt to inject it into the supply chain. Another innovation is pick-to-voice. The picker is outfitted with a wireless device that communicates with a central computer that translates pick instructions to the picker in his or her native language. Such technology ensures the right item in the right quantity gets picked and that no item on the customer's order is left behind.

Whenever you can trade information for inventory, operating costs will come down. The interface between logistics and distribution provides several excellent opportunities to do this. First, a full container of a single SKU can be cross-docked to load multiple containers with multiple SKUs going to multiple locations. Cross-docking can be viewed as low-cost route switching. Second, pallet loads can be built from mixed SKUs to make store-specific loads. Additionally, these mixed SKU pallets can be packaged store-ready. As soon as the shipment is received at the store, the SKUs go directly on the shelf or on the rack, ready for customer shopping. Third, distributors can perform postponement by completing a product's assembly or by adding the right accessories after the customer order has been released. Postponement reduces inventory investment while achieving high service levels across a product mix.

Inventory security is yet another area where IT can be applied in distribution. There are fire detection, motion detection, and camera systems for physical security. These monitors and alarms can be tied to the local fire and police. Fire detection alarms can have options for synthesized voice instructions telling personnel how to exit the building. You should also think of other kinds of activities as security related. ASNs make the customer aware that their shipment is imminent and to look for it. And export compliance regulations dictate that the ship-to address of every export has to be checked against continuously updated Denial Lists.

Select the Best Distribution Network

A key topic of this chapter is learning how to make a good distribution organization selection to meet your supply chain construction requirements specification. If your organization is the distributor, then this section speaks on how to best position your organization to grow your business. The decision criteria in Table 7.3 enable you to quickly eliminate possible distributor choices that do not fit in order to spend your time evaluating criteria that are more difficult to determine. The "must" criteria are normally documented in the supply chain construction requirements specification. If a candidate distributor does not satisfy all the "musts," then do not waste any more time with that candidate. Evaluating pricing is hard; it will take some time, particularly if the candidate distributor does not want to share confidential information. The "want" criteria will be satisfied, to a greater or lesser degree, depending on the candidate. While it is easy to add more "wants," you can make a good decision with just this set. Execute a nondisclosure agreement with each candidate distributor before sharing information.

Table 7.3 Distributor Selection Decision Criteria

Priority	*Criteria*	*Validation*	*Numerical Value*
Must 1	Requirements specification: market access	1. The right geographical reach? 2. The right commodity expertise? 3. Supports the required delivery lead time?	
Must 2	Requirements specification: landed cost at volume	1. Driven by distributor markup? 2. Driven by distributor labor costs? 3. Driven by outbound logistics?	$Landed Cost
Must 3	Requirements specification: inventory capacity	1. Rack space and floor capacity? 2. Perpetual inventory accounting? 3. Demonstrated inventory accuracy?	#Pallet Spaces
Must 4	Requirements specification: throughput capacity	1. Your percentage of their throughput? 2. Number of loading/unloading docks? 3. Constraints to doubling growth?	20%–35%
Must 5	Specialized capability	1. Postponement? 2. Refrigeration? 3. High-value, high-security inventory? 4. Hazardous material?	
Want	Consistent service level	1. Low, measured delivery variability? 2. High, measured picking accuracy?	
Want	Information systems	1. Information completeness? 2. Good application of technology?	
Want	Management team	1. Cultural compatibility? 2. Experience in risk management? 3. Financial track record?	

(Continued)

Table 7.3 (Continued) Distributor Selection Decision Criteria

Priority	*Criteria*	*Validation*	*Numerical Value*
Want	Flexibility and responsiveness	1. Can respond easily to mix change? 2. Can respond easily to rate change?	
Want	Approach to quality	1. Workforce turnover and training? 2. ISO certification? 3. Details of specific quality programs?	
Want	Sustainability	1. Has computed its carbon footprint? 2. Environmentally responsible packaging? 3. Environmentally responsible recycling?	

Keep in mind that for a multiechelon distribution network, you will apply these criteria in the context of echelon 2 and again in a different context for echelon 3. The specifications for landed cost, geographical reach, inventory capacity, and throughput will be varied accordingly. An echelon 3 distributor feeding a network of echelon 2 distributors will require a broader geographic reach, will hold more days of inventory, and will process a higher throughput than the individual echelon 2 distributors.

There is a high probability that the distributor you choose will also be handling inventory owned by your competitor. You need to have a frank discussion with the distributor's management early in the relationship to ensure that the distributor can build and maintain a "firewall" between the two supply chains. This firewall must cover both the physical inventory with no comingling of items and the proprietary information aspects, like customer names, sales volumes, and product pricing markups.

Optimize Outbound Logistics Costs

Outbound logistics connects the distributor with the end customer. While outbound logistics may involve motor freight, rail freight, ocean freight, or air freight shipping either domestically or internationally, one characteristic of outbound logistics is that each origin-to-destination pair is potentially a new routing. This variable transportation network is called upon to deliver both high SKU mix and high SKU volume. This section describes the main considerations for outbound freight. Refer to Chapter 5: "Make" for a description of palletization, containerization, mode of transportation, and midbound logistics considerations. Refer to Chapter 6: "Source" for a description of inbound logistics and import regulatory considerations, which can become the case when an exported product must be returned to the DC. Distributors maintain inbound logistics connections with packing materials suppliers, printers, and with suppliers for postponed parts.

Domestic Outbound Logistics

The following are the most common forms of outbound logistics:

- *Small-Parcel UPS, FedEx, US Postal Service (USPS)*—UPS, FedEx, and USPS accounts have negotiable rates based on the total volume conducted by the business. Rates and delivery lead times are based on geographical zones. UPS and FedEx typically deliver in the morning and pick up in the afternoon. Both provide special computer terminals to enter shipment descriptions and destination information to print shipping labels. This has the added advantage of maintaining accurate ship-to addresses on the system. There is a wealth of information about shipping rates, packaging requirements, and point-to-point transit times on their respective websites: http://www.ups.com, http://www.fedex.com, and http://www.usps.com.
- *Customer pickup*—Some customers insist on picking up a shipment themselves. This saves cost for the customer. But the pickup time is often unreliable; it can add cost to the distributor as they have to work around freight that should have been already shipped.
- *Customer-specified carriers*—Customers sometimes specify shipping against their own UPS or FedEx account or their preferred LTL carrier to save on transportation costs. The distributor should accommodate these requests whenever possible.
- *LTL*—Distributors often have agreements with local LTL carriers to handle the occasional large quantity, large cubic volume, and/or large weight shipment.
- *Full truckload (TL)/full container load (CL)*—Larger customers with larger orders going to the same destination may require a TL or CL shipment. This can be 20 pallets single stacked or 40 pallets double stacked.
- *Freight forwarders for rail freight, airfreight, and ocean freight*—Shipments sent by rail freight, airfreight, or short-haul ocean freight will be delivered to a freight forwarder for consolidation and documentation preparation before being transferred to the modal carrier.

- *Routing optimization*—When one carrier is tasked with delivering many small shipments, it is cost effective to optimize the sequencing and routing of the deliveries. One famous example is the UPS policy of making only right-hand turns to increase driver efficiency and reduce fuel costs from idling at stop lights waiting to make a left turn.
- *Expediting*—Pay attention to your operations and minimize outbound expediting to eliminate outbound logistics cost surprises. Many freight cost reporting systems report well after the fact, making it impossible to correct bad situations in real time.
- *Special handling considerations*—Certain types of commodities such as refrigerated freight or radioactive isotopes or corrosive hazardous materials require special handling. There are airfreight restrictions on concentrated packaging of lithium batteries. It is imperative that you know and adhere to the transportation regulations for such shipments. Your freight forwarder can put you in touch with the most up-to-date regulatory requirements.

International Outbound Logistics and Exporting

When the outbound logistics connection involves the distributor exporting and the customer importing, the shipment involves international logistics. Remember that if the product has to be returned for any reason, then the customer is exporting and the distributor is importing. The seller and the buyer must comply with all export regulations according to the laws of their respective countries. Export regulations define restricted shipments requiring an export license, denied parties who cannot receive a shipment legally, and embargoed countries who cannot receive a shipment legally.

The International Chamber of Commerce, http://www.iccwbo.org, provides access to internationally recognized purchasing terms and conditions, INCOTERMS, explanations of how to use letters of credit (LOC), and arbitration services. The US Census Bureau website, http://www.census.gov, publishes and maintains Schedule B for the classification of exports. The Bureau of Industry and Security of the US Department of Commerce website, http://www.bis.doc.gov, provides information on Export Control Classification Numbers (ECCN), the Commercial Control List (CCL), export licensing, and the Denial List. While Chapter 6: "Source" discusses import compliance, here are the key considerations for export compliance:

- *Bill of lading*—This transfers title to the goods from the seller to the carrier.
- *Commercial invoice*—This is a document signed by the seller or his agent providing the following kinds of information: port of entry; names of buyer and seller; if consigned, names of shipper and receiver; description of the merchandise; number of packages, weights, and measures; purchase price of each item and its currency; charges upon the merchandise such as freight,

insurance, and commissions; allowed rebates and drawbacks; country of origin; and more.

- *Advance manifest rules*—The number of hours before arrival that customs must be notified of an inbound shipment. Advance manifest rules are transportation mode specific: ocean freight 24 hours before landing, airfreight 4 hours before wheels up, rail freight 2 hours before arrival, and motor freight 1 hour before arrival.
- *Country of origin certification*—The distributor passes along the producer's country of origin certification to validate preferential duty treatment.
- *Customs power of attorney for the exporter of record*—This is the customs broker given legal authority by the exporter to represent the exporter to customs.
- *Schedule B classification*—Exported goods are statistically compiled according to their classification under Schedule B. Schedule B is very similar to the Harmonized Tariff Schedule (HTS) used for import classification. This is a 10-digit code expressed as xxxx.yy.zzzz, which is determined by the manufacturer, sometimes with the help of a customs broker. Like the HTS, Schedule B is divided into chapters dealing separately with merchandise in broad categories.
- *Export Classification Control Number (ECCN)*—This is an alpha-numeric code that describes the item and identifies the level of export control required. Manufacturers may self-classify products with the exception of items containing encryption functionality. A custom broker can also classify products.
- *CCL*—The US Government controls the export of certain types of technology to protect national security, economic security, cyber security, and homeland security. This document lists all ECCN numbers arranged into 10 categories, each with five product groupings. The CCL lists the licensing requirements for each ECCN and the reason for the export control.
- *Dual use*—Certain products and components of these products are capable of both their intended commercial use and an unintended illegal use.
- *Export licensing*—The need for export licensing has to be determined for each export shipment, each time, even if the distributor is shipping the same product to the same customer. Export licenses fall into three categories: no license required (NLR), an individual validated license, and, in special cases, a special comprehensive license, which does allow repeated shipments.
- *EAR99*—Certain low-technology consumer goods that are not listed in the CCL and do not require export licensing.
- *Denied persons list*—The US Government expects all manufacturers and distributors to know the ultimate end customer and end usage for their products. This is a heavy responsibility as the product may be redistributed and reexported several times. Each export shipment must be checked against the most current denied persons list before the shipment is made.

- *Embargoed countries list*—The US Department of State maintains a list of embargoed countries where all trading is denied.
- *Carnets*—A carnet is an internationally recognized temporary import/export document. It allows commercial samples, demo equipment for trade shows, and professional equipment to clear customs without paying duty and taxes. The carnet must be processed through customs both upon arrival and again at departure. The item must be reexported within 12 months. Certain categories of goods and equipment such as seeds, fertilizer, pesticides, and explosives do not qualify for a carnet.

Not Knowing Is No Excuse

A young product development engineer, who had never traveled outside the United States, was asked to spend two weeks in Taiwan to resolve a design problem on a sophisticated microprocessor mother board. At the last minute, the engineer was told to hand carry the only working prototype of the mother board to Taiwan and to return home with it. As the project was on a very tight schedule, the engineering manager felt that the prototype board would be very helpful in troubleshooting any differences with the production board being manufactured in Taiwan. The company never filed for a carnet, and the engineer did not know any better.

Upon arrival, a random check by customs discovered the prototype board in the engineer's luggage. When asked, the engineer explained how this was a state-of-the-art, high-clock-speed microprocessor with deep memory and encrypted input/output ports. The engineer then admitted no knowledge of export licensing requirements or the need for a carnet. The prototype board was confiscated by customs, and the engineer personally fined. Needless to say, the project fell far behind schedule.

In Summary

This chapter shows how to select a distributor that fits your supply chain construction requirements specification. Market segmentation and delivery channel configurations are discussed. The characteristics that differentiate a distribution relationship from other kinds of supply chain relationships are revealed. A distributor selection criterion with musts and wants is presented. The product landed cost to the end customer is determined by the length and breadth of the delivery channel. Finally, the details of outbound logistics and exporting are discussed.

Chapter 8

Return

This chapter addresses two topics: how to construct a reverse supply chain and how to apply the Supply Chain Construction Blueprint when building a reverse network. Components are returned and recycled, and products are returned, refurbished, repaired, remanufactured, and recycled all the time. A reverse supply chain network, different from a forward supply chain network, must be specifically designed and operated to support such actions. This chapter applies the template of the Supply Chain Construction Blueprint from Chapter 2: "The Blueprint" in a very detailed manner to a reverse supply chain scenario. This reinforces the methodology in a multiechelon setting, and it illustrates the differences in building and operating a reverse supply chain.

No Deposit, No Return

When the pallets finally arrived on the 17th, there were three pallets on the bill of lading instead of two. The 28 cartons on the first pallet looked to be in reasonably good shape. The cartons on the second pallet were visibly damaged. And somewhere along the way, these cartons had been haphazardly restacked.

"What a mess!" Tony, the cost accountant, said as the Supply Chain Construction Project Team assembled on the receiving dock. "What do we do now?"

Bill, the project manager, answered, "First, take digital photos of everything. We can probably start testing units from the good pallet. We will need to open a damaged goods claim with the shipper for the bad pallet and start a trace on the location of the missing third pallet. Let's see if we can figure out what happened."

After the photos had been taken, John, from Engineering, opened two of the crushed cartons, "Look, the front frames on both of these units have slipped off their plastic cushions inside the carton. The frames are badly deformed, probably because of the weight of the unit moving around."

"Engineering tested the frame design months ago with shake and vibration testing done by a third-party environmental testing lab. The product enclosure design came through with flying colors. But these units came by airfreight through Seoul, Korea, through Chicago, and finally into Newark. That's three sets of takeoff and landing accelerations and decelerations. I don't think we ever designed the packing carton for that!" Bill surmised.

"We can't repair these units here," said Donna, the buyer. "We don't carry any spare parts yet. By the way, what's our support plan for the uninterruptable power supply (UPS) product line?"

"It's going to be really expensive to ship these heavy units back to Malaysia for repairs," said Tony. "Who is going to pay for that?"

"OK, so we have a little setback. It's much better to face these problems early in our business start-up than to have 1,000 defect units onboard a ship for a month before we even know about the problem," said Bill. "We need to regroup and work through each issue in a logical fashion."

John had finished opening three more units, "The good news is that all five crushed cartons show the same product damage inside. The bad news is that going to a packing carton design with higher burst strength, and adding surface area to the plastic cushions will add material cost to our product."

"We need at least 36 functional units to complete our testing plan on time," Bill commented. "If the first pallet of 28 units all look OK, turn on, and pass their initial performance checks, then we only need eight more. Let's open all of the damaged products, choose the eight best, and order replacement frames and other parts from Malaysia to repair the damaged units here. We can probably use these repaired units for some engineering work and other testing. All 56 units in the pilot run were to be owned by Engineering and not to be saleable to customers anyway. Maybe a few can be even be prettied up for sales demos."

John said, "I think we need to return a couple of units to Malaysia so that they can see what happened."

"We will need a return material authorization (RMA) from Astec to return these units. And we should rebox these units in their original, damaged packing cartons and deformed floaters and carefully pack all that into a larger master carton for the return shipment. That way, Malaysia can see exactly the state of how we received these units," said Donna.

"Good idea," added Bill. "Don't forget that we are now exporting these returns, and Astec is importing. I'll contact the forwarder about the required documentation. Have we classified the UPS product for export licensing yet?"

Meanwhile, the contract manufacturer was having its own problems. In setting up their insertion programming for the first production run of the control board assembly, they had identified an incorrect part number in the product bill of materials (BOM) for a precision resistor network. A reel of these precision resistors networks had been shipped to Astec from the Power Products inventory. The part's only use was in an analog-to-digital converter circuit on the new UPS control board.

Aznul, the production manager, on Safdar's manufacturing staff had sent an e-mail to Donna, which read, "Send a reel of the correct part number 0811-0124 precision resistor networks. We are returning the reel of 0811-0123 precision resistor networks to you."

Donna had replied by e-mail, "Thanks Aznul. It is best if you can return these parts directly to Vishay, the manufacturer, for a credit."

Aznul had responded, "That is impossible. The part is manufactured by a Vishay plant in Israel. Don't you know that Malaysia has a trade embargo with Israel?"

Donna went looking for John to see what other suppliers were capable of making the precision resistor network. This could cause a major project delay if the circuit had to be redesigned and retested.

Later, when the team was assembled again for their weekly meeting, Donna began, "I think we have to talk about how we plan to support customers in the field after the UPS product ships."

Harry, in Product Marketing, said, "We are offering a two-year warranty. That is based on the expected battery life and the fact that the product may be in finished goods for a few months before it gets shipped to the customer."

Tony asked, "Are we planning to replace defective battery cells during the warranty period? Would customers do that themselves?"

John replied, "I don't think we want customers replacing any battery cells. The product was not designed for easy battery access. In fact, it requires a fair amount of disassembly just to get at the battery. This was done to reduce the overall size and cost of the product."

"One solution is to have some number of spare UPS units here that could be immediately swapped with a unit under warranty that is found to be defective in the field. Hopefully, the number of field defects will be very small. This is supposed to be a highly reliable product," said Bill.

"It is. We calculated a four-year theoretical mean time between failures (MTBF)," said John.

Bill continued, "Then, Donna, the solution is not so much having a repair facility, but more carrying some replacement inventory and having an environmentally responsible process to disassemble and recycle returned defective units. Let's see, each additional 1% of annual failure rate (AFR) per 2,500 units shipped would be an additional 25 defective units returns. If we had a 3% AFR the first year, then we would need to replace 75 units. I'll discuss this approach with George, our vice president of quality."

Harry suggested, "We probably need to set a trigger point. If we got more than a couple of defective units in any month, we should understand the failure mechanism and revisit our support plan."

"I think we have to be careful that defective units don't just accumulate. As time goes by, Engineering will be less willing to immediately devote resources to investigate potentially latent product failures. And we are already experiencing that it takes days and sometimes weeks to get basic questions answered from our factory halfway around the world," Bill reminded everyone.

Harry said, "It's really important that we stay on top of this, as the sales team is building our brand in the marketplace. An unreliable product would be devastating."

"John, it would be helpful if you could work with Donna to break the UPS BOM down into commodity buckets like sheet metal, batteries, plastics, printed circuit assemblies, etc. Then, this team can determine a set of preferred companies to handle the recycling of each type of commodity," said Bill. With that, the meeting broke up, and everyone headed for lunch in the cafeteria.

Accommodate Returns in the Forward Network

There are two sets of returns generated within a supply chain (see Figure 8.1). First, each echelon of the forward network can generate a component return upstream to its source. These are normally caused by quality defects found while building the product. Sometimes, material is returned upstream to a supplier simply because the demand forecast has been found to grossly overstate supply requirements. Second, completed products sold to customers can generate returns to a downstream reverse supply chain. These are normally warranty returns for repair and recalibration or out-of-warranty defective products, called cores, for remanufacturing and recycling.

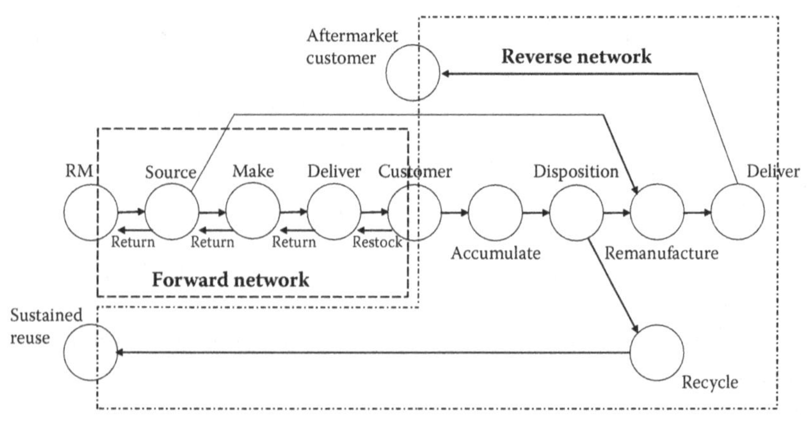

Figure 8.1 Forward and reverse supply chain networks.

Warranty

A warranty is often provided with a manufactured product or component part. Such a warranty may be a minimal 90-day guarantee on material and workmanship or a full-year warranty to replace the product against any defect. Some businesses sell extended warranties for a monthly premium. This secondary revenue stream can be profitable as long as the warranty costs do not exceed the revenue collected. A warranty is not the same as an offer to accept a return for credit with no questions asked. A warranty is meant to make the customer whole should the product develop a defect during its intended use; under a warranty, the customer always ends up with a working product.

Product serialization is the normal method of determining whether or not a product is covered under a warranty. The customer must contact the seller and request a return material authorization (RMA). The seller then compares the serial number of the product being returned with a list of authorized serial numbers and warranty periods. Your information system must be capable of capturing, sorting and continually updating serial number information. When a defective product is found to be in-warranty, a replacement product can be shipped to the customer; the customer is provided a means of returning the defective product, or core, back to the seller. If the customer fails to return a core after receiving a replacement product, then after 90 days, the customer is invoiced for the replacement product. When a product is found to be out-of-warranty, the customer is given a choice of purchasing a new product at its full price or a refurbished product at a reduced price.

Component and Raw Material Returns

Component and/or raw material returns occur in all echelons of the forward supply chain, as shown in Figure 8.1.

- *Rework in-house*—A defective component is identified during production. The assembly is rejected to a previous work center, where the assembly is reworked and put back into play.
- *Repackage and relabel*—Sometimes, shipping cartons get damaged with handling and/or shipping labels need to be reprinted with a different ship-to address or to fix a damaged bar code. These tasks are handled in-house.
- *Return to supplier for restock and credit*—When an overstock condition exists, it is sometimes possible to negotiate a return of stock to the supplier or supplier's distributor for a credit. You would want to write this possibility into your annual pricing contract. In large corporations, it is sometimes possible to sell overstocks to a sister division that has demand for the same item.
- *Return to supplier for rework and replacement*—Defective components are identified during production. Production is stopped. All components with the specific date code are collected from the production floor and from stock.

Sometimes, select date codes are deemed "bad," while earlier or later date codes after critical testing are deemed "good." The supplier is contacted for a return authorization, and the entire defective inventory is shipped back to the supplier. Disciplined stock rotation and split location tracing are essential to identify all potentially defective components within a facility. Production may be placed on hold until good components can be supplied to replace the defective ones.

- *Scrap*—When there is no opportunity to rework or return material, it ends up getting scrapped. This goes directly against the profit margin, and it must be done in an environmentally responsible way.
- *Factory outlet store*—Some manufacturers operate a small number of factory outlet stores to handle inventory from discontinued lines and production overruns. These stores sell the inventory in volume at a discount rather than writing it all off.

Forward Network Returns Infrastructure

Information systems developed to operate a forward supply chain do not run backward. Therefore, additional infrastructure must be in place to manage the material, information, and cash flows associated with forward network returns. Keep in mind that such returns are sporadic, and they usually involve situations with high product mix and low volume.

The information flow begins with the buyer requesting a return authorization from the seller. The material flow is the return of the defective component or raw material, often valued at $1. When replacement material is provided, the supplier initiates the order internally and the material is processed as with any other forward network order fulfillment. The cash flow is usually the seller giving the buyer an equivalent dollar credit on their next order; the seller does not make any cash payment. In a few special cases replacement material may be consigned to the buyer for evaluation and acceptance, the buyer has a fixed period in which to accept or return the consigned inventory. Once the material is accepted, the buyer must pay the seller.

Product Returns

Finished goods product returns normally pass between a forward supply chain network and a reverse supply chain network under the following circumstances, as shown in Figure 8.1:

- *Restock*—Product restocks flow back to the forward supply chain. There are strict accounting rules about what can be considered a new product. Some businesses apply a tamper-proof label, or seal, to prove that the customer did not try to use the product before returning it.

- *Repair*—The defective product is shipped to a reverse network repair depot. If the product is under warranty, it is repaired and returned without charge. If the product is determined to be out-of-warranty, it may be repaired and returned for a fee. The customer normally loses the use of the product during the repair time.
- *Recalibrate*—The product is shipped to a reverse network calibration site and recalibrated for a fee. The customer normally loses the use of the product while it is out for calibration.
- *Remanufacture*—Product cores are accumulated into a reverse network, its component parts dispositioned as to fitness for reuse. The core is then remanufactured and sold for a lower price in an aftermarket.
- *Recycle*—Product cores are accumulated into a reverse network, its component parts dispositioned as to fitness for reuse, disassembled by commodity groupings, and processed for environmentally responsible recycling.
- *Scrap*—Product cores are accumulated into a reverse network, determined to be unfit for use and unfit for component recycling, and scrapped. This goes directly against the profit margin, and it needs to be done in an environmentally responsible way.

Build a Reverse Supply Chain—A Comprehensive Example

The following comprehensive case study details how to complete each step of the Supply Chain Construction Blueprint to build a reverse supply chain. This case study is a compilation of experiences designed to teach the application of The Blueprint for a multiechelon reverse supply chain with lumpy throughput. Follow each of these steps, in sequence, to build your own multiechelon, high-throughput reverse supply chain. Note that the construction steps for a reverse supply chain are the same as in Chapter 2: "The Blueprint" for a forward supply chain except that the trading partner names and functions are different.

Step A: Set the Business Objective Connecting the Market Segment and Product (Chapter 1)

In step A, you set the business context for the market segment and product being returned to your reverse supply chain. A technology company is developing its business plan for the third-generation launch of its bestselling product. The company provides telematics for over-the-road trucking companies in the United States. The telematics product, called "Tractor Tracker," sends GPS location, engine RPM, and engine fuel consumption to customer fleet operations centers by means of cellular phone technology. This competitively priced, high-volume product consists of a plastic encapsulated head unit containing a GPS radio, cellular radio, internal antennas, and microprocessor which bolts to the back of a tractor cab. A family of custom cables, designed specifically for different truck manufacturers like Peterbilt, Kenworth, Freightliner, Volvo, etc., connects the head unit with the tractor's battery, tachometer, and fuel sensor.

The customer base for this product is located throughout the United States, with some concentration in the Midwest. Customer fleets run coast-to-coast and to all points between the borders with Canada and Mexico. Larger fleet operators have their own maintenance organizations install the telematics product, while smaller fleets contract with third-party truck maintenance organizations for installation. Each of the installers is trained and certified as a service provided by the technology company. The operating environment for the equipment is especially harsh from blinding rain storms to tractor power washing and from the heat of the Mojave Desert to the altitude of Denver to the subzero weather of North Dakota. This third-generation product is being sold with a three-year warranty and an extended warranty plan covering years four and five. The technology company reserves the right to supply customers with refurbished product under its extended warranty agreement.

Step B: Staff the Construction Project, Develop the Timeline, and Plan the Budget (Chapters 3, 4)

In step B, you staff the supply chain construction project, develop the project timeline with milestones, and plan the project budget. This reverse network supply chain construction project might take three or four people about eight months to complete. Besides the expense of staffing the project, the project budget would depend largely upon the necessary investment for the information system, outfitting facilities, and inventory.

Step 1: Write the Network Container SCCRS (Chapters 1, 11)

In step 1, you describe the reverse supply chain network and document the top half of the SCCRS for the network container. The technology company has been in business for several years. It has an installed base of customers, a market reputation for high-performance quality products, the experience of designing and manufacturing two previous product generations, and the warranty expense experience from its earlier product generations. The basic plan is to seed the extended warranty program with new product inventory until the technology company has recovered enough product cores to support a remanufacturing operation. The technology company has no experience with the actual construction of a reverse supply chain network.

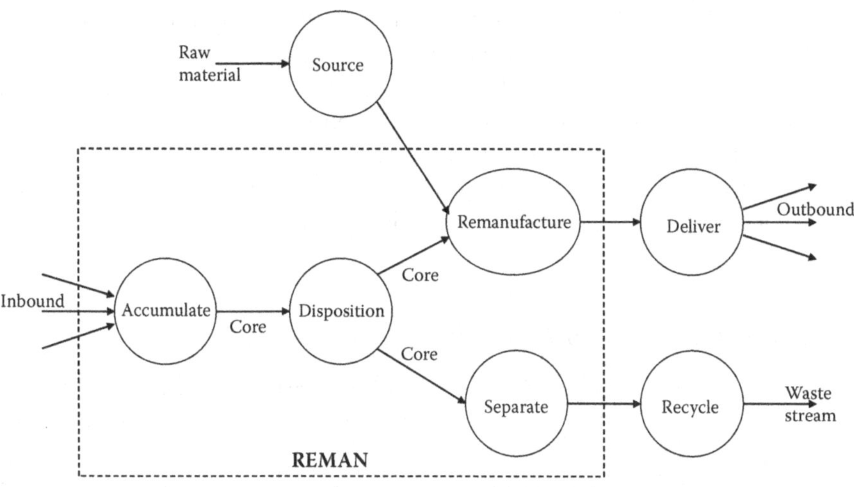

Figure 8.2 Reverse supply chain echelon map for the Tractor Tracker.

To begin documenting the requirements specification, the technology company needs a supply chain echelon map along with an estimate of replacement volumes and remanufacturing costs for the reverse network. These initial ideas and estimates are then refined by iterating the remaining steps of the Supply Chain Construction Blueprint. The iterations are to (1) make it work, (2) make it work well, and (3) make it work in a flexible and risk tolerant manner.

The reverse supply chain echelon map documents the process relationships necessary to remanufacture a Tractor Tracker (see Figure 8.2). Under the proposed business plan, defective product cores are accumulated from all customers, whether or not they have purchased an extended warranty. Each core is dispositioned to be either remanufactured or recycled. Remanufactured cores require a source of certain replacement parts and then distribution to customers with extended warranty. Recycled cores require separation by commodity type and then appropriate, environmentally responsible recycling. The vertical alignment in Figure 8.2 does not represent the final echelons of the reverse network, as the decision to combine processes within a single echelon has not yet been made.

How to Estimate Throughput

Next, throughput and remanufacturing costs need to be estimated. Throughput is a function of the growth of the installed base and the annual failure rate (AFR) of the product. The size of the installed base will grow over time, while the AFR may decrease over time as latent product design problems are identified and resolved within the forward supply chain.

Forecast three-year base of installed product: 25,000 installed units
Expected AFR: 10% or 0.833% per month
Forecast monthly throughput: (25,000 units) × (0.833%) = 208 units per month
Extended warranty pricing: \$5 per unit per month
Expected percentage of customers purchasing extended warranty: 35%
Forecast reverse network revenue: (25,000 units) × (35%) × (\$5 per unit per month) = \$43,750 per month by end of third year

How to Estimate Cash-to-Cash Velocity

Velocity is the mean number of days, positive or negative, of the remanufacturer's cash-to-cash cycle. The remanufacturer plans to hold a month and a half of finished goods, which is 45 days of inventory. The extended warranty is invoiced midmonth with NET45 day terms; therefore, the remanufacturer has 45 days of accounts receivable. Replacement parts and period expenses are paid with NET30 day terms; therefore, the remanufacturer has 30 days of accounts payable. The cash-to-cash velocity is 45 days of inventory plus 45 days of accounts receivable minus 30 days of accounts payable, or a positive 60 days. Step 9 presents a detailed analysis to calculate cash-to-cash velocity and to estimate cash-to-cash variability.

How to Estimate Price/Landed Cost

Remanufacturing costs break down into three buckets. First, there are significant logistics costs for both inbound cores and outbound warranty replacement units. Second, there are replacement material costs. Although the usable material content of a returned core is free, the plastic case and antenna are damaged beyond repair when the enclosure is opened. Other components have a probability of replacement depending on the cause of the defect. For example, water ingression into the enclosure will send the unit to recycling, while defects from excessive tractor shock will send the unit to remanufacturing. Third are the labor and overhead costs to accumulate, disposition, source, remanufacture, deliver, separate, and recycle. The customer pays to remove and reinstall the unit. You will see later that this first pass tends to underestimate the real landed cost.

First-pass logistics costs:	\$25 per unit
First-pass material costs:	\$55 per unit
First-pass labor + overhead costs:	\$56 per unit
Total landed cost:	\$136 per unit

The network container portion of the SCCRS can now be completed (see Table 8.1).

Table 8.1 SCCRS for the REMAN Network Container

Attribute	*Description*		
Network type	Remanufacturing reverse network		
Market segment	Over-the-road fleet logistics in the United States		
Product family	Third-generation Tractor Tracker		
Project objective	We are constructing a reverse network to support fourth and fifth year extended warranty demand with a supply of remanufactured Tractor Trackers.		
Specification	*Value*	*Dimensions*	*Validation*
Throughput	208	Units per month	☐Accept ☐Reject
Cash-to-cash cycle	Velocity +60	Days	☐Accept ☐Reject
Price/landed cost	$136	Dollars per unit	☐Accept ☐Reject
Inventory			
Delivery lead time			
ROIC			

Step 2: Budget Price/Landed Cost End-to-End Echelon by Echelon (Chapters 1, 3, 4)

In step 2, you determine whether or not the number of supply chain echelons can yield profitable margins at the expected throughput. Since the Tractor Tracker Reverse Network is a low-volume operation, you want to leverage from the forward supply chain network as much as possible. You plan to connect with the forward network's source and deliver trading partners. Any replacement part required for the remanufacturer will be the same as a new part. You should be able to get item pricing for the reverse network based on the total annual demand for that item, as it is used in the forward network. Since your customer base for extended warranty is the same as your customer base for new products, it makes sense to use the same distributor network. This can be accomplished by giving the remanufactured Tractor Tracker a different part number. There will be some cores that cannot be salvaged. These cores will be disassembled and their parts separated into commodity streams to be sent to third-party recyclers.

Therefore, there are two material flow inputs: inbound cores and replacement parts. And there are two material flow outputs: outbound remanufactured Tractor Trackers and separated commodities streams for recycling. Estimated cost factors

Table 8.2 Margin Analysis per Unit per Month

Income Statement	*Initial Estimate*	*Iterate Steps 3, 4, 5*	*Explanation*
Revenue			
Extended warranty	$210.34	$210.34	$43,750 Revenue/208 Remanufactured units
Recycled material	$8.00	$1.00	Sell plastic for recycling
Total revenue	$218.34	$211.34	
Cost of Goods Sold (COGS)			
Inbound logistics	$12.00	$14.00	Loose control over inbound cost
Midbound logistics	$8.00	$1.00	Facilities in close proximity
Outbound logistics	$8.00	$7.85	Forward network average
Total logistics	$28.00	$22.85	Total network logistics cost
Core	$0.00	$0.00	Returns
New plastic enclosure	$5.75	$5.75	Enclosure lost upon cutting enclosure open
New antenna	$16.50	$16.50	Antenna lost upon cutting enclosure open
Other parts replaced	$32.75	$31.00	Parts kits from forward network
Total material	$55.00	$53.25	Total direct material cost
Accumulate	$4.00	$4.00	100% × 15 minutes of labor at $16/hour
Disposition	$5.33	$5.33	100% × 20 minutes of labor at $16/hour
60% Remanufacture	$4.80	$4.80	60% × 30 minutes of labor at $16/hour

(*Continued*)

Table 8.2 (Continued) Margin Analysis per Unit per Month

Income Statement	*Initial Estimate*	*Iterate Steps 3, 4, 5*	*Explanation*
40% Separate	$2.13	$2.13	40% × 20 minutes of labor at $16/hour
Total direct labor	$16.26	$16.26	Total direct labor cost
Purchasing overhead	$4.00	$4.00	Remanufacturing purchasing
Operations overhead	$8.50	$8.50	Remanufacturing operations
Rent and utilities	$27.50	$27.50	Remanufacturing facility
Total overhead	$40.00	$40.00	Total remanufacturing overhead
Distribution	$15.00	$14.75	DC cost to distribute through forward network
Recycling	$20.00	$20.00	Waste transport and recycling fees
Total deliver	$35.00	$34.75	
Total REMAN COGS	$174.26	$167.11	Remanufactured product COGS
Gross Margin			
Gross margin	$44.08	$44.23	

for the remaining reverse network organizations are shown in the margin analysis of Table 8.2 supposing that 60% of the cores go to the remanufacturer and 40% of the cores go to the recyclers. The point of the margin analysis is to see if you have acceptable margins before continuing. This plan looks workable. It will be refined with more detail following steps 3, 4, and 5. For example, the actual revenue from recycled plastic turns out to be just a fraction of its initial estimate.

Step 3: Start with Remanufacturer-to-Midbound-to-Distributor Material Flow (Chapters 5, 7)

In step 3, you choose the separator and remanufacturing organizations and their locations and the transportation mode for midbound logistics. Referring again to Figure 8.2, the Tractor Tracker reverse supply chain echelon map has two distinct make-to-deliver relationships. One is remanufacture-to-deliver for the remanufactured product. The other is separate-to-recycle for recycled commodities.

The separator and remanufacture organizations can be located within the same facility, along with the accumulate and disposition organizations discussed later. This can all be considered as a single echelon. This facility should be located to optimize the tradeoff between logistics costs and direct labor costs. With the forward network distribution center (DC) located in Allentown, Pennsylvania, the question becomes, where is the best location for the remanufacturing facility among Allentown, Atlanta, Chicago, or Oakland? Table 8.3 shows a very simplified location optimization analysis based on a total annual throughput of 2,500 units split 30% in the East, 45% in the Midwest, and 25% in the West. Road mileages are based on http://www.google.com/maps and labor rates are based on state mean wage estimates for 51-2022 electrical and electronic equipment assemblers found on the Bureau of Labor Statistics website (http://www.bls.gov). A total of 2,500 units of throughput at an estimated 61 minutes per unit equal 2,542 hours. The actual weight of a unit and the average dollars per ton-mile are necessary to dollarize the unit-mile calculations. Equation 8.1 is used to calculate the ton-miles for each of the three inbound and the one outbound logistics segments in Table 8.3.

$$\text{Ton-miles} = \frac{(\text{Annual volume}) \times (\text{Pounds/unit}) \times (\%\text{Split by customer}) \times (\text{Road distance})}{(2{,}000 \text{ pounds per ton})} \quad (8.1)$$

The logistics cost total is added to the direct labor cost total, and the scenario with the minimum total cost is selected. Since the difference in labor rates across the four scenarios is only $0.66/hour, about 4%, the difference in annual unit-miles dominates this decision. While a more detailed analysis of actual customer locations may yield a different result, Table 8.3 suggests that scenario 1 is best with the remanufacturer located close to the forward network DC in Allentown, Pennsylvania. The midbound logistics cost to connect the remanufacturer with the DC is then minimal. The selection criteria shown in Table 8.4 are now used to select an actual facility.

Step 4: Detail the Supply Base-to-Inbound-to-Remanufacturer Material Flow (Chapter 6)

In step 4, you determine supply base relationships and inbound logistics connections. The Tractor Tracker reverse supply chain echelon map has two material inputs: the accumulation of defective cores from the field and the supply of new component parts to replace those found to be defective. The list of potential replacement parts is essentially the entire BOM for the product. As described later, each item in the product's item master is assigned a probability for replacement. This is the probability that when the core is inspected, each component is found

Table 8.3 Optimal Remanufacturer Facility Location

		Inbound	*Outbound*	*Logistics*	*Direct Labor*
Scenario 1					
Distributor	Allentown, Pennsylvania			Total: 3,202,500 unit-miles	$15.38/hour × 2,542 hours = $39,096
Remanufacture	Allentown, Pennsylvania		100% × 0 miles		
30% Customer	Atlanta, Georgia	30% × 800 miles			
45% Customer	Chicago, Illinois	45% × 730 miles			
25% Customer	Oakland, California	25% × 2,850 miles			
Scenario 2					
Distributor	Allentown, Pennsylvania			Total: 4,362,500 unit-miles	$15.90/hour × 2,542 hours = $40,418
Remanufacture	Atlanta, Georgia		100% × 800 miles		
30% Customer	Atlanta, Georgia	30% × 0 miles			
45% Customer	Chicago, Illinois	45% × 700 miles			
25% Customer	Oakland, California	25% × 2,520 miles			

(*Continued*)

Table 8.3 (Continued) Optimal Remanufacturer Facility Location

		Inbound	*Outbound*	*Logistics*	*Direct Labor*
Scenario 3					
Distributor	Allentown, Pennsylvania			Total: 3,675,500 unit-miles	\$15.24/hour × 2,542 hours = \$38,740
Remanufacture	Chicago, Illinois		100% × 730 miles		
30% Customer	Atlanta, Georgia	30% × 700 miles			
45% Customer	Chicago, Illinois	45% × 0 miles			
25% Customer	Oakland, California	25% × 2,120 miles			
Scenario 4					
Distributor	Allentown, Pennsylvania			Total: 11,400,500 unit-miles	\$15.35/hour × 2,542 hours = \$39,020
Remanufacture	Oakland, California		100% × 2850 miles		
30% Customer	Atlanta, Georgia	30% × 2,520 miles			
45% Customer	Chicago, Illinois	45% × 2,120 miles			
25% Customer	Oakland, California	25% × 0 miles			

Table 8.4 Selection Criteria for the Remanufacturer

Priority	*Criteria*	*Validation*	*Value*
Must 1	Requirements specification: transformation capability	1. Remanufacture processes? 2. The right commodity expertise?	Yes Light electronics
Must 2	Requirements specification: landed cost at volume	1. Logistics costs driven by location? 2. Driven by labor costs?	Mileage centroid <$16/hour
Must 3	Requirements specification: throughput capacity	1. Your volume of their throughput? 2. Any constraints to doubling growth?	208 units/ month No
Want	Management team	1. Financial track record? 2. Experience in risk management?	Yes Yes
Want	Flexibility	1. Can respond easily to mix change? 2. Can respond easily to rate change?	High probability High probability
Want	Engineering support	1. Sustainability engineering? 2. Process engineering?	Yes Yes
Want	Information systems	1. Information completeness? 2. Can handle serialized product?	Yes Yes
Want	Inventory management	1. Perpetual inventory accounting? 2. Product separation by revision?	Yes Yes

to be reusable to remanufacture the product. Aside from the plastic enclosure and internal antenna, which must be replaced 100% of the time, the result is a very-low-volume, high-mix replacement parts inventory profile. An economical approach to sourcing a low volume of replacement parts is for the reverse network to buy a small number of complete part kits from the forward network. Then, after some experience determining which core parts are being found defective with higher rates of incidence, the reverse network can establish direct relationships with just the appropriate forward network suppliers. The reverse network should be able to leverage component pricing agreements established by the forward network with these suppliers.

The accumulate and disposition organizations are colocated in the same facility with the remanufacture and separate organizations. The front end of the reverse network must begin an immediate sortation process feeding into disposition. Customers will return a product in all manner of packaging, sometimes causing additional damage to the cores. Different generations and different serialization of the Tractor Tracker will be accumulated. The product will be received sometimes with cabling and sometimes with metal brackets attached. It will be difficult to read labels because of the dirt and grime from being used in the field. Sometimes, unrelated products and components and truck parts will be returned. The cubic volume and shelving available to hold returns at the input of the accumulator should be kept flexible, as returns are often batched by customers and arrive unexpectedly in waves. There must be a strict first-in, first-out processing of all returns so that earlier arrivals do not get lost later in a big pile of junk.

The reverse network is paying the inbound freight costs because the reverse network needs the source of cores to keep operational. You will want to put firm controls on inbound freight; otherwise, it will rapidly get out of control and devour your profit margin. One approach to control inbound freight costs is to assign a transportation mode, carrier, bill of lading, and prepaid freight account plus print a "ship to" label at the time the customer requests the return authorization. Since the accumulate organization is in nearly the same location as the forward supply chain DC, and since returns customers are one-in-the-same as forward path customers, the inbound routes from customers to the accumulation site can parallel the outbound routes from the DC to the customer.

Step 5: Detail Remanufacturer-to-Outbound-to-Delivery Channel Material Flow (Chapter 7)

In step 5, you determine the aftermarket and recycling relationships and outbound logistics connections. The Tractor Tracker reverse supply chain echelon map has two material outputs: the delivery of remanufactured product for warranty replacement and the delivery of separated waste streams to third-party recyclers. Delivery of the remanufactured product is straightforward. A different stock-keeping unit (SKU) number is assigned to the remanufactured product and set up within the DC of the forward network. The reverse network remanufacturer forwards its product output to the input of the forward network DC at a minimal midbound logistics cost.

After a core is dispositioned, the separator organization receives cores deemed to be unfit for remanufacture. The separator disassembles these units into discrete commodity waste streams: plastic from enclosures, printed circuit assemblies, copper from copper wire, etc. When a printed circuit assembly is in good shape and without water damage, it may be possible to use special equipment and electrostatic discharge safeguards to carefully remove high-value components, like radios and microprocessor chips, for reuse. There is a different cost to transport and recycle each type of commodity waste stream. There may be some revenue opportunity in selling certain commodities; this depends on the commodity, the volume of material being recycled, and the purity of the separation. Table 8.5 shows a high-level BOM for the Tractor Tracker mapped into its possible commodity recycling streams. Plastic from 100% of the returned enclosures appears to be the greatest opportunity for a recycled material revenue stream. It is estimated that only 5% of the wiring harness copper gets returned as the head unit can be replaced without touching the wiring harness. While the volumes of the other commodities are too low to generate any real revenue, there is a cost to recycle them.

Table 8.6 lists selection criteria for the plastics recycler. The main focus is due diligence on risk management regarding recycling. The recycler that is chosen must be one that is established and financially stable and follows environmental and labor laws. In this scenario, your volume is too small to influence any change in the way the recycler does business.

Step 6: Add Any Service Element (Chapter 7)

In step 6, you add any service that the reverse network delivers to complement the product. Some customers have made internal information system investments to match equipment serial numbers to internal company operational statistics and performance measures. These customers prefer to have replacement equipment shipped with a serial number that is identical to the serial number on the defective unit under warranty. As a service to the customer, at the customer's request, the remanufacturer can transfer the original serial number from a defective core to the remanufactured replacement unit. This becomes a new requirement for the remanufacturer's information system. However, the remanufacturer needs some mechanism to track the timing of such a serial number reassignment. The warranty clock, started when the original unit first shipped, is not reset when the same serial number is reassigned to a replacement unit. Otherwise, the extended five-year warranty would effectively become a perpetual warranty.

Table 8.5 Recycling Drivers for Commodity Waste Streams

BOM Level	*Commodity*	*Qty Per*	*Recycle Plastic*	*Recycle Copper*	*Recycle PC Board*	*Recycle Electronics*
0.	Head unit	1				
..1	Enclosure	1	100%			
..1	Printed circuit assembly	1			×	
....2	Cellular radio	1				×
....2	GPS radio	1				×
....2	GPS antenna	1				
....2	Microprocessor	1				×
....2	Memory	1				×
....2	Other electronics	25				×
......3	Printed circuit board	1			×	
..1	Cellular antenna	1				100%
0.	Wiring harness	1		5%		

Step 7: Connect Demand Broadcast Information with Material Flow and Test (Chapters 7, 9)

In step 7, you match the information flows to replenish inventory with the material flows and test each connection. The Tractor Tracker Reverse Network ships the replacement product under warranty from its shipping buffer at the forward network DC. The disposition organization is the network constraint, as it takes successive attempts and variable amounts of time to identify the good cores out of all the accumulated cores. Table 8.7 describes how the demand signal flows from the customer's RMA order in parallel to the shipping buffer and to the network constraint in the disposition organization. A constrained demand signal is then broadcast by the network constraint in parallel to the remanufacturer organization, the accumulate organization, and external suppliers. The customer is reminded of the obligation to return the defective core along with its RMA number.

Table 8.6 Selection Criteria for the Plastics Recycler

Priority	*Criteria*	*Validation*	*Numerical Value*
Must 1	Revenue potential exceeds landed cost	1. Price offered? 2. Minimum weight per sale? 3. Transportation cost?	Net positive revenue
Must 2	Recycler meets all environmental regulations	1. Federal regulations? 2. State regulations? 3. Clean water, clean air? 4. HAZMAT certified?	Evidence provided
Must 3	Recycler meets all employee safety regulations	1. OSHA? 2. Child Labor Laws?	Evidence provided
Want	Receipt documentation	1. Documented/dated proof of received weight and quantity for recycling? 2. Title to material transferred?	Yes
Want	Geographical proximity	1. Minimize logistics cost? 2. Recycler provides pickup?	Yes
Want	Payment terms	1. NET30 day payment?	Yes
Want	Flexibility and responsiveness	1. Can respond easily to change in pickups?	Yes

Step 8: Connect Request for Payment with Cash Payments and Test (Chapters 4, 7)

In step 8, you match requests for payment information flow with its respective payment cash flow and test each connection. There is a request for payment information-to-cash loop for each seller–buyer interface in the network. The sequencing of the request for payment information-to-cash loops will be somewhat different from the sequencing of the demand broadcast information-to-material loops. Table 8.8 details each of the seller/buyer interfaces with the REMAN organization. REMAN is the name of the reverse network trading partner, which, in this case, includes the accumulate, disposition, remanufacture, and separate organizations. That is, the four organizations exist as a single echelon and do not pass along cash with each inventory transaction. Rather, the REMAN echelon is a black box that only buys and sells with other external reverse network organizations.

Table 8.7 Reverse Network Demand Broadcast Information-to-Material Loops

Step	*Order Sent from*	*Order Sent to*	*Inventory Action*
Seed Inventory			
0	Forward distributor	Forward factory	Seed inventory with new Tractor Trackers
Demand Information Flow for Remanufactured Unit			
1	Customer RMA order	1A. Forward DC 1B. Network constraint	Ship Tractor Tracker(s) from stock Send good core(s) to remanufacture Send bad core(s) to separate
2	Demand broadcast from the network constraint (disposition)	2A. Remanufacture 2B. External suppliers 2C. Accumulate	Replenish forward DC inventory Source component(s) to remanufacture Release core(s) to disposition
3	Accumulate	Customer	Reminder to customers to return defective unit against the RMA number
Demand Information Flow for Recycling Commodities			
4	Separate	Recycler(s)	Accumulating commodities trigger pickup orders to recyclers

Step 9: Detail the REMAN Steady-State Cash-to-Cash Cycle (Chapter 4)

In step 9, you analyze the steady-state cash-to-cash cycle velocity and variability for the remanufacturer. The Tractor Tracker Reverse Network has the following peculiarities in its cash-to-cash cycle.

Table 8.8 Reverse Network Request for Payment Information-to-Cash Loops

Action	*Payment Information Flow*	*Cash Flow*	*Reason*
Sell	Factory invoices distributor	Distributor pays factory	Seed initial warranty inventory with new product.
Sell	REMAN invoices customer	Customer pays REMAN	Monthly extended warranty revenue. This periodic payment is not tied to material flow.
Sell	REMAN invoices customer	Customer pays REMAN	Payment for replacement product when core not returned.
Sell	REMAN invoices distributor	Distributor pays REMAN	Remanufactured warranty inventory. This may be a zero dollar transfer payment.
Sell	REMAN invoices recycler	Recycler pays REMAN	Sales of plastic for recycling.
Buy	Distributor invoices REMAN	REMAN pays distributor	Monthly distribution services for remanufactured product.
Buy	Supplier(s) invoice REMAN	REMAN pays supplier(s)	Replacement parts for cores.
Buy	Recycler(s) invoice REMAN	REMAN pays recycler(s)	Payment for recycling services.
Buy	Carrier(s) invoice REMAN	REMAN pays carrier(s)	Payment for logistics services.

- The timing of the revenue generated from monthly extended warranty invoicing is independent of the timing of any product inventory receipt and issue events.
- The cash-to-cash velocity is the combination of 80% of payments issued by day 30, 99% of revenue received by day 45, and 20% of payments issued by day 60 as shown in Table 8.9.
- The majority of accumulated cores are received against an RMA. However, a number of cores are just returned from customers who have not purchased

Table 8.9 The REMAN Steady-State Cash-to-Cash Velocity and Variability

Item	*Velocity*	*Variability*	*Sell/Buy*	*Monthly Cash Flow*
1	45 days	±5 days	99% sell	Extended warranty
2	90 days		1% sell	Plastic for recycling
3	30 days	±3 days	32% buy	Replacement parts inventory
4	30 days	±3 days	16% buy	Inbound, midbound, and outbound logistics
5	30 days	±3 days	32% buy	REMAN labor and overhead
6	60 days		9% buy	Distribution services
7	60 days		11% buy	Recycling services
8	52 days	±15 days		Inventory holding period

Days of Inventory = 52 days (see step 15)

$$\text{Days of Receivables} = \frac{99\% \times 45\text{ days} + 1\% \times 90\text{ days}}{100\%} = 45.4\text{ days}$$

$$\text{Days of Payables} = \frac{80\% \times 30\text{ days} + 20\% \times 60\text{ days}}{100\%} = 36\text{ days}$$

From Equation 4.5: Cash-to-Cash Velocity = 52 days + 45.4 days − 36 days = +61.4 days

Cash-to-Cash Variability = 52 ± 15 days + 45 ± 5 days − 36 ± 3 days = +61 ± 9.3 days

$$\text{RMS Series Variability} = \sqrt{\frac{((15)^2 + (5)^2 + (3)^2)}{3}} = 9.3\text{ days}$$

an extended warranty. These unauthorized returns do not add to warranty revenue, but they can add significantly to processing and recycle expense.

- Reverse networks experience significantly higher cash-to-cash variability than forward networks. This is because throughput can become constrained by lumpy demand and/or a complete lack of cores and because material flow is intentionally batched in an attempt to minimize logistics costs.

Table 8.9 details the steady-state cash-to-cash cycle for the remanufacturer. The customer is invoiced for extended warranty on the 15th of the month under NET45 day terms.

Step 10: Plot a Value Circle to Validate Network Container Performance Measures (Chapter 11)

In step 10, you plot the top half of the Value Circle related to the network container. This includes supply chain performance for throughput, cash-to-cash velocity, landed cost, and cash-to-cash variability. You are looking to validate the Tractor Tracker Network container construction by answering these three questions: Can your choice of REMAN network relationships maintain the required throughput? Can you operate the end-to-end network profitably? Can you predict the cash-to-cash cycle velocity for the REMAN echelon and understand its probable variability? Figure 8.3 shows the partial Value Circle associated with the network container SCCRS of Table 8.1. The unit circle represents the first set of estimates; each axis of the Value Circle improves moving toward the origin.

Throughput is achievable at 208 units/month, with the relationships established in steps 3, 4, and 5. The more careful cost analysis completed in step 2 shows a still profitable landed cost/unit of $167 versus the first estimate of $136. The cash-to-cash analysis completed in step 9 shows a positive 61.4 days of velocity with 9.3 days of variability. The supply chain construction of a workable network container is now complete.

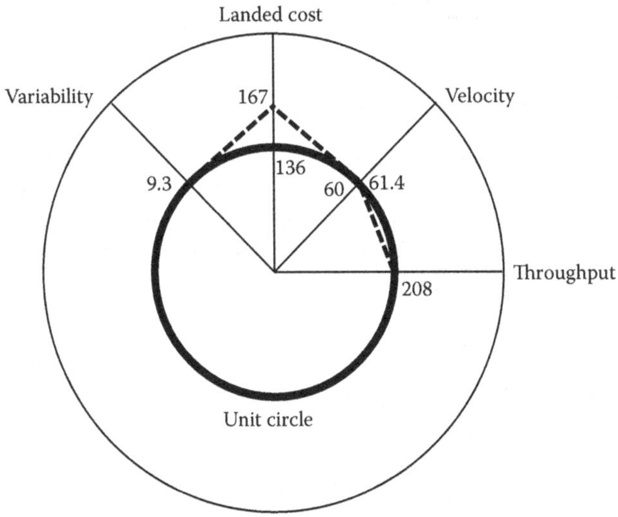

Figure 8.3 Value Circle for the Tractor Tracker reverse network container.

Step 11: Write the Product Contents SCCRS (Chapters 1, 11)

In step 11, you complete the bottom half of the SCCRS related to filling the network container with the product contents. The Tractor Tracker is a single product with potentially several different hardware and firmware revisions. The exact revision needs to be determined and isolated between the time of accumulation and the time of disposition.

Demand for warranty replacements in the fourth and fifth years is expected to be lumpy. The push/pull boundary is the remanufactured finished goods inventory location within REMAN. There is a demand forecast for accumulated cores pushed through disposition to remanufacture. There is also a second component-by-component forecast for the probability of returned core components being good. Replacement parts are pushed into remanufacture based on this second forecast. Stocking orders from the distributor pulls remanufactured finished goods inventory out of REMAN. Small quantities of the remanufactured product can be shipped immediately from the shipping buffer. Disposition is expected to be the network constraint. This is because a shortage of good cores will constrain returned material and/or limited technical labor hours will constrain capacity.

The separate-to-recycle path is operated asynchronously. Bad cores are delivered to the separate queue. Separate works until a given commodity stream accumulates enough weight and volume to trigger an economical transport and recycle purchase. Then, a recycle pickup is scheduled. In addition, recycle pickups are scheduled twice a year for every commodity regardless of their accumulated weight and volume. This is to ensure that returns cast into some dark corner of the facility do not hang around for years and years.

How to Determine Inventory Value

There are nine inventory locations to be valued within the accumulate, disposition, remanufacture, distribute, and separate organizations (see Figure 8.4). These include the push/pull boundary in remanufacture and the shipping buffer in distribute. Cost factors from step 2 plus lot sizes and other details from step 15 are used to value each inventory location.

- *Accumulate*—Core returns are counted but carried at zero book value. This is because the value of any given core has not yet been determined.

$$\text{Average accumulate inventory} = \$0$$

- *Disposition*—Core returns are counted but carried at zero book value. As soon as a core is determined to be good, it is given a different part number.

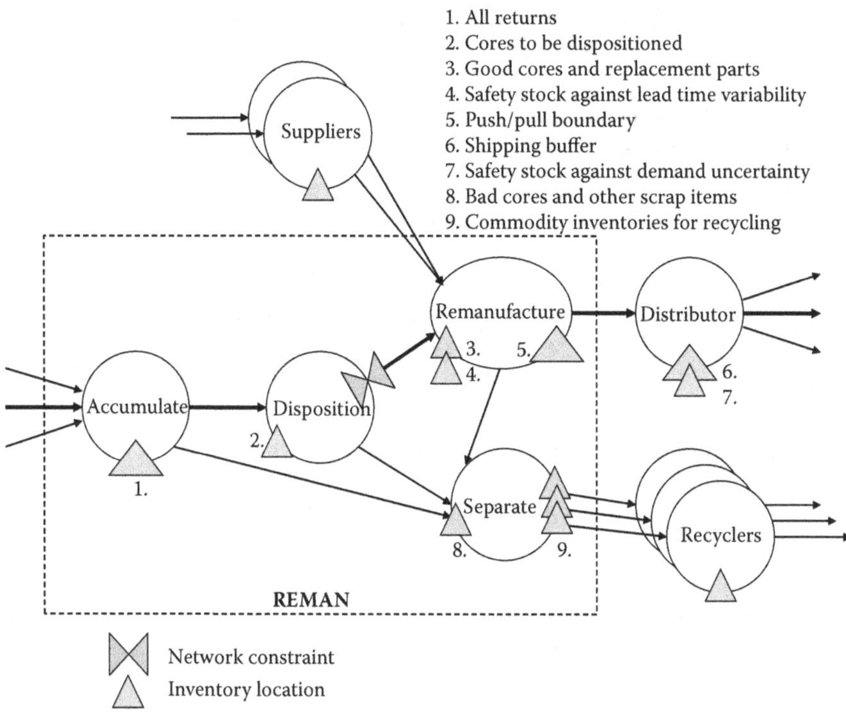

Figure 8.4 Tractor Tracker reverse network inventory locations.

However, a good core adds $0.00 of material cost to the cost of goods sold (COGS) for a remanufactured Tractor Tracker.

Average disposition inventory = $0

- *Remanufacture good cores*—Good cores at the front end of the remanufacturing process are counted but carried at zero book value.

Average remanufacture good core inventory = $0

- *Remanufacture components including safety stock*—Replacement raw materials and component parts plus safety stock against supply lead time variability are valued in dollars at their material cost.

Average remanufacture raw material inventory
= (1/2) × (354 units) × ($53.25 parts) = $9,425

Average remanufacture safety stock inventory
= (57 units) × ($53.25 parts) = $3,035

- *Remanufacture push/pull boundary*—The remanufactured product is valued in dollars at COGS. Average remanufacture push/pull inventory = (1/2) × (354 units) × ($167.11 COGS) = $29,578.
- *Distributor shipping buffer*—Remanufactured product is valued in dollars at COGS.

Average distributor shipping buffer inventory
= (1/2) × (224 units) × ($167.11 COGS) = $18,716

- *Distributor safety stock*—Remanufactured product safety stock against demand uncertainty is valued in dollars at COGS.

Average distributor safety stock inventory
= (24 units) × ($167.11 COGS) = $4,011

- *Separate bad cores*—Bad cores sent to recycling are counted but carried at zero book value.

Average separate inventory = $0

- *Separate commodity waste streams for recycling*—Commodity waste streams separated for recycling pickup are counted but carried at zero book value.

Average separate commodity waste stream inventory = $0

The total network inventory is valued at $64,765 with 7.0 inventory turns.

$$\textit{Inventory turns} = \frac{\text{2,500 Units annual throughput}}{\text{354 Units in push/pull boundary}} = 7.0 \text{ turns}$$

How to Estimate Delivery Lead Time

Delivery lead time is the time from when the customer requests an RMA until the customer receives the warranty replacement Tractor Tracker. Since replacement units are always in stock, delivery lead time is dominated by the outbound logistics time to the customer's location. With the distributor located in Allentown, Pennsylvania, delivery lead time is estimated to be two to five days depending on the customer's location. The shipping buffer at the distributor is replenished from the push/pull boundary at the remanufacturer. The replenishment lead time is three days. Vocalize is the lead time to pull inventory from the push/pull boundary and deliver it to the customer; in this reverse supply chain, it is the delivery lead time plus the replenishment lead time, or a total of five to eight days. Visualize is the planning horizon to push inventory to the push/pull boundary. The planning horizon is the longest cumulative path through the Tractor Tracker BOM for any item. It is estimated at 175 days to cover long lead time parts such as memory and the cellular radio.

How to Estimate Return on Invested Capital

Return on invested capital (ROIC) combines the profit after taxes from the income statement with the inventory, production capacity assets, accounts receivable assets, and accounts payable liabilities from the balance sheet. The following steps give an approximate estimate of ROIC for the REMAN organization:

1. Estimate the monthly profit after tax as 1/4 × Gross Margin = (1/4) × (208 units) × (\$44.23) = \$2,300

   The 1/4 factor comes from gross margin divided among sales, general, and administrative (SG&A), interest expense, taxes, and profit. (Note: Use an actual figure for monthly profit after tax once it is known. Until that time, when making comparison calculations, be consistent with the 1/4 factor for monthly profit after tax and with the value of production capacity assets.)
2. Dollarize the average inventory for REMAN. This does not include inventory at the distributor.

   \$42,038 from the above analysis.
3. Compute accounts receivable as one month of annual revenue from extended warranty purchased on a fraction of the installed base = \$43,750.
4. Compute accounts payable as one month of COGS on replacement units = (208 units) × (\$167.11) = \$34,759.
5. Suppose production capacity assets are valued at \$200,000.

   (Note: Use an actual figure for the value of production capacity assets once it is known. Until that time, when making comparison calculations, be consistent with the 1/4 factor for monthly profit after tax and with the value of production capacity assets.)
6. Calculate ROIC for REMAN using Equation 1.2:

$$\text{ROIC} = \frac{\$\text{After tax profit/month} \times 12 \text{ months} \times 100\%}{\$\text{Inventory} + \$\text{Production capacity assets} + \$\text{Accounts receivable} - \$\text{Accounts payable}}$$

$$\text{ROIC} = \frac{\$2{,}300 \times 12 \times 100\%}{\$42{,}038 + \$200{,}000 + \$43{,}750 - \$34{,}759} = 11.0\%$$

Table 8.10 SCCRS for the REMAN Product Contents

Attribute	*Description*		
Network type	Remanufacturing reverse network		
Market segment	Over-the-road fleet logistics in the United States		
Product family	Third-generation Tractor Tracker		
Project objective	We are constructing a reverse network to support fourth- and fifth-year extended warranty demand with a supply of remanufactured Tractor Trackers.		
Specification	*Value*	*Dimensions*	*Validation*
Throughput	208	Units per month	X Accept
Cash-to-cash cycle	Velocity +61 Variability ±9.3	Days Days	X Accept
Price/landed cost	$167	Dollars per unit	X Accept
Inventory	$64,765 7.0	Dollars Turns	☐Accept ☐Reject
Delivery lead time	Delivery LT = 2 to 5 Vocalize = 5 to 8 Visualize = 175	Days based on location Days based on location Days	☐Accept ☐Reject
ROIC	11.0	Percentage	☐Accept ☐Reject

The product contents portion of the requirements specification is now complete (see Table 8.10).

Step 12: Decide the Operating Strategy and Locate the Push/Pull Boundary (Chapter 9)

In step 12, you decide the operating strategy, locate the push/pull boundary inventory location, and identify the network constraint to achieve a competitive delivery lead time. The Tractor Tracker Reverse Network is operated under a build-to-stock operating strategy. Warranty replacement units must be immediately available when customers place their RMA requests. An inventory of the remanufactured product is kept in the shipping buffer at the forward network distributor. The remanufactured finished goods inventory at the remanufacturer is the push/pull boundary. A forecast for warranty replacement demand pushes inventory to the push/pull boundary. The distributor's replenishment order pulls inventory from the push/pull boundary. The shipping buffer keeps a small safety stock to protect against demand uncertainty, and the remanufacturer's component inventory keeps a small safety stock to protect against supply lead time variability. Both the remanufacturer's component inventory and its safety stock include quantities of good cores protecting the remanufacturer against supply variability in the accumulation, disposition, and current yields of cores returned from the field.

Since Tractor Tracker warranty replacement units are shipped from the forward network distributor, the delivery lead time seen by the customer is the sum of RMA processing time plus cycle stock pick and pack time at the distributor plus outbound logistics transit time. The replenishment lead time seen by the distributor is the sum of the replenishment order processing time plus remanufactured finished goods pick and pack time at remanufacture plus midbound logistics transit time.

$$\text{Delivery LT}_{\text{Customer}} = \text{RMA processing time} + \text{Pick/pack time}_{\text{Distributor}} + \text{Outbound transit time} \quad (8.2)$$

$$\text{Replenish LT}_{\text{Distributor}} = \text{Order processing time} + \text{Pick/pack time}_{\text{REMAN}} + \text{Midbound transit time} \quad (8.3)$$

The disposition organization is the network constraint, as shown in Figure 8.4. Network constraints can be caused by material shortages, skilled labor shortages, or machine hour shortages. When customers fail to return their defective products, the disposition organization can run out of cores. When core returns show multiple issues that are difficult to diagnose or show a mix of product revision levels, the number of skilled labor hours available in disposition may not yield a sufficient quantity of good cores. Tractor Tracker Reverse Network throughput is tied directly to the number of cores that REMAN can process.

Another artificially introduced constraint can be the customer batching of returns to save on logistics costs. When a customer requests an RMA, a warranty replacement is shipped immediately; the customer has 30 days to return their defective unit before getting invoiced. The customer may decide to wait 25 days to see if anything else fails, then batch units in a single return shipment. This can become an issue for REMAN because there is no return material flow for 25 days, and then a bulk quantity overwhelms the accumulate and disposition organizations with all manner of returns including unrelated junk. For instance, friends at a Hewlett-Packard Service Center tell the story of receiving Apple Laser printers and an unmarked box with eight complete table settings of dinner plates, cups, saucers, and soup bowls as typical customer returns.

Step 13: Compile the Composite BOM (Chapters 6, 10)

In step 13, you compile the composite BOM item master and map the instance of each part number across end-to-end supply chain inventory locations. There are four separate SKU numbers for (1) cores awaiting disposition, (2) bad cores, (3) good cores, and (4) remanufactured Tractor Tracker product. There is also a SKU for a kit containing a complete set of lower-level core replacement parts. Since value-adding and value-subtracting transformations occur in the remanufacture and separate organizations, these two have two inventory locations each: one location for material input and a second location for material output. The remanufacturer organization rebuilds product (output) from good cores and other components (input). The separate organization disassembles bad cores (input) into commodity waste streams for recycling (output). Table 8.11 details the composite BOM across the Tractor Tracker Reverse Network.

Step 14: Forecast Demand (Chapter 9)

In step 14, you forecast the demand to push inventory into the push/pull boundary. Demand planning is especially difficult for a reverse supply chain because each forecast has three parts. Returns first consist of some mix of [cores of different revision] or [noncores], then second [good and repairable cores] or [bad cores to recycling], and third [good cores with good parts] or [good cores requiring replacement parts]. Expect each of these three splits to be dynamic over time. Of course, the criteria for a good core and for good components must be well documented and understood.

- *Forecast the rate of returns*—The rate of return is a function of the quantity of product in the installed base, the field failure rate of the product, the product's warranty period, the percentage of customers purchasing an extended warranty, and the sense of customer urgency to return defective units.
- *Forecast the yield of good cores versus bad cores*—The yield of good cores depends upon the field failure mode, the training of the technicians working in the disposition organization, and the reliability and repeatability of the equipment used to sort the core inventory.
- *Forecast the probability that each part in a good core is a good part*—100% good parts on a given core depends upon the customer's application of the product and its failure mechanism. For example, does "no trouble found" mean that the core is good and the customer did not understand how to use the product, or does it mean the product has a latent design defect and the customer is correct?

Table 8.11 The Tractor Tracker Reverse Network Composite BOM

Item	*Accumulate*	*Disposition*	*Remanufacture*	*Separate*
Core awaiting disposition	In Out	In		
Good core		Out	In	
Bad core		Out		In
Rebuilt Tractor Tracker			Out	
Enclosure			In	
Plastic for recycling				Out
Printed circuit assembly			In	
PC assembly for recycling				In Out
Cellular radio			In	
Cellular antenna			In	
GPS radio			In	
GPS antenna			In	
Microprocessor			In	
Memory			In	
Other electronics			In	
Electronics for recycling				Out
Printed circuit board			In	
Replacement parts kit			In	

Two different revisions of the third-generation Tractor Tracker are forecast in Table 8.12. Revision A was released to production with a design defect that surfaced later in the field. Revision A's field failure rate is still on the rise. Revision B is newly released; its field failure rate is declining as the installed base of revision B product continues to grow. A good revision A core can be converted to a good revision B core with the addition of three parts and a firmware upgrade. Table 8.12 shows a six-month forecast for product returns, good cores, and known replacement parts issues. The forecast for good cores is also the forecast that drives the product remanufacture. Some of the product returns are not covered by warranty and will not need replacements. However, if the good core/REMAN product forecast line cannot meet the replacement demand, then new Tractor Trackers will have to be sent out as replacements.

The RevA to RevB conversion kit forecast brings the Gen3.RevA good cores up to the Gen3.RevB design. Part 1 and part 2 are components that have shown a historically high component failure rate on good cores. In addition, a particular customer wants a Gen3.RevB upgrade made to 75 of their units to be done in April.

Table 8.12 Tractor Tracker Core Six-Month Demand Forecast

Product Return Forecast	*Jan*	*Feb*	*Mar*	*Apr*	*May*	*June*
Tractor Tracker—Gen3.RevA	285	292	311	321	330	337
Tractor Tracker—Gen3.RevB	60	60	54	54	50	50
Product total	345	352	365	375	380	387
Good Core Forecast	*Jan*	*Feb*	*Mar*	*Apr*	*May*	*June*
Good cores/REMAN product—60%	207	211	219	225	228	232
Bad cores—40%	138	141	146	150	152	155
Core total	345	352	365	375	380	387
Replacement Parts Forecast	*Jan*	*Feb*	*Mar*	*Apr*	*May*	*June*
Replacement enclosure	207	211	219	225	228	232
Replacement antenna	207	211	219	225	228	232
RevA to RevB conversion kit	171	175	187	268	198	202
Complete parts kit	40	40	40	40	40	40
Part 1 (historical)	75	86	67	77	88	69
Part 2 (historical)	31	31	30	30	30	28

Step 15: Budget Inventory Echelon by Echelon (Chapters 1, 3, 10)

In step 15, you budget inventory across the supply chain network by determining the lot size, reorder point, inventory turns, and safety stock for each inventory item at each inventory location echelon by echelon. Figure 8.5 shows the Tractor Tracker Reverse Network inventory locations focused on core inventory: all returns, good cores, remanufactured cores, and remanufactured finished goods. The table below each inventory location in Figure 8.5 specifies the method used to calculate lot size, inventory turns, reorder point, and safety stock. The starting point is the annual demand estimate of 2,500 units/year.

Ordering Cost and Inventory Holding Cost Estimates

- *Ordering cost*
  From Table 8.2, REMAN purchasing overhead is $4.00 per unit per month, or nearly $10,000 per year. If the REMAN organization processes 200 orders per year, then the ordering cost is $50.00 per order.
- *Inventory holding cost*
  From Table 8.2, REMAN rent and utilities is $27.50 per unit per month, or $68,640 per year. Suppose the remanufacturing operation requires stocking 32 replacement parts.

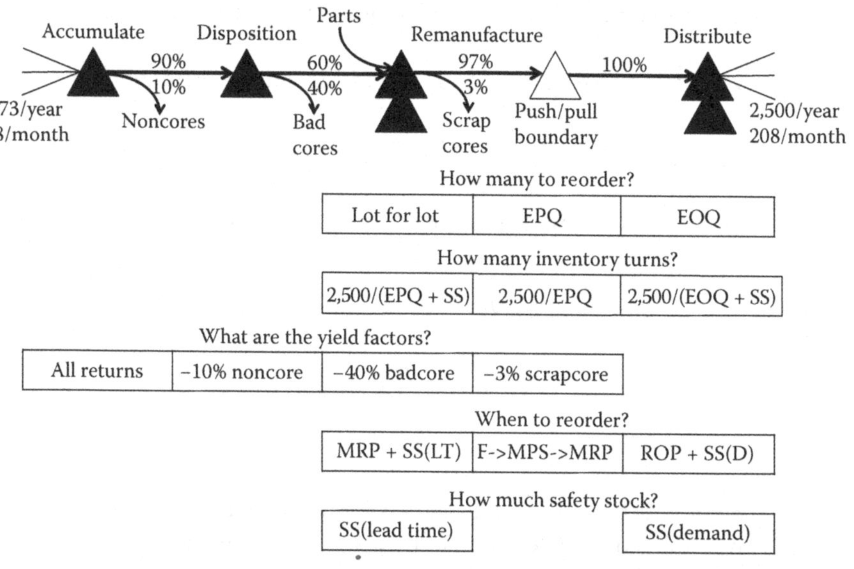

Figure 8.5 Tractor Tracker Reverse Network inventory parameter calculations.

(411 units of good core inventory + safety stock) × (1 item)
= 411 unit-items

(411 units of component part inventory + safety stock) × (32 items)
= 13,152 unit-items

(354 units of remanufactured finished goods) × (1 item)
= 354 unit-items

Total = 13,917 unit-items

$$\text{Holding cost} = \frac{\$68{,}640 \text{ per year}}{13{,}917 \text{ unit-items}} = \$4.93 \text{ per unit/per item/per year.}$$

Distributor Cycle Stock (Shipping Buffer)

■ *Lot size using Equation 10.9 for an economic order quantity (EOQ)*

$$\text{EOQ} = \sqrt{2DS/H} \text{ in units}$$

where
D = annual demand in units;
S = the cost to place an order in dollars; and
H = the cost to hold one unit of one item of inventory for one year in dollars.

D = 2,500 units/year; S = \$50; H = \$5 per unit/per item/per year

$$\text{EOQ} = \sqrt{(2) \times (2{,}500) \times (50)/5} = 224 \text{ units}$$

= distribution requirements planning (DRP) lot size

■ *Safety stock using Equation 10.16 for demand uncertainty safety stock*

$$\text{SS}_\text{d} = z\sigma_\text{d}\sqrt{\text{LT}} \text{ in units}$$

where
z = number of standard deviations for the desired service level;
σ_d = the standard deviation of demand per period; and
LT = lead time with the unit of measure for the period the same as for d and LT.

z = 1.645 for a 95% service level; σ_d = 10 units/day standard deviation versus a mean demand of (2,500 units/365 days) = 6.85 units/day; LT = 2 days

$$SS_d = (1.645) \times (10) \times (\sqrt{2}) = 24 \text{ units rounded up} = \text{DRP safety stock}$$

- *Inventory turns*

$$\text{Turns} = \frac{2{,}500 \text{ units/year}}{(224 \text{ units/order} + 24 \text{ units safety stock})} = 10 \text{ turns;}$$

36.5 days for the shipping buffer

- *Reorder point using Equation 10.14 for a fixed order quantity reorder point with safety stock*

$$\text{ROP} = (d)(\text{LT}) + SS_d \text{ in units}$$

where

ROP = reorder point in units;
d = demand rate in units per day;
LT = lead time using a consistent measure of time in days; and
SS = safety stock in units.

d = 6.85 units/day; LT = 2 days; SS_d = 24 units

$$\text{ROP} = (6.85) \times (2) + 24 = 38 \text{ units rounded up} = \text{DRP reorder point}$$

Remanufacturer Finished Goods Inventory (Push/Pull Boundary)

- *Lot size using Equation 10.10 for an economic production quantity (EPQ)*

$$\text{EPQ} = \left(\sqrt{2DS/H}\right) \times \left(\sqrt{p/(p-u)}\right) \text{in units}$$

where

D = annual demand in units;
S = the cost to place an order in dollars;
H = the cost to hold one unit of one item of inventory for one year in dollars;
p = the production rate in units per week; and
u = the usage rate in units per week.

D = 2,500 units/year; S = \$50; H = \$5 per unit/per item/per year; p = 80 units/week; u = 48 units/week

$\text{EPQ} = \left(\sqrt{(2)(2{,}500)(50)/5)}\right) \times \left(\sqrt{80/(80-48)}\right) = 223.6 \times 1.581 = 354$ units rounded up = master production schedule (MPS) lot size

- *Inventory turns*

$$\text{Turns} = \frac{2{,}500 \text{ units/year}}{354 \text{ units/order}} = 7.1 \text{ turns;}$$

52 days of inventory in the push/pull boundary

- *Reorder point for a fixed order quantity reorder point*

$$\text{ROP} = (d)(\text{LT}) \text{ in units}$$

where
ROP = reorder point in units;
d = demand rate in units per day; and
LT = lead time using a consistent measure of time in days.

$$d = 6.85 \text{ units/day; LT} = 10 \text{ days}$$

$$\text{ROP} = (6.85) \times (10) = 69 \text{ units rounded up} = \text{MPS reorder point}$$

Remanufacturer Component Inventory

- *Lot size using lot-for-lot*

Materials requirements planning (MRP) lot size = 354 units = MPS lot size

- *Safety stock using Equation 10.17 for supply lead time variability safety stock*

$$SS_{LT} = zd\sigma_{LT} \text{ in units}$$

where
z = number of standard deviations for the desired service level;
d = demand rate in units per day; and
σ_{LT} = the standard deviation of lead time in days.

$z = 1.645$ for a 95% service level; $d = 6.85$ units/day; LT = 15 days; $\sigma_{LT} = 5$ days

$$SS_{LT} = (1.645) \times (6.85) \times (5) = 57 \text{ units rounded up} = \text{MRP safety stock}$$

This safety stock applies to both good cores and other replacement component inventory.

- *Inventory turns*

$$\text{Turns} = \frac{2{,}500 \text{ units/year}}{(354 \text{ units/order} + 57 \text{ units safety stock})} = 6.0 \text{ turns;}$$

61 days of component inventory

- *Reorder point*

MRP reorder point equals the safety stock = 57 units

Step 16: Plan and Control the Push Zone (Chapter 10)

In step 16, you construct the inventory and capacity planning and control system used to push inventory into the push/pull boundary. The Tractor Tracker Reverse Network uses a demand forecast and DRP at the distributor feeding into an MPS and MRP at REMAN to drive inventory locations. These planning tools are thoroughly explained in Chapter 10: "Inventory Management."

Figure 8.6 details the linkages from DRP to MPS to MRP for remanufactured Tractor Trackers and for good cores. In this example, the planning horizon changes from months for DRP to weeks for MPS and MRP. The lot size, reorder point, and safety stock quantities calculated in step 15 are key parameters in the planning tools of step 16. The shipping buffer at the forward network distributor is seeded with a starting inventory 250 new Tractor Trackers to get operations started. The next critical inventory questions is whether or not the disposition organization can process enough good cores to deliver 354 units to the remanufacturer by week 4 against an order released earlier in January.

Step 17: Plan and Control the Pull Zone (Chapter 10)

In step 17, you ensure that the pull zone has sufficient capacity and inventory to handle maximum throughput.

In the Tractor Tracker Reverse Network, the customer pulls from the shipping buffer, and the shipping buffer pulls its replenishment from the push/pull boundary. Each customer order shipped from the shipping buffer generates a demand signal to pull an identical unit from the push/pull boundary, thus replenishing the shipping buffer. Although step 16 suggests monthly replenishment of the shipping buffer with lots of 224 units, the pull zone continuously replenishes inventory reflecting the actual customer RMA demand pattern. Should cumulative shipments for the month exceed 224 units, then the shipping buffer must be replenished with new production from the forward supply chain.

REMAN tractor tracker DRP		Lot Size	224 units	Reorder Point	38 units	Lead Time	2 days
		January	February	March	April		
Demand forecast		207	211	219	225		
Net requirements			56	61	60		
Starting inventory	250	43	−168	−163	−164		
Scheduled receipts							
Planned order			224	224	224		

REMAN tractor tracker MPS		Lot size	354 units	Reorder point	69 units	Lead time	10 days
		January	February				March
		Week 4	Week 5	Week 6	Week 7	Week 8	Week 9
Period demand			224				224
Projected available balance			130				200
Starting inventory	0	0	−224	130	130	130	−94
Scheduled receipts							
Master schedule receipt			354				354
Master schedule release		354				354	

Good core MRP		Bill of materials			1 per		
		Lot size	354 units	Reorder point	57 units	Lead time	15 days
		January	February				March
		Week 4	Week 5	Week 6	Week 7	Week 8	Week 9
Gross requirements		354				354	
Net requirements		75				75	
Starting inventory	75	−279	75	75	75	−279	75
Scheduled receipts		354					
Planned order receipt						354	
Planned order release				354			

Figure 8.6 Push planning for the remanufactured Tractor Tracker.

- *Pull capacity*—The distributor must have the capacity to sustain a throughput of 208 units/month. Notice that the demand forecast shows throughput slowing increasing over the next year.
- *Pull inventory*—The push/pull boundary must hold a quantity of inventory at least equal to the maximum monthly throughput of 208 units/month.

Step 18: Plot a Value Circle to Validate Product Contents Performance Measures (Chapter 11)

In step 18, you plot the bottom half of the Value Circle related to the product contents. This includes supply chain performance measures for inventory, vocalize,

ROIC, and visualize. You are looking to validate the Tractor Tracker product contents construction by answering these three questions: What is the right level of product inventory, and where is it to be located? Can you completely visualize the push zone and properly vocalize the pull zone to achieve a competitive delivery lead time? Does the pricing leading to profit on the income statement and the cash flow leading to inventory assets, receivables, and payables on the balance sheet support a favorable investment return? Figure 8.7 shows the partial Value Circle associated with the product contents portion of the SSCRS in Table 8.10. The unit circle represents the first set of estimates with each axis of the Value Circle improving toward the origin.

The push/pull boundary is operated with 7.1 inventory turns, as determined in step 15. The shipping buffer maintains a safety stock of 24 Tractor Trackers to protect against demand uncertainty. The REMAN component inventory maintains a safety stock of 57 good cores to protect against lead time variability in the disposition operations. However, the greatest risk is not accumulating enough core returns to support the planned throughput. Delivery lead time, step 12, is two to five days depending on the customer's distance from the Allentown distributor. Vocalize is five to eight days from the push/pull boundary. Visualize is 175 days to cover the longest lead time replacement components. ROIC is estimated to be 11% in step 11. ROIC improves when profit is increased and the inventory asset is decreased. The supply chain construction for the product content is now complete.

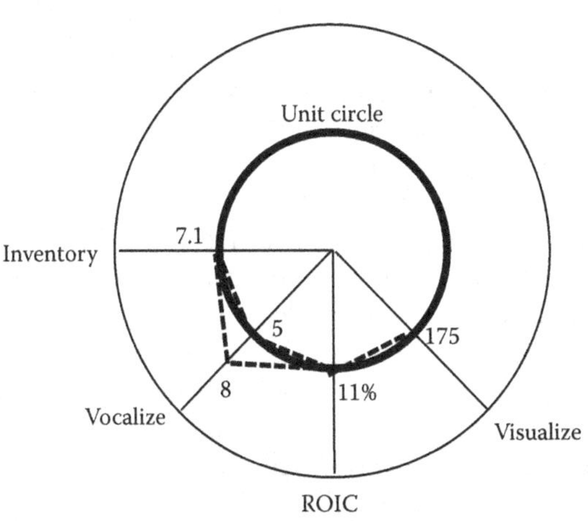

Figure 8.7 Value Circle for the Tractor Tracker Reverse Network product contents.

Step 19: Stabilize Supply Chain Operations and End the Construction Project (Chapters 11, 12)

In step 19, you stabilize supply chain operations until the required level of performance is reached. Then the supply chain construction project is formally ended and the project team disbanded.

- *Example large order dynamic*

  Sometimes, customers request special upgrades to their equipment purchases. The customer will want to convert their entire fleet within a few months. However, when a customer's fleet size is large, attempting to quickly turn the entire conversion can put your parts inventory plan at risk for supporting normal warranty replacements. You will want to carefully plan supply quantities and lead times for every part in both the existing warranty replacement program and the incremental upgrade program before you let sales make any calendar time commitment to the customer. There is also a high probability that the customer will not deliver their equipment to be upgraded when they said they would.

Step 20: Manage Supply Chain Risk (Chapter 12)

In step 20, you assess highly probable risk scenarios that might disrupt your supply chain network.

- *Example of a medium-probability, high-severity scenario: a shortage of cores*

  At a 60%/40% split between returned good cores and returned bad cores approximately 4,168 core returns per year need to be collected by the accumulator organization to support 2,500 remanufactured Tractor Trackers per year. There are no guarantees that customers will provide this rate of core returns. A short fall will severely constrain annual throughput. If the shortfall is caused by a better-than-expected field failure rate, then the shortfall is a good thing. But if remanufactured Tractor Trackers have to be allocated among customers who have paid for extend warranty, there will be serious customer dissatisfaction issues, including some customers wanting refunds. If such a core shortage is resolved by shipping the difference in new products, then profit margins come into serious question. It is important to carefully monitor the core return rate and to ensure timely processing through the accumulate and disposition organizations.

In Summary

This chapter describes how to construct the inner workings of a reverse supply chain network. The chapter illustrates how to apply the Supply Chain Construction Blueprint from Chapter 2: "The Blueprint" to build the Tractor Tracker Reverse Network. The network container is constructed from accumulate, disposition, remanufacture, distribute, separate, and recycle organizations and their material, information, and cash interconnections. The end-to-end margin is checked for profitability. The product content construction is detailed from the composite BOM, through the push/pull boundary, through the planning parameters, to the inventory investment. The ROIC percentage gives a reasonable check that this reverse supply chain is a good investment. Certain steps in The Blueprint are iterated to meet price/landed cost targets and inventory turns targets. These iterations are (1) make it work, (2) make it work well, and (3) make it work in a flexible and risk tolerant manner.

Chapter 9

Demand Planning

With the construction of the network container complete, the next task is to fill the container with product contents. The network container has the capability of combining any set of raw materials and component parts from SOURCE through multiple product structures within MAKE to DELIVER the range of products demanded by specific market segments. This chapter begins the construction of the PLAN to fill the network with the right inventory in the right quantity at the right place and the right time. The next chapter completes construction of the PLAN. Keep in mind that the network's supply capabilities are different from the customer's actual demand. Demand planning is meant to align demand and supply.

This chapter is organized into four sections. The first looks at how your customer views customer service. The second section describes alternative operating strategies to achieve a competitive delivery lead time. The third section explains how to forecast the right thing in a network context and then how to forecast things right relative to different forecasting methods. The last section details how to capture customer orders downstream and broadcast customer orders upstream in a way that defeats the bullwhip effect. This is followed by Chapter 10: "Inventory Management," which covers push planning methods, pull planning methods, and how to set inventory levels throughout the supply chain.

All Forecasts Are Wrong

The Supply Chain Construction Project Team was preparing for their quarterly review meeting with the divisional vice presidents. George, the executive champion for the project team, had joined their meeting to review their preparations.

"I'm hearing this team is making great progress. That's very important to Steve, our chief executive officer, because his reputation is on the line with the request to Corporate to fund the uninterruptable power supply (UPS) business venture," began George.

"Thanks. Everyone on the project team is really pulling their weight," replied Bill, the project manager.

"What's on the agenda for today's meeting?" asked George.

"We are going to walk you through our PowerPoint presentation for the quarterly review, but first, Harry has an update on the forecast from Product Marketing," said Bill.

Tony from Cost Accounting spoke, "The forecast is really important because it drives the revenue number, the size of our inventory investment, and the capacity we need in manufacturing and distribution. The forecast needs to be really accurate."

"What is the forecast?" asked George.

Before Harry could respond, Bill jumped in, "We have built our operating assumptions around four numbers, knowing that they were placeholders, until we could get the real forecast from Computer Products. For some reason, Computer Products has been reluctant to share much information about their new server program."

"OK. So, what are the four numbers?" asked George again.

"I don't want to put Harry on the spot because our starting numbers have been mostly working assumptions about probable demand. We said total first year throughput, once shipments began, would be about 20,000 units. We said the run rate at the end of the 12th month would be 2,500 units per month. We said the connect rate between Computer Products servers and our UPS would be 90%. And we said UPS products would sell through a network of 100 value-added resellers (VARs). All of our work to-date has been based on these four numbers," replied Bill.

"How does that translate into revenue for the first year?" asked George.

Again, Tony answered, "Using end-customer pricing of $500 for the Product 500 model, and giving the VARs a 30% discount, then 20,000 units per year times $500 per unit times 70%, which is the distributor price out of our division to the VARs, is $7 million. At a connect rate of 90%, we see $6.3 million."

"The $6.3 million of revenue to Power Products is $10 million of revenue at the VARs," clarified Bill.

"Make sure the team talks in terms of dollars of revenue, and keep the explanation simple. That's language the vice presidents understand. Steve is going to want to hear $10 million," replied George.

Not wanting to wait any longer to speak, Harry finally jumped in, "Those are the numbers we used months ago to get the project rolling, but there are better numbers now. For some reason, I had to get assistance from both Jerry, my boss, and Steve to pry the server forecast out of Computer Products."

"Probably because the numbers for the new server program are supposed to be company private information," suggested George.

"Anyway, this is what I learned just yesterday. I haven't even had a chance to share this new information with the team, although Steve has heard these numbers. First, the servers will be rolled out in phases. The first phase will be piloted through 23 VARs. Computer Products will not allow our sales force to talk with any of the other VARs until the next phase of server introduction begins," said Harry.

"That's a little parochial," commented Donna from Purchasing.

Harry continued, "Yes, but it is really their program, and we are a tag along sale. Next, my counterpart at Computer Products thinks the connect rate will be closer to 75%, but she doesn't really have any compelling argument for this. It's mostly a gut feel on her part."

"That makes a big difference on our revenue number," exclaimed Bill.

"I know," said Harry. "I'm saving the worst for last, so please don't shoot the messenger."

"Oh?" responded Bill. He already did not appreciate that Steve had this information and that he was being blindsided in front of George.

Harry cleared his throat and went on, "Well, the first year server volume is forecast to be 18,000 units, or 1,500 servers per month. I just got these numbers."

Tony quickly recalculated, "A $500 customer price per unit times 18,000 units times 70% customer to distributor pricing times a 75% connect rate is $4.725 million."

"That's a problem," said George quietly.

"Well, maybe not," said Harry. "This is the first phase selling through only about a quarter of the VARs. Computer Products would not give up the information regarding their timing of the second phase."

"We need to work with the best information that we have at the time. This new forecast means we'll have to get busy and revise a number of PowerPoint slides before the review meeting tomorrow," said Bill.

John from Engineering had been listening carefully to the first part of the meeting, "Maybe we show a table with a side-by-side comparison of our supply chain construction work based on the starting forecast and Computer Product's latest forecast."

"That's a great idea, thanks John," said Bill.

"What was the source of your starting forecast?" asked George pointedly. This was the pivotal question.

Bill felt defensive, but replied truthfully, "When the team was at first unable to get a server forecast from Computer Products, we asked what would it take for our supply chain to support $10 million in throughput on a $500 product and then worked backwards."

"I see. So, your forecast has always been inflated?" asked George looking to point blame. "This puts Steve in a very tough spot asking Corporate for financing. He might not get it."

"So many decisions in starting up a new supply chain are based on the forecast. Without some kind of target number, we couldn't even begin the project let alone give Steve an estimate of the size of the investment. You know as well as I that this is an iterative process," said Bill looking directly at George.

Donna jumped into the fray, "Look, the team had no idea how to begin the project. Bill knew exactly how to connect the dots. We have made amazing progress under his leadership."

Tony added, "This information was asked for repeatedly. If you remember, George, the team asked you and Jerry months ago to help Harry get the server forecast."

"Yes, I remember," admitted George reluctantly.

"Forecasts are always wrong. If we made a mistake in our approach, it was only that we focused on a fixed demand number rather that a probabilistic range. But, the team had to start somewhere, and no one had any better ideas," said Bill.

"So, maybe this summary table with columns for different forecast that we have been talking about needs to show a high forecast and a low forecast range that captures the probable forecast error," offered John.

"Again, that is an excellent idea," replied Bill. "Let's look at the slide set, while George is here, and determine which slides have to change with the reduction in the demand forecast. This will not change the decision to go with Astec as our manufacturer, but we will have to inform Astec of the potentially smaller unit volume. It will not change the decision to use our division as the distributor. But it will increase the market price of the product and decrease the total inventory investment."

"And, we still don't understand the parts volume split among the Product 250, the Product 500, and the Product 1000," added Donna.

"This is not going to be a very pleasant quarterly review for the team, but let's present our best work in ranges of price, cost and, unit volumes as candidly as we can," concluded Bill.

Focus on Consistent, Reliable Delivery

Customer service is all about managing expectations. Your customers believe that they can get most of your product's functionality for a fraction of your product's price; never mind that the missing functionality is probably what differentiates your value proposition. Your customers can get instant gratification on other types of purchases, and they expect the same from you; never mind that your commodity has a different sourcing pattern. Your customers believe that they can get a response 24 hours/day, 7 days/week, 365 days/year from your competitor, and they expect the same from you; never mind that your entire company has a small total number of employees. Your customers are delighted by the free return service wrapped around your competitor's product, and they expect the same from you; never mind that your product has high recycling costs.

Perfect order fulfillment is said to be the right product, at the right price, delivered at the right time, delivered in the right quantity, delivered to the right place, with the right quality, with the right invoice, with no returns and with no hassle. These are the "seven rights" of excellent customer service. Where do you start? Start by focusing on providing consistent, reliable delivery.

Good Intentions but Poor Performance

A high-mix business ran a small distribution center that picked, kitted, and shipped-to-order. A typical order consisted of eight line items. One of the kitted parts was a sheet metal bracket. There were 30 sheet metal bracket stock-keeping units (SKUs) in inventory and several that, with a quick glance, looked the same. The bracket design failed to call out stamping the part number and revision letter on each part; this critical information was stapled to the skid provided by the bracket supplier. The business also had a high volume of replacement and spare part orders. While a typical replacement part order had only one line item, that line item had potentially three product options to be replicated. The replacement part had to be routed back through the main production process to confirm or add product options before being moved to shipping.

The distribution process proceeded as follows. A pick list was generated from the customer's order. In the case of a standard order, the pick list documented each of the individual SKUs by part number, by description, and by the quantity per order. Product options were listed as separate line items. There was no revision information on the pick list. In the case of a replacement order, the pick list documented the SKU by part number, by description, and by the quantity per order and listed each product option separately as required. Again, there was no revision information on the pick list. Neither the items themselves nor the pick list was bar coded. A picker walked the stockroom floor pulling quantities of SKUs and putting them on a cart, which was then wheeled to the shipping department. The picker initialed each line item for quality control. In shipping, a different person, the packer, pulled items from the cart to complete the packing list for the customer's order. The body of the packing list was identical to the pick list except that the customer's name, ship-to address, freight method, and due date were added to the header. The packer also initialed each line item for quality control. If the picker pulled the wrong bracket, the packer could not catch the mistake. If the picker failed to route a replacement order through production for an options validation, the packer could not catch the mistake. Many calls to customer service complained about the wrong part being shipped, the wrong revision of right part being shipped, and replacements with missing options being shipped. Customer service, which was located in another city, had little insight into the root cause of this poor performance.

Delivery Lead Time

Customers expect a competitive delivery lead time for your product. If your delivery channel involves the customer going to a retail store and making a cash purchase, then your customer expects to walk out of the store with the product. If your delivery channel involves ordering over the Internet, then your customer expects next-day delivery regardless of what time the order was placed or where the deliver-to address is located. If your delivery channel involves a common carrier shipment and NET30 day payment terms, then your customer expects a fixed delivery lead time with an on-time delivery. Attributes of delivery lead time include variability and reliability. You may also have to take into account any difference in time zones between the end customer and the distributor that can impact time windows for ordering and delivery. Table 9.1 shows some typical examples.

$$\begin{gathered}\text{Delivery lead time is expressed in days and is defined starting}\\ \text{at the date/time the customer enters his or her order and ending at}\\ \text{the date/time product arrives at the customer's receiving dock.}\end{gathered} \tag{9.1}$$

When product is in inventory at the shipping buffer:

$$\begin{gathered}\text{Delivery lead time} = \text{Ordering time} + \text{Pick and pack time}\\ + \text{Outbound transit time}\end{gathered} \tag{9.2}$$

When product is not in inventory at the shipping buffer and has to be replenished:

$$\begin{gathered}\text{Delivery lead time} = \text{Ordering time} + \text{Replenishment lead time}\\ + \text{Pick and pack time} + \text{Outbound transit time}\end{gathered} \tag{9.3}$$

Table 9.1 Example Delivery Lead Times

Ordering Method	*Delivery Method*	*Delivery Lead Time*
Customer shops in store	Customer pickup in store	0 days
Customer shops online	Overnight shipment from warehouse	1 day
Customer e-mails purchase order	Eastern factory ships by truck to East coast	1–2 days
Customer e-mails purchase order	Eastern factory ships by truck to Midwest	3–4 days
Customer e-mails purchase order	Eastern factory ships by truck to West coast	5–6 days

Whether or not the inventory required for the order is on hand often depends on the product quantities ordered. While there should be no problem in shipping one or two products, especially as demos for new customers, there may be significant issues in shipping 100 units of the product. In small business situations, delivery lead time may vary as a function of the demand volume.

Taking Variability Out of Delivery Lead Time

Suppose over a large number of order-to-delivery cycles, each term in Equation 9.2 can be described as a mean time with a standard deviation. Then, because the three terms [Mean_1, Standard Deviation_1], [M_2, SD_2], and [M_3, SD_3] are in series, from Equation 4.11 in Chapter 4, the following is known:

Delivery lead time mean = Ordering mean + Pick and pack mean + Outbound transit mean

$$\text{Delivery lead time mean} = M_1 + M_2 + M_3 \text{ in days} \tag{9.4}$$

Delivery lead time standard deviation = Root mean squared (Ordering SD, Pick and pack SD, and Outbound transit SD)

$$\text{Delivery lead time standard deviation} = \sqrt{\frac{(SD_1)^2 + (SD_2)^2 + (SD_3)^2}{3}} \text{ in days} \tag{9.5}$$

The predictability of delivery lead time depends upon minimizing delivery lead time variability. Whichever standard deviation is largest in Equation 9.5 will dominate the total variability of the delivery lead time. You minimize delivery lead time variability by addressing the largest standard deviation component first. For example, if a single distribution center services the entire United States, then the logistics variability from one to six days will be driven by geography. The variability of pick and pack becomes significant when packaging materials such as cartons, floaters, labels, or pallets are not immediately available and when a shipment must be held for an outside inspector to release the goods. Ordering variability is most often erratic when a customer order is frozen for a credit hold or when adding new customer information to the database requires log-in access from an employee who is out sick or on vacation. Customer self-service approaches take out some of the ordering time variability because the delivery lead time clock does not start until the customer completes inputting all the required information.

Building Reliability into Delivery Lead Time

Setting aside variability for the moment, delivery lead time reliability means the supply chain will deliver the same product in the same time, every time. This is all about operational consistency. Reliability requires having both the product inventory and the process capacity where and when you need it. Product inventory depends on reasonable forecasts with excellence in planning and execution. On-hand inventory depends upon the order quantity mix. A shipment of 100 units at once might totally deplete the inventory for a given item, where 10 smaller shipments of 10 units each for the same product spread over several days might still provide inventory coverage for the next order. It is common practice to buttress inventory against demand uncertainty with safety stock as addressed in Chapter 10: "Inventory Management."

Delivery lead time reliability can be lost due to inadequate capacity. Capacity must be sized for the maximum expected volume plus some peak capacity capability. Since delivery lead time must be executed in hours or days, capacity alternatives that take weeks or months to implement are not good solutions in the near term. Failing to achieve adequate capacity in real-time means you are limiting your throughput and leaving revenue money on the table. Again, since an order-to-delivery cycle has ordering, pick and pack, and outbound logistics processes in series, each of these three processes must have adequate capacity. The smallest of the three capacities will set the limits for the entire delivery operation.

Let the Vocalize and Visualize Principles Guide Construction

Just as cash flow in the network container is driven by the cash-to-cash cycle velocity and variability, inventory turns of the product content are driven by vocalizing the customer's demand and visualizing the forecast supply. Vocalize and visualize are two more of the 5V Principles. They are applied to the product contents portion of a supply chain construction project.

Vocalize Principle

The *Vocalize Principle* states that throughput is maximized by pulling the right inventory out of the push/pull boundary to fulfill demand orders vocalized across the pull zone.

This principle directs how the end customer's demand gets communicated upstream in a supply chain to ensure that the mix (and rate) of inventory is available downstream. This principle is used to determine the best methods for capturing the customer order and broadcasting it to the right inventory locations across the supply chain in real-time.

Visualize Principle

The *Visualize Principle* states that throughput is maximized by pushing the right inventory into the push/pull boundary from a supply forecast visualized across the push zone.

This principle directs how a forecast gets communicated across the supply chain to give visibility to the trading partners providing the right rate (and mix) of inventory that will become available downstream. This principle is used to determine the best methods for forecasting supply requirements, supplying these requirements to the right inventory locations and providing the means to see actual inventory balances across the supply chain in real-time.

Work from the Big Picture

Your supply chain network is constructed from a requirements specification to connect a supply base with a set of raw materials and production capability with a delivery channel connected to a specific market segment. The SOURCE, MAKE, and DELIVER aspects of the network container are done. Supply chain construction now moves to the steps necessary to fill the network container with product contents following the steps in The Blueprint.

Push Zone and Pull Zone

The material flow for every multiechelon supply chain network is split end-to-end into two sections. The upstream section is called the push zone, while the downstream section is called the pull zone. The push zone begins with the raw material supplier and ends at a physical inventory location called the push/pull boundary. The pull zone begins at the push/pull boundary and ends with delivery to the end customer. Product inventory is driven from a supply forecast into the push/pull boundary. Product inventory is pulled from the push/pull boundary to fulfill customer demand. Product inventory transverses the push/pull boundary becoming throughput, only when both the rate and mix of demand on the customer order can be exactly matched with the rate and mix of supply from the forecast.

The big picture of supply chain operations focuses on the two sides of the push/pull boundary. The upstream side develops a product forecast that is used to drive quantities of raw materials, component parts, products, product options,

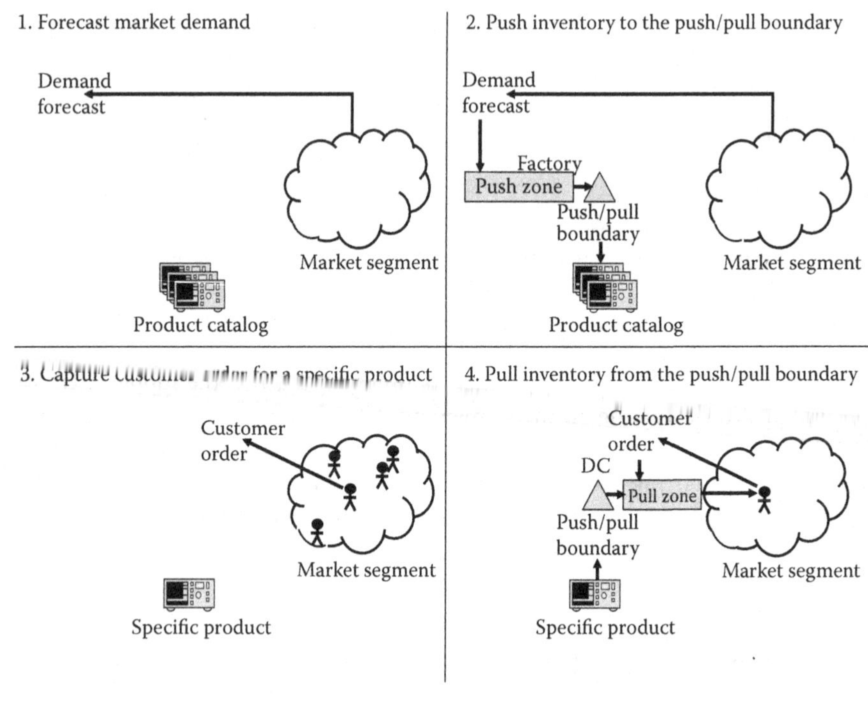

Figure 9.1 The big picture.

and product accessories through the push zone into the push/pull boundary. The downstream side captures and processes the customer orders that are used to pull the customer-required product and system configurations and quantities from the push/pull boundary through the pull zone. Figure 9.1 depicts the big picture.

Four Operating Strategies

The push/pull boundary can be located in different positions along a supply chain network. Each position has advantages and disadvantages in terms of delivery lead time, total inventory investment, and flexibility to meet demand mix (see Table 9.2). Your decision regarding which operating strategy to use is a competitive decision. Depending on your industry and product, you may want to use build-to-stock (BTS) to match a competition's short delivery lead time. Or, you may prefer to run your business from an order backlog using a build-to-order (BTO) operating strategy. For example, for many years, Harley Davidson ran their business from a backlog, with customers waiting nearly a year for their customized bikes. Harley Davidson held a unique position in their market and used order backlog to build allure for their product.

Table 9.2 The Four Operating Strategies

Strategy	*Push/Pull Location*	*Advantage*	*Disadvantage*	*Inventory or Backlog*
Build-to-stock (BTS)	Downstream	Shortest delivery lead time	Largest inventory investment	FG inventory
Postponement and assemble-to-order (ATO)	Downstream or midstream	Mix flexibility	Medium inventory investment	Module inventory; product backlog
Build-to-order (BTO)	Midstream	Build exact mix	Long delivery lead time	Backlog
Engineer-to-order (ETO)	Upstream	Smallest inventory investment	Longest delivery lead time	Long LT inventory; product backlog

Postponement is an excellent alternative if your business runs a high mix. Postponement involves completing a small part of a product's assembly after the customer order is received. Postponement might involve putting a different colored case on a nearly complete cell phone or loading different firmware into a nearly complete personal computer. Assemble-to-order involves assembling the final product by combining several modules held in inventory. Assemble-to-order might involve assembling a pickup truck by combining an eight-cylinder engine with a five-speed transmission with a king cab and an extended bed.

Locating the Push/Pull Boundary

The push/pull boundary is one of the physical inventory locations found in a supply chain network (see Table 9.3). It is commonly the distributor's cycle stock inventory location for a BTS operating strategy or the factory's finished goods inventory location for a BTO operating strategy. The push/pull boundary is often different from the shipping buffer, which is the most downstream, customer-facing physical inventory location. The shipping buffer determines the delivery lead time, while the push/pull boundary separates planning to a forecast from executing to an order. In some cases, the shipping buffer and the push/pull boundary may be the same physical inventory location. Businesses often run parallel operating strategies with their main products in backlog as BTO and their accessory products in inventory as BTS. Once the main product is ready to ship, you cannot afford to wait until a secondary accessory becomes available.

Table 9.3 Locating the Push/Pull Boundary

Network	*Inventory Location*	*BTO*	*Postponement*	*BTS*
Echelon 6: raw material	Raw material stock			
Echelon 5: supplier	Supplier raw material			
	Supplier finished goods			
Echelon 4: factory	Factory raw materials			
	Factory finished goods	Push/pull boundary		
Echelon 3: distributor	Distributor cycle stock	Shipping buffer	Push/pull boundary Shipping buffer	Push/pull boundary
Echelon 2: store	Retail store cycle stock			Shipping buffer
Echelon 1: customer				

Forecast the Order

The demand forecast drives product inventory into the push/pull boundary. It determines the rate and mix of raw materials, component parts, and complete products flowing through the upstream SOURCE and midstream MAKE portions of your supply chain network. The demand forecast is the first point of connection in the big picture between a market segment and a product offering. When the demand forecast is too high, your inventory investment will grow needlessly using up valuable cash. When the demand forecast is too low, your delivery lead time lengthens because there are not enough products in the pipeline. But how do you even know where to start with forecasting?

There are three important aspects to forecasting. First, you want to forecast the right thing. This is about understanding the network context of the forecast. Where in their life cycles are the market, the supply chain relationships, and the product? Do you need to forecast inventory or capacity? Where is the demand independent versus where is the demand dependent? Second, you want to forecast things right. Which echelon should make the forecast? What forecasting technique should be used and over what planning horizon? When should the forecast be updated? And third, you want to continuously improve upon your forecast accuracy, as assumptions change, markets change, and products change.

Forecast the Right Thing

Before you ever start to develop a forecast, it is important to correctly define its context. There is both a demand side and a supply side to any supply chain forecast. The demand side may be driven by market density, by competition, by deep pricing discounts, by seasonality, or by leapfrogging technology, to name a few. The supply side may be driven by raw material scarcity or seasonality, by capacity constraints, by leapfrogging technology, or by trading partner acquisitions and divestitures, to name a few. Here are some relevant contextual factors to consider:

- *Life cycle of the market*—Does this market have a growing, mature, seasonal, or declining demand for the type of product your supply chain is delivering?
- *Life cycle of the network relationships*—Network trading partner relationships that are merging or diverging have a different dynamic from those that are stable.
- *Life cycle of the product*—Demand for recently introduced product ramps up. Demand for mature product is level or seasonal. Demand for soon-to-be-discontinued product ramps down.
- *Independent demand driving inventory*—Under a BTS operating strategy, the network constraint is inventory.
- *Independent demand driving capacity*—Under a BTO operating strategy, the network constraint is capacity.
- *Dependent demand*—Dependent demand items are lower-level components to an end product. Dependent demand is never forecast; it is calculated from the forecast demand for the parent product.

One special case of dependent demand is being a supplier to an original equipment manufacturer (OEM). In this case, you most likely have a pricing contract for a certain quantity of a known product configuration. The only uncertainty is variability in the delivery dates stipulated by the pricing contract. Product going to an OEM should not be forecast; rather, it should be computed from the OEM's production schedule of the parent product being produced at the OEM.

The following examples describe a contextual starting assumption for a product forecast:

- "This product is made from ingots of a sole-sourced compound material that is forged once a year. There are 30 units left in stock, and the next ingot, scheduled for production next month, should yield about 625 units if the pouring is successful." This implies the product forecast has either a fixed total quantity over the planning horizon or an acute shortage if the ingot pouring is unsuccessful.

- "This product has been on the market for the past five years. The market is responding to new, lower-cost competition for other products having better capabilities." This implies the product forecast should be trending down.
- "This product will be introduced to new markets in Europe and Asia as a result of the recent merger of the two companies and access to the new company's distribution network." This implies the product forecast should show a step function in international growth.

Three Kinds of Forecasts

Three kinds of forecasts are used to drive inventory into the push/pull boundary (see Figure 9.2). The first, called the demand rate forecast, is a top–down aggregate rate forecast of revenue dollars prepared annually by the VP of finance with input from the VP of sales and marketing. The planning horizon is one year minimum.

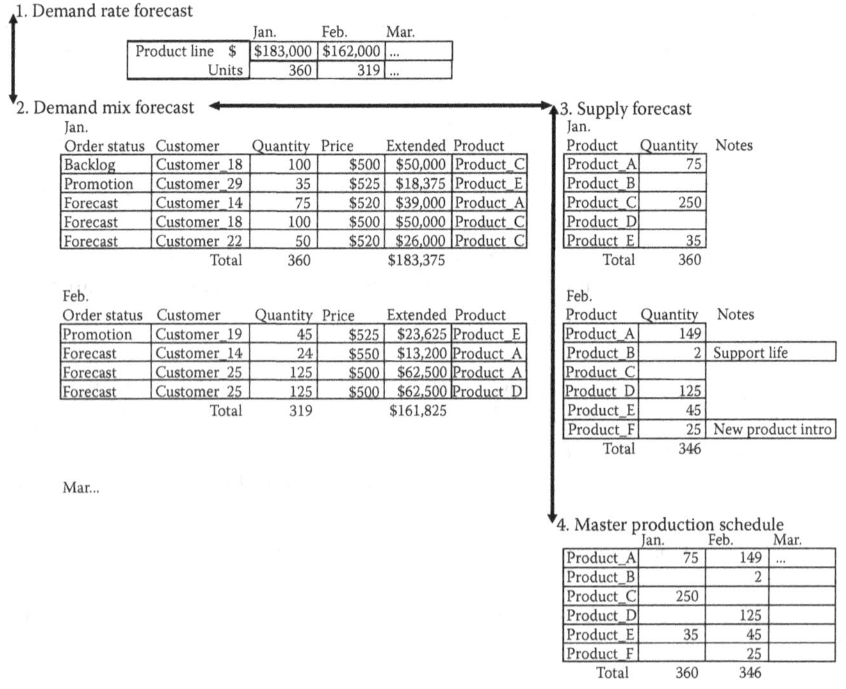

1. Demand rate forecast

	Jan.	Feb.	Mar.
Product line $	$183,000	$162,000	...
Units	360	319	...

2. Demand mix forecast

Jan.

Order status	Customer	Quantity	Price	Extended	Product
Backlog	Customer_18	100	$500	$50,000	Product_C
Promotion	Customer_29	35	$525	$18,375	Product_E
Forecast	Customer_14	75	$520	$39,000	Product_A
Forecast	Customer_18	100	$500	$50,000	Product_C
Forecast	Customer_22	50	$520	$26,000	Product_C
	Total	360		$183,375	

Feb.

Order status	Customer	Quantity	Price	Extended	Product
Promotion	Customer_19	45	$525	$23,625	Product_E
Forecast	Customer_14	24	$550	$13,200	Product_A
Forecast	Customer_25	125	$500	$62,500	Product_A
Forecast	Customer_25	125	$500	$62,500	Product_D
	Total	319		$161,825	

Mar...

3. Supply forecast

Jan.

Product	Quantity	Notes
Product_A	75	
Product_B		
Product_C	250	
Product_D		
Product_E	35	
Total	360	

Feb.

Product	Quantity	Notes
Product_A	149	
Product_B	2	Support life
Product_C		
Product_D	125	
Product_E	45	
Product_F	25	New product intro
Total	346	

4. Master production schedule

	Jan.	Feb.	Mar.
Product_A	75	149	...
Product_B		2	
Product_C	250		
Product_D		125	
Product_E	35	45	
Product_F		25	
Total	360	346	

Figure 9.2 Three kinds of forecasts.

Each row is the aggregation of all the expected revenue dollars for a single product line; i.e. one product line is one row, two product lines are two rows. The columns are months grouped into quarters typically based on a fiscal year. This forecast is used both by Finance for setting budgets and by Operations to gauge inventory purchases.

The second kind of forecast, called the demand mix forecast, is a bottom–up customer-by-customer forecast prepared monthly by Sales. It is based on Sales' understanding of which products existing customers are likely to buy and what new customers are likely to become new accounts. Each row is a major product and customer pair stated in both units per month and extended dollars per month. Each row is given a status of backlog, forecast, or sales promotion. The planning horizon extends at least as far as the master production schedule (MPS) planning horizon. The totals of extended dollars and aggregated units are reconciled month by month with the demand rate forecast. The demand mix forecast is used by Sales to manage their quotas and by Operations to prepare the third kind of forecast, the supply forecast.

The third forecast, the supply forecast, is a bottom–up product quantity mix forecast prepared monthly by Operations. It is based on the demand mix forecast dropping the customer information and consolidating similar products across all customers within each time period. The supply forecast incorporates additional information about new product introductions, old product discontinuances, component part allocations, additional product support requirements, and critical capacity constraints. Each row is a major product in both units per month and extended dollars per month. Each column is a month. The planning horizon covers the MPS's planning horizon. Total quantities are reconciled product by product with the demand mix forecast; total extended dollars are reconciled month by month with the demand rate forecast. The supply forecast is used to drive the MPS at the factory, which in turn drives inventory into the push/pull boundary.

Note that there is no one right answer between the aggregate dollar rate/unit rate and the disaggregated dollar mix/unit mix. In fact, there are an infinite number of possible combinations of the sum of the products of price times quantity being equal to a specific number. What really happens is that demand rate forecast and the demand mix forecast are worked together. Finance has an idea of the total revenue dollars needed to make the targets. Sales has an idea of the quantities and pricing for a few individual large orders in a given month. The difference is called the "plug." The plug is exploded into a set of probable product types, quantities, and prices based on historical demand data and is iterated until the mix forecast and the rate forecast match. The forecasting techniques described later in this chapter are used to take the historical demand data and project it across the planning horizon as level, trending, or seasonal patterns.

Forecast Things Right

Which echelon should prepare the forecast? It is important to realize that each of your trading partners probably participates in several different supply chain networks. That is, they buy from other supply bases and sell to other demand channels the same and/or different inventory items (see Figure 9.3). The end customer represents the in-network independent demand that is driving your supply chain. This independent demand becomes dependent demand as it propagates upstream. Therefore, the demand forecast should be made as close to the end customer as possible and probably by the distributor so that all of the small retail store demands are consolidated. The demand forecast for your supply chain network should be separated from the other pairs of out-of-network independent and dependent demand shown in Figure 9.3 as demands 2, 3, 4, and 5.

When should a new forecast be made? In most business settings, a demand rate forecast is generated once a year to set financial targets and is regenerated once a quarter, i.e., every three months, to account for major changes in the business climate. The demand mix forecast and the supply forecast are regenerated every month, preferably at the same time of the month. The supply forecast is completed after the demand mix forecast is completed. The monthly sales and operations planning meeting is held after the supply forecast is completed. In addition, whenever a major sales event occurs, such as winning a new contract or losing a large customer order, the supply forecast is immediately regenerated and the changes are immediately communicated upstream to the factory and all relevant suppliers.

How far into the future should a forecast be made? A forecast prepared mid-month for this month and next month is not a forecast. The planning horizon on the demand rate forecast covers a minimum of 12 calendar months. It is not

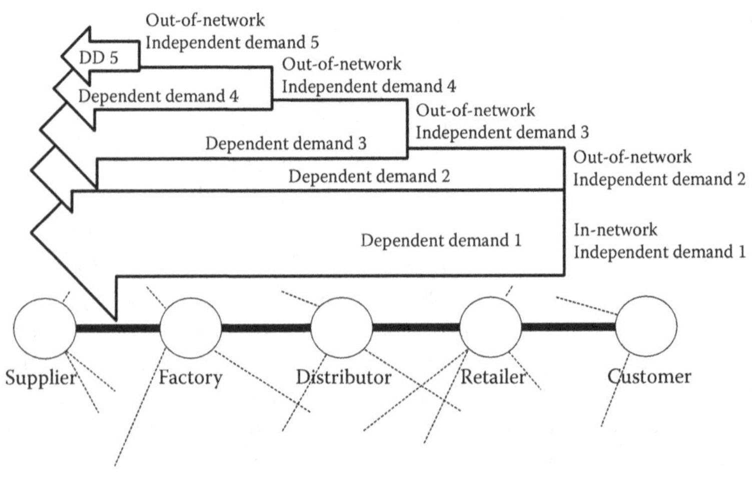

Figure 9.3 In-network and out-of-network demand.

unusual for the demand rate forecast to cover five quarters, or 15 months, to give coverage during the period that the next year's targets are being prepared. The demand mix forecast and the supply forecast have to have planning horizons covering a minimum of the longest path of lead times plus cycle times plus transit times of any of the product structures delivered through your supply chain. This planning horizon has to load the master production schedule far enough out in time to drive inventory requirements down through the lowest level of any of the product bills of material (BOMs).

Forecasting Techniques

The elements of any forecast include a set of historical time periods, the present plus a set of future time periods called the planning horizon, historical actual demand, the forecast demand, and the forecast accuracy. The forecasting techniques discussed in this section include forecasting for level demand, forecasting for trending up or trending down demand, and forecasting for demand with seasonality. Calculating and improving forecast accuracy are discussed after the forecasting techniques.

Demand patterns tend to follow shorter life cycles of product to market acceptance and longer life cycles of trading partner to supply chain network relationships. Over a complete life cycle, demand ramps up from zero to its mature level, then remains flat perhaps with some seasonal variation, and then drifts down toward zero demand, ending with a small support life requirement. Demand forecasts can therefore be modeled with an upward trending forecast, followed by a level or seasonal forecast, followed by a downward trending forecast depending upon the product's place along its life cycle. Here are forecasting techniques for each of these.

- *Start by graphing the latest available demand information*

  Get a sense of the magnitude and the direction of demand by graphing available historical information. If the data are clearly trending up or down, start with a trend forecasting method. Otherwise, start simply with a level forecast and work up to a more complex seasonality forecast when level or trend methods generates too much forecast error. Do not forecast dependent demand.
- *Three-period moving average (level) forecast*

  The forecast for the current period and all future periods equals the average of the sum of the last three period's actuals: A_{-3}, A_{-2}, and A_{-1}. The 3 in MA_3 designates the number of periods to be averaged. An MA_4 moving average would use four periods. Graphing a moving average forecast over several periods shows that this technique lags the actual demand pattern.

  Period T_{-3}: A_{-3} Actual demand from three months ago
  Period T_{-2}: A_{-2} Actual demand from two months ago
  Period T_{-1}: A_{-1} Actual demand from one month ago
  Period T_0: The period being forecast

$$\text{Forecast} = \text{MA}_3 = \frac{A_{-3} + A_{-2} + A_{-1}}{3} \tag{9.6}$$

Period T_1: Forecast = MA_3 for one month from now
Period T_2: Forecast = MA_3 forecast for two months from now
All future periods: Forecast = MA_3

For example:

$$T_{-3} = 14 \text{ units}, T_{-2} = 18 \text{ units}, T_{-1} = 17 \text{ units}$$

$$\text{MA}_3 = (14 + 18 + 17)/3 = 49/3 = 16.3 \text{ units}$$

$$T_0 = T_1 = T_2 = T_{\text{Future}} = 16 \text{ units rounded down}$$

- *Simple exponential smoothing (level) forecast*

  Simple exponential smoothing requires knowing the last period's actual A_{-1} and the last period's forecast F_{-1}. The smoothing constant, α, is a number between 0 and 1. When α is close to 0, the new forecast is the same as the last forecast. When α is close to 1, the new forecast is the same as the last actual. α can be optimized by calculating a least sum of the squares error over 10 samples, or use $\alpha = 0.3$ as a good starting point. Graphing a simple exponential smoothing forecast over several periods shows that this technique lags the actual demand pattern.

Period T_{-1}: A_{-1} Actual demand from one month ago

F_{-1} Forecast from one month ago

Period T_0: The period being forecast

$$\text{Forecast} = F_0 = F_{-1} + \alpha(A_{-1} - F_{-1}) \tag{9.7}$$

Period T_1: Forecast $F_1 = F_0$ forecast for one month from now
Period T_2: Forecast $F_2 = F_0$ forecast for two months from now
All future periods: Forecast = F_0

For example:

$$\alpha = 0.3, A_{-1} = 17 \text{ units}, F_{-1} = 15 \text{ units}$$

$$F_0 = 15 + 0.3(17 - 15) = 15 + 0.3(2) = 15.6 \text{ units}$$

$$T_0 = T_1 = T_2 = T_{\text{Future}} = 16 \text{ units rounded up}$$

■ *Linear regression (trending up or trending down) forecast*

Linear regression is a sum of the least squared error method of computing the best fit of a straight line through a group of (period, demand) pairs. It returns the equation of a straight line and works for both increasing and decreasing trend lines. It is preprogrammed into most scientific and business calculators. The easiest way to hand compute a linear regression is by using the format of Table 9.4. For example, suppose you know the following five historical (period, demand) pairs: (period 1, demand 20 units), (period 2, demand 23 units), (period 3, demand 24 units), (period 4, demand 29 units), and (period 5, 32 units). Plotting these data would show an upward trend. Table 9.4 applies the format to compute a straight line best fit to this data.

Table 9.4 Linear Regression Calculation

	Period T	*Demand A*	$T \times A$	$T \times T$
	1	20	20	1
	2	23	46	4
	3	24	72	9
	4	29	116	16
	5	32	160	25
Count n	*SUM(T)*	*SUM(A)*	*SUM(TA)*	*SUM(T^2)*
5	15	128	414	55

$$m = \frac{n\text{SUM(TA)} - \text{SUM(T)SUM(A)}}{n\text{SUM(T}^2) - \text{SUM(T)SUM(T)}} \quad \text{Slope} \qquad (9.8)$$

$$m = \frac{(5)(414) - (15)(128)}{(5)(55) - (15)(15)} = \frac{150}{50} = 3.00$$

$$b = \frac{\text{SUM(A)} - m\text{SUM(T)}}{n} \quad \text{Demand intercept} \qquad (9.9)$$

$$b = \frac{(128) - (3.00)(15)}{5} = \frac{83}{5} = 16.60$$

Forecast = $mT + b$ Line equation (9.10)

Forecast $F_T = 3T + 16.6$ units

Then $T_6 = (3)(6) + 16.6 = 34.6$ units, and $T_7 = (3)(7) + 16.6 = 37.6$ units, etc.

- *Seasonal forecast*

  Winter's method is a way of computing a set of seasonal relatives expressed as percentages derived from the historical details of the last two complete cycles. Eyeball a plot of historical data to gauge the length of one cycle. Within each period, the period demands from two cycles are added and then divided by the sum of the demand totals for the same two cycles. This results in a seasonal relative as a percentage of the average total cycle. The sum of the seasonal relatives must add to exactly 100%. The seasonal relatives are then applied to a level or trend forecast for the total demand projected for the next cycle. This method is most easily understood by studying an example calculation formatted as in Table 9.5. More than two cycles can be averaged, and the cycles can have more than four periods.

  Two steps are necessary to forecast the next cycle. First, use a linear or trend method to forecast the total demand for the next cycle. This is 410 units in the example. Second, apply the seasonal relatives to each period in the next cycle. The first period in the example is 410 units × 17.8%, or 73 units.
- *Forecasting product line mix*

  Ideally, you want to forecast as small a number of items as possible over as short of a planning horizon as possible. When a product line involves a high product mix, the following method can be an alternative approach to forecasting each product individually.

Table 9.5 Seasonal Forecasting Example

Period	*Last Cycle*	*This Cycle*	*2 Cycle Total*	*Seasonal Relative*	*Next Cycle Forecast*
1	47	60	107	107/600 = 0.178 17.8%	410 × 17.8% = 73.0
2	53	64	117	117/600 = 0.195 19.5%	410 × 19.5% = 80.0
3	65	80	145	145/600 = 0.242 24.2%	410 × 24.2% = 99.2
4	100	131	231	231/600 = 0.385 38.5%	410 × 38.5% = 157.8
Totals	265	335	600	Total = 100.0%	Total = 410 units

Forecast total demand for the next cycle as follows:

265 + 70   335 + 75

265 units last cycle → 335 units this cycle → 410 units next cycle

- Capture a few months of actual demand history for each product.
- Group products as (1) main products, (2) products sold in pairs or as system components, and (3) product options or accessories.
- Sum the historical monthly demand product by product, then calculate the mean and standard deviation of the demand for each product. Use Equation 9.11 to calculate the coefficient of variation for each product.

$$\text{Coefficient of variation} = \frac{\text{Standard deviation}}{\text{Mean}} \tag{9.11}$$

- Split the list of main products into two groups: those with a coefficient of variation less than 1 and those with a coefficient of variation greater than 1.
- Use the linear, trend, and seasonality techniques to forecast main products when the coefficient of variation is less than 1. These main products have demands with low volatility.
- In low-volatility situations, a planning BOM, which relates the connect rate of another product as a fixed percentage of the main product's demand, can be used to forecast groups of secondary products. For example, if the forecast for Main Product_A is 40 units, and the planning BOM indicates that the connect rate for Secondary Product_B is 75%, then the forecast for Secondary Product_B is 30 units.
- When the coefficient of variation is greater than 1, then (1) have Sales work very closely with the main customer, or (2) try forecasting down one BOM level especially for system components, or (3) check that this product is not really a dependently demanded product that should not be forecast. These main products have demands with high volatility where the application of simple level, trend, or seasonality forecasting methods may generate large forecast errors.

■ *Forecasting a new product with no demand history*

Work with a probabilistic range consisting of an upper trend line and a lower trend line. That is, the demand is expected to be no more than the upper number and no less than the bottom number. The lower trend line can be based on early customers committed to purchasing the product. As actual product demand history develops, adjust the two trend lines. The upper trend line drives inventory planning so that there is enough product to satisfy the upside demand. The lower trend line drives breakeven profitability and cash replenishment so that the business has enough cash flow to survive.

Tracking Forecast Accuracy for Continuous Improvement

Different figures of merit are commonly used to track forecast accuracy. The mean absolute deviation (MAD) weighs the forecast error of each period evenly. The mean absolute percentage error (MAPE) weighs the forecast error of each period according to its relative error. Use Table 9.6 below to quickly compute forecast accuracy. A smaller number indicates a more accurate forecast. Very large numbers indicate that a different forecasting method should be used.

$$\text{Forecast error}_T = \text{Actual}_T - \text{Forecast}_T \quad \text{for period } T \tag{9.12}$$

$$\text{MAD} = \sum_T \frac{|\text{Forecast error}_T|}{n} \quad \text{for } n \text{ periods} \tag{9.13}$$

$$\text{MAPE} = \frac{\sum_T \frac{|\text{Forecast error}_T|}{\text{Actual } T} \times 100\%}{n} \tag{9.14}$$

As time goes by and data from more periods become available, MAD can be used in a tracking signal equation to detect forecast bias. A control chart with control limits set to ±3 MADs can identify the presence of nonrandom forecast errors, i.e., outliers, error trends, or error cycling. Table 9.7 is an example of using a rolling three-period moving average forecast, with a tracking signal based on a rolling four-period accumulation of errors, and a rolling four-period (n = 4) MAD.

Table 9.6 Computing Forecast Accuracy

Period	*Actual (A)*	*Forecast (F)*	*FC Error (A–F)*	*|FC Error|*	*% |FC Error| / Actual*
1	20	19.6	0.4	0.4	2.0%
2	23	22.6	0.4	0.4	1.7%
3	24	25.6	–1.6	1.6	6.7%
4	29	28.6	0.4	0.4	1.4%
5	32	31.6	0.4	0.4	1.3%
			SUM	3.2	13.1%
			n Factor	*n* = 5	*n* = 5
				MAD	*MAPE*
				0.64	2.6%

Table 9.7 Example Forecast Error Tracking Signal Calculation

Period	*Actual (A)*	*MA_3 Forecast (F)*	*FC Error (A–F)*	*|FC Error|*	*MAD (n = 4)*	*Tracking Signal (n = 4)*
1	20					
2	23					
3	24					
4	29	22.3	6.7	6.7		
5	32	25.3	6.7	6.7		
6	31	28.3	2.7	2.7		
7	35	30.7	4.3	4.3	5.1	20.3/5.1 = 3.98
8	36	32.7	3.3	3.3	4.3	17.0/4.3 = 3.95
9	29	34.0	–5.0	5.0	3.8	–5.3/3.8 = –1.39
10	27	33.3	–6.3	6.3	4.8	–3.7/4.8 = –0.77
11	31	30.7	0.3	0.3	3.8	–7.7/3.8 = –2.02
12	33	29.0	4.0	4.0	3.9	–7.0/3.9 = –1.79
					Control Limits +/– 3MAD	

$$\text{Tracking signal} = \sum_T \frac{\text{Forecast error}_T}{\text{MAD}_n} \tag{9.15}$$

Capture the Order

Referring once again to the big picture, Figure 9.1, the forecast drives inventory into the push/pull boundary; this is demand planning. The customer's order pulls inventory out of the push/pull boundary; this is demand management and fulfillment. This section describes the construction of a process to capture the customer's order.

Sources of Revenue

The income statement is driven from top line revenue. Simplistically, revenue is the payment of one price for shipping one unit of product to one customer at one location. The reality is much more complex with multiple prices and discounts, multiple quantities, multiple products, multiple customers, multiple customer locations, returns, and credits. Your supply chain may generate some or all of the following types of revenue:

- *One-time product sales in the forward supply chain*—This is the most common form of sale. Keep in mind that revenue may be impacted by volume discounts and credits for returns.
- *Contracted product sales in the forward supply chain*—Customers ordering high volumes of the same product configuration often sign contracts with volume pricing discounts and delivery schedules stretching across several months. This makes for easy revenue forecasting.
- *Spare parts sales in the forward supply chain*—Customers often buy spares to maintain the products they have purchased.
- *Subscription service sales in the forward supply chain*—This is monthly revenue generated from services such as customer access to telecommunications networks or websites.
- *Information or consulting services in the forward supply chain*—Specialty information or consulting capability developed within the business may be packaged and sold as another source of service revenue.
- *One-time services in the forward supply chain*—This is revenue generated from services such as installation or training.
- *Product rentals or leasing services in the forward supply chain*—These are alternative forms of financial service arrangements to assist the buyer in paying for the product.
- *Extended warranty in the reverse supply chain*—This service revenue generator from supporting an installed base of customer products long after their initial sale drives reverse supply chain operations.
- *Aftermarket sales in the reverse supply chain*—Remanufactured product can be sold at a lower price into a different market segment.
- *Calibration and repair services in the reverse supply chain*—This is service revenue from the calibration and repair of product.
- *Recycling recovery in the reverse supply chain*—This is revenue gained from the sale of recycled raw materials.

Scrolling through the Customer Order States

Think of the flow of customer orders using the analogy of a scroll. The scroll unwinds from the top and rewinds at the bottom, with the unrolled portion of the scroll in plain view in the middle. The top of the scroll is the future; the middle of the scroll is the present; the bottom of the scroll is the past. A customer order can be in one of four states: (1) a target, (2) a forecast, (3) a backlog, or (4) a shipment, as it transverses time on the scroll.

- *Target (future state)*—When financial targets are set based on past revenue dollars, customer–product pairs are usually unknown. For example, if this quarter is targeted to be 105% of this quarter last year, you may not know the customer details of exactly how you are going to achieve the new target.

- *Forecast (future or present state)*—The demand forecast contains the detail of the customer, the product, the price, the quantity, and the extended dollars. Sometimes, a quotation is prepared for the customer. But while a quotation may provide some detail to the forecast, it cannot be considered an order. A customer order in the forecast state is not booked until the product is completely specified and the order margin approved; the order quantity, price, ship-to address, and shipping method are confirmed in writing by the customer; and the customer has passed credit approval.

Note: When the sum of the demand forecast dollars plus the backlog dollars plus the shipment dollars does not add up to the financial target for a given period, there may be a plug row in the forecast. The plug row forces the dollar total to match the financial target; however, there is significant risk that sales will be unable to identify a real customer–product opportunity to convert the plug row into a real backlog within the specified timeframe.

- *Backlog (present state)*—The customer order, which was once part of the demand forecast, is now booked but has not yet been shipped. A customer order can remain in a backlog state for a few hours or a few months. For example, the customer may specify a "do not ship before" date or the use of a specific logistics carrier or require an inspection before shipment. Or the distributor may be waiting on the factory to replenish inventory.
- *Shipped (present or past state)*—The customer makes a product pickup and makes payment for the product. Or the customer's product has left the shipping dock complete, an invoice has been sent to the customer, and an advance shipping notice (ASN) has been sent to the customer. You have to decide under what circumstances, if any, your business may allow a partial shipment, as this can be a big dissatisfier for your customer.

Revenue Reporting

Each shippable customer order is a line item on the revenue report. Each line item can have a status of shipped, backlog, or forecast. Backlog status is from the perspective of Operations and not Sales. Backlog means the customer order has been booked and acknowledged with a promise date but has not yet been shipped. The Sales process from forecast through quotation to order booking on each customer deal is largely invisible to Operations. An order is not booked until the seller makes an offer having reviewed the margin and checked the buyer's credit limit and the buyer signs off on the product configuration, quantity, and terms. Each of these decision points can result in a wait loop that contributes to the variability of the order-to-delivery-to-cash$_{\text{Demand}}$ cycle. The revenue report is in continuous flux because there is shipment, order booking, and order acknowledgment activity every day, sometimes every hour.

Table 9.8 shows an example of three months of rolling revenue reporting. Future orders projected by Sales come onto the report under a forecast status. Once an order is booked with its pricing, quantity, and product configuration locked down, the order status changes to backlog, and the order is moved above any forecast orders for that month. Once the order is shipped, the order status changes to shipped and

Table 9.8 Rolling Revenue Report

Order	*Status*	*Ship Date*	*Customer*	*Net Price*	*Net Qty*	*Net Revenue*	*Product*
January							
4852	**Shipped**	Jan. 4	Customer_D	$675	100	$67,500	
4853	**Shipped**	Jan. 10	Customer_G	$805	75	$60,375	
4855	**Shipped**	Jan. 12	Customer_B	$805	200	$161,000	
4856	**Shipped**	Jan. 22	Customer_H	$650	85	$55,250	
4857	**Shipped**	Jan. 28	Customer_E	$1,210	50	$60,500	
					510	**$404,625**	**Total**
					500	**$400,000**	**Target**
February							
4858	**Shipped**	Feb. 5	Customer_B	$805	200	$161,000	
4793	Backlog	Feb. 12	Customer_J	$700	75	$52,500	
4794	Backlog	Feb. 22	Customer_J	$700	75	$52,500	
4859	Backlog	Feb. 25	Customer_E	$1,210	100	$121,000	
	Forecast		Customer_L	$700	100	$70,000	
					550	**$457,000**	**Total**
					500	**$400,000**	**Target**
March							
4854	Backlog	Mar. 3	Customer_M	$805	50	$40,250	
	Forecast		Customer_G	$805	150	$120,750	
	Forecast		Customer_N	$700	100	$70,000	
	Forecast		Plug	$805	200	$161,000	
					500	**$392,000**	**Total**
					550	**$440,000**	**Target**
				Quarterly total	**1,560**	**$1,253,625**	
				Quarterly target	**1,550**	**$1,240,000**	

the line item is moved above any order backlog for the month. Line items are listed within their status groupings in ship date or promise date order. Each month and quarter, the total quantity and the total revenue are compared against monthly and quarterly revenue targets for the business. January shipments exceeded the target, February appears to be on track to exceed the target, but March, even with its plug number, is in trouble. If customer demand for the March forecast plus the plug number can be made, then the actual shipments for the quarter will be slightly better than target.

Product mix can have a big impact on making the revenue numbers. For example, higher volume sales of a lower priced product or deeply discounted pricing on a high-volume contract can result in total revenue being lower than desired. On the other hand, healthy parts sales and/or subscription service revenue can improve total revenue over what was expected.

Information Technology Applied to Order Capture

There are several important information technology applications that can be applied to the process of capturing the customer's order. Some of these come under an umbrella application called customer relationship management (CRM), while others provide standalone functions that can be linked together to form a complete order management process. CRM gathers everything about each customer into one database including contact information, ship-to and bill-to addresses, past quotes, past purchases, links to credit checking, open orders, customer feedback, customer service requests, product warranty, report generators, and more. The following basic process steps can be easily automated and made accessible over the Internet:

- *Electronic catalogs*—A website displays your complete product catalog with product photographs, descriptions, and pricing. Products can be grouped into product lines. Pricing and promotional sales can be continuously updated. Discontinued products can be easily deleted.
- *Electronic shopping cart*—Off-the-shelf retail products chosen from the catalog are added to an electronic shopping cart. The shopping cart application keeps a running total of the dollar and quantity amounts to be purchased, and it allows shoppers to easily add more purchases or change their minds and put something back on the shelf electronically.
- *New customer setup*—Each new customer must be properly entered into the information technology system before order processing can proceed. This includes gathering basic information about the customer, including name and contact information, a ship-to address, a bill-to address, method of payment, etc. New customers applying for a line of credit must be properly vetted through Finance before continuing.

- *Quoting packages*—Industrial products often have custom requirements, which must be quoted before a purchase is made. The same customer may ask for multiple quotes covering different product configurations and/or different delivery scenarios. The quote is entered into an electronic form, which can then be printed for the customer. Later, when approved by the customer, the quote converts directly into the customer's order.
- *Configurators*—Complex products and systems can have technical incompatibilities among their various components. A configurator is application software that translates a customer-friendly ordering scheme into an operations-friendly set of inventory part numbers. At the same time, the configurator holds a set of component combining rules that will stop processing an order should the combination be known to be incompatible.
- *Credit checking and credit card validation*—Customers buying on credit and/or with a credit card or procurement card must have their purchase checked against fraudulent activity and their current credit limits verified before the order can be booked. Credit customer accounts are checked against an aged accounts receivable report. Credit card and procurement card customers are checked via third-party credit checking applications run by VISA, MasterCard, American Express, etc., which also provide additional security checks.
- *Booking the order*—Once the product is completely specified as to price, quantity, and configuration; once the delivery is completely specified as to ship-to location, delivery date, and delivery logistics; once payment is completely specified as to available credit, terms, method of payment, bank account name, account number, and routing number or credit card type, name, account number, expiration date, security code, and bill-to address; and once the customer has signed the order, then the customer's order is booked.
- *Order confirmation*—Once booked, the order is confirmed back to the customer along with the additional information of an estimated delivery date, estimated freight charges, and actual sales tax.

Broadcast the Order

The manner in which a point-of-sale customer order is communicated upstream is critical. The customer order drives the fulfillment operation, the replenishment of certain inventories, and longer-term forecasting. When the details of sales events are corrupted or lost in translation moving upstream, supply chain operations get blindsided by unexpected changes in mix and rate requirements. Upstream operations scramble to try to meet these new requirements, which often result in unmet expectations, inefficiencies, excess inventories, and unnecessary costs.

Bullwhip Effect

The round-trip customer order and product delivery, coupled with the round-trip replenishment signal and inventory restock, represents a feedback loop across the end-to-end supply chain network. Just as a microphone placed in the wrong position in front of a high gain public address speaker will howl from feedback oscillations, a supply chain network can break into order-to-replenishment oscillations. Small changes in customer demand downstream that occur with the right timing and that get amplified by various lot sizing rules moving upstream can result in the supply base getting slammed by demands for full capacity to demands for no capacity. The supply base is called to either produce excessive amounts of inventory or to completely halt production. This is called the bullwhip effect. A small flick of the wrist at the handle, i.e., customer demand, causes the end of the whip to strike an arc causing supplier whiplash.

Studies of feedback control systems from other disciplines have shown that oscillations are caused by the simultaneous occurrence of all the amplification factors around the feedback path being greater than 1 and by the next input being in-phase with the last output. Delays along the feedback path are a major cause of keeping the next input in phase with the output, thus adding to demand.

The bullwhip effect in a supply chain is caused largely by lot sizing amplification along the serial path that the replenishment signal travels upstream and by the logistics transit time delays along the serial paths that inventory restocks travel downstream. The replenishment signal moves from the retail store to the distributor, where it gets lot sized; then it moves from the distributor to the factory, where it gets lot sized; and finally it moves from the factory to the supplier, where it again gets lot sized. The resulting restock inventory, when it arrives back at the retail store, may well be larger than the original demand. Then, as inventory moves downstream, there is a delay with inbound logistics, another delay with midbound logistics, and finally a delay with outbound logistics. The supply chain's feedback path now has the amplification factor and the phase delay factor to sustain an inventory oscillation.

The bullwhip effect can be conquered effectively by broadcasting the replenishment signal to the trading partners in parallel rather than in series to reduce the lot sizing amplification, and by synchronizing inbound, midbound, and outbound logistics transit times such that there is effectively one delay and not three.

How to Synchronize the Replenishment of BTS Products

The last physical inventory location closest to the end customer is called the shipping buffer. This would be at the retail store for a two-echelon delivery channel, at the distributor for a one-echelon delivery channel, or at the factory for a zero-echelon delivery channel. Under a BTS operating strategy, the shipping buffer and the push/pull boundary are often the same physical inventory locations.

Initially, a demand forecast pushes product inventory into the push/pull boundary, which is the BTS shipping buffer. When a point-of-sale customer order gets released for shipment, product inventory is immediately pulled from the shipping buffer and delivered to the customer. The point-of-sale customer order is also broadcast upstream to become a replenishment order for product inventory.

A supply forecast is regenerated monthly, as was explained earlier in this chapter. Then, as explained in Chapter 10: "Inventory Management," lead time offsets and fixed lot sizing are applied in DRP, in MPS, and in MRP to bring in materials with long lead time. This results in a planned replenishment quantity of inventory being delivered to the push/pull boundary and shipping buffer at a specified time. The daily point-of-sale order broadcast modifies the replenishment according to the following guidelines to defeat the bullwhip effect. The use of fixed period replenishment synchronizes the logistics transfers.

- A supply forecast is regenerated monthly, and sometimes weekly, to drive inventory into the push/pull boundary, which is also the shipping buffer.
- Point-of-sale demand is connected directly to the shipping buffer and to the network constraint.
- The customer-facing echelon delivers the ordered quantity and mix from the shipping buffer.
- The network constraint accumulates daily demand information and broadcasts this demand to each of the other trading partners in a parallel information transmission (see Figure 9.4).

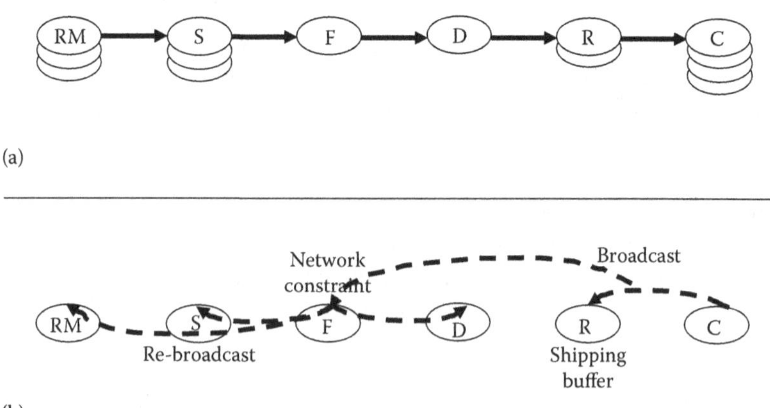

Figure 9.4 Threading the point-of-sale demand signal: (a) material flow; (b) point-of-scale order broadcast. C = customer; D = distributor; F = factory; R = retailer; RM = raw material; S = supplier.

- If the network constraint can meet the actual order rate and mix, then it broadcasts the actual order rate and mix to all trading partners for next day replenishment (see Table 9.9).
- If the network constraint cannot meet the actual order rate or mix, then it advises an adjusted delivery date for the customer, broadcasts a constrained rate or mix for next-day replenishment, and manages the order backlog (see Table 9.9).

Table 9.9 Sample Order Broadcast

Replenishment Broadcast				*Network Constraint*				*Point-of-Sale*			
				Constraint = 20 Units							
Products				*Products*				*Products*			
A	*B*	*C*	*D*	*A*	*B*	*C*	*D*	*A*	*B*	*C*	*D*
For day 2								Day 1			
3	5	8	2	3	5	8	2	3	5	8	2
				0	0	0	0				
				Day 1 backlog							
For day 3								Day 2			
4	7	6	3	4	7	**6**	3	4	7	9	3
				0	0	**3**	0				
				Day 2 backlog							
For day 4								Day 3			
4	4	9	3	4	4	**9**	3	4	4	8	3
				0	0	**2**	0				
				Day 3 backlog							
For day 5								Day 4			
4	5	8	2	4	5	**8**	2	4	5	6	2
				0	0	0	0				
				Day 4 backlog							

- The trading partners plan using fixed-order interval replenishment rather than fixed-order quantity replenishment.
- The point-of-sale demand is accumulated SKU by SKU and consumes the forecast. At the end of each fixed period, the replenishment quantity equals the accumulated point-of-sale demand.
- Each period, the trading partners produce the number of products, assemblies, or components that match the accumulated point-of-sale rate and mix broadcast.
- The most upstream suppliers plan raw materials to match the rate of incoming customer orders.

Some large distributors will drop factories and/or suppliers that have backorders in their daily replenishment performance. It is worth noting that many apparel and fast moving consumer goods (FMCG) companies follow a nine-step process called Collaborative Planning Forecasting and Replenishment (CPFR), which is a trademark of the Voluntary Interindustry Commerce Standards Committee (VICS) (http://www.gs1us.org). VICS has also standardized electronic data interchange protocols and Universal Product Code bar codes and is working on standards for radiofrequency identification tags.

How to Fulfill BTO Products

While there is product mix among the various SKUs under the BTS operating strategy above, the products themselves are not customized. In a retail setting, the same set of products gets replenished over and over. Daily and/or weekly seasonal and/or promotional changes in the SKU mix are fulfilled by the planning cycle. Under a BTO operating strategy, products are replenished differently. Every product is potentially customized. Some products pictured in the catalog are never built because there will never be customer orders for them. Under a BTO operating strategy, the push/pull boundary is located farther upstream at the distributor for postponement or at the factory for full customization. In an industrial setting, there is no downstream shipping buffer because a customized product is never stocked. There is less probability of the bullwhip effect because upstream inventory is released against specific downstream customer orders. Inventory moves to fulfill specific orders, rather than as replenishment. It is harder for arriving inventory to be larger than the customer's order demands.

Consistent, reliable delivery for a BTO business depends upon having both the capacity and the raw material inventory when and where it is needed. You want to broadcast the order backlog in a way that facilitates capacity constraint and raw material inventory mix decisions. If the required work center capacity is not available and/or if the required BOM is not available, then the promise date to the customer cannot be met. BTO products should be managed using the following guidelines.

- A supply forecast is regenerated monthly to order long-lead-time raw materials, to drive long-lead-time BTS component inventory into the push/pull boundary, and to replenish safety stocks.
- Purchasing agreements are in place to ensure timely access to seldom used, high-mix items.
- Point-of-sale demand is connected directly with the push/pull boundary and with the network constraint.
- The network constraint accumulates daily demand information and broadcasts this demand to each of the other trading partners in a parallel information transmission.
- If the network constraint can meet the required delivery date for the actual order rate and mix, then it broadcasts the actual order rate and mix to all trading partners.
- If the network constraint cannot meet the actual order rate or mix, then it advises an adjusted delivery date for the customer, broadcasts a constrained rate or mix, and manages the order backlog.
- The trading partners plan using fixed-quantity reorder points rather than a fixed-interval reorder points.
- The point-of-sale demand is accumulated SKU by SKU and consumes the forecast. At the end of each fixed period, MRP is regenerated across the actual order mix, and on-hand and on-order inventories are checked against actual requirements.
- The ordered quantity and mix is shipped from the push/pull boundary through the delivery channel to the customer.
- The raw material suppliers plan long-lead-time raw materials to match the rate of actual customer orders plus a safety stock.

How to Fulfill Services

Services are sold to differentiate product offerings, to provide more complete customer solutions, and to generate recurring revenue. Some typical examples of services include one-time product training and system installation. Monthly reoccurring services might include product leasing, business information services, telecommunication network access, and extended warranty. Services entail an information flow and a cash flow, but no material flow. Therefore, the customer's order for services is treated a little differently at the Operations interface.

A service supply forecast is for capacity rather than for inventory. Service capacity is perishable; i.e., unused capacity cannot be recovered. Services can be defined by a bill of capacity with lead times rather than a BOM with lead times. For example, the service order is about scheduling a capable service technician for a specific time at a specific location. Every attempt should be made to schedule services in a way that maximizes capacity utilization. However, it is often the case that a high-revenue product inventory sale is tightly coupled to a low-revenue service capacity sale, and the product inventory sale will take priority.

In Summary

This chapter describes demand planning including establishing a delivery lead time and operations strategy, forecasting the order, capturing the order, and broadcasting the order. It details how to forecast the right thing, how to forecast things right, and how to compute forecast accuracy for the purpose of continuous improvement. The chapter describes the application of information technology to order processing. Finally, the chapter explains how to replenish inventory while eliminating the bullwhip effect.

Chapter 10

Inventory Management

The big picture in Chapter 9: "Demand Planning" showed how the supply chain network splits into a push zone and a pull zone. The location of the push/pull boundary determines whether the operating strategy is build-to-stock (BTS) or build-to-order (BTO). Forecasting techniques for demand planning anticipate product inventory requirements, while order processing and delivery complete the fulfillment of the customer's order from inventory. Keeping inventory turning throughout the supply chain network is one of the key success factors in operating a great supply chain. This chapter presents a method to manage inventory turns across the supply chain network. In this chapter, you learn how to use push planning methods to convert the demand forecast into item-specific purchase orders and work orders released to drive inventory into the push/pull boundary. You also learn how to use pull planning methods to ensure reliable, predictable inventory matching when specific customer orders are pulled from the push/pull boundary.

In Stock, No Problem

Just as Bill, the Supply Chain Construction Project Team manager, had suspected, the quarterly review meeting was difficult. They were in a tough spot. The revenue number was almost too small to make the Corporate hurdle rate for starting a new business. Steve, the chief executive officer, totally understood that demand for the new uninterruptable power supply (UPS) product family was dependent upon server sales that were outside of his control. Steve would try to sell Corporate on the idea that a more complete product offering would boost sales for both Computer Products and Power Products. Steve challenged Marketing to improve the connect rate and to accelerate engagement with the value-added resellers (VARs). The Supply Chain Construction Project Team was told to plan at a rate of 1,800 units per month.

"Whew, I glad that meeting is over," exclaimed Donna from Purchasing as they gathered for a postmortem analysis of the quarterly review in a different conference room. "Now what?"

"Now we turn our attention to filling the network container with product content," said Bill.

"How do we do that?" asked John from Engineering.

"Let's go back to the network for a minute," said Bill stepping up to the whiteboard. "We have SOURCE + MAKE + DELIVER. Under that we have Raw Materials + Suppliers for SOURCE, Astec for MAKE, and Power Products + VARs + Customers for DELIVER…a total of six echelons. Harry, explain to the team again how Product Marketing sees the VARs' role in delivery."

Harry explained, "After the VAR forwards the customer's order, the VAR consolidates all the hardware at their location, you know the server, the router, the UPS, the LAN cable, etc. In most cases, the VAR preloads the server operating system and customer-specific application software. Last, the VAR delivers the system to the customer's location and helps the customer install the system."

"So, it would be correct to say that our customer is really the VAR and that our delivery lead time is relative to the VAR rather than the end customer?" asked Bill.

"Yes, that's right. We need three to five days of delivery lead time for the VAR," said Harry.

Back at the whiteboard Bill said, "OK. Suppliers for SOURCE, Astec contract manufacturer for MAKE, Power Products Distribution for DELIVER, VAR for customer. Let's focus on these four echelons and split the supply chain into two sections: a push zone and a pull zone."

"What's a push zone and what's a pull zone?" asked Tony from Cost Accounting.

Bill replied, "The push zone pushes inventory from a forecast into an inventory location called the push/pull boundary. After a matchup, the pull zone pulls inventory out of the push/pull boundary to fulfill the customer order. The push/pull boundary location determines the delivery lead time that the customer sees."

"Oh, I get it," said Tony. "If the push/pull boundary is downstream close to the customer, the delivery lead time is short. But if the push/pull boundary is upstream close to the supplier, the delivery lead time is long. Why would anyone want a long lead time?"

"Because with a downstream location, the supply chain is operated in a build-to-stock mode with lots of inventory investment, while with a midstream location, rather than an upstream location, the supply chain is operated in a build-to-order mode, which is better suited for high mix," said Bill.

Harry chimed in, "We need a short delivery lead time, just a couple of days."

"Yes, our push/pull boundary inventory location will be the cycle stock here at the Power Products Distribution Center. Our supply chain operating strategy should be BTS," agreed Bill.

Everyone around the table shook their heads in agreement.

Bill continued, "The next order of business is to list a composite bill of materials (BOM) and decide how the 1,800 units per month will be split across the Product 250, Product 500, and Product 1000 models. The composite BOM item master lists every unique part number for all the materials we need to build any of the three UPS products. From there, we will determine which part numbers are common to all three products and which part numbers are product specific."

Donna replied, "John and I can do that pretty quickly. What do we need to convert the forecast into my purchase orders?"

"What we have so far is just a forecast for an aggregate run rate of 1,800 per month, as we exit the first year of shipments. We have to plan how this aggregate rate starts from zero and builds to 1,800 per month. Then we have to determine the parts mix to build this rate," answered Bill.

"Yes, but why wouldn't Astec figure out the parts that they need?" Donna wanted to know.

"That's a good point," admitted Bill. "However, there are a few long lead time, strategic materials that we said we would plan and purchase for Astec during the first year. This would include the battery cells and the front and rear frames. We agreed to do this to manage supply risk on these key parts."

"From the forecast, we place purchase orders with Astec for three models of complete products to be delivered to our distribution center (DC), and we place purchase orders with the battery supplier and the frame extruder to deliver lower level parts to Astec," summarized Donna.

"As an overview yes, but we need a bit more detail," continued Bill. Back at the whiteboard, he wrote "Planning = FC + S&OP/RCCP + DRP + MPS + MRP/CRP" and began, "Normally, the forecast (FC) drives a sales & operation plan (S&OP) with rough cut capacity planning (RCCP), which drives a distribution requirements plan (DRP), which drives a master production schedule (MPS), which drives material requirements planning (MRP) with capacity requirements planning (CRP). The input is the rolling monthly forecast, and the output is a set of weekly purchase orders and work orders."

"So how does that work out?" asked John.

"Hold on. Let me simplify this a little. DRP is only necessary when there are multiple DCs; we can eliminate DRP for now. Astec runs capacity planning, so we can also eliminate CRP from our planning. Our model becomes: 'Planning = FC + S&OP/RCCP + MPS + MRP.' "

"Why do we need MRP?" asked Tony.

"That is because for material planning, we will use a modified BOM to split out the battery cells and the frames while ordering the finished product from Astec.

The planning BOM might be something like: "level 0 = (quantity 1) Product 500 UPS, level 1 = (quantity 1) Partial Product 500 UPS, level 1 = (quantity 3) battery cell, level 1 = (quantity 1) front frame, level 1 = (quantity 1) rear frame." We plan the Product 500 UPS, battery cell, front frame, and rear frame. Astec plans the rest of the product as Partial Product 500 UPS with all its lower-level parts. We will use RCCP to plan distribution capacity and Astec will use their internal CRP to plan factory capacity," explained Bill.

"What does MRP add to the planning?" asked John.

Donna answered his question, "MRP allows us to plan using lot sizing and lead time offsets. MRP suggests purchase orders far enough in advance and in the right quantity for the number of products needed in distribution. It will be in stock, no problem!"

"What if we need a different quantity of the Product 250 or Product 1000 models?" asked Harry.

"Why don't you just give us the right forecast?" remarked Tony.

"Look! My hands are tied. Computer Products has been uncooperative!" shot back Harry.

"Well, maybe we won't have enough cash to buy the entire inventory you think you need," said Tony.

"Hold it!" commanded Bill. "We need to stay supportive of each other, if we hope to pull off this supply chain construction project as planned. One answer to Harry's question is to overplan the Product 250 and Product 1000 models to build a small safety stock of each. We will need to develop some understanding of the demand uncertainty over lead time. Otherwise, Tony's point is valid, and we run out of cash."

"We're certainly not going to hold 1,800 Product 250, plus 1,800 Product 500, plus 1,800 Product 1000 UPS in finished goods. That is nearly $1.4 million tied up in just-in-case inventory," countered Tony.

"The total mixed model inventory we choose to hold will be more than 100% of 1,800 units per month, but certainly not 300%. We also have to determine how many days of supply to hold at the push/pull boundary in the DC to maintain our delivery lead time. The key is to keep high inventory turns on all this material." concluded Bill.

Ask These Eight Inventory Questions

Inventory is like the balance on your personal credit card. The balance can be maintained anywhere you want from zero dollars to the maximum allowed. There is no right amount, although there are understandable reasons for either a zero balance or a maximum balance. Some people have a credit card just-in-case. The balance tends to drift upward unless you have discipline and a written budget. Once you start a credit balance, the minimum cash payment is tied up forever, or at least until the balance is fully paid. And, it takes even more cash to pay off growing credit card debt.

The following eight questions are fundamental to an understanding of inventory management.

1. *Why is inventory required in a supply chain?*

   Inventory is used to buffer operations timing. The inventory of other parts can be accumulated until the last part becomes available and the product can be built. Customer shipments can be made from inventory when there is insufficient capacity available right now to build the product. Inventory can be held until the customer is able to make their payment. Inventory can be accumulated to keep full-time employees working. Inventory can be held to mitigate certain kinds of risk. Inventory can help an organization achieve its desired service level.
2. *What are the natural demand patterns for the business?*

   Different businesses have different demand patterns. Fast moving consumer goods (FMCGs) demand regular, repetitive replenishment of the same set of products. Textile and apparel have four or six seasons per year with 100% turnover of product styles and colors. Industrial customers demand highly customized, complex products on an irregular basis. Demands for pharmaceutical products compete between high-priced originals and low-cost generics that hopefully are not counterfeit. Demand for capital equipment sold to the government can take years for approvals. Demand for services can be influenced by consumer ratings and social media.
3. *How much inventory investment is needed to run the business?*

   The inventory investment depends upon many factors including the volume of business, the product mix, the length of the supply chain, lot sizing rules, service level targets, and more. This chapter provides an answer to the question of how much inventory is needed.
4. *Where should this inventory be located?*

   Inventory can be held in every echelon of a supply chain network. Longer supply chains hold more total inventory than shorter supply chains do. The breadth of each echelon, meaning, for example, the number of suppliers in an upstream echelon or the number of retail stores in a downstream echelon, multiples the total inventory. Inventory can also be found in transit in every active logistics connection. This chapter addresses the question of where to best locate inventory.
5. *How much should be reordered at any one time?*

   This question is about lot sizing. There are costs to holding inventory, from the rental on the warehouse and its associated utilities to inventory loss due to pilferage, spoilage, and obsolescence. There are costs to process the orders to replenish inventory; the smaller the lot, the more ordering drives up this cost. Lot sizing strives to balance holding costs with ordering costs. This chapter provides answers to lot sizing questions.

6. *When should the replenishment orders be placed?*
   Inventory is best replenished just before it is needed. Some inventory requirements are driven by independent demands. Other inventory requirements are driven by dependent demand. The timing of replenishment depends upon knowing the type of demand, the replenishment lead time, and the rate of demand during the replenishment lead time. This chapter details a set of planning tools that answer the question of when to replenish inventory.
7. *When is safety stock a good idea?*
   Lead time has variability, and demand has uncertainty. Safety stocks are kept to counteract these risks. This chapter advises when to consider safety stock, how much safety stock to keep, and where to place such inventory.
8. *How are inventory turns related to working capital?*
   A huge amount of working capital is tied to inventory. This cash is not available for any other purpose, unless the total inventory investment can be reduced. Inventory that turns frequently will release its cash investment sooner. Stranded inventory, on the other hand, never turns. It is dead. It never gives up its cash investment, and it never provides any return.

This book is focused on the planning and execution of a workable inventory solution across an end-to-end supply chain network. This is particularly relevant during the start-up of a new supply chain and during the merger of two existing supply chains. As your supply chain matures, you may want to consider applying Lean production techniques to your factory and supplier operations. Lean production includes execution techniques that can improve inventory turns, but it requires a planning method such as presented in this book. An in-depth discussion of Lean production is outside the scope of this book.

Get the Lay of the Land

It is very helpful to think through this mental exercise. Image your end product all packaged and palletized sitting on the factory's shipping dock waiting to be picked up. What are the cubic dimensions of the pallet? How many products does it hold? What does the pallet weigh? Look upstream toward raw materials (RMs) and image the product exploding backward into assemblies, then into components, and finally into RMs. How does each of these items look as they flow into the factory? What lot sizes and lead times dominate the supply? How are these items packaged and transported? How often does the upstream inventory for these items turn? Now, look downstream toward the end customer and image how the product is handled through the delivery channel. What kind of transportation moves the product? Where is safety stock kept? How many times does the product get touched? Is the product ever repackaged? How often does the downstream inventory for these products turn?

The end-to-end supply chain network, i.e., the network container, has a fixed number of locations that can hold inventory. The operations plan includes which of these locations are to be used, which items are assigned to each location, and how much inventory of each item is to be held at each location. The product flowing through the network, i.e., the product contents, has certain characteristics. Each product in the product set has its own rate, mix, and seasonality. Not every product requires inventory from every supplier, and not every product has inventory flowing through every delivery channel to every customer. One of the trading partners in the network is the network constraint. The network constraint may move to a different trading partner should the product mix experience a large shift.

Forward Network Inventory Locations

Consider a typical six-echelon supply chain network: echelon 6–RM, echelon 5–supplier, echelon 4–factory, echelon 3–distributor, echelon 2–retail store, echelon 1–customer (see Figure 10.1). The inventory locations listed below are the possible places to hold inventory. There may be more than one echelon of suppliers, factories including contract manufacturers and copackers, and/or distributors in your

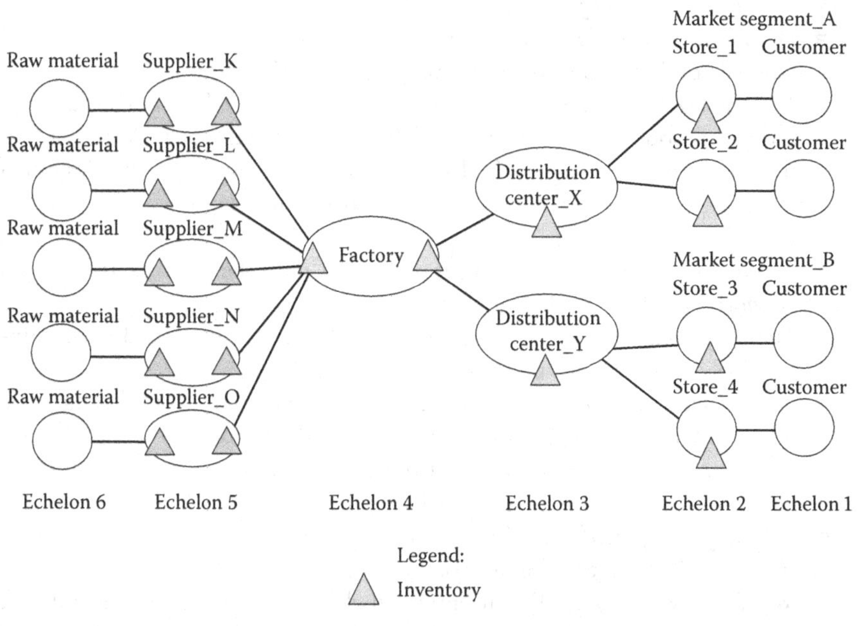

Figure 10.1 Inventory locations across a forward supply chain network.

network, which will increase the number of potential inventory locations. Reverse supply chain network inventory locations are discussed in Chapter 8: "Return."

- *Supplier RM inventory*—RM held at the supplier's facility.
- *Supplier quarantined inventory*—RM that has failed incoming inspection and is waiting a material disposition action.
- *Supplier work-in-process (WIP) inventory*—In-process inventory on the supplier's production floor. This book does not focus on WIP because in many cases, WIP is a fast-turn inventory, making the RM input and the finished good (FG) output inventories much more relevant. WIP increases the complexity of internal inventory accounting for suppliers.
- *Supplier FG inventory*—Finished component parts held at the supplier's facility or in the supplier's distribution network which is an additional echelon.
- *Inventory transported by inbound logistics*—Cartons, pallets, and/or containers of finished component parts and RMs in-transit to the supplier or factory.
- *Consignment inventory*—Inventory located at one organization to reduce lead time but owned by another organization. Consignment inventory is paid for as it is consumed. Vendor-managed inventory is consignment inventory where the vendor comes on-site to stock, count, and order.
- *Factory RM inventory*—RM held at the factory.
- *Factory quarantined inventory*—RM and component part inventory that has failed incoming inspection and is waiting a material disposition action.
- *Factory WIP inventory*—In-process inventory on the factory's production floor. This book does not focus on WIP because in many cases, WIP is a fast-turn inventory, making the RM input and the FG output inventories much more relevant. WIP increases the complexity of internal inventory accounting for the factory.
- *Factory FG inventory*—FGs held at the factory or in the factory's distribution network, which is an additional echelon.
- *Inventory transported by midbound logistics*—Cartons, pallets, and/or containers of FGs in-transit to the distributor.
- *Postponement inventory*—Component inventory required to build out generic subassemblies into end products held at either the factory or the distributor.
- *Distributor cycle stock*—FGs held at the distributor or in a multitiered distribution network, which adds an additional echelon.
- *Inventory transported by outbound logistics*—Cartons, pallets, and/or containers of FGs in-transit to the store or customer.
- *Retail store cycle stock*—FG inventory stocked on the store shelves and in a backroom.

- *Field inventory*—Inventory held by a sales representative to facilitate the selling process. This can also be inventory on consignment with an important customer perhaps to ensure equipment uptime.
- *Support inventory*—Component parts and FGs held in distribtion, but set aside for the immediate replacement of a product found to be defective in the field.

Inventory Items by Location

Before you can start planning inventory, you need to develop a list of each inventory item held at each inventory location. In this chapter, the terms *item*, *part*, and *stock keeping unit* (SKU) are used interchangeably. Clearly, only RMs are to be found at the extreme upstream, and only end products are to be found at the downstream extreme. But which inventory items are located in between? Figure 10.2 shows that not every product requires inventory from every supplier and not every market requires a product from every delivery channel.

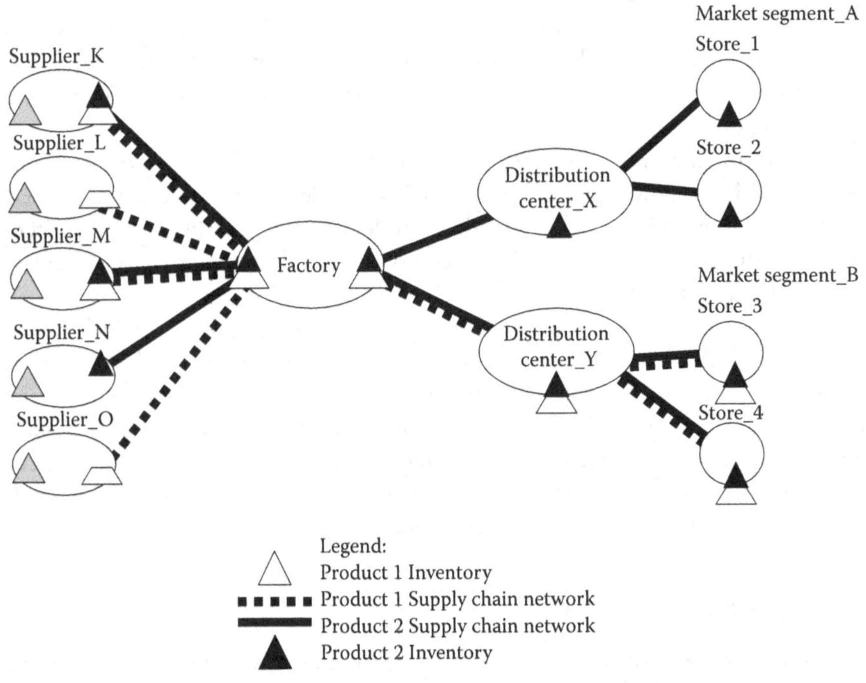

Figure 10.2 Inventory flows specific to products and markets.

Table 10.1 Products Mapped to Market Segments from Table 6.4

Market	*Market Segment Y*			*Market Segment Z*	
Product offering	Product set 1	Product set 2	Product set 3	Product set 4	Product set 5
Product	1× Product A	1× Product A	1× Product B		
Accessory		1× Accessory1		1× Accessory1	2× Accessory2

The composite BOM item master, introduced in Chapter 8: "Source," is used to define the exhaustive list of unique item numbers including product and system SKUs found throughout the end-to-end supply chain network. Each product and system SKU from the composite BOM item master is tracked forward through its downstream delivery channel ending at its respective market segment. Each lower-level item in the composite BOM item master is traced backward through its respective upstream suppliers, ending at its respective RM source.

Return to the product line example from Chapter 6, Table 6.4, the five product sets are offered to two market segments, as shown again in Table 10.1. Notice that a product set can have multiples of a specific product as in Product Set 5 with two per of Accessory2.

Return to Chapter 6, Table 6.5, the individual product BOMs and their composite BOM are shown again in Table 10.2. BOM levels are indicated to the left of the item description in the individual product BOMs. An FG is level 0. Item sources are indicated to the right in the composite BOM item master. The quantity per is not relevant at this time.

Figure 10.3 answers the question of which items are assigned to which inventory locations. Each item has an inventory origin echelon location and one or more inventory destination echelon locations. Assemblies and subassemblies built by the factory have their inventory origin and destination locations within the same echelon. The remaining sections of this chapter explain how to determine the level of inventory, the replenishment timing, the lot sizing, and the amount of safety stock to hold for each item at each inventory location.

Driving Inventory Turns

Inventory consumes the largest amount of working capital. Therefore, it is important to understand and manage your inventory investment to preserve your cash flow. Inventory turns are a key tool in managing network inventory. Once an item is ordered, received, and the cash paid for it, that item sits in an inventory location until consumed by demand. When 100% of that item is consumed and the cash

Table 10.2 The Composite BOM Item Master from Table 6.5

First BOM	*Second BOM*	*Third BOM*	*Nth BOM*	*Composite BOM Item Master*
0Product A	0Product B	0Accessory1	0Accessory2	
..1Carton F	..1Carton F	..1Carton G	..1Carton G	0Product A->Factory
..1Assembly S	..1Assembly S	..1Assembly H	..1Assembly H	0Product B->Factory
....2Part C	....2Part H	....2Part J	....2Part J	0Accessory1->Factory
....2Part D	....2Part J	....2Subassy N	....2Subassy O	0Accessory2->Factory
......3RawMat I	....2Subassy K	......3Part P	......3Part P	..1Part E->Supplier2
..1Part E	......3Part L	......3Part Q	......3Part R	..1Carton F->Supplier1
	..1Part T			..1Carton G->Supplier1
				..1Assembly S->Factory
				..1Assembly H->Factory
				..1Part T->Supplier3

(Continued)

Table 10.2 (Continued) The Composite BOM Item Master from Table 6.5

First BOM	*Second BOM*	*Third BOM*	*Nth BOM*	*Composite BOM Item Master*
				....2Part C->Supplier4
				....2Part D->Supplier2
				....2Part H->Supplier5
				....2Part J->Supplier6
				....2Subassem K->Factory
				....2Subassem N->Factory
				....2Subassem O->Factory
				......3RawMat I->Supplier7
				......3Part L->Supplier8
				......3Part P->Supplier9
				......3Part Q->Supplier9
				......3Part R->Supplier10

Echelon 5	**Echelon 4**	**Echelon 3**	**Echelon 2**	**Echelon 1**
Supplier 7---------	-Suppliers 1–6---------	-Factory---------------	-Distributor---------	-Customer
	Suppliers 8–10			

Raw material inventory items	**Supply base inventory items**	**Factory inventory items**	**Distributor inventory items**
			Origin-product set 1
			Origin-product set 2
			Origin-product set 3
			Origin-product set 4
			Origin-product set 5
		Origin-product A	Destination-product A
		Origin-product B	Destination-product B
		Origin-accessory1	Destination-accessory1
		Origin-accessory2	Destination-accessory2
	Origin-carton F	Destination-carton F	
	Origin-carton G	Destination-carton G	
		O-assembly S-D	
		O-assembly H-D	
	Origin-part E	Destination-part E	
	Origin-part S	Destination-part S	
	Origin-part T	Destination-part T	
	Origin-part C	Destination-part C	
	Origin-part D	Destination-part D	
Origin-raw material I	Destination-RawMat		
	Origin-part I	Destination-part I	
	Origin-part J	Destination-part J	
		O-subassembly K-D	
		O-subassembly N-D	
		O-subassembly O-D	
	Origin-part L	Destination-part L	
	Origin-part P	Destination-part P	
	Origin-part Q	Destination-part Q	
	Origin-part R	Destination-part R	

Figure 10.3 Inventory item origin and destination locations by supply chain echelon.

paid for that item is recovered through product sales, its inventory has had one turn. Inventory turns are defined by the number of times such a cycle occurs in one calendar year. For example, if an item cycles through inventory receipt, cash payment, inventory issue, and cash recovery once a quarter, then that item has four inventory turns. Inventory that turns frequently replenishes working capital frequently. Low-turn or no-turn inventory consumes working capital but does not replenish working capital. Stranded inventory is a cash sink.

The financial ratio for inventory turns,[3] shown in Equation 10.1, is typically for one trading partner and unfortunately does not help identify how to manage the network inventory investment to improve inventory turns.

$$\text{Inventory turns} = \frac{\text{Annual cost of goods sold}}{(\text{Starting inventory} + \text{Ending inventory})/2} \tag{10.1}$$

For example, Turns = 5.06 with \$6,500,000 Annual COGS and \$1,285,000 Average inventory.

$$\text{Days of inventory} = \frac{365 \text{ days}}{\text{Inventory turns}} \tag{10.2}$$

For example, Days of inventory = 365/5.06 = 72 days.

Inventory must be connected to some demand to turn. Table 10.3 shows the common drivers that increase or decrease inventory turns in the push zone and in the pull zone. As product structures for new products are developed, the product is added to the MPS and connected with a demand forecast. Inventory becomes stranded when all demand for that item is disconnected because of a parts substitution, product discontinuance, or product line divestiture.

Table 10.3 Inventory Turns Drivers

Push Inventory into the Push/Pull Boundary	
Increase turns	Demand forecast
	Additional demand for support requirements
Decrease turns/stranded inventory	Excess inventory caused by the multiplicative nature of forecast error with lot size
	Safety stock
	New products not yet tied to the master schedule
	An engineering change order switches to different part
	Old revision from failure to rotate stock
Pull Inventory from the Push/Pull Boundary	
Increase turns	Customer orders
Decrease turns/stranded inventory	Obsolescence
	Inventory past its expiration date
	Next generation product replaces current generation product

Push Inventory into the Push/Pull Boundary

Push planning is an established methodology that is usually encapsulated within a modern computer system application such as enterprise resource planning (ERP) or the older manufacturing resources planning (MRP II). If you are running a small company, it is possible with today's technology to put all this methodology on a personal computer or to license pay-as-you-go time from a third party running ERP on the Cloud. APICS, www.apics.org, is the authority for and provides certification in this body of knowledge. It is important for you to understand what goes on inside such a computer system application. First, unless you understand the detail of how resources are planned, it is difficult to deploy such a system in its most advantageous way. Second, the embedded parameters, timing, and decisions are the levers to managing inventory turns.

An Overview of the Push Planning Methodology

A delivery lead time of a few days is decoupled from the cumulative material lead time plus manufacturing cycle time plus logistics transit time of many weeks through one of four operating strategies: BTS, assemble-to-stock, BTO, and engineer-to-order. Chapter 9: "Demand Planning" discusses how the placement of the push/pull boundary determines the operating strategy. But to be able to pull inventory out of the push/pull boundary, there must already be inventory in the push/pull boundary. And each and every inventory item must have some demand driver for that inventory to turn. A forecast is the demand driver that pushes inventory, while a customer order is the demand driver that pulls inventory. The push planning tools start with the forecast and end with the right quantity of inventory for every item at each inventory location (see Figure 10.4). The push planning methodology discussed in this chapter is driven by the steady-state or "small-signal" demand in your business. An approach to "large-signal" or disruptive demand that your business might experience is discussed in Chapter 12: "Risk Management."

The push planning tools include the following:

- *BOM*—The item master and product structure for each product.
- *Routing file*—The sequence of work centers and standard hours per work center to build an item.
- *Inventory balances*—The current quantity on hand for each item in the item master.
- *Demand rate forecast*—A top–down aggregate rate forecast of revenue dollars prepared annually by Finance (see Chapter 9).
- *Demand mix forecast*—A bottom–up customer and product by customer and product forecast in dollars and units prepared monthly by Sales (see Chapter 9).
- *Supply forecast*—A bottom–up product by product quantity mix forecast in units prepared monthly by Operations (see Chapter 9).

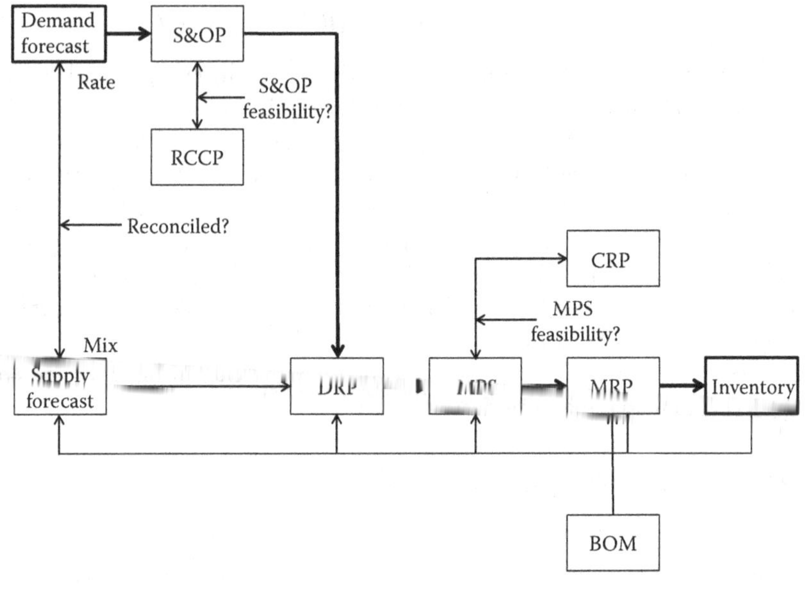

Figure 10.4 Push planning tools.

- *Sales and operations plan (S&OP)*—12-month plan to balance customer service, inventory investment, and shipment revenue with validated rough cut capacity.
- *Rough cut capacity planning (RCCP)*—Capacity plan validation of the S&OP that does not account for lead time offsets.
- *Distribution requirements planning (DRP)*—Maintains product specific inventory levels for independently demanded product in supply chains with multiple DCs to achieve desired service levels. Considers lot sizing and lead time offsets.
- *Master production schedule (MPS)*—Maintains product-specific FG levels independently demanded at the factory to achieve the desired service levels. Considers lot sizing and lead time offsets.
- *Materials requirements planning (MRP)*—Used to manage dependently demanded lower-level parts and RM inventory across the product mix. Considers lot sizing and lead time offsets.
- *Capacity requirements planning (CRP)*—Used to manage work center capacity across the product mix. Considers lot sizing and lead time offsets.

Push planning is regenerated once a month. Organizations with multiple product lines usually regenerate different product lines each week and the whole plan once a month. In addition, whenever the organization wins or loses a very large order, the push plan is regenerated. Modern computer systems offer a "what-if?" capability that can check inventory and capacity availability by adding or subtracting incremental explosions for specific product BOMs before committing to a large customer order.

S&OP and RCCP

The S&OP is an aggregate rate plan that starts the push planning process. It is a cross-function discussion among Sales, Operations, Engineering, and Finance to balance organizational resources to meet customer service levels, inventory and capacity investment levels, new product introduction delivery dates, and monthly revenue targets. The S&OP is regenerated once a month over a planning horizon of typically 12 months. This planning horizon provides sufficient lead time to implement increases or decreases to aggregate production rates and capacity alternatives. The S&OP strives to validate the feasibility of available capacity and cash while minimizing cost premiums to achieve the desired balance point. Once the S&OP plan is developed, it should be reviewed and approved by Sales, Operations, Engineering, and Finance before regenerating the MPS.

Table 10.4 shows an example S&OP including an RCCP driven from the demand rate forecast discussed in Chapter 9: "Demand Planning." Once completed, Table 10.4 provides monthly numbers for a production rate, employment and overtime, and the incremental investment level for production inventory. If the S&OP is achievable in terms of capacity and investment, then the business is one step closer to making its revenue target.

Here is an explanation of the S&OP table:

- *Columns: months*—The columns are forward-looking months starting from the current month. The number of working days per month impacts both regular time and overtime capacity.
- *Demand*—This section is the demand rate forecast in revenue dollars and aggregate units over the planning horizon.
- *Maximum capacity*—This section presents possible and feasible capacity alternatives over the planning horizon. The rightmost column details the per-unit cost premium by capacity alternative.
- *S&OP/RCCP*—This section is the monthly plan of the number of units to be sourced by each capacity alternative and/or from previously built FG inventory. Each capacity alternative is assumed to be available in the quantity and period stated. RCCP does not consider lead time offsets. This example shows steady employment for the number of days per month.
- *FG inventory*—This section details the accumulation of FG inventory.
- *Cost premium*—This section is used, through trial and error, to find the combination of capacity alternatives that provide the desired monthly shipment level for the lowest total cost premium.

The S&OP is optimized using the following heuristics:

1. Fill in the months, days per month, forecast, starting inventory, and cost premium information.
2. Sum the total unit demand across the planning horizon.

Table 10.4 Example Sales and Operations Plan with an RCCP

Demand	*Jan*	*Feb*	*Mar*	*Apr*	*May*	*June*	*Measured in*
Forecast dated January	183,000	162,000	201,000	213,500	188,000	207,300	Dollars
	360	346	400	425	375	410	Units
			1,106			1,210	Quarter total
Maximum capacity–units/month							Per unit cost
Working days	21 days	19 days	22 days	20 days	20 days	21 days	
Regular time capacity	350	320	365	335	335	350	
Overtime capacity	30	30	33	30	30	15	$35/unit
Subcontract capacity	100	100	100	100	100	100	$55/unit
Inventory							$2/unit/month
S&OP/RCCP	*Jan*	*Feb*	*Mar*	*Apr*	*May*	*June*	*Unit Totals*
From regular time	350	320	365	335	335	350	2,055
From overtime	20	28	33	30	30	15	156
From subcontracting				60		45	105

(Continued)

Table 10.4 (Continued) Example Sales and Operations Plan with an RCCP

Demand	*Jan*	*Feb*	*Mar*	*Apr*	*May*	*June*	*Unit Totals*
To inventory	–10	–2					–12
From inventory			2		10		12
Total supply	360	346	400	425	375	410	2,316
FG inventory							Measured in
Starting inventory	0	10	12	10	10	0	Units
+Production	370	348	398	425	365	410	Units
–Shipments	360	346	400	425	375	410	Units
Ending inventory	10	12	10	10	0	0	Units
Cost Premiums	*Jan*	*Feb*	*Mar*	*Apr*	*May*	*June*	
Overtime premium	$700	$980	$1,155	$1,050	$1,050	$525	Plan S&OP to minimize the cost premium.
Subcontract premium				$3,300		$2,475	
Inventory holding cost	$20	$24	$20	$20			
Total premium	$720	$1,004	$1,175	$4,370	$1,050	$3,000	$11,319

3. Starting with the lowest cost capacity alternative, load the regular time capacity and compare its sum of 2,055 against the total required of 2,316 units.
4. Working from the other capacity alternatives in the order of their cost premiums, notice that not all of the overtime capacity is required in January and February to meet monthly demand. It is cheaper to use the remaining January and February overtime capacity to build inventory at \$35 + \$2 per unit for March and May than to use subcontracting at \$55 per unit.
5. Use the most expensive capacity alternative as the last resort.
6. If regular time generates excess capacity, build inventory for the future to keep people employed.
7. Finally, check that the column totals support the month-by-month financial revenue targets.

Reconcile Three Forecasts and the S&OP

The demand rate forecast drives sufficient inventory and production starts to enable making your monthly finance revenue targets. Should you experience having customer demand without enough product supply, then you cannot achieve your desired level of throughput. The demand mix forecast is the first look at matching customers to product mix. It is often a struggle to motivate Sales to forecast anywhere near enough months to cover the planning horizon. In the near term, the demand mix forecast is reconciled with the S&OP plan month by month. The S&OP plan ensures that there is sufficient capacity and cash to meet monthly targets. The supply forecast drives inventory into the push/pull boundary and must cover the full planning horizon. The supply forecast is reconciled with the demand mix forecast over the near term and with the demand rate forecast over the far term. This means the supply forecast will reflect the best information from Sales regarding anticipated customer rate and mix requirements over the first few months, and it will reflect inventory rates to meet Finance revenue targets through the end of the planning horizon.

Distribution Requirements Planning

When the same independently demanded product is distributed from more than one DC, DRP is inserted between the supply forecast and the MPS. DRP maintains the desired stocking level for each product at each DC. Depending on the geography of market segmentation and the density of customers, there can be good reasons for stocking different levels of the same product at different DCs. When factory FGs are shipped direct to the end customer, and/or when factory FGs are distributed through a single DC, then the DRP tool is not used. Figure 10.5 shows the DRP record for a single product–distributor pair. Under DRP, every distributor that carries Product_A would have its own DRP record for Product_A. For example, if there were three DCs that each carried 50 product SKUs, then there would be 150 DRP records like Figure 10.5.

Product_A and Distributor_Y	**Gross requirements rule**			Take larger value of the forecast or the backlog for each period		
	Lot size	225 units	**Reorder point**	50 units BTS	**Lead time**	1 week
			Safety stock	+12 units		

	January				**February**	
	Week 1	**Week 2**	**Week 3**	**Week 4**	**Week 5**	**Week 6**
Forecast	150		200		150	150
Backlog	200	75	50			
Gross requirements	200	75	200	0	150	150
Net requirements		227	252			177
Starting inventory 52	77	2	27	252	102	-48
Scheduled receipts	225					
Planned order receipt		225	225			225
Planned order release	225	225			225	

Figure 10.5 DRP record.

Here is an explanation of the DRP record:

- *Columns: week N*—The columns are time periods in weeks. Modern computer systems operate using a "bucket-less" approach.
- *Row: forecast*—This is the quantity split of the total supply forecast of the demand for Product_A at Distributor_Y.
- *Row: backlog*—This shows the quantity of customer orders booked but not yet shipped.
- *Row: gross requirements*—This shows the total product demand quantity for that period following the gross requirements rule.
- *Header: gross requirements rule*—This is the rule on how to combine forecast and backlog demands.
- *Row: net requirements*—These are the period-by-period calculations of supply minus demand explained below.
- *Row: starting inventory*—This shows the starting quantity of Product_A inventory held at Distributor_Y.
- *Row: scheduled receipts*—These are expected receipts of product inventory that were ordered at a time prior to the starting period of the DRP record.
- *Header: lot size*—This refers to the replenishment unit quantity of product inventory ordered at any one time. It answers the question of how much to order.
- *Row: planned order receipt*—In any period when the net requirement calculation falls below its reorder point, a planned order receipt for one lot size is placed in that period.
- *Header: reorder point*—This is the unit quantity that triggers a planned order receipt. It answers the question of when to reorder. The reorder point takes

into account demand over lead time and the need for safety stock to protect against demand uncertainty.

- *Row: planned order release*—This is the time period when the next order for a lot size must be released taking lead time into account. The period-by-period quantity in this row drives the period demand for the MPS.
- *Header: lead time*—This is the distributor order-to-factory delivery lead time in weeks or days.
- *Header: safety stock*—This is the quantity of safety stock held, if any, to protect against demand uncertainty.

The DRP record is completed as follows:

1. Fill in the header information and the starting inventory
2. Split the product forecast row from the supply forecast DC by DC.
3. Enter any customer order backlog into the appropriate time periods for each respective DC.
4. Complete the gross requirements row working from left to right following the gross requirements rule.
5. Week by week, working from left to right:

$$\text{Net requirements} = \text{Total supply} - \text{Gross requirements} \tag{10.3}$$

6. Calculate total supply:

For the first week, Total supply = Starting inventory + Scheduled receipts

For the following weeks, Total supply = Previous net requirements + scheduled receipts

7. When net requirements are greater than or equal to the reorder point, continue to the next week.
8. When net requirements are less than the reorder point, strike out the net requirement quantity. Place the quantity of one lot size in that same period in the planned order receipt row. Recalculate net requirements placing the new number above the strikeout, where:

New total supply = Previous net requirements + Scheduled receipts + Planned order receipt

9. Back up the number of lead time weeks from the period of the planned order receipt as shown by the diagonal arrow and place one lot size quantity in the appropriate planned order release period. This drives the period demand for the MPS.

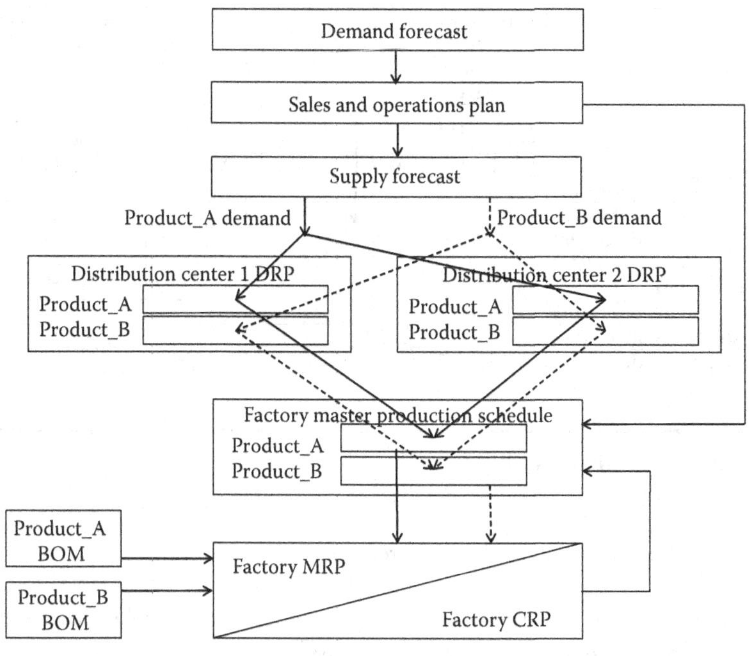

Figure 10.6 Push planning tool linkages.

Figure 10.6 illustrates the linkages from the demand forecast to S&OP to the supply forecast to DRP to MPS to MRP. In particular, notice that for a multiple distributor supply chain network, planning for each product splits among the DCs then is consolidated back at the MPS for factory production.

Master Production Schedule

When an independently demanded product is distributed from just one DC or directly from the factory, the supply forecast drives the MPS directly. The MPS maintains the desired FG stocking levels for each product. Figure 10.7 shows the MPS record for a single product. If there were 50 products in the business, then there would be 50 MPS records like Figure 10.7.

All required part inventory and work center capacity must be available in their required timeframes for the MPS to be feasible. Material shortages determined later in the planning process through MRP and/or capacity shortages determined later in the process through CRP are fed back to the MPS; the MPS would then have to be regenerated to regain feasibility. A factory with excessive amounts of past due production is the sign of an infeasible MPS.

Product_A (BOM level 0)		Period demand rule with DRP			Add product_A demands from all distributors in each period		
		Lot size	300 units	Reorder point	50 units BTS	Lead time	1 week
		January Week 1	Week 2	Week 3	Week 4	February Week 5	Week 6
Forecast							
Backlog							
Period demand		225	225	0	0	225	0
PAB			237			312	
Starting inventory	87	162	−63	237	237	12	312
Scheduled receipts		300					
Master schedule receipt			300			300	
Master schedule release		300			300		

Figure 10.7 The MPS record.

Here is an explanation of the MPS record:

- *Columns: week N*—The columns are time periods in weeks. Modern computer systems operate using a "bucket-less" approach.
- *Row: forecast*—This is the supply forecast of the demand for Product_A at the factory.
- *Row: backlog*—This is the quantity of customer orders booked but not yet shipped.
- *Row: period demand*—This this the total product demand quantity for that period following the period demand rule. When DRP drives the MPS, period demand equals the period by period sum of the DRP planned order release rows from each DC for Product_A.
- *Header: period demand rule*—This is the rule on how to combine forecast demand with backlog or how to sum DRP planned order releases.
- *Row: projected available balance (PAB)*—This is the period-by-period calculation of supply minus demand (see step 4 under MPS record).
- *Row: starting inventory*—This is the starting quantity of Product_A inventory held in FGs at the factory.
- *Row: scheduled receipts*—These are the expected receipts of a master scheduled lot that was ordered at a time prior to the starting period of the MPS record.
- *Header: lot size*—This is the replenishment unit quantity of the product ordered at any one time. It answers the question of how much to order.
- *Row: master schedule receipt*—In any period when the PAB calculation falls below its reorder point, a master schedule receipt for one lot size is placed in that period.
- *Header: reorder point*—This is the unit quantity that triggers a master schedule receipt. It answers the question of when to reorder. The reorder point takes

into account demand over lead time. When DRP is not used, the reorder point may also include a safety stock to protect against demand variability.

- *Row: master schedule release*—This is the time period when the next manufacturing order for a lot size must be released taking lead time into account. The period-by-period quantity in this row times the quantity per from the product BOM drives the gross requirements for MRP.
- *Header: lead time*—This is the factory cycle time to build the product in weeks or days.

The MPS record is completed as follows:

1. Fill in the header information and the starting inventory.
2. Copy the forecast row from the supply forecast and enter any customer order backlog.
3. Complete the period demand row working left to right. When DRP is not used, follow the header period demand rule, such as period demand is the larger of forecast or order backlog, period by period. When DRP is used, the MPS period demand equals the period-by-period sum of the DRP planned order releases.
4. Week by week, working from left to right, calculate the PAB:

$$\text{PAB} = \text{Total supply} - \text{Period demand} \tag{10.4}$$

5. Calculate total supply:

   For the first week, Total supply = Starting inventory + Scheduled receipts

   For the following weeks, Total supply = Previous net requirements + Scheduled receipts

6. When PAB is greater than or equal to the reorder point, continue to the next week.
7. When PAB is less than the reorder point, strike out the PAB quantity. Place the quantity of one master schedule lot in that same period in the master schedule receipt row. Recalculate PAB placing the new number above the strikeout, where:

$$\text{New total supply} = \text{Previous net requirements} + \text{Scheduled receipts} + \text{Master schedule receipt}$$

8. Back up the number of lead time weeks from the period of the master schedule receipt as shown by the diagonal arrow and place one lot size quantity in the appropriate master schedule release period. This times the quantity per from the BOM drives the gross requirements for the next BOM level in MRP. And this becomes a new manufacturing order to the factory.

Planning Horizons and Available-to-Promise

The MPS drives MRP and is used to determine product availability. The MPS planning horizon has to be long enough to drive through the longest cumulative manufacturing cycle time plus transit time plus purchasing lead time down through the lowest level of any product structure. For example, if a BOM has four levels requiring eight weeks of cycle time and three weeks of logistics time and has a part requiring 28 weeks of lead time, then the planning horizon needs to be a minimum of 8 + 3 + 28 = 39 weeks. It is common practice to "freeze" the first few weeks of the master schedule to prevent nervous schedules starting and stopping and restarting the production floor.

Product available to promise (ATP) is calculated from the MPS. ATP is the total accumulated supply minus total accumulated backlog. Therefore, the demand is determined by summing the backlog and disregarding the forecast. ATP is used to answer the question "Can the customer take delivery of this many units in that particular week?" Figure 10.8 shows an example of an ATP calculation.

ATP is calculated as follows:

1. Work left to right period by period:

$$\text{ATP} = \text{Accumulated supply} - \text{Accumulated backlog} \tag{10.5}$$

2. For the first period:

$$\text{Period supply} = \text{Starting inventory} + \text{Scheduled receipts} = 87 + 300 = 387$$
$$\text{Period demand} = \text{Backlog} = 200 + 90 = 290$$

Product_A (BOM level 0)	Period demand rule without DRP			Let backlog consume the forecast for each period		
	Lot size	300 units	Reorder point	50 units BTS	Lead time	1 week
	January				February	
	Week 1	Week 2	Week 3	Week 4	Week 5	Week 6
Forecast	150		200		150	150
Backlog	200	90	50			
Period demand	200	90	200	0	150	150
PAB			197		347	
Starting inventory 87	187	97	~~-103~~	197	~~47~~	197
Scheduled receipts	300					
Master schedule receipt			300		300	
Master schedule release		300		300		
Available-to-promise	97	97	347	347	647	647

Figure 10.8 Master schedule ATP.

3. For all other periods:

Sum of period supply = Starting inventory + Scheduled receipts + Sum of master schedule receipts

Sum of period demand = Sum of backlogs

Material Requirements Planning

Dependently demanded items are calculated from the BOM, current inventory balances, and MPS-driven requirements using MRP. Figure 10.9 shows the MRP record for an item. If there were 200 items in the BOM item master, then there would be 200 MRP records like Figure 10.9. The example in Figure 10.9 shows the BOM level 1 MRP record for child Assembly_S under parent Product_A driving down to the BOM level 2 MRP record for child Part_C under parent Assembly_S from the BOM product structure for Product_A. Notice that Product_A requires one per of Assembly_S

Assembly_S (BOM level 1)		**Gross requirements rule**			Gather all demands from any parent of this child and multiply by the appropriate quantity per. Use 1 per for Product_A		
		Lot size	400 units	**Reorder point**	0 units	**Lead time**	1 week
		January				**February**	
		Week 1	**Week 2**	**Week 3**	**Week 4**	**Week 5**	**Week 6**
Gross requirements		300	0	0	300	0	0
Net requirements					250		
Starting inventory	50	150	150	150	−150	250	250
Scheduled receipts		400					
Planned order receipt					400		
Planned order release				400			

Part_C (BOM level 2)		**Gross requirements rule**			Gather all demands from any parent of this child and multiply by the appropriate quantity per. Use 2 per for Assembly_S		
		Lot size	2,000 units	**Reorder point**	0 units or safety stock	**Lead time**	2 weeks
				Safety stock	+136 units		
		January				**February**	
		Week 1	**Week 2**	**Week 3**	**Week 4**	**Week 5**	**Week 6**
Gross requirements		0	0	800	0	0	0
Net requirements				1,950			
Starting inventory	750	750	750	−50	1,950	1,950	1,950
Scheduled receipts							
Planned order receipt				2,000			
Planned order release		2,000					

Figure 10.9 MRP record.

and that Assembly _S requires two per of Part_C. If other products on the MPS have Part_C in their BOMs, then MRP gathers together all of the demands for Part_C on its gross requirements row. The same is true for all the other items at every BOM level.

Here is an explanation of the MRP record:

- *Columns: week N*—The columns are time periods in weeks. Modern computer systems operate using a "bucket-less" approach.
- *Row: gross requirements*—This is the total part quantity required in that period after gathering all demands from any parent of this child and multiplying these demands by the appropriate quantity per. Demand comes from MPS releases and from upper-level MRP planned order releases.
- *Header: gross requirements rule*—This rule states: gather all demands from any parent of this child, all master scheduled releases and all upper level MRP planned order releases, and multiply each by their appropriate quantity per.
- *Row: net requirements*—These show period-by-period calculation of supply minus demand (see step 2 under the MRP record).
- *Row: starting inventory*—This is the starting inventory unit quantity held at the factory.
- *Row: scheduled receipts*—These are the expected receipts of a planned lot that were ordered at a time prior to the starting period of the MRP record.
- *Header: lot size*—This is the replenishment unit quantity of the part ordered at any one time. It answers the question of how much to order.
- *Row: planned order receipt*—In any period, when the net requirements calculation falls below its reorder point, a planned order receipt for one lot size is placed in that period.
- *Header: reorder point*—This is the unit quantity that triggers a planned order receipt. It answers the question of when to reorder. The reorder point takes into account demand over lead time and may also include safety stock to protect against lead time variability.
- *Row: planned order release*—This is the time period when the next order for a lot size must be released taking lead time into account. Order types include purchase orders for suppliers and work orders for the factory.
- *Header: lead time*—This is the factory order-to-supplier delivery time in weeks or days.
- *Header: safety stock*—This is the quantity of safety stock held, if any, to protect against lead time variability.

The MRP record is completed as follows:

1. Fill in the header information and the starting inventory.
2. Complete the gross requirements row working left to right following the header gross requirements rule to gather demands and multiply each by the quantity per on the respective BOM.

3. Week by week, working from left to right:

$$\text{Net requirements} = \text{Total supply} - \text{Gross requirements} \tag{10.6}$$

4. Calculate total supply:

For the first week, Total supply = Starting inventory + Scheduled receipts

For the following weeks, Total supply = Previous net requirements + Scheduled receipts

5. When net requirements are greater than or equal to the reorder point, continue to the next week.
6. When net requirements are less than the reorder point, strike out the net requirements quantity. Place the quantity of one lot size in that same period in the planned order receipt row. Recalculate net requirements placing the new number above the strikeout, where:

New total supply = Previous net requirements + Scheduled receipts + Planned order receipt

7. Back up the number of lead time weeks from the period of the planned order receipt as shown by the diagonal arrow and place one lot size quantity in the appropriate planned order release period. This becomes a new purchase order to a supplier or a new work order to the factory.

Capacity Requirements Planning

There will be a network capacity constraint somewhere within your supply chain. This network capacity constraint limits the end-to-end throughput. Moreover, the network capacity constraint may be a trading partner outside your own organization, yet it will surely limit your throughput. And it is probable that the network capacity constraint will move as the product mix through your supply chain shifts.

CRP is used to plan the loading of individual work centers to identify constraints and to test MPS feasibility. Unlike RCCP calculated from the S&OP plan, CRP takes into account MRP lot sizing and MRP lead time offsets. When MRP generates a planned work order release for a product, assembly, or subassembly, the work order gets assigned a work center routing. The product, assembly, or subassembly is assigned a standard setup plus run time in hours per unit for each work center in its routing file. CRP takes the lot size from MRP times the standard hours from the routing file plus the setup time to compute the total hours of load on the work center in the time period planned by MRP. CRP then sums all of the load hours per week for each job at each work center and plots the work center's load profile.

CRP takes the accumulated hours of loading by work center by week and identifies any times when the load profile exceeds the work center capacity. The front end of a production schedule may be capacity infeasible when the correct priority of job releases has been lost because of excessive past due hours. When work center capacity is exceeded, the following outcomes are possible:

- Use a more expensive alternative routing through a different work center to build the item on time.
- Regenerate the MPS with different mix timing to make the schedule capacity feasible.
- Do nothing and accept that all jobs will be late.

Set Lot Size, Reorder Point, Lead Time, and Safety Stock

In each instance of DRP, MPS, and MRP, the questions to be asked include the following: How much replenishment inventory should be ordered, i.e., what is the lot size? When is the replenishment inventory needed, i.e., where is the reorder point? When should the replenishment inventory order be placed, i.e., what is the lead time offset? How can the service level be protected, i.e., should a safety stock be assigned? Table 10.5 identifies the right numerical method to use when answering these questions. Numerical examples for the different cases are shown below. Lot size, reorder points, lead times, and safety stock levels should be reevaluated at least annually, as demand and variability assumptions will change.

How to Estimate Ordering Cost and Inventory Holding Cost

Suppose your business has a composite BOM with 1,000 items in the item master. It is common practice to assign an "A," "B," or "C" designation to each item based on a rank order of each item's extended annual inventory purchase. For example, an item that costs $2.00 with an annual usage of 500 units has an extended annual inventory purchase of $1,000. "A" items might represent 20% of the item numbers and get ordered once a month. "B" items might represent 30% of the item numbers and get ordered once a quarter. "C" items might represent the last 50% of the item numbers and get ordered once a year. The total number of orders becomes (1,000 × 20% × 12) + (1,000 × 30% × 4) + (1,000 × 50% × 1) = 4,100 orders per year.

- *Ordering cost (S)*

  Ordering cost is the average cost per year to process one purchase order. Consider your staff who spend part of their time planning, purchasing,

Table 10.5 Solutions for Lot Sizing, Reorder Point with Lead Time, and Safety Stock

	Application		
	DRP	*MPS*	*MRP*
Lot size: How much to order?	EOQ—economic order quantity	EPQ—economic production quantity	EOQ or discounted EOQ when purchasing large volumes
Reorder point: When is it needed?	Independent demand ROP + SS_{demand} Reorder point with safety stock	Independent demand With DRP: ROP Without DRP: ROP + SS_{demand} Fixed interval for BTS Fixed quantity for BTO	Dependent demand MRP + $SS_{Lead\ Time}$ MRP with safety stock MRP reorder point without safety stock = 0
Lead time offset: When to order?	Distributor order to factory delivery (days) includes lead time and midbound transit time	Factory order to factory delivery (days) includes cycle time	Factory order to supplier delivery (days) includes lead time and inbound transit time
Safety stock level: service level protection	SS_{demand} Demand uncertainty safety stock here, when DRP is used	SS_{demand} Demand uncertainty safety stock here, when DRP is not used	$SS_{Lead\ Time}$ Lead time variability safety stock here

invoicing, doing accounts payable, and doing ordering-related administration. Estimate the approximate number of hours per year in these activities times the dollars/hour of salary paid. Use 2,000 hours/year for a 50-week work-year and estimate what fraction each type of position puts into ordering activities. Then divide the total dollars by the total number of orders per year.

Suppose a distributor spends $143,500 on staff costs for ordering related activity and the distributor processes 4,100 replenishment orders per year, then the distributor's ordering cost would be as follows:

$$S = \frac{\text{Annual related staffing costs}}{\text{Total number of replenishment orders}} = \frac{\$143{,}500}{4{,}100} = \$35 \text{ per order} \tag{10.7}$$

- *Inventory holding cost (H)*

  Inventory holding cost is the average cost to hold one unit of one item number for one year. A distributor will operate a larger warehouse than a factory will and will therefore have a higher total warehouse cost for rent, utilities, insurance, etc. But a distributor will carry a smaller total number of item numbers than a factory will, and most of those items will displace a larger cubic volume per unit than many smaller component parts found in the factory warehouse.

  Suppose the same distributor has a warehouse that costs $2.05 million a year to operate. This distributor places 4,100 replenishment orders per year. If the mean lot size of each replenishment order is 100 units, then 410,000 item-units pass through the warehouse in a year.

$$H = \frac{\text{Annual warehouse opening expense}}{\text{Total annual item-units}} = \frac{\$2{,}050{,}000}{410{,}000} = \$5/\text{item/unit/year} \tag{10.8}$$

How to Determine Lot Size

- *Use economic order quantity (EOQ) to lot size independently demanded items for the DRP.*

$$\text{EOQ} = \sqrt{2DS/H} \text{ in units} \tag{10.9}$$

where D = annual demand in units; S = the cost to place an order in dollars; and H = the cost to hold one unit of one item of inventory for one year in dollars.

For example: A distributor ships 3,600 units of Product_A per year. A replenishment order costs $35 to process, and the distributor has an inventory holding cost of $5/item/unit/year.

$$\text{EOQ} = \sqrt{(2)(3{,}600)(35)/5} = 225 \text{ units} = \text{DRP lot size}$$

- *Use economic production quantity (EPQ) to lot size independently demanded items for the MPS.*

$$\text{EPQ} = \left(\sqrt{2DS/H}\right)\left(\sqrt{p/(p-u)}\right) \text{ in units} \tag{10.10}$$

where D = annual demand in units; S = the cost to place an order in dollars; H = the cost to hold one unit of one item of inventory for one year in dollars; p = the production rate in units per week; and u = the usage rate in units per week.

For example: A factory ships 5,400 units of Product_A per year. A replenishment order costs $42 to process, and the factory has an inventory holding cost of $10/unit/item/year because Product_A is physically large. The factory can build Product_A at a rate of 200 units/week, and the factory ships Product_A at a rate of 100 units/week.

$$\text{EPQ} = \left(\sqrt{(2)(5,400)(42)/10}\right)\left(\sqrt{200/(200-100)}\right)$$

$$= 213 \times 1.41 = 300 \text{ units} = \text{MPS lot size}$$

- *Use ABC analysis to lot size dependently demanded "B," "C," and "D" items for MRP.*

  The total inventory is segmented into value classes to better manage the inventory investment. Inventory items are classified as "A," "B," "C," and "D" items. "A" items represent about 80% of the top material dollars and about 20% of the top item numbers. "B" items represent about 15% of the middle material dollars and about 30% of the middle item numbers. "C" items are the remaining 5% of the bottom material dollars and the remaining 50% of the bottom item numbers. Since the highest value items have the most impact on total inventory investment, these "A" items are purchased or built lot-for-lot or else replenished once a month. "B" items are purchased or built once a quarter. "C" items are purchased or built annually. "D" items are no-turn stranded inventory items, items held for a product's support life and safety stock items. Excess inventory from "B" and "C" items having quantities well in excess of one year's supply can degenerate into no-turn inventory.

Classify all dependently demanded items as "A," "B," "C," or "D" based on an analysis of expected annual throughput. See the detailed inventory model later in this chapter.

Lot size "A" items lot-for-lot as discussed below.

"B" item lot size = annual demand quantity divided by four orders (10.11)

"C" item lot size = annual demand quantity divided by one order (10.12)

Lot size "D" item safety stock as discussed below.

- *Use lot-for-lot to lot size dependently demanded "A" items for MRP.*
  "A" items are your highest value inventory items. Use lot-for-lot lot sizing for these items taking into account any quantity per multipliers in the product structure. Add additional usage for spares or known quality yield issues.
  For example: A master schedule release calls for 100 units; the product structure calls for a quantity of two per order; there is a support requirement for five units; and there is a probability of losing two units from quality yield factors.

Lot-for-lot: 100 units of master schedule release = 100 units

Lot-for-lot taking into account the quantity per:
100 units × 2 per = 200 units

Lot-for-lot, with quantity per, with spares and yield factor:
200 units + 5 units + 2 units = 207 unit lot

How to Determine the Reorder Point

- *Use fixed-order interval replenishment with a BTS operating strategy.*
  A fixed-order interval approach is part of the solution to eliminate any possible bullwhip effect.

$$\text{ROP} = (d)(\text{OI} + \text{LT}) - A \text{ in units} \quad (10.13)$$

where ROP = reorder point in units; d = demand rate in units per week; OI = order interval in weeks; LT = lead time in weeks; and A = number of units on hand at the reorder time. Note: Use a consistent measure of time in weeks or days.

For example: A distributor ships 3,600 units of Product_A per year or 69 units per week using a BTS strategy. The lead time for the distributor to place a replenishment order with the factory and take delivery of FGs is one week. The order interval is two weeks. At the time of this order, there were 157 units left in stock.

$$\text{ROP} = (69)(2 + 1) - 157 = 50 \text{ units}$$

Lead time = 1 week

- *Use fixed-order quantity replenishment with a BTO operating strategy.*

$$\text{ROP} = (d)(\text{LT}) \text{ in units} \quad (10.14)$$

where ROP = reorder point in units; d = demand rate in units per week; and LT = lead time in weeks. Note: Use a consistent measure of time in weeks or days.

For example: A factory ships 5,400 units of Product_B per year or 104 units per week using a BTO strategy. The lead time for the factory to place a manufacturing order on the factory floor and take delivery of FGs is one week.

$$\text{ROP} = (104)(1) = 104 \text{ units}$$

$$\text{Lead time} = 1 \text{ week}$$

- *Use a reorder point of zero with MRP.*
  When a dependently demanded item does not have a safety stock, use zero as the reorder point.
- *Use a reorder point equal to the safety stock quantity with MRP.*
  When a dependently demanded item has a safety stock, use the safety stock level as the reorder point.

How to Determine Safety Stock

Once a replenishment order is released, three things can go wrong to upset customer service. First, demand can increase more than expected, consuming your remaining inventory faster than expected. Second, the supply lead time can take longer than expected, again consuming your remaining inventory faster than expected. And third, there can be a supply quality problem, resulting in the shipment of a replenishment quantity that is smaller than expected. While you use safety stock to buffer against such problems, safety stock adds to your total inventory investment and may become no-turn inventory.

- *Safety stock adds to the reorder point quantity.*
  Safety stock provides a higher probability that you can maintain your desired service level by adding to the reorder point.

$$\text{ROP}_\text{W}\text{SS} = \text{ROP} + \text{SS in units} \quad (10.15)$$

where $\text{ROP}_\text{W}\text{SS}$ = reorder point with safety stock in units; ROP = reorder point in units; and SS = safety stock in units.

For example: A distributor uses a reorder point of 225 units and wants to maintain a safety stock level of an additional 50 units.

$$\text{ROP}_\text{W}\text{SS} = 225 + 50 = 275 \text{ units}$$

- *Use inventory service level.*
  Service level is the expected probability of not experiencing a stock out based on a normal distribution curve. A positive *Z* score normal distribution

table can be found on the Internet at https://www.easycalculation.com/statistics/positive-z-score-chart.php. This table relates the desired service level as a decimal to a *z*-factor, which is the number of standard deviations required in the safety stock calculations below. A higher service level requires a greater safety stock investment.

For a 95% service level: locate SL = 0.950 in the table and read off
$z = 1.645$ standard deviations

For a 98% service level: locate SL = 0.980 in the table and read off
$z = 2.055$ standard deviations

- *Use safety stock with DRP or MRP to protect the service level against demand uncertainty.*

  Products with high demand uncertainty are best dealt with at the top of their product structures, i.e., with safety stock added to the DRP reorder point for distributor cycle stock or with safety stock added to the MPS reorder point for factory FGs, but not both.

$$SS_d = z\sigma_d\sqrt{LT} \text{ in units} \tag{10.16}$$

where z = number of standard deviations for the desired service level; σ_d = the standard deviation of demand per period; and LT = lead time. Note that the unit of measure for the period in weeks or days must be the same for d, σ_d, and LT.

For example: Calculate the safety stock to maintain a 95% service level when Product_A has a standard deviation of demand of seven units per week and a lead time of one week.

$$SS_d = (1.645)(7)\left(\sqrt{1}\right) = 12 \text{ units rounded up}$$

- *Use safety stock with MRP to protect the service level against lead time variability.*

  Products with high lead time variability from suppliers are best dealt with at the bottom of their product structures, i.e., with safety stock added to the MRP reorder point on specific components.

$$SS_{LT} = zd\sigma_{LT} \text{ in units} \tag{10.17}$$

where z = number of standard deviations for the desired service level; d = demand per period in units; and σ_{LT} = the standard deviation of lead time.

Note that the unit of measure for the period in weeks or days must be the same for d, σ_{LT}, and LT.

For example: Calculate the safety stock to maintain a 98% service level when Part_C has a demand of 200 units/week and a standard deviation of lead time of 0.33 weeks.

$$SS_{LT} = (2.055)(200)(0.33) = 136 \text{ units rounded up}$$

An Inventory Model

The following inventory model example is based on the BOM for a single product; however, the method is also used working with a composite BOM. Begin with the item master list with the item value for each item and the expected annual throughput for each item. Create an ABC inventory analysis based on annual throughput, as shown in Table 10.6. An extended value is calculated for each and every item by

Table 10.6 ABC Inventory Analysis Based on Annual Product Throughput

Item	*Annual Throughput*	*Item Value*	*Extended Value*	*Cumulative Value*	*ABC*	*Cut Point*
Product_A	1,200	$400	$480,000	$480,000	A	
Part_C (2 per)	2,400	$80	$192,000	$672,000	A	
Assembly_B	1,200	$150	$180,000	$852,000	B	80% = $793,920
Part_F (3 per)	3,600	$20	$72,000	$924,000	B	
Assembly_E	1,200	$40	$48,000	$972,000	C	95% = $942,780
Assembly_H	1,200	$8	$9,600	$981,600	C	
Part_D	1,200	$2	$2,400	$984,000	C	
Part_G	1,200	$2	$2,400	$986,400	C	
Part_I	1,200	$2	$2,400	$988,800	C	
Part_J	1,200	$2	$2,400	$991,200	C	
Carton_K	1,200	$1	$1,200	$992,400	C	
		Total value	$992,400			

multiplying the item's value by the item's expected annual throughput. The set of extended values is sorted with the largest on the top to the smallest on the bottom. The cumulative value column starts with the largest extended value and accumulates each smaller extended value until the last cumulative value equals the total extended value. Since "A" items represent 80% of the inventory dollars, a cut is made to the cumulative value column at 80% of the total extended value. Since "A" plus "B" items represent 95% of the inventory dollars, a cut is made to the cumulative value column at 95% of the total extended value. Each row is then designated as an "A," "B," or "C" item.

The next step is to determine the lot size, reorder point, and possible safety stock for each and every inventory item–inventory location pair. This is shown for factory RM inventory locations and factory FG inventory locations in Table 10.7. Product_A uses EPQ to set lot size and ROP to determine its reorder point and has no safety stock. Part_C uses lot-for-lot to set lot size and safety stock as its reorder point and has safety stock. "B" and "C" items use the ABC analysis to set lot size, use zero as their reorder point, and have no safety stock. Shipping Carton_K is a special case. You do not want to run out of this $1 part and hold up shipments, yet these cartons can take up a large cubic volume. The supplier delivers once a week, plus you decide to carry one week of safety stock; do not forget to rotate safety stock with the main stock.

Total network inventory is the sum of the inventories associated with each product. Total product inventory is the sum of the FG inventories in the pull zone plus the sum of the component and RM inventories in the push zone. Within the pull zone, FG and system component cycle stocks can be classified as "A," "B," "C," or "D" items relative to value and turns. Within the push zone RMs, component parts and subassemblies can be classified as "A," "B," "C," or "D" items relative to value and turns. Figure 10.10 shows a typical single product inventory profile at the factory. In this figure, no-turn inventory represents "D" items, excess inventory, and safety stocks.

Suppose Figure 10.10 is representative of your highest volume product. Then the following set of equations, based on the average area enclosed by a triangular shape, approximates the average inventory value for this single product at the factory. There will also be in-transit inventory pulsing through inbound, midbound, and outbound logistics paths. Note that each equation relates to timing in months and that some quantities are lot size quantities while others are annual quantities.

$$\text{Average inventory value} = (0.500) \times \text{Lot size} \times \$/\text{unit} \tag{10.18}$$

"A" average inventory value = (0.0417) × Annual quantity × ("A" item $/unit)
For inventory items purchased one month at a time or lot-for-lot. (10.19)

"B" average inventory value = (0.125) × Annual quantity × ("B" item $/unit)
For inventory items purchased three months at a time. (10.20)

Table 10.7 Lot Size, Reorder Point, and Safety Stock for Each Item–Location Pair

		Factory RMs			*Factory FGs*		
Item	*ABC*	*Lot Size*	*Reorder Point*	*Safety Stock*	*Lot Size*	*Reorder Point*	*Safety Stock*
Product_A					EPQ	ROP	No
Assembly_B	B				3 months	Zero	No
Assembly_E	C				6 months	Zero	No
Assembly_H	C				6 months	Zero	No
Carton_K					Weekly	Safety	Yes
Part_C	A	Lot 4 Lot	Safety	Yes			
Part_D	C	6 months	Zero	No			
Part_F	B	3 months	Safety	Yes			
Part_G	C	6 months	Zero	No			
Part_I	C	6 months	Zero	No			
Part_J	C	6 months	Zero	No			
		Distributor Cycle Stock					
Item	*ABC*	*Lot Size*	*Reorder Point*	*Safety Stock*			
Product_A		EOQ	ROP + SS	Yes			

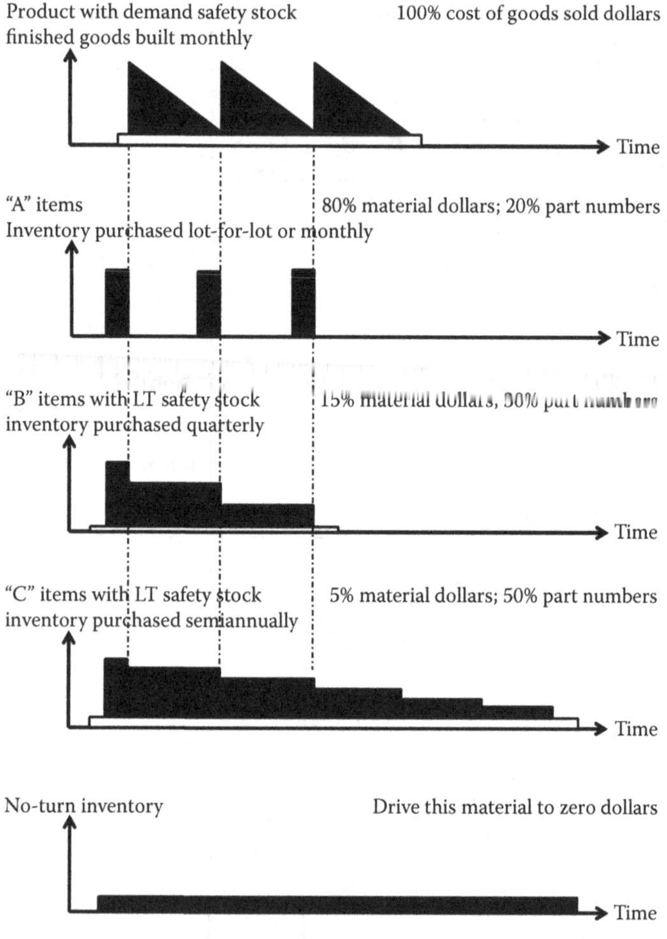

Figure 10.10 Typical single product inventory profile at the factory.

$$\text{"C" average inventory value} = (0.250) \times \text{Annual quantity} \times (\text{"C" item \$/unit}) \tag{10.21}$$

For inventory items purchased six months at a time.

$$\text{"D" average inventory value} = (1.000) \times \text{Lot size} \times (\text{"D" item \$/unit}) \tag{10.22}$$

For no-turn inventory and/or safety stock.

Since each product can be modeled the same way, the total average inventory at each supplier, factory, and distributor inventory location is given by:

$$\text{Total Average Inventory} = \sum_{\text{Inventory}} \text{"A" Items} + \sum_{\text{Inventory}} \text{"B" Items} + \sum_{\text{Inventory}} \text{"C" Items} + \sum_{\text{Inventory}} \text{"D" Items} \quad (10.23)$$

Finally, the expected average value of the factory RM inventory and the factory FG inventory comes together in Table 10.8. Each item with a safety stock is broken out into two rows with the top row for the main quantity and the bottom row for the safety stock quantity. The multiplier is determined by the part classification, the equations above, and the number of times the item is replenished in a year. The set of extended values for items found in one inventory location are summed to determine the average expected inventory. In general, this table is expanded to also include supplier and distributor inventories across the full set of items in the composite BOM item master.

$$\text{\$Extended value} = (\text{\$/unit of item value}) \times (\text{Lot size in units}) \times (\text{Multiplier}) \quad (10.24)$$

Pull Inventory Out of the Push/Pull Boundary

Inventory and capacity planning and control in the pull zone are fundamentally different and simpler than the push planning described above. Inventory has to be matched to the customer order in both rate and mix at the push/pull boundary for throughput to occur. Trading partners downstream from the push/pull boundary need to be maximum capacity capable for the order to deliver unimpeded to the end customer.

Pulling Inventory under a Synchronized BTS Scenario

Under this scenario, standard product, for example, FMCGs, is replenished from a push/pull boundary close to the end customer. Demand information broadcast upstream is synchronized across echelons in its timing. Supply inventories transported downstream are synchronized across echelons in their movement. The rate of RMs brought into the supply chain is matched with the rate of FGs shipped to customers. This synchronization eliminates the bullwhip effect.

- *Maximum daily throughput capacity*

  Each trading partner and logistics connection downstream of the push/pull boundary must be capacity capable of supporting the maximum daily throughput.

Table 10.8 Calculating Expected Average Inventory at the Factory and the Distributor

				Factory RMs			*Factory FGs*		
Item	*ABCD*	*Item Value*	*Multiplier*	*Lot Size*	*Safety Stock*	*Extend Value*	*Lot Size*	*Safety Stock*	*Extend Value*
Prod_A		$400	×0.500				225	0	$45,000
Assy_B	B	$150	×0.125 ×4				300	0	$22,500
Assy_E	C	$40	×0.250 ×2				600	0	$12,000
Assy_H	C	$8	×0.250 ×2				600	0	$2,400
Carton_K		$1	×0.500				24	0	$12
	D	$1	×1.000				0	24	$24
Part_C	A	$80	×0.042 ×5.3	450	0	$7,956			
	D	$80	×1.000	0	100	$8,000			
Part_D	C	$2	×0.250 ×2	600	0	$600			
Part_F	B	$20	×0.125 ×4	900	0	$9,000			
	D	$20	×1.000	0	375	$7,500			
Part_G	C	$2	×0.250 ×2	600	0	$600			

(Continued)

Table 10.8 (Continued) Calculating Expected Average Inventory at the Factory and the Distributor

				Factory RMs			*Factory FGs*		
Item	*ABCD*	*Item Value*	*Multiplier*	*Lot Size*	*Safety Stock*	*Extend Value*	*Lot Size*	*Safety Stock*	*Extend Value*
Part_I	C	$2	×0.250 ×2	600	0	$600			
Part_J	C	$2	×0.250 ×2	600	0	$600			
						$34,856			$81,936
				Average RM Inventory			Average FG Inventory		
				Distributor Cycle Stock					
Item	*ABCD*	*Item Value*	*Multiplier*	*Lot Size*	*Safety Stock*	*Extended Value*			
Product_A		$400	×0.500	200	0	$40,000			
	D	$400	×1.000	0	75	$30,000			
						$70,000			
				Average DC inventory					

For example: Suppose a delivery channel consists of a single distributor feeding 20 retail stores. A product has a maximum throughput of 100 units per day at the DC and (100 units per day)/20 stores or 5 units per day at each of 20 retail stores. The DC must have labor capacity to deliver 100 units per day, and each retail store must have labor capacity to receive, stock, and sell 5 units per day. If the distributor uses two trucks to make daily deliveries to the 20 retail stores, then each truck must be capacity capable of transporting (100 units per day)/2 trucks or 50 units per day per truck.

- *Distributor cycle stock inventory*

  The cycle stock inventory held at the distributor depends on the maximum daily throughput.

$$I_{\text{Cycle}} = T_{\text{Max}} d_{\text{supply}} \text{ in units} \tag{10.25}$$

where I_{Cycle} = cycle stock inventory in units; T_{Max} = maximum throughput in units per day; and d_{supply} = days supply in days.

For example: Continuing the scenario from above, the distributor wants to keep 14 days' supply of inventory. The 14 days comes from the two-week fixed interval replenishment cycle used to synchronize the supply chain.

$$I_{\text{Cycle}} = (100 \text{ units/day})(14 \text{ days}) = 1{,}400 \text{ units}$$

- *Retail store cycle stock inventory*

  The cycle stock inventory held at each retail store depends upon the following relationship:

$$I_{\text{Cycle}} = \frac{T_{\text{Max}} d_{\text{supply}}}{\#\text{Stores}} \text{ in units} \tag{10.26}$$

where I_{Cycle} = cycle stock inventory in units; T_{Max} = maximum throughput in units; d_{supply} = days supply in days; and #Stores = number of stores in the network.

For example: Completing the scenario from above, each of the 20 retail stores is within a two-hour drive of the distributor and gets replenished each day. However, the stores decide to carry an additional day of safety lead time to protect against weather-related delays in delivery. The stores allocate shelf space to display five units and reserve part of their very limited backroom storage for the five units of safety stock. Store management must ensure first-in/first-out stock rotation of the entire inventory on the shelf and in the backroom.

$$I_{\text{Cycle}} = (100 \text{ units/day})(2 \text{ days})/20 \text{ stores} = 10 \text{ units}$$

In reality, this maximum-capacity, maximum-inventory model gets multiplied by the number of SKUs sold in each store.

Pulling Inventory under a Postpone-to-Order Scenario

Under this scenario, a high-mix or customized product, for example, an industrial good, is postponed and delivered from the push/pull boundary to the end customer. The emphasis is on completing the product to match an actual customer order within a short delivery lead time rather than investing in FG inventory of the wrong mix. The product has to be designed for postponement. Because each product is customized, product flows directly to the end customer and does not stick in any downstream inventory location. Postponement reduces the inventory mix investment, and it provides an opportunity to reduce the cost of generic assembly because of higher consolidated volume.

- *Network capacity* is sized to handle the maximum rate of throughput across any mix.
- *Generic cycle stock inventory*

  The factory pushes the generic portion of the product into the push/pull boundary at the postponement center using the push planning methodology detailed earlier in this chapter. The generic product's monthly rate of production is driven from the supply forecast.
- *Postponement inventory*

  Purchasing at the postponement center maintains an inventory of every unique postponed item in quantities equal to the generic product's monthly rate. These items are pushed into the push/pull boundary based on the supply forecast for the generic product. Each of the items in postponement inventory is of low value relative to the value of the finished product; this reduces the total inventory investment significantly.

  For example: Suppose there are three products. Product_H = Generic Assembly + Part_H; Product_J = Generic Assembly + Part_J; Product_K = Generic Assembly + Part_K. If the Generic Assembly is planned at a rate of 200/month, then purchasing at the postponement center maintains an inventory level of 200 Part_H, 200 Part_J, and 200 Part_K so that 200 complete products with any mix can be built and shipped that month.
- *Fulfillment*

  The postponement center matches the correct configuration with the customer order. The product is completed, tested, inspected, and shipped. See the example in Figure 10.11.

Product structure before postponement			
Bills of materials	**Cable_H**	**Cable_J**	**Cable_K**
Near connector end	8 pin male twistlock	8 pin male twistlock	8 pin male twistlock
Cable body	14 ft 8 wire 20 AWG	14 ft 8 wire 20 AWG	14 ft 8 wire 20 AWG
Far connector end	6 pin male delphi	4 pin male delphi 4 pin female delphi	4 pin male delphi 2 pin male delphi 3 pin female twistlock

Push items	Push/pull boundary inventory	Pull items
Generic assembly		Cable_H
3 pin female twistlock		Cable_J
4 pin female delphi		Cable_K
2 pin male delphi		
4 pin male delphi		
6 pin male delphi		

Product structure after postponement			
Bills of materials	**Cable_H**	**Cable_J**	**Cable_K**
Generic cable		8 pin male twistlock 14 ft 8 wire 20 AWG	
Postponed connectors	6 pin male delphi	4 pin male delphi 4 pin female delphi	4 pin male delphi 2 pin male delphi 3 pin female twistlock

Figure 10.11 Example of a postponed cable.

In Summary

This chapter describes how to flow product inventory through the supply chain network container and the importance of keeping this inventory turning. The selection of an operating strategy together with the location of the push/pull boundary determines the delivery lead time to the customer. A push planning methodology that drives inventory into the push/pull boundary from a forecast is detailed. Inventory is then matched with the customer order and pulled from the push/pull boundary to complete the order fulfillment. Such normal operations are considered small signal static operations. Chapter 12: "Risk Management" describes how to deal with large signal dynamic situations.

Chapter 11

Performance Measures—"Make It Work Well"

Supply chain construction starts and ends with your customer. It is a process that iterates through the Supply Chain Construction Blueprint. Chapter 2: "The Blueprint" presents a detailed example of how to apply The Blueprint to a forward supply chain, and Chapter 8: "Return" presents a detailed example of how to apply The Blueprint to a reverse supply chain. The optimal design and operation of a supply chain are not merely the sum of local optimizations. It is much more complex systems approach because of its integrated nature. Performance measures, key performance indicators (KPIs), and metrics are all names for gauging how the system is working relative to its Supply Chain Construction Requirements Specification. This chapter presents diagnostics and troubleshooting techniques that can be applied as a new or modified supply chain is first turned on should its performance not measure up. This chapter closes the loop between the architecture and the construction of a supply chain network. It closes the loop back to your customer.

You Get What You Measure

Harry from Product Marketing had been visiting a few of the value-added resellers (VARs) with his Computer Products counterpart. He had learned that a number of sales were anticipated to be for sets of three servers. He had some ideas about how to make the uninterruptable power supply (UPS) product more attractive in the delivery channel. One idea was to bundle a Product 1000 with two Product 500s and with a set of cables and rack mounting kits to be sold under a single system number at a discounted price. The Supply Chain Construction Project Team was debating the challenges of fulfilling product bundles at the distribution center (DC).

"How many bundles would we need to set up?" asked Donna from Purchasing.

Harry replied, "Just this one."

"We've been down this path before with our power supplies. Next, you'll want the same bundle without rack mounting. Then you'll want the bundle with two Product 1000s and one Product 500. Then you'll want the bundle with… There are endless combinations," said Donna exasperated.

"Yes, so? What's the real problem if our customers want to buy in bundles?" questioned Harry.

"But, isn't that part of the value added of the VARs?" asked Tony from Cost Accounting.

"Maybe, but we cannot afford to give the VAR any excuse not to order a UPS," replied Harry.

Bill, project manager, entered the conversation, "Let's humor Harry and talk about how we would implement bundling in the DC. When a VAR order comes to the push/pull boundary, we would have to have the UPS products, the cables, and the rack mount kits already there. I think one key issue is how we measure inventory availability."

"The Product 1000 UPS and the Product 500 UPS will be coming from Astec by ocean freight. Would we put a mixed shipment in one container? I will order power cables from Belden using UPS Ground delivery. I will order rack mount kits from our supplier also with a motor freight delivery," said Donna.

Moving to the whiteboard, Bill continued, "So, let's draw an inventory map and then talk about inventory measurement. I'll draw four triangles that represent individual part number inventories at the push/pull boundary in the DC: one each for the Product 1000 UPS, the Product 500 UPS, the cable, and the rack mount kit. Next, I'll connect the DC with Astec twice and represent Astec's two finished goods part numbers with inventory triangles and two in-transit ocean freight finished goods part numbers with inventory triangles. Finally, I'll connect each of the other suppliers with their own finished goods inventory triangles and in-transit motor freight finished goods inventory triangles. That gives a total of four inventory locations at the DC, plus four in-transit inventories, plus four inventory locations at suppliers."

"To fulfill one of Harry's product bundles, we would need the right quantities of inventory for each of the four part numbers to be in stock at the DC," said Donna.

"Or be able to reliably predict when each of the in-transit inventories would be received at the DC," added Bill.

"Then, the earliest ship date from the DC would be the latest inventory receipt date at the DC," concluded John from Engineering, who was starting to understand supply chain inventory concepts.

"How do we measure inventory?" asked Tony.

"We want to focus on measuring the quantity of inventory. Other measures include inventory turns and inventory dollar value. The inventory quantity can be dollarized in a secondary calculation because its dollar value depends upon which accounting system Tony is going to use, i.e., standard cost, last cost, or average cost," said Bill.

Donna said, "For the DC inventory, we can just look up the item's inventory quantity on our material management system. In the inventory view, you enter a part number and the system returns the current inventory balance by inventory location. There may be several locations. For example, a DC will often have both a pick face and a bulk storage location. The total inventory on hand is the sum of the quantities at each location. In the purchasing view, the system gives the expected delivery date for open purchase orders."

"How accurate is that?" asked Harry.

"It can be off a little because it is based on the average lead time that I have entered into the item master for a given part number," explained Donna. "When I place a purchase order, I usually get a confirmation of the expected ship date. Then, when the order ships from the supplier, I get the UPS tracking number, unless the supplier makes a less-than-truckload shipment."

"Do we have anything set up with Astec regarding inventory reporting?" asked Tony.

"Astec runs an independent enterprise requirements planning (ERP) system. They can provide a weekly summary of our inventory balances. We can also query them about the inventory level of specific items at any time, but their response will not be instantaneous because of time zone differences," said Bill.

"That could be a real problem," said Tony.

Bill continued, "A big issue with the kind of supply chain construction project we are doing is that each of the trading partners has their own independent information systems. We will have to cobble together information feeds for the measurements we need. This often means either the time to manually process small pieces of information or the expense of paying someone to customize an automated interface. With the volume of information to be processed, manual calculations are usually out of the question."

"Can the international procurement operation (IPO) help us get inventory balance information?" asked Donna.

"The IPO can at least validate when inventory arrives dockside in Singapore and provide an estimated time of arrival for the ocean freight going into Oakland, California," said Bill. "Again, this is a small piece of the total information we need to measure the performance of our supply chain."

Harry summarized what he was hearing, "When the VAR orders the bundle, we have to first check the inventory balances of the four part numbers in the DC; then, if something is out of stock, look up its expected delivery date; and then determine the earliest date that the required quantities of all parts are in stock at the DC. How do we know whether the inventory quantities are even accurate?"

Donna answered, "We can cycle count any item whose inventory balance is in question. That means someone is sent to every physical inventory locations for that item, counts the item, and compares the count with the inventory balance on the system. If there is any discrepancy, the person tracks down the root cause, for example, a quantity of parts misplaced on an adjacent rack shelf and corrects the inventory record."

Bill said, "There is another complication to determining inventory availability for the customer. This has to do with allocated versus nonallocated inventory. In most inventory management systems, inventory can be allocated to specific customer orders. If there are 100 units in stock with an order backlog for 60 units, then only 40 units are available for new orders. The first 60 are already allocated to other customer orders."

"I understand that," said Harry.

"But inventory allocation is determined on a first-come, first-serve basis. The question becomes when does the latest customer order become a released order? When does the allocation start?" said Bill.

"The VAR order has to have a complete product specification including all product options and bundles. The VAR order has to pass credit checking before being released to the DC. And, of course, we need the ship-to address, the preferred shipping method, and the bill-to address," answered Harry.

"That's right. Our available inventory measure starts when the right quantity of the last item in the product bundle gets received into stock; it ends when the next customer order is completed and released to shipping after credit check. Performance measurement is all about the source and timing of the data being sampled," stated Bill.

"I may need to rethink my UPS bundling idea," concluded Harry.

Measure KPIs

A supply chain is a very complex, highly integrated, nonlinear set of relationships, resources, and constraints. Most people want to view the supply chain as a black box with inputs and outputs plus a few meters to read the internal workings of the network. The car you drive is a good analogy. Your car is a black box, perhaps in some other color, with gasoline as its input and your physical transportation as its output. Your car has a speedometer based on the rotation of the car's tires and a fuel gauge to measure the engine's consumption of gasoline over time. But, internally, the engine, exhaust, transmission, steering, brakes, and chassis comprise a very complex, highly integrated, nonlinear set of relationships, resources, and constraints. Speed and fuel economy are necessary but insufficient measures of an automobile's construction.

And when you decide to buy a car, you have particular requirements in mind, namely, the price, body style, color, and fuel economy. You want immediate delivery. When you accept delivery of your new car, your acceptance is based on an agreed-upon price, a test drive, the observable body style and color, and the manufacturer's certified fuel economy. Your customer acceptance is the payment that you hand over to the car distributor before driving your new car off the lot. This chapter continues the journey having started from customer needs documented in the Supply Chain Construction Requirements Specification, through the formation of a project team and through the Supply Chain Construction Blueprint to the Value Circle and performance validation, ending back with customer acceptance. The objective is, of course, to make it work well.

A good performance measure, KPI, or metric has a long list of definitional attributes including a purpose, a description, a target value, a defined source of data, a defined repetition, a defined calculation algorithm, a single owner, network accountability, etc. But there is more to understanding the nature of a good performance measure.

The act of measurement can disturb the underlying performance. Consider this actual situation. It is the end of the quarter, and your shipments are far off your revenue target. You have open warranty repair orders that customers want right away that generate no revenue. And you have an order backlog that could be used to make your target, but the customer has requested delayed delivery until next month because of a cash flow issue on their end to make the payment. The completion of this order requires inventory that should be used for the warranty replacements. The management team struggles to decide what to do: ship the warranty replacements, or ship the backlog early, pulling inventory designated for warranty repair, dissatisfying the customer, and making the target? This is an example of the revenue measurement disturbing the system priorities.

Work with This Basic Performance Measurement System

A question often asked is, "How many performance measures should you have?" Some companies prefer a few robust metrics, while other companies employ a staggering number of metrics slicing and dicing each and every operation. The APICS Supply Chain Council, www.apics.org/sites/apics-supply-chain-council, has defined a set of standard hierarchical measures that many companies use.

The focus of this book, however, is a concise set of just eight basic performance measures that are both essential to supply chain construction and illustrative of additional metrics you might employ. Four of the performance measures and the overarching Value Circle are derived from the 5V Principles of supply chain management as stated in Chapter 3: "Building Relationships." Four of the performance measures are traditional financial measures. From another perspective, four of the measures look at the network container and four of the measures look at the product contents. Table 11.1 shows the relationships among the eight basic performance measures. The paragraphs following Table 11.1 describe the measurement system used in this book. Later sections in this chapter describe how to use this measurement system to

Table 11.1 Basic Performance Measure Relationships

Supply chain construction requirements specification			
	Network container	Product contents	
5V Principles	Cash-to-cash velocity Cash-to-cash variability	Visualize to pull Visualize to push	
	Value principle Value Circle		
Financial measures	End-to-end throughput Landed cost	Inventory turns ROIC	
			Validated supply chain performance

compare supply chain construction alternatives, how to use this measurement system to validate supply chain performance, and how to use this measurement system to diagnose supply chain start-up problems.

Throughput (Chapter 4)

- *How is throughput measured?* Throughput is measured end to end in revenue dollars. To be counted as throughput, payment from the end customer must result in cash flows all the way back upstream to the raw material supplier. Throughput is recorded as shipment revenue net of returns.
- *Where is throughput measured?* The throughput measure has an echelon context (see Figure 11.1). Factory output is the best measure of total throughput. Moving downstream, the unit quantity of this total throughput splits among DCs and splits again among retail stores and any inventory held in reserve at the DC. Moving upstream, the unit quantity of total throughput

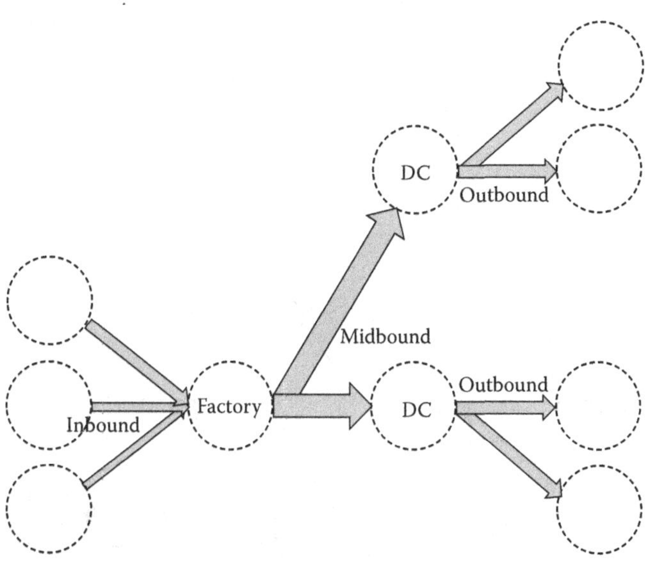

Figure 11.1 Throughput.

splits among parts inventory held in reserve at the factory and the first tier parts suppliers, then splits again among second tier parts suppliers, and so on.

- *What is the throughput leverage point?* The network constraint is the leverage point for throughput. Any adjustment to the network constraint's capacity will increase, or decrease, end-to-end throughput.

Landed Cost (Chapter 4)

- *How is landed cost measured?* The buyer's landed cost is the sum of the seller's price plus the carrier's price for logistics. These prices are determined from the supplier's and carrier's invoices.
- *Where is landed cost measured?* Landed cost has an echelon context (see Figure 11.2). Landed cost at the input to the factory is the sum of supplier material prices plus the price of inbound logistics. Landed cost at the input to the DC is the sum of the factory product price plus the price of midbound logistics. Landed cost at the store is the sum of the distributor product price plus the price of outbound logistics.
- *What are the landed cost leverage points?* Landed cost has four leverage points: network length, material cost in the product bill of materials (BOM), the factory labor rate, and logistics cost. As more echelons are added to the network length, the end product becomes more expensive because of additional echelon markups. The more direct material cost that is built into a product's

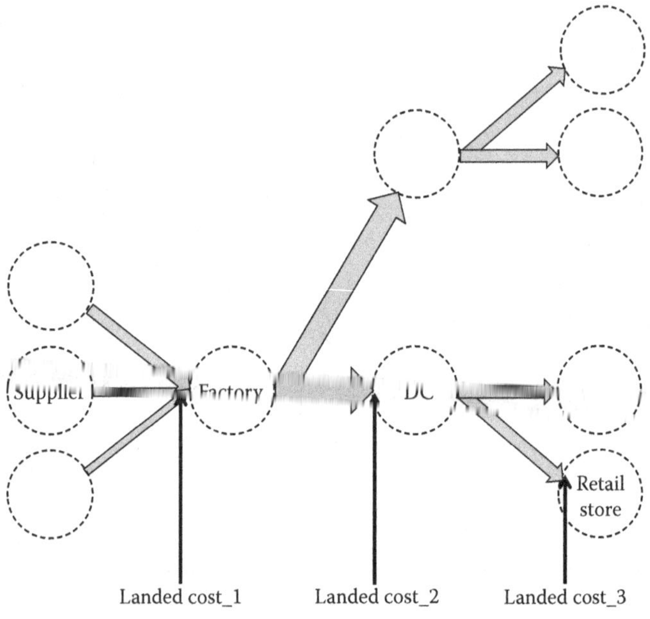

Figure 11.2 Landed cost.

design, the more expensive is the product. The higher the factory labor rate determined by the factory's geographical location, the more expensive is the product. The longer the distance the product inventory travels and the higher the weight and/or cube of the product inventory, the more expensive logistics cost becomes.

Cash-to-Cash Velocity (Chapter 4)

- *How is cash-to-cash velocity measured?* Cash-to-cash velocity is the time difference in days between the completion of the order-to-delivery-to-cash$_{\text{Supply}}$ cycle and the completion of the order-to-delivery-to-cash$_{\text{Demand}}$ cycle relative to the same point in time. Cash-to-cash velocity can be positive or negative depending on whether the supply or demand subcycle is completed first. Specifically, determine a primary component part that is out of stock with a corresponding product that is out of stock. Identify the purchase order sent to the supplier for the component part. Record the date/time stamp the supplier is paid for the component's purchase order. Record the date/time stamp the customer pays for the first of the product inventory. The cash-to-cash velocity is the difference between the two dates/times.
- *Where is cash-to-cash velocity measured?* Cash-to-cash velocity has an echelon context (see Figure 11.3). It is measured separately for the factory and for the DC.

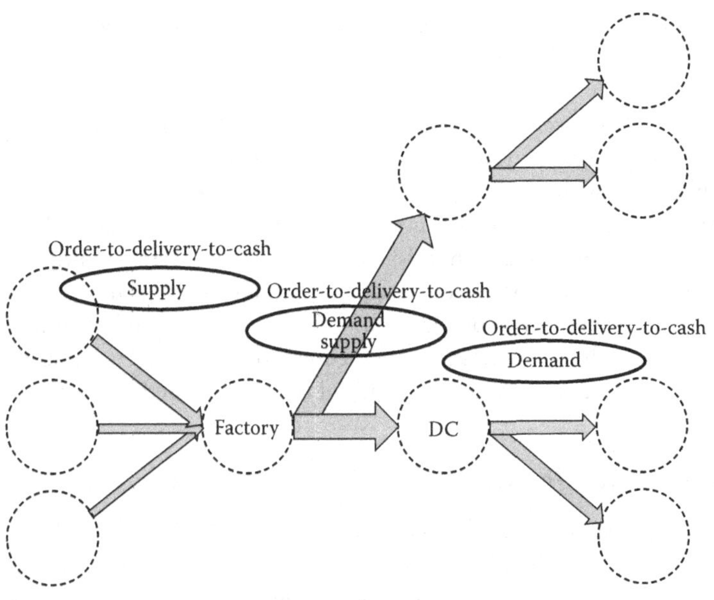

Figure 11.3 The cash-to-cash cycle velocity and variability.

- *What is the cash-to-cash velocity leverage point?* You want the downstream buyer to pay before having to pay the upstream seller. You want the seller's terms to be longer than the buyer's terms. You want to avoid giving credit to the buyer and/or having to prepay the seller. With a build-to-stock strategy, cash-to-cash velocity improves when the product's manufacturing cycle time is reduced and when the average number of days the product is held in inventory is reduced. With a build-to-order strategy, cash-to-cash velocity improves when the ordered material's lead time is reduced and when the product's manufacturing cycle time is reduced.

Cash-to-Cash Variability (Chapter 4)

- *How is cash-to-cash variability measured?* Cash-to-cash variability is the measure of how much cash-to-cash velocity changes from one cycle to the next. This should be measured across a small sample of cash-to-cash cycles. The mean of the set of samples is the cash-to-cash velocity and the standard deviation of the set of samples is the cash-to-cash variability.

$$\text{Cash-to-cash velocity} = \text{Mean of the set}_i \text{ of (cash-to-cash velocity}_i) \quad (11.1)$$

$$\text{Cash-to-cash variability} = \text{Standard deviation of the set}_i \text{ of (cash-to-cash velocity}_i) \quad (11.2)$$

- *Where is cash-to-cash variability measured?* Cash-to-cash variability has an echelon context (see Figure 11.3). It is measured separately for the factory and for the DC.
- *What is the cash-to-cash variability leverage point?* When large customers do not pay on time, cash-to-cash variability is dominated by payment delinquency. Otherwise, with a build-to-stock strategy, when everything else is under good control, cash-to-cash variability is dominated by differences in the length of time the product is held in finished goods inventory across multiple customer orders. When customers order a given product infrequently, the inventory duration variability is outside your control. With a build-to-order strategy, when everything else is under good control, cash-to-cash variability is dominated by differences in the longest lead time for ordered materials.

Inventory (Chapter 10)

- *How is inventory measured?* Inventory can be measured in units, dollars, turns, and/or days of supply. Inventory can be counted periodically or counted on request. Perpetual inventory systems accumulate the quantities of every inventory receipt and every inventory issue starting from a known quantity for each and every inventory item-location pair. Inventory counts are validated once a year with a physical inventory or continuously with cycle counting.

  Basic Equation 11.3 applies to single items in units or dollars and to groups of items in dollars.

$$\text{Ending inventory} = \text{Starting inventory} + \text{Receipts} - \text{Issues} \tag{11.3}$$

Inventory is dollarized by multiplying the quantity count of each item by the dollar value of each item and summing over all items in inventory in that warehouse.

$$\text{Total warehouse inventory \$} = \sum_i (\text{Item}_i \text{ count} \times \text{Item}_i \text{ \$Value}) \tag{11.4}$$

Inventory turns are related to inventory days of supply based on a 365-day year.

$$\text{Days of supply} = \frac{365 \text{ days}}{\text{Inventory turns}} \tag{11.5}$$

ABC analysis is a powerful inventory control and measurement tool. ABC analysis done commodity by commodity, for example, all sheet metal items, all plastic items, all fastener items, etc., yields the best inventory control. Refer to Table 11.2 where part values range from \$2.50 to \$45.00 and part annual volumes range from 800 units to 60,200 units. Each inventory item is dollarized, and then the extended dollar value list is sorted in descending order. The cumulative dollar column starts at the top row, with the highest extended dollar item, then adds each successively smaller extended dollar value item until the total inventory value is reached in the last row. A cut is made at the cumulative dollar value separating "B" items from "A" items. A second cut is made at the cumulative dollar value separating "C" items from "B" items. The ABC classifications are filled in accordingly between the two cuts.

Table 11.2 An ABC Inventory Analysis for a Single Commodity

Inventory Item	*Annual Unit Demand*	*Unit \$Value*	*Extended \$Value*	*Cumulative \$Value*	*ABC Classification*
C	45,000	\$40.00	\$1,800,000	\$1,800,000	"A"
B	21,000	\$45.00	\$945,000	\$2,745,000	"A"
F	9,800	\$28.50	\$279,300	\$3,024,300	"A"
H	60,200	\$4.00	\$240,800	\$3,265,100	"B"
J	14,500	\$12.00	\$174,000	\$3,439,100	"B"
A	7,500	\$22.00	\$165,000	\$3,604,100	"B"
I	33,100	\$4.00	\$132,400	\$3,736,500	"C"
G	6,250	\$9.00	\$56,250	\$3,792,750	"C"
D	20,000	\$2.50	\$50,000	\$3,842,750	"C"
E	800	\$20.00	\$16,000	\$3,858,750	"C"
			\$3,858,750	Total	
			ABC criteria		
			80% dollars	\$3,087,000	"A" Item
			15% dollars	\$578,813	"B" Item
			5% dollars	\$192,938	"C" Item
				\$3,858,750	

"A" items are defined to be 80% of the dollars and 20% of the part numbers, cut at 80% of the total.
"B" items are defined to be 15% of the dollars and 30% of the part numbers, cut at 95% of the total.
"C" items are defined to be $\frac{5\%}{100\%}$ of the dollars and $\frac{50\%}{100\%}$ of the part numbers.

Once the ABC analysis has been completed, a cycle counting program can be established. Under cycle counting, a small number of inventory items are counted every day. Typically, a computer program generates a daily list of part numbers and stocking locations. The count is blind, meaning the counter does not know the system value until after the physical count has been made. The purpose of cycle counting is to validate the current inventory count against the inventory record shown in the information system. When these two counts do not match, the process root cause is investigated the same day, and the process is fixed immediately. A robust cycle counting program can eliminate the need for an expensive shutdown to perform a multiday physical inventory.

"A" items are counted once a month.

"B" items are counted once a quarter.

"C" items are counted once every 6 or 12 months.

The most efficient counting time is when the inventory count balance is supposedly zero.

- *Where is inventory measured?* Inventory has an echelon context (see Figure 11.4). For the purposes of this book, suppliers have component-level finished goods, the factory has component-level raw material and product-level finished goods, distributors have product-level cycle stock, and retail stores have product-level cycle stock. This book does not distinguish the added complexity of work-in-process inventory at the factory or inventory held by the customer. The push/pull boundary is most likely either the distributor's cycle stock location or the factory's finished goods location.
- *What is the inventory leverage point?* Inventory has three leverage points. First, large lot sizes get multiplied by forecast error. This means an error in forecasting can easily cause the reorder of an additional product lot. Second, safety stocks get multiplied by higher-than-required service-level factors. Safety stock should be carefully positioned downstream to protect against demand uncertainty and upstream to protect against lead time variability. Third, low-value, high-mix inventory gets improperly classified as an "A" or "B" item. Low-usage, high-mix inventory in distribution is better handled through postponement.

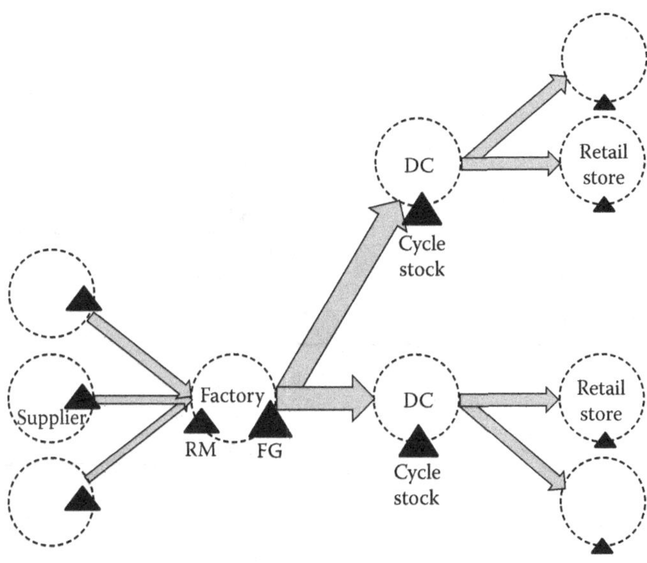

Figure 11.4 Inventory.

Delivery Lead Time Vocalize Pull (Chapter 9)

- *How is vocalize measured?* Vocalize is the delivery lead time in days from the push/pull boundary to the end customer. It starts with the customer placing their order and ends with the customer receiving their product. Vocalize includes three process steps with high degrees of variability: order booking, customer credit checking, order picking and packing, plus outbound logistics transit time. The time spent in order booking depends upon the complexity of the product configuration choices. The time spent in customer credit checking depends upon the customer being a new or a repeat customer and the dollar amount of open accounts receivable for repeat customers. The time spent in transit depends upon the geographical location of the customer relative to the DC and the transportation mode selected. The internal vocalize time can be measured from the date/time stamp an order is booked until the date/time stamp the product is shipped. The external vocalize time can be measured using the date/time stamp on the UPS or FedEx proof of delivery.
- *Where is vocalize measured?* Vocalize includes the order processing path from the end customer to order release at the push/pull boundary, potentially waiting for the finished goods to be received into the push/pull boundary from production, picking and packing at the push/pull boundary, and shipping the product to the end customer using a common carrier (see Figure 11.5).
- *What is the vocalize leverage point?* With the product in stock, the largest variability for vocalize is usually found in the credit checking process. Streamlining credit checking, simplifying product configurations for

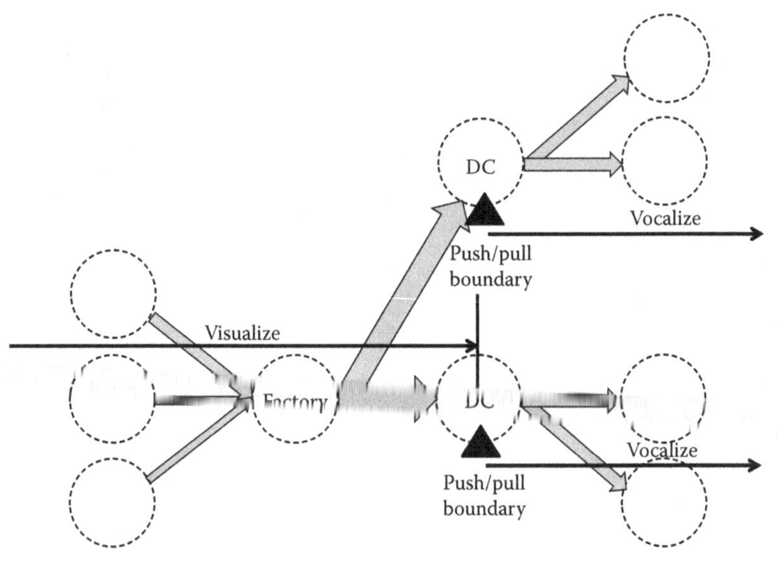

Figure 11.5 Delivery lead time and the planning horizon.

ordering, and paying attention to the number of signatures required to release an order are the leverage points to consistent, competitive delivery lead time.

Visualize Push (Chapter 10)

- *How is visualize measured?* Visualize is the planning horizon in days from the longest lead time raw material to the push/pull boundary. It starts with the approval of the monthly supply forecast and ends with the finished goods built from that forecast being received into the push/pull boundary. Material lead times are not static. Therefore, the duration of the planning horizon should be reassessed twice a year. Identify the longest lead time item that needs replenishment to build a specific future product inventory. Record the date that the purchase order for that long-lead-time item is released. Record the date that the specific product built from the replenishment purchase order for the longest lead time part is received into the push/pull boundary. Note that this may be many weeks or months later. Visualize is the number of days difference between these two dates.
- *Where is visualize measured?* Visualize is the longest cumulative path of planning cycle time, plus queue time, plus purchasing lead time, plus manufacturing cycle time, plus logistics transit and customs clearance times through the deepest, longest product structure for any of your products (see Figure 11.5).

- *What is the visualize leverage point?* Ideally, you want the planning horizon to be as short as possible because you want to be as independent of the forecast as possible. Visualize has four leverage points: the depth of the BOM product structure, forecast mix accuracy, the single longest lead time for material, and any material delivered using ocean freight. Work to flatten the product structures of your product BOMs so that lead times do not stack up serially. Improve forecast mix accuracy so that the parts mix coming into inventory is what is really needed for customer orders. Determine materials with exceptionally long lead times and work with the supplier to ensure consistency in their actual delivery time. Perhaps, a substitute material or a different supplier can shorten the lead time. Carefully monitor demand and supply of any material arriving by ocean freight.

Return on Invested Capital (Chapter 2)

- *How is return on invested capital (ROIC) measured?* ROIC is not really a measurement because it is a percentage calculated from the profit and loss (P&L) statement and the balance sheet. Profit after taxes in the numerator comes from the P&L statement. If the P&L statement is available, use it. The following estimate can be used for profit after taxes when a complete P&L statement is not available. The 1/4 factor comes from dividing the gross margin among sales, general, and administrative (SG&A), depreciation and interest expense, taxes, and profit. This is a very crude estimate; but if used consistently, it can be useful for comparing alternatives.

$$\text{Profit after taxes} = (\text{Revenue} - \text{Cost of goods sold [COGS]}) \times 1/4 \quad (11.6)$$

Inventory, production assets, accounts receivable, and accounts payable in the denominator come from the balance sheet. If the full balance sheet is available, use it. Otherwise, the following crude estimates may be used. Under NET30 day terms, accounts receivable can be estimated as equal to one month of revenue. Under NET30 day terms, accounts payable can be estimated as equal to one month of COGS. Inventory can be dollarized based on inventory turns and the dollar value of COGS.

$$\$\text{Inventory} = \frac{\$\text{COGS}}{\text{Inventory turns}} \quad (11.7)$$

There will be times when you do not know the dollar value for fixed assets, or you may only know the dollar value for production equipment being purchased or sold as part of the supply chain construction project. If you have access to the full balance sheet, use it. Otherwise, for estimating purposes, double the value of the "as-is" inventory to cover the fixed assets. Adjust the "to-be" production assets by the purchase or sale of any project-related production assets. In such a case, the calculated ROIC will not reflect the actual ROIC; however, when computed consistently, this ROIC estimate is useful for comparing alternatives. Table 11.3 shows an example of how to estimate

Table 11.3 Example of ROIC Comparison Using Estimated Amounts

	"As-Is" Supply Chain	*"To-Be" Supply Chain*
Expected change		5% reduction in direct material Inventory turns improved to 5.5 from 4.0
Annual revenue	$10,000,000	$10,000,000
Annual cost of goods sold	$7,200,000	$7,200,000 – $150,000 = $7,050,000
Direct material	$3,000,000	$2,850,000 with 5% reduction
Annual estimated profit after taxes	($10,000,000 – $7,200,000) × 1/4 = $700,000	($10,000,000 – $7,050,000) × 1/8 = $737,500
Accounts receivable	$10,000,000 × 1/12 = $833,333	$10,000,000 × 1/12 = $833,333
Accounts payable	$7,200,000 × 1/12 = $600,000	$7,050,000 × 1/12 = $587,500
Inventory turns	4.0	5.5
Inventory dollars	$7,200,000/4.0 = $1,800,000	$7,050,000/5.5 = $1,281,818
Estimated production assets	$1,800,000	$1,800,000; same as "As-Is"
Calculated ROIC denominator	$1,800,000 + $1,800,000 + $833,333 – $600,000 = $3,833,333	$1,281,818 + $1,800,000 + $833,333 – $587,500 = $3,327,651
Calculated ROIC	$700,000 × 100%/$3,833,333 = 18.3%	$737,500 × 100%/$3,327,651 = 22.2%

ROIC when you do not have a complete P&L statement or a complete balance sheet.

- *Where is ROIC measured?* ROIC has an echelon context. It is calculated separately for the factory and for the DC.
- *What is the ROIC leverage point?* Profit dominates the numerator of the ROIC equation and inventory dominates the denominator of the ROIC equation. Therefore, while holding revenue constant, decreasing product cost and increasing inventory turns are leverage points for ROIC.

Use a Value Circle to Make Comparisons

Reassembling the eight performance measures and combining Figures 11.1 through 11.5 into Figure 11.6, you can see that it is complicated. A better way to see the interactions and compare alternatives is to construct separate Value Circles for the factory and for the distributor. A Value Circle is a graphical representation of the relative interaction of a number of supply chain performance measures. The Value Circle portrays the throughput, velocity, landed cost, and variability attributes associated with the network container. The Value Circle portrays the inventory, vocalize, ROIC, and visualize attributes associated with the product contents.

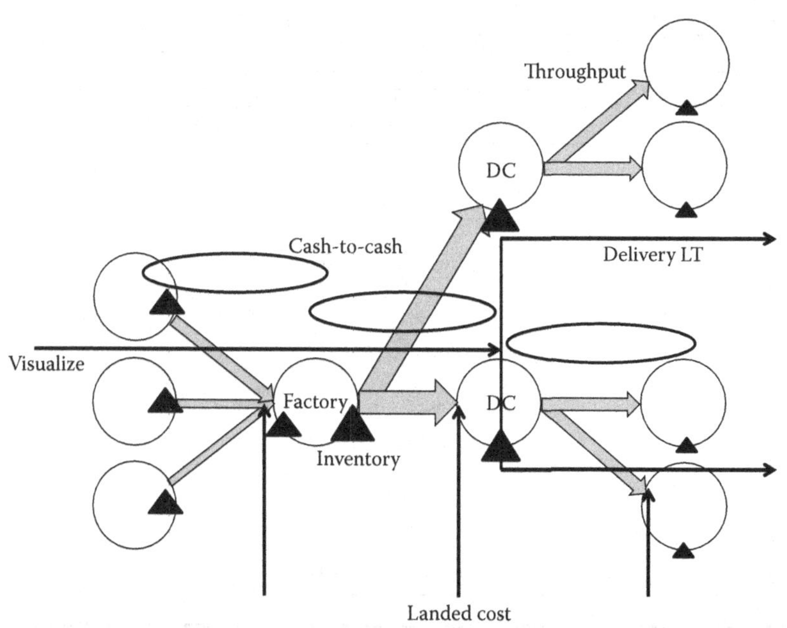

Figure 11.6 The set of basic performance measures.

How to Draw a Value Circle

The Value Circle is drawn as a circular radar diagram, also called a spider diagram, with a number of axes radiating from its center point, or origin (see Figure 11.7). Each axis has an independent scale, but in all cases, the performance measurement improves toward the origin. These independent scales may be linear or nonlinear. A reference circle, called the unit circle, is drawn half way out from the origin. As individual points on each axis are connected successively, they enclose an eight-sided shape and some area relative to the circular area of the unit circle. The smaller the area enclosed by the eight-sided shape, the more competitive is the supply chain.

The axes on the Value Circle are the same as the specifications on the Supply Chain Construction Requirements Specification. There are four financial axes: throughput (K$), price/landed cost ($), inventory (days), and ROIC (percentage). There are four operational axes: velocity (days), variability (days), visualize (days), and vocalize (days). The order of the eight axes is fixed. These axes are drawn in a particular counterclockwise order starting from the right center: throughput, velocity, price/landed cost, variability, inventory, vocalize, ROIC and visualize. The eight-sided shape improves along each axis as it moves toward the origin shrinking in its total enclosed area. The Appendix at the end of this chapter describes how to use Excel to plot a Value Circle.

To-be	As-is	Dimensions	Axes titles	To-be	Unit circle As-is
585	600	$	Price/landed cost ($)	1.0	1.0
10	10	Days	Velocity (days)	1.0	1.0
275	250	K$	Throughput (K$)	0.9	1.0
180	180	Days	Visualize (days)	1.0	1.0
8.6	12	%	ROIC (%)	1.4	1.0
3	5	Days	Vocalize (days)	0.6	1.0
125	75	Days	Inventory (days)	1.7	1.0
15	12	Days	Variability (days)	1.0	1.0

To-be	As-is
0.345	0.354
0.322	0.354
0.322	0.354
0.494	0.354
0.296	0.354
0.354	0.354
0.590	0.354
0.345	0.354
Total area	Total area
3.068	2.832

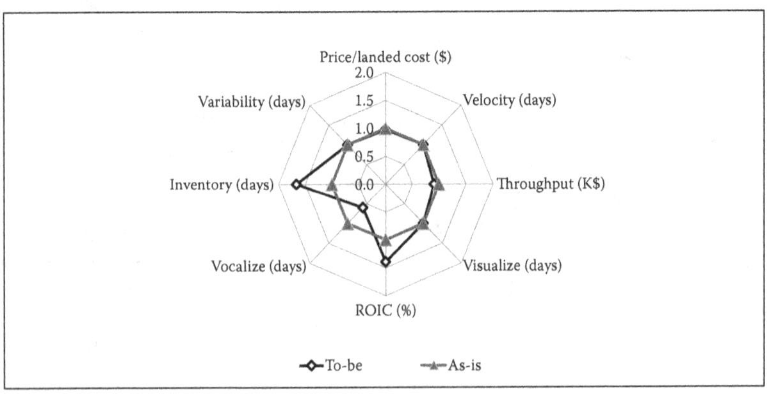

Figure 11.7 A Value Circle.

How to Scale Each Value Circle Axis

The scale of each axis is independent with its numerical value getting smaller moving toward the origin except for throughput, visualize, and ROIC, whose numerical values get larger moving toward the origin.

- Scale the "as-is" unit circle equal to 1.00 by dividing the "as-is" number by the "as-is" number.
- Scale velocity, landed cost, variability, inventory, and vocalize by dividing the "to-be" number by the "as-is" number so that a larger "to-be" number moves away from the origin.
- Scale throughput, visualize, and ROIC by dividing the "as-is" number by the "to-be" number so that a larger "to-be" number moves toward the origin.

How to Make Relative Comparisons Using the Value Circle

The Value Circle, derived directly from the Supply Chain Construction Requirements Specification, is an easy way to compare alternative approaches during a supply chain construction project. There will be times when you are presented with a choice, a fork in the road, about how to proceed. You will want to "true up" your construction progress to that point, much as a carpenter uses a level to true up his carpentry progress. Supply chain networks are complex systems with tight couplings and complicated interactions. While you can understand the dynamics of any one performance measure, it is difficult to see the resulting simultaneous interaction of eight performance measures. Plot each alternative on the Value Circle and then use the smaller of the two areas enclosed by each Value Circle as a relative indication of which alternative is the better choice. You can use a Value Circle to compare the following:

- Your current supply chain network "as-is" against your future supply chain network "to-be."
- Your supply chain network against your competitor's supply chain network.
- Your supply chain network against a best-in-class benchmark supply chain network.

How to Calculate the Enclosed Area on a Value Circle

The unit circle divided by the eight axes is like eight slices of pizza pie. With a perfect circle, each slice is a 45-degree equilateral triangle with both sides having equal lengths of one. The length of the side is the distance from the origin to the point on the unit circle. The whole unit circle pizza pie contains eight identical slices.

$$\text{Unit circle area of one slice} = (1/2) \times (\text{Sine of 45 degrees}) \times (\text{Length of side 1}) \times (\text{Length of side 2}) = 0.5 \times 0.707 \times 1.0 \times 1.0 = 0.354 \quad (11.8)$$

$$\text{Unit circle total area} = \text{Sum of areas of each slice} = 8 \times 0.354 = 2.832 \quad (11.9)$$

Value Circle total area =
0.354 × (Length of price/landed cost side) × (Length of velocity side)
+ 0.354 × (Length of velocity side) × (Length of throughput side)
+ 0.354 × (Length of throughput side) × (Length of visualize side)
+ 0.354 × (Length of visualize side) × (Length of ROIC side)
+ 0.354 × (Length of ROIC side) × (Length of vocalize side)
+ 0.354 × (Length of vocalize side) × (Length of inventory side)
+ 0.354 × (Length of inventory side) × (Length of variability side)
+ 0.354 × (Length of variability side) × (Length of price/landed cost side)
(11.10)

where each of the side lengths has been normalized relative to the unit circle.

Comparing the area of the "to-be" eight-sided shape against the area of the "as-is" unit circle is done by adding the areas of each of the eight "to-be" triangles and comparing this total area with 2.832. Each triangular area will vary according to the change in the length of the sides. If the "to-be" area is smaller than the "as-is" area, then the overall "to-be" network is an improvement to the supply chain.

A Value Circle Comparison Example

A factory delivering a high-mix product line through a distributor is contemplating on switching from a build-to-stock operating strategy to a build-to-order operating strategy. Finance believes that the factory's inventory investment can be cut by one third, which will also improve ROIC. Marketing believes that revenue will drop 20% because delivery lead times will double to 10 days. Product pricing remains unchanged. Operations realizes that while the planning horizon remains unchanged, the factory's cash-to-cash velocity will improve from having to finance 20 days of cash flow to having to finance 10 days of cash flow. But when the Value Circle is constructed and the "to-be" and "as-is" areas are computed, the management team realizes that 2.847 versus 2.832 is probably too close to call a clear winner. The advantages of reduced inventory investment, improved ROIC, and

Table 11.4 Example Value Circle Areas Comparison

To-Be	*As-Is*	*Dimensions*	*Axes*	*Scaled To-Be*	*As-Is Unit Circle*		
200	200	Dollars	Price/ landed cost	1.000	1.000	*To-Be Area*	*As-Is Area*
10	20	Days	Velocity	0.500	1.000	0.177	0.354
2,400	3,000	Dollars ×1,000	Throughput	1.250	1.000	0.221	0.354
180	180	Days	Visualize	1.000	1.000	0.443	0.354
13.5	12.0	Percent	ROIC	0.889	1.000	0.315	0.354
10	5	Days	Vocalize	2.000	1.000	0.629	0.354
50	75	Days	Inventory	0.667	1.000	0.472	0.354
10	10	Days	Variability	1.000	1.000	0.236	0.354
						0.230	0.354
						Area Totals	
						2.847	2.832

improved cash-to-cash cycle are cancelled out by the disadvantages of less than competitive delivery lead time and reduced revenue. The decision is postponed until soft feelings can be turned into hard data (Table 11.4).

Validate Performance to Gain Customer Acceptance

The project team needs to formally gain customer acceptance of the results of the supply chain construction project before being assigned to other tasks and other priorities. Customer acceptance is required from both the external end customer and key internal customers.

Always Document What the Customer Expects (Chapter 1)

The full Supply Chain Construction Requirements Specification from Chapter 1: "Eight Steps," shown again in Table 11.5, documents customer requirements at the start of a supply chain construction project. The rightmost column is completed, as supply chain performance is demonstrated and each of the specifications

Table 11.5 Validation of the Supply Chain Construction Requirements Specification

Attribute	*Description*		
Network type	[*Forward Network*] or [*With Service Component*] or [*Reverse Network*]		
Market segment	[*Enter*] or [*Switch*] or [*Existing*] or [*Exit*]		
Product family	[*New*] or [*Rollover*] or [*Existing*] or [*Obsolete*]		
Project objective	We are constructing a [*network type*] to connect this [*product family*] supply with this [*market segment*] demand.		
Specification	*Value*	*Dimensions*	*Validation*
Throughput		Dollars per month or units per month	X Accept
Factory Cash-to-cash cycle	Velocity Variability	Days +/– +/– Days	X Accept
Distributor Cash-to-cash cycle	Velocity Variability	Days +/– +/– Days	X Accept
Factory/distributor price/landed cost		Dollars per unit	X Accept
Distributor/store price/landed cost		Dollars per unit	X Accept
Factory RM and FG inventory		Days or turns	X Accept
Distributor Cycle stock inventory		Days or turns	X Accept
Delivery lead time	Vocalize delivery LT Visualize planning horizon	Days Days	X Accept
Factory return on invested capital		Percent	X Accept
Distributor return on invested capital		Percent	X Accept

is validated. There are three key external and internal customers for any supply chain construction project.

- *The end customer*—Product price/landed cost and delivery lead time.
- *The distributor*—Throughput, price/landed cost, inventory, the cash-to-cash cycle, and ROIC.
- *The factory*—Throughput, price/landed cost, inventory, the cash-to-cash cycle, ROIC, and planning horizon.

External and Internal Customer Acceptance

The real question is, "How do you demonstrate a supply chain's performance before building and operating one?" This is an excellent question. In some cases, it is possible to simulate a supply chain with a computer program, but computer simulations are outside the context of this book. The approached taken here is to focus on a subset of the performance measures and have a detailed understanding of the expected results and a diagnostic to apply should the actual results not reach expectations.

Your end customer is really concerned only about price and delivery. The end customer's "what-if" questions facing the project team at project completion are the following:

- *Can the resulting supply chain sustain delivery lead time at double the targeted throughput?*

  The answer depends upon (1) the time and the investment it would take to expand the network constraint and (2) the time and the cash flow it would take to double throughput inventory.
- *Can the resulting supply chain sustain customer pricing at half the targeted throughput?*

  The answer depends upon (1) the volume sensitivity of the most expensive direct material components and (2) the ability of the factory and distributor to absorb their fixed overhead costs under conditions of reduced revenue.

Notice that this is a 4:1 dynamic range for typical "small signal" network operations. Unusual "large signal" situations are taken up in Chapter 12: "Risk Management." The project team should conduct a conference room walk-through of doubling throughput and halving throughput. Where is the network constraint? Does the constraint move? How much incremental cash is needed for inventory, for accounts receivable? Can current sales generate this cash in time? What volume triggers a rise in material cost? How long can the factory and the distributor absorb fixed overhead without adequate sales? What prevents the factory and the distributor from stockpiling unnecessary inventory? As actual throughput begins to flow through the network, record the actual pricing and actual delivery lead time.

Compare this with the expected price and delivery at one and a half time, one time, and two times the expected throughput.

Your internal customers respond to other performance measures.

- *The factory's Value Circle*—Focus on factory throughput, price/landed cost to the distributor, and factory raw materials and finished goods inventory turns. Use velocity, variability, vocalize, and visualize to tune the factory's operational performance. ROIC is calculated from the financials.
- *The distributor's Value Circle*—Focus on distributor throughput, price/landed cost to the customer, and distributor cycle stock inventory turns. Use velocity, variability, vocalize, and visualize to tune the distributor's operational performance. ROIC is calculated from the financials.

Performance Diagnostics

The distributor and the factory want to see demonstrated supply chain capabilities for throughput, price/landed cost, and inventory. Use the performance diagnostics below to troubleshoot the start-up of your supply chain construction project.

Throughput Diagnostic

The virtual supply chain contracted with a third-party manufacturer to both build its product and act as its distributor. The DC, located in the same building as manufacturing, kitted complete systems from system components built by the contract manufacturer and those purchased from other suppliers. The DC's cycle stock inventory was the push/pull boundary. The business continuously monitored operations at the push/pull boundary. It compared monthly shipments plus backlog against a throughput forecast, and it compared the cumulative demand against the cumulative supply for each system component. Throughput was not up to plan for some of its product, but how does the business determine where to address the throughput issue?

Throughput can be updated daily from shipments through the push/pull boundary. Throughput is either demand limited or supply limited. Supply-limited throughput has either an inventory limit or a capacity limit. Product A in Table 11.6 is supply limited and short 35 units for the month. Demand-limited throughput either lacks shippable backlog or has product mix forecast error. Product B in Table 11.6 is demand limited and short $106,220 for the month.

Monitor throughput at the push/pull boundary. When throughput is supply limited, look first at the network constraint. Is the network constraint currently working at full capacity? Can its capacity be increased by working longer hours, working a split shift, or offloading some work to an alternate routing? Lead time is involved in increasing, or decreasing, capacity to get people to change their schedules, to get

Table 11.6 Supply Limited or Demand Limited at the Push/Pull Boundary?

Status	*Quantity*	*Price*	*Throughput*	*Shipped*	*Inventory Units*	*Restocked*
Product A—supply limited						
					350	Start inventory
Shipped	100	$825	$82,500	Jan. 6	250	
Shipped	150	$805	$120,750	Jan. 8	100	
					300	+200 on Jan. 14
Shipped	75	$835	$62,625	Jan. 14	225	
Backlog	35	$770	$26,950	Due Jan. 21	190	
Backlog	225	$805	$181,125	Due Jan. 28	–35	
					–35	End inventory
Totals	585	*Actual*	$473,950			
		Forecast	$470,000			
Product B—demand limited						
					120	Start inventory
Shipped	50	$1,075	$53,750	Jan. 3	70	
Shipped	25	$1,250	$31,250	Jan. 7	45	
					120	+75 on Jan. 8
Shipped	35	$1,250	$43,750	Jan. 10	85	
					85	End inventory
Totals	110	*Actual*	$128,780			
		Forecast	$235,000			

people trained, and to purchase additional equipment. If the network constraint is not working at full capacity, identify the material shortage that has become the constraint and determine how to quickly supply more of the material. Was the material underplanned? Is there a quality yield problem? Is the material on allocation? Is the material available elsewhere in the distribution network? When throughput is demand limited, work with sales. Does the forecast error suggest a big disconnect? Is the forecast realistic? Are product quality issues impeding sales? Has something changed competitively in terms of price and/or delivery? Have you lost a big order?

Price from the Seller as Landed Cost to the Buyer Diagnostic

The Dollar Store decided to introduce a new product into the store lineup to freshen its product offering. The new product was to be manufactured in the Shenzhen area of China, trucked to Hong Kong, and shipped by ocean freight to the Port of Oakland, where it would be trucked to the company's west coast DC. From there, the new product would be cross-docked through the company's distribution network and on to each retail outlet. The new product had to meet the distributor's per unit landed cost objective of 64 cents, but the distributor was invoiced 70 cents on the first shipment. This meant the Dollar Store would take a loss on selling the new product. The business either had to quickly fix the cost issue before the second shipment or make a decision to drop the new product. But how does the business determine where to address such a cost issue?

It is essential to document the expected price/landed cost landscape from a complete cost rollup for your highest volume and highest margin products before starting operations in your newly constructed supply chain (see Table 11.7). Work in per unit dollars and not in total dollars. Unfortunately, costs typically get reported weeks after the fact. Also, prices are easier to obtain than costs. As data become available, fill in the "actual" column of Table 11.7. As soon as any price exceeds its expected value, start communicating with the trading partner or carrier. In Table 11.7, supplier direct material pricing exceeds expectation by $0.03 per unit, or 18.8%; midbound logistics exceeds expectation by $0.02 per unit, or 16.7%. These are huge differences because the numbers are so small. Work from raw materials up to the end customer because factory, distributor, and store markups are each multipliers of lower-level discrepancies. Pay particular attention to logistics costs; most carriers can provide one-time actual costs within a couple of days. Follow the business news regarding local labor rate increases, raw material commodity price trends, and logistics fuel surcharges.

Inventory Turns Diagnostic

The supply chain construction project included a goal of halving the inventory dollar investment by doubling inventory turns from 6 per year to 12 per year on "A" products. This was to be accomplished by changing the forecasting method to halve

Table 11.7 Expected End Customer per Unit Landed Cost

Price/Landed Cost Rollup	*Expected*	*Actual*	*Root Cause—Action to Be Taken*
Supplier price for direct material	$0.16	$0.19	Root cause A: high parts count, low material yields, increasing labor rates. Action: ____________
Inbound logistics	$0.01	$0.01	Additive
Factory landed cost	$0.17	$0.20	
Factory direct labor	$0.09	$0.09	Additive
Factory overhead	$0.09	$0.09	Additive
Factory markup	$0.16	$0.18	Multiplier
Factory price	$0.51	$0.56	
Midbound logistics	$0.12	$0.14	Root cause B: forgot to include port and fuel surcharges on ocean freight container. Action: ____________
Distributor landed cost	$0.63	$0.70	
Distributor direct labor	$0.05	$0.05	Additive
Distributor overhead	$0.07	$0.07	Additive
Distributor markup	$0.12	$0.13	Multiplier
Distributor price	$0.87	$0.95	
Outbound logistics	$0.04	$0.04	Additive
Retail store landed cost	$0.91	$0.99	
Store markup	$0.09	$0.10	Multiplier
Retail store price	$1.00	$1.09	
Outbound logistics	$0.00	$0.00	Customer shops at retail store
End customer landed cost	$1.00	$1.09	

forecast error and by halving the lot sizing on "A" products and on "A" and "B" components. Inventory was handled first in, first out. The business picked five high-dollar "A" product numbers, 10 high-dollar "A" component part numbers, and 10 high-dollar "B" component part numbers to track inventory turns. On the next stock replenishment, the first product and the first component from each lot were tagged with a colored, bar-coded tag. The item number and date/time were recorded as these items were received into inventory. As soon as the first products and first components of each lot were issued from inventory, the colored tag was removed and the item number and date/time were recorded. The process was repeated matching specific red tags back with specific item numbers and tagging the first item of their next replenishment lot. The results were averaged as in the example below. Referring to Table 11.8, it was found that "A" products were only turning 10.3 times at the factory and a slower 9.8 times at the distributor. Likewise "A" and "B" components were turning slower than planned in the factory's raw material inventory.

Product A — First lot received January 16	
Product A — First lot issued February 20	Delta 35 days
Product A — Second lot issued March 25	Delta 33 days
Product A — Third lot issued May 2	Delta 38 days
	Average 35.3 days

Inventory turns = 365 days/35.3 days = 10.3

Table 11.8 Expected Inventory Turns

	Factory Raw Material Turns		*Factory Finished Goods Turns*		*Distributor Cycle Stock Turns*	
	Plan	*Actual*	*Plan*	*Actual*	*Plan*	*Actual*
"A" products			12.0	10.3	12.0	9.8
"B" products			8.0	5.5	8.0	3.3
"C" products			2.0	1.2	2.0	1.1
Demand safety stock					0.0	0.0
"A" components	12.0	11.5				
"B" components	8.0	3.8				
"C" components	2.0	1.9				
Lead time safety stock	0.0	0.0				

Again, it is essential to document the expected turns for the complete inventory plan before starting operations in your newly constructed supply chain. Inventory turns are easier to measure, using the technique described above, than trying to compile inventory dollars from purchasing invoices. Inventory measurement takes some calendar time; it is not instantaneous. When an item turns too slowly, investigate why its demand is too low or its supply is too high. Item demand may be low because the item is not properly connected through the product structures or because there is a large error in forecasting mix. Item supply may be too high because forecast error and lot sizing are multiplying, because of a minimum buy quantity, or because purchasing is buying too much to achieve a price breakpoint. Safety stock generally will not turn. If safety stock turns, then the service level factors may not be set high enough.

Improve the Margin

There is constant pressure on businesses of all stripes to improve their margins. This is because margin improvement provides businesses with the flexibility to either lower their product pricing to be more competitive or raise their profitability to achieve higher cash flow. Within the supply chain construction methodology of this book, is to (1) make it work, (2) make it work well, and (3) make it work in a flexible and risk-tolerant manner, margin improvement spans all three efforts. A supply chain will not work at all if the margins force pricing to be above what the market segment is willing to pay. A supply chain will not reimburse its cash fast enough if the margins generate too little profit. A supply chain will have very low risk tolerance if the margins cannot accommodate unexpected inflationary shocks. How does a business go about improving its margin?

Consider Each Income Statement Line Item as an Opportunity

Businesses improve their margins by looking for opportunities to impact each and every line item on the income statement. The following list is a sampling of approaches that have been successful at many companies:

- *Reevaluate the returns policy*—If the return policy of a business is too easy, some purchases become frivolous, masking the fact that real demand is less than was forecast.
- *Take control of logistics costs*—Outbound, midbound, and inbound logistics costs can add up to big dollars. Logistics costs are often reported too late to take action. A single mismanaged unusual airfreight or international shipment can obliterate the entire logistics budget.
- *Consolidate volume in material purchases*—Increasing volume is the key to decreasing purchasing costs. Look for opportunities to consolidate more purchases across fewer suppliers.

- *Move production to a lower labor rate*—Labor rates are not homogeneous within countries or among countries. The labor cost savings from moving to contract manufacturing or outsourcing in another country have to be weighed against increased logistics costs, increased total network inventory investment, and less operational flexibility.
- *Move production to a lower-cost building*—Margins improve when there is no longer a mortgage on the building and when the building is located in an area with lower-than-average utility costs. Sustainability initiatives such as solar panels, energy efficient lighting, warehouse lighting control motion sensors, etc., can have a significant impact on utility costs.
- *Take control of employee travel costs*—Travel costs are an area of discretionary expense that can quickly exceed budgets. Air travel booked one or two days before traveling can have exorbitant cost.
- *Reduce and redirect advertising dollars to websites and social media*—Print advertising expense may be reduced through increased usage of the Internet and social media.
- *Improve product quality*—Yield issues in manufacturing increase COGS, while warranty expense reduces gross margin. Product quality improvements flow directly to the bottom line.
- *Lease versus depreciate equipment*—In some instances, it may be more cost effective to lease capital equipment rather than purchase it. Such a decision needs to be weighed against the number of years the specific production or computing capability is expected to be online.
- *Refinance debt at a lower interest rate*—Depending on the movement of interest rates, there may be an opportunity to refinance outstanding debt at a lower interest rate.
- *Look for local government tax incentives or property reevaluation*—Tax incentives for business start-ups, energy conservation, reevaluation of commercial properties paying disproportionate local taxes, sustainability initiatives, and free trade zones are a few examples of tax savings that can improve margins.

How to Accelerate Cash Reimbursement from the Bottom Line

Suppose you decided to improve your bottom line by 1%. For example, using the income statement shown in Table 11.9, a 1% improvement on $10 million of revenue would increase net profit from $500,000 to $600,000. Since the tax rate in this example is 33%, $150,000 in savings would have to be realized to gain a $100,000 improvement in the bottom line.

Table 11.9 shows $150,000 in cost savings targeted across four areas: returns, COGS, quality, and SG&A. If these savings can be realized, then net profit will improve by 1%. How could this be done? The next step is to detail an action plan to achieve each cost saving, assign responsibility, and set a timeframe. The

Table 11.9 Example Plan to Improve Margins

Income Statement	*Starting Amount*		*Target Savings*	*Ending Amount*	
Gross product revenue		$8,400,000			$8,400,000
Service revenue		$2,000,000			$2,000,000
Discounts	$300,000			$300,000	
Returns	$100,000		$10,000	$90,000	
Net revenue		$10,000,000			$10,010,000
COGS	$6,500,000		$100,000	$6,400,000	
Cost of quality	$150,000		$15,000	$135,000	
Gross margin		$3,350,000			$3,475,000
Selling, general, admin	$2,050,000		$25,000	$2,025,000	
Depreciation	$350,000			$350,000	
Operating profit		$950,000			$1,100,000
Interest expense	$200,000			$200,000	
Profit before taxes		$750,000			$900,000
Income tax	$250,000		<$50,000>	$300,000	
Net profit		$500,000			$600,000

action plan is reviewed monthly. Some line items will track well to the plan. Some line items will turn out to be unachievable for a variety of reasons. Some line items will be completed, but with less-than-expected savings. Other line items will take more resource and more time than expected to implement. All company employees, suppliers, and customers can contribute cost saving ideas. In fact, you should keep a continuously running log of cost savings ideas. Call it your "Margin Book." Table 11.10 shows an action plan to achieve the targeted cost savings. At the bottom of Table 11.10 are three next best opportunities for cost savings. These can be used to offset any dollars that turn out to be unachievable from the original plan.

Table 11.10 Action Plan to Achieve Cost Savings

Line Item	*Savings Target*	*Action Plan*
Returns	$10,000	1. Require a return authorization and adherence to prescribed return packaging and labeling before issuing a credit. Person Responsible: ________ Completion Date:________
COGS	$26,000 $60,000 $10,000 $4,000	2. Switch metal suppliers, saving 500 miles per trip on logistics cost Person Responsible: ________ Completion Date:________ 3. Negotiate 5% price reduction on ferrite commodity based on volume. Person Responsible: ________ Completion Date:________ 4. Rationalize connector suppliers from seven to three to consolidate volume. Person Responsible: ________ Completion Date:________ 5. Reduce electric costs by switching to compact fluorescent lighting. Person Responsible: ________ Completion Date:________
Quality	$6,000 $9,000	6. Replace worn gear on machine 8 to improve material yield by 3%. Person Responsible: ________ Completion Date:________ 7. Revise material handling procedures to eliminate cover scratches. Person Responsible: ________ Completion Date:________

(*Continued*)

Table 11.10 (Continued) Action Plan to Achieve Cost Savings

Line Item	*Savings Target*	*Action Plan*
SG&A	$10,000 $15,000	8. Require signature authorization before booking air travel. Person Responsible: ________ Completion Date:________ 9. Redirect advertising from print media to social media. Person Responsible: ________ Completion Date:________
Total plan	$150,000	
		Three Next Best Cost Reduction Opportunities
Depreciation	$4,400	A. Sell a two-year-old milling machine worth $22,000 new.
SG&A	$1,500	B. Recycle copy paper: Print weekly reports on the back of old reports.
COGS	$1,000	C. Readjust the parking lot lights timer for two hours less light.

Decrease the Network Inventory Investment

Take action to reduce network inventory and increase inventory turns. Write down your inventory reduction improvement target, and then plan how you will get there within a set timeframe. See the example in Table 11.11. Use the list of possible inventory reductions following the table to generate your action plan.

- *Reduce the number of network echelons*—Each echelon in a supply chain network adds incremental inventory. The first way to reduce inventory is to rationalize the total number of echelons.
- *Size DCs to encourage smaller inventories*—Keep smaller cubic volumes and floor spaces in distribution to force the management of higher inventory turns. Shine a light on stranded inventory rather than casting it into a dark corner.
- *Shorten transportation distances*—Keep raw materials and suppliers close to the factory. Keep distributors close to stores and customers. Otherwise, there will be significant amounts of inventory in transit at all times.

Table 11.11 Example Inventory Reduction Plan

Objective: Increase inventory turns from 5× to 8× over the next six months. Current inventory valued $1,285,000. Future inventory target $803,125. Inventory reduced $481,875.			
Reduction Component	*Target*	*Actual*	*Action Steps*
Forecast error Forecast error lot size Multiplication	$150,000		Change forecast method on products with MAPE >10%. Do not add additional lot on products with MAPE <5%.
Product and "A" items	$240,000		Cut product lot sizes by 25%. Reorder "A" items lot-for-lot.
"B" items	$45,000		Reorder every 2.5 months instead of 3 months.
"C" items	$14,000		Reorder every 5 months instead of 6 months.
Safety stock	$26,000		Recalculate with 95% service level with $z = 1.65$. Rather than 97.5% service level with $z = 1.96$.
Excess inventory	$6,875		Inventory write down.
Totals	$481,875		

- *Reduce forecast error*—Forecast error drives more inventory into the push/pull boundary than is necessary. In addition, forecast error can trip higher multiples of a lot size, adding considerably more inventory. For example, suppose product demand is forecast at 95 units but comes in with an actual demand of 85 units. Then the 10 units of forecast error drive 10 unnecessary sets of inventory. Now, suppose the product demand is forecast for 105 units and the finished goods lot size is 100 units with the same actual demand of 85 units. Then the 20 units of forecast error drive 115 unnecessary sets of inventory (2 × lot size of 100 − 85 actual). Always review the demand forecast and recent forecast error relative to the distribution requirements plan (DRP) and master production schedule (MPS) finished goods lot size.
- *Reduce "A" item lot size*—Lot sizing is a tradeoff between the cost of ordering and the cost of holding inventory. If you are ordering "A" items monthly, see

if lot-for-lot ordering can reduce the "A" inventory. "A" items should be on blanket orders with suppliers so that the per-item price will not be impacted. It may be well worth small increases in ordering and logistics costs to turn "A" items more often to increase working capital.

- *Reduce the months of supply for "B" and "C" lot sizing*—Ordering "B" items every 2.5 months instead of three and ordering "C" items every five months instead of six will have a favorable impact.
- *Ensure that low-value, high-mix items are not improperly classified as "A" or "B" items*—Sometimes, "C" parts get misclassified. Review the BOM periodically to check each item's ABC classification.
- *Eliminate safety lead times*—Safety lead time causes items to be brought into inventory early and held longer than necessary.
- *Reduce safety stock levels*—Safety stock exists to ensure a service level despite demand uncertainty and/or lead time variability. When safety stock is properly maintained by the push planning system, the stocking level remains nearly constant and looks like no-turn inventory. As the service level increases, the safety stock multiplier increases. You have two choices. The best choice is to minimize the root cause of the variability. A second choice is to operate with a lower service level.
- *Connect demand to stranded inventory*—Inventory cannot turn without being connected through a product structure and master schedule to some demand. For new products, make sure the product structure linkages exist and that product demand is loaded into the MPS. For mature products, when an engineering change order eliminates all usage, sell inventory back to its supplier, or auction off excess inventory through a broker, or sell raw materials to a recycler. For obsolete products, keep just enough inventory for warranty and support life.
- *As a last resort, write down excess and no-turn inventory*—Move aggressively to get excess inventory off your balance sheet. You will never use 10 years of supply of that one item. Dead inventory has many hidden costs, including the cost of storing and counting the excess, higher inventory insurance costs, and the potential for an earlier revision of an item finding its way into production, causing an expensive product quality problem with recalls and rework.
- *Eliminate consignment inventory*—Consignment inventory is located with one organization but owned by another organization. It is often out of sight and out of control.
- *Outsourcing does not reduce total network inventory*—From an inventory perspective, outsourcing can be viewed as gamesmanship, as you are moving inventory off your balance sheet onto someone else's balance sheet. The network inventory investment does not go away. Total network inventory will probable increase, as lot sizes increase to cover longer transit times. There is more in-transit inventory using ocean freight than using motor freight.

Track Project Team Progress against the Plan

The final section of this chapter addresses measuring the supply chain construction team's progress against the project objective while meeting schedule and budget constraints. The project team's performance should be measured by the project manager, monitored by the project champion executive, and reviewed periodically by senior management.

Keep the Focus

As has been noted, there are many potential supply chain lifecycle events. It is not unusual for a second or third event to occur after your supply chain construction project team has been commissioned. Resist the temptation to modify the project team's statement of work. In the best case, this will slow the completion of any of the project work; in the worst case, the team's statement of work will continuously evolve with nothing being accomplished. Instead, staff and commission a second project team on the heels of the first, and finish what you started with the first project team. Experience shows that sequential tightly focused, highly motivated, short projects accomplish far more than single, large-staff, multiple-objective projects that never end.

Communicate, Communicate, Communicate

Senior management wants to know where you are with the project, and when it will be finished. Some kinds of work, like software development, are difficult to judge and even more difficult to communicate. One creative project manager, when pressed during a project review to be definitive about his team's progress, held up a floppy disk (an ancient technology) and taking a pair of scissors cut off a quarter of the disk, announcing, "We are now 75% done with our project. Would any of you like to test the results?"

Communication is an important task for the project manager. This communication needs to be 360 degrees, frequent, and repetitious. 360 degrees means that you communicate with your superiors, your peers, and your subordinates. You communicate within the company and outside to other trading partners up and down your supply chain network. Frequent communication means that you communicate every couple of weeks and at least once a month. Repetitious communication means that you say the same thing multiple times using different media: coffee talks, e-mail, blogs, private social media, video conferences, project reviews, and personal visits with trading partners.

How to Know When Your Project Is Off the Rails

Every supply chain construction project will hit a snag or two. But how do you know when your project is going off the rails toward impending disaster? Use the one-page project timeline from Chapter 3: "Building Relationships" and the one-page project cash flow budget from Chapter 4: "Cash Flow" to measure your progress. These two documents need to be completed and approved before any significant project work is begun.

When actual project timing or cost begins to deviate from the plan, good judgment is required to know if the deviation is minor or major. Keep a mindset that the project end date and the project total cost cannot expand. How you and the team get there is another matter altogether. The first question to ask is, what other tasks are impacted by delays or complications from this task? The second question to ask is, how can this delayed or complicated task be taken off the critical path? Put pride aside and ask for help sooner rather than later. Be honest with your project champion executive about the difficulty in fixing the problem and the implications of any delay.

Iterate or "Plan B"

The approach of layering a supply chain construction project allows the project team ample opportunities to gauge the ability of their approach to the network container and product contents to meet the Supply Chain Construction Requirements Specification. Any inability to meet price/landed cost targets or inventory turns targets early in the project needs to be addressed immediately. The project team may have to iterate back and revisit key decisions from earlier steps in the Supply Chain Construction Blueprint. In the worst case, the project team may be forced to abandon "plan A" to embrace a different "plan B." The trick is to keep all this on-schedule and within budget.

Keep at Least One Degree of Freedom

As discussed in Chapter 3: "Building Relationships," supply chain construction projects should be commissioned with at least one degree of freedom from among calendar time, project cost, and project staffing. When an intractable problem emerges, the one degree of freedom becomes your trump card. The project manager and the project champion executive must be accurate, honest, and convincing in presenting the essence of the problem. Only then can the project get completed with senior management's agreement to add project staffing, to allow a project cost overrun, or to allow a calendar time extension.

Performance Measurement Comparisons… When to End the Project

There are two different kinds of performance measurement comparisons to use when deciding whether a supply chain construction project is finished. The first consists of "as-is" to "to-be" performance comparisons of the throughput, price/landed cost, inventory, and ROIC basic financial measures when a network container and/or product contents are changed. Examples of this kind of project include starting a new supply chain, outsourcing a significant portion of the business, or acquiring and merging the supply chain from another's business. These performance measure comparisons are used to validate that the new has been made to work at least as good as the old.

The second kind of comparison consists of operational changes that improve, or tune up, the velocity, variability, vocalize, and visualize business performance measures without changing the market segment, the end product, or the network container. Examples of this kind of project include serial-to-parallel process improvements that accelerate cash-to-cash velocity and reduce cash-to-cash variability, BOM flattening and lead time reduction to improve planning horizon visualization, and credit checking process improvements to improve delivery lead time vocalization. These performance measure comparisons are used to bring actual performance in line with the plan.

When each specification has been demonstrated and validated to your internal and external customers, formally end the project. If you decide to leave one project team member assigned to project maintenance beyond the completion date, then make sure you have recognized that person's contribution in the main effort.

Celebrate Success

In today's business world, supply chain life cycle events come fast and furious. Businesses are acquired and divested. Supply chains are disrupted and terminated. Competitors proliferate. Key relationships are acquired or go into bankruptcy. Sole-sourced components go on allocation. Product lines are outsourced and insourced. New products are launched, while old products enter support life. New designs become more sustainable. New information system architectures and software applications enter the market. Extreme weather conditions wipe out critical factories and transportation networks, etc. The events that demand your attention to supply chain changes are endless.

In such an environment, it is easy to burn out your best people. Instead, run short, highly focused projects and celebrate success at the end of each project. Let people know you value their contribution in the area of supply chain construction. Give them a party, a bonus or a raise, and your respect. Use the celebration to formally end the project. Then ask them to do it all over again.

In Summary

This chapter describes how to use performance measures to make your new or modified supply chain work well. A small set of eight integrated performance measures—throughput, velocity, price/landed cost, variability, inventory, vocalize, ROIC, and visualize—are defined and applied in their appropriate echelon context. The Value Circle is introduced as a method of using these eight measures to compare supply chain alternatives. Throughput, price/landed cost, and inventory diagnostics are provided for the start-up and tune up of new or modified supply chains. Finally, this chapter offers advice on measuring the progress of the project team against the project objective. The last chapter, Chapter 12: "Risk Management," describes how to deal with large signal and dynamic situations.

Appendix: Using Excel to Plot a Value Circle

Refer to Figure 11.8 and use the following steps to create a Value Circle in Excel. You can then reuse this spreadsheet again and again for later analysis.

1. Create a table 8 columns across and 13 rows down from cell B2 to cell I14.
2. Label the columns from left to right in row 3 as "To-Be" in cell B3, "As-Is," "Dimension," "Axes Titles," "To-Be," and "As-Is" in cell G3. Enter "To-Be" in cell H4 and "As-Is" in cell I4. Enter "Unit Circle" in cell C2 and in cell G2.
3. Enter the Value Circle dimensions from top to bottom in column D as "$" in cell D4 and "Days," "K$," "Days," "%," "Days," "Days," and "Days" in cells D5 through D11, respectively.
4. Label the axes titles from top to bottom in column E in the following order: "Price/Landed Cost ($)" in cell E4 and "Velocity (Days)," "Throughput (K$)," "Visualize (Days)," "ROIC (%)," "Vocalize (Days)," "Inventory (Days)," and "Variability (Days)" in cells E5 through E11, respectively.
5. Enter the equations shown in Figure 11.8, column F into cells F4 through F11. Note that cells F6 through F8 have inverted equations because each axis increases toward the origin to improve.
6. Enter the equations shown in Figure 11.8, column G, into cells G4 through G11.
7. Enter the equations shown in Figure 11.8, column H, into cells H5 through H12 and cell H14. Notice that these equations are offset one row from those in column G. Label cell H13 as "Total Area."
8. Enter the equations shown in Figure 11.8, column I, into cells I5 through I12 and cell I14. Label cell I13 as "Total Area."
9. Numerical values for "To-Be" are entered in column B, cell B4 through cell B11. Numerical values for the unit circle ("As-Is") are entered in column C, cell C4 through cell C11.

	B	C	D	E	F	G	H	I
2		Unit circle				Unit circle		
3	To-be	As-is	Dimensions	Axes titles	To-be	As-is		
4	575	200	$	Price/landed cost ($)	=B4/C4	=C4/C4	To-be	As-is
5	10	20	Days	Velocity (days)	=B5/C5	=C5/C5	=0.354*F4*F5	=0.354*G4*G5
6	2,400	3,000	K$	Throughput (K$)	=C6/B6	=C6/C6	=0.354*F5*F6	=0.354*G5*G6
7	180	180	Days	Visualize (days)	=C7/B7	=C7/C7	=0.354*F6*F7	=0.354*G6*G7
8	13.5	12	%	ROIC (%)	=C8/B8	=C8/C8	=0.354*F7*F8	=0.354*G7*G8
9	10	5	Days	Vocalize (days)	=B9/C9	=C9/C9	=0.354*F8*F9	=0.354*G8*G9
10	50	75	Days	Inventory (days)	=B10/C10	=C10/C10	=0.354*F9*F10	=0.354*G9*G10
11	10	10	Days	Variability (days)	=B11/C11	=C11/C11	=0.354*F10*F11	=0.354*G10*G11
12							=0.354*F11*F4	=0.354*G11*G4
13							Total area	Total area
14							=sum(H5:H12)	=sum(I5:I12)

Chart data range: =e3:g11

	Unit circle				Unit circle		
To-be	As-is	Dimension	Axes titles	To-be	As-is		
200	200	$	Price/landed cost ($)	1.0	1.0	To-be	As-is
10	20	Days	Velocity (days)	0.5	1.0	0.177	0.354
2400	3000	K$	Throughput (K$)	[illegible]	1.0	0.221	0.354
180	180	Days	Visualize (days)	1.0	1.0	0.443	0.354
13.5	12.0	%	ROIC (%)	0.9	1.0	0.315	0.354
10	5	Days	Vocalize (days)	2.0	1.0	0.629	0.354
50	75	Days	Inventory (days)	0.7	1.0	0.472	0.354
10	10	Days	Variability (days)	1.0	1.0	0.236	0.354
						0.354	0.354
						Total area	Total area
						2.847	2.832

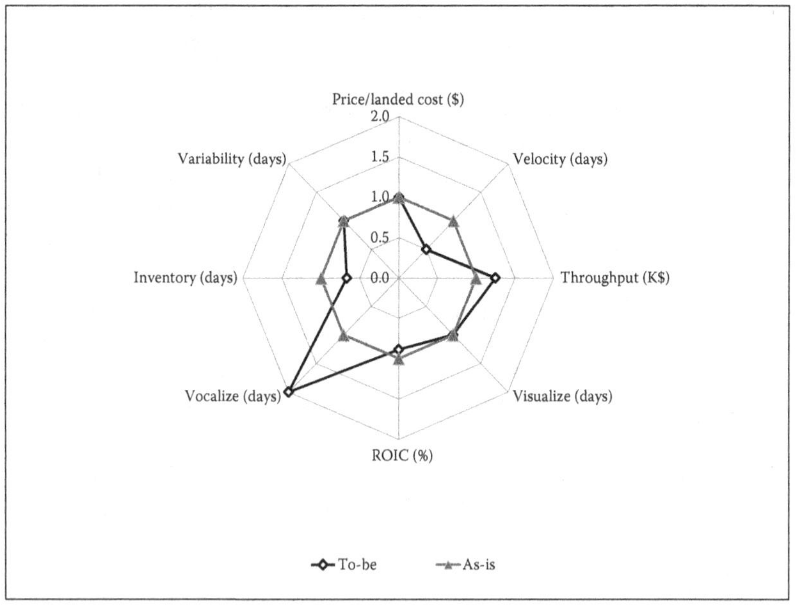

Figure 11.8 The Value Circle drawn with Excel.

10. In Excel, <select the cell range E3 through G11>, then use the follow keystrokes in Excel.
11. <Insert>/<Other Charts>/<Radar>.
12. Select the Radar Chart, then move and size the graph.
13. <Chart Tools>/<Layout>.

14. Edit the Title and <Show Legend at Bottom>.
15. Double click an axis, <Scale>/<Format Axis>/<Axis Options>/<Set Maximum to Fixed 2.0>.
16. Double click an axis, <Scale>/<Format Axis>/<Axis Options>/<Set Axis Labels to None>.
17. Double click a data point on circle 1, <Set Format Data Series>/<Marker Option>/<Automatic>.
    Note: that the line color can also be changed.
18. Double click a data point on circle 2, <Set Format Data Series>/<Marker Option>/<Automatic>.
    Note: that the line color can also be changed.
19. The equations in cells H5 through I14 compute and compare the areas enclosed by the two circles.

Once this Excel spreadsheet and the Value Circle plot are complete, a new analysis can be displayed by entering a new data set into columns B and C, cells B4 through C11.

Chapter 12

Risk Management—"Make It Work in a Flexible, Risk-Tolerant Manner"

As your supply chain construction project is completed and you begin operations, it is fairly common to encounter the following situation: demand is down, cost of goods sold (COGS) is higher than expected, and the inventory investment is greater than expected. All three work to strain your cash flow. You may become concerned that your cash reserve is too small to carry you through, until the new or modified supply chain is working to plan. The last chapter, Chapter 11: "Performance Measures," presented diagnostics to get throughput, landed cost, and inventory turns back on plan. Tuning supply chain "small-signal" performance is not the focus of this last chapter. Rather, this chapter looks at "large-signal" situations and external dynamics outside your control that could sink your boat. You need to understand the degree to which your supply chain can be made flexible and risk tolerant before it is stretched to its breaking point.

During the 2014 World Cup, Brazil played superb soccer through the quarter-finals, winning against Columbia 2:1. Then with top player, Neymar, sidelined with a fractured vertebra and the yellow card suspension of team captain, Thiago Silva, Brazil's team performance came unglued against Germany's 7:1 rout in the semi-final. Although well versed in the basics, Team Brazil Operations had succumbed to forces outside its control, namely, player injury and penalties called by the referee.

Risky Business

It was the week before their first customer shipment. The project team had successfully completed each step in the Supply Chain Construction Blueprint to build the network container and to fill it with product contents. A pricing contract agreement had been reached with Astec. They had first-year inventory commitments with the supply base for 22,000 units. The Power Products Distribution Center had been expanded, and the first containerized pallets of product have been received. Engineering had completed specification testing on the pilot run units, and they had all passed. The shipping container had been redesigned to better protect the product. Sales had mailed a slick data sheet and price list to all the value-added resellers (VARs); Sales was scheduled to meet personally with each VAR over the next six weeks. The uninterruptible power supply (UPS) business information had been loaded into the Power Products information system. The Supply Chain Construction Project was on time and within budget. Everything was a "go."

Harry left the Product Marketing offices late, delaying the start of the team meeting. He looked white as a ghost.

"What's the matter with you?" Donna asked. "Are you sick? We have some aspirin back in Purchasing, if you want it."

"I think I'm going to be sick," replied Harry. "APC, our primary competitor, just announced a $100 price reduction on all their models. This is a huge blow to our chances in the marketplace."

"Say that again," commanded Tony. His financial mind was recalculating the gross margin.

"Just put me out of my misery," wailed Harry. "APC's $500 product now sells for $400. The team knows how hard we worked to get our final selling price down to $515 for our equivalent product."

"Now what are we going to do?" the team asked Bill.

"Look, I don't know how much impact this will have. Remember, ours is a system sale. It probably depends on whether the individual VAR is going for the absolute lowest price solution or is selling a single-vendor solution to their end customer. We have very little visibility into that," replied Bill, the project manager.

John said, "Engineering just cannot take another $100 out of our product's selling price. It is impossible."

Donna said, "And we're not going to be able to walk away from the inventory commitment for 22,000 units, especially not after we all worked so hard to make it happen."

Harry said, "I don't want to, but I need to go brief Steve and Jerry and the rest of our senior management on this latest development."

"Wait! Risk management is an important part of supply chain management. In fact, it is the last step on the Supply Chain Construction Blueprint after stabilizing the start-up. Let's see if we can approach this a little more rationally," offered Bill.

"What are you suggesting?" John asked.

"Situations like this create very high anxiety. But we have to learn to separate the things that are out of our control from the things that are in our control. We have no control over APC's product pricing strategy," continued Bill. "So, let's put our energy into talking about the things we can control."

"...But this is a really tough situation," said John.

"I know. However, a competitor's price reduction is not the only disastrous event that the UPS business might ever encounter. What about Computer Products dropping the midrange server business? What about labor rates rising in Malaysia? What about our battery manufacturer coming under some new regulatory requirement? What about the impact of extreme weather on logistics, or computer hackers disrupting our information, or ...? We don't control any of these factors. We can, however, collect and categorize external factors through a process called environmental scanning," explained Bill.

"What does that do for us?" asked John.

"Environmental scanning leads into a second phase of risk management called scenario planning. Here, we look at the probability of occurrence, the severity of occurrence, action plans for recovery, and the time to recovery. In supply chain risk management, the outcome is more important than the cause," said Bill.

"Sorry, I'm not on the same page; I still don't understand what you are saying," replied John.

"OK. This time, there is no need to do environmental scanning because we have a real scenario. APC has decided to undercut our pricing. Maybe they knew that we were ready to launch a competitive product line. The probability of occurrence is 100%. Now, we have to figure out the severity, our response plan, and the time duration until the risk is mitigated," said Bill. "What is the immediate impact on our business?"

"That's easy. Sales will ramp up much slower than we planned. We will be awash in inventory commitments. In a little while, we will run out of space to store product inventory in the distribution center. Later, we will run out of cash to pay for all the product inventory accumulating in the distribution center," said Tony.

"I'm glad you didn't make it sound too depressing, Tony," replied Bill sarcastically. "Under scenario planning, we break what Tony just said down into a set of occurrences, each with a probability and a severity. I heard four things: (1) sales ramps too slowly, (2) fixed inventory commitments, (3) we run out of space at the DC, and (4) we run out of cash because of slower-than-expected sales. What is the probability and severity grading as high, medium, or low for the first item: sales ramps too slowly?"

"The probability is high and the severity is high," said Harry.

"Any thoughts on a recovery plan?" asked Bill.

"Prioritize the time each salesperson spends with the VARs. Give the VARs superior service. The downside is that Computer Products will not allow us to spend too much time with the VARs because ours is just a tag-along sale," replied Harry.

"Could we reach out to a couple of the largest end customers to try and accelerate their first purchases?" suggested Bill.

"That would be difficult because the sale is controlled by Computer Products," said Harry.

"Would Computer Products switch to the lower-cost competitor's UPS?" asked Donna.

"I don't think so, because we have customized a number of our UPS features explicitly for the Power Products servers," replied Harry.

"I think we have some wiggle room with our inventory commitments," said Donna. "After all, we are buying the batteries and frames for Astec. If we slowed the rate of battery and frame purchases, we could delay some logistics costs and maybe avoid running out of space here to store finished product."

"Astec wouldn't like that," said Tony.

"No, that's right," replied Donna. "We would have to be sure and pay them as per our agreement. It would push the inventory space problem back to them. We still have to have taken all 22,000 units after 16 months, but at least it spreads things out."

"Donna, you just gave a perfect example of considering an occurrence, developing a recovery action plan, and determining a duration for the recovery," said Bill.

"We could rent a warehouse for product overflow," suggested John.

"What we need to do is to take all these great ideas and organize them into a scenario plan. Then we can prioritize the resources necessary to implement each response and present this to senior management as more of a solution and less of a problem. Harry will be in a much better place when he gives the news of APC's pricing reduction, if he also has the team's scenario planning of possible responses for the vice presidents to consider," said Bill.

"Thank you team," replied Harry.

Complete the Current Supply Chain Construction Project

It is human nature in both large and small organizations to start new projects before completely finishing the current project. The rate of change in business only acerbates this issue. Stop! The very first step toward making your supply chain robust and risk tolerant is to compete your current supply chain construction project. Table 12.1 is a completion checklist based on the Supply Chain Construction Blueprint. Now, dot your i's and cross your t's to finish the job.

Table 12.1 Answer Each Question to Complete the Supply Chain Construction Blueprint

Completed	*Step*	*Key Supply Chain Construction Project Questions*
☑	A	Document the Business Objective Do you have a *written* description of the market segment and customer needs that your product addresses?
☑	B	Document the Supply Chain Construction Project Have you *tracked project staffing* against the construction project timeline? Have you *tracked project costs* against the construction project budget?
Completed	*Step*	*Key Network Container Questions*
☑	1	Write the Network Requirements Specification for the Network Container Do you have a *numerical value* or range of values assigned to each specification?
☑	2	Budget the Network Container's Price/Cost Echelon by Echelon Do you have a *detailed* budget across the *end-to-end supply chain* including material costs, labor costs, logistics costs, and trading partner markups?
☑	3	Select the Factory and Midbound Logistics Do you have a *written* factory pricing agreement and *all* midbound logistics details?
☑	4	Select the Supply Base and Inbound Logistics Do you have a *complete* list of suppliers and *all* inbound logistics details?
☑	5	Select the Distributor and Outbound Logistics Do you have a *written* distributor agreement and *all* outbound logistics details? Have you updated the network price/cost budget with *actual costs.*

(*Continued*)

Table 12.1 (Continued) Answer Each Question to Complete the Supply Chain Construction Blueprint

Completed	*Step*	*Key Supply Chain Construction Project Questions*
☑	6	Implement the Service Element Have you *implemented* any related services?
☑	7	Connect Order Broadcast through Network Constraint to Material Delivery Does the *customer's order connect with last echelon and the network constraint*? Does the *network constraint rebroadcast customer orders to all other echelons*? Does the *factory and distribution ordering connect with the supply base*? Have you *exercised all the loops from supplier to factory to DC to customer*?
☑	8	Connect Invoicing with Cash Payments *Have you exercised all invoice-to-cash loops in every echelon?*
☑	9	Quantify Cash-to-Cash Cycle Velocity and Variability *Do you know the days of cash-to-cash cycle for the factory?* *Do you know the days of cash-to-cash cycle for the distributor?*
☑	10	Plot the Network Container on a Value Circle Have you plotted the network container on a *Value Circle*?
Completed	*Step*	*Key Product Contents Questions*
☑	11	Write the Network Requirements Specification for the Product Contents Do you have a *numerical value* or range of values assigned to each specification?
☑	12	Integrate Product BOMs into a Composite BOM Have you incorporated *every* product into the composite BOM?

(Continued)

Table 12.1 (Continued) Answer Each Question to Complete the Supply Chain Construction Blueprint

Completed	*Step*	*Key Supply Chain Construction Project Questions*
☑	13	Locate the Push/Pull Boundary; Identify the Network Constraint Do you have an inventory location for the push/pull boundary on *each* product? Do you have a build-to-stock or build-to-order operating strategy for *each* product? Do you know *how the network constraint moves with changes to product mix?* Have you *identified the network constraint?*
☑	14	Develop the Demand Forecast Do you have a *12-month aggregate demand forecast?* Do you have a *supply mix forecast over the planning horizon?*
☑	15	Budget Inventory Turns Echelon by Echelon Do you have an *inventory turns budget for the shipping buffer?* Do you have an *inventory turns budget for the push/pull boundary?* Do you have an *inventory turns budget for store cycle stock?* Do you have an *inventory turns budget for distribution cycle stock?* Do you have an *inventory turns budget for factory finished goods?* Do you have an *inventory turns budget for factory raw material?* Do you have an *inventory turns budget for supplier finished goods?*
☑	16	Implement Push Zone Planning and Control Have you implemented *S&OP, RCCP, DRP, and MPS for all products?* Have you implemented *MRP and CRP for all lower level parts?*

(Continued)

Table 12.1 (Continued) Answer Each Question to Complete the Supply Chain Construction Blueprint

Completed	*Step*	*Key Supply Chain Construction Project Questions*
☑	17	Implement Pull Zone Planning and Control Have you implemented *pull maximum capacity for all relevant inventory items*? Have you implemented *pull maximum inventory for all relevant inventory items*?
☑	18	Plot the Product Contents on a Value Circle Have you plotted the product contents on a *Value Circle*?
Completed	*Step*	*Key Operations Stabilization Questions*
☑	19	Stabilize Supply Chain Operations Have you achieved your *throughput, cost, and inventory specifications*?
☑	20	Risk Management Have you evaluated how the project changed *risk tolerance* in your supply chain?

Separate What You Can Control from What You Cannot Control

Your organization has limited resources. The supply chain construction project, just completed, has probably stretched company resources to its limit. But as days, weeks, and months go by with a constant struggle to sustain demand and keep a positive cash flow, you may begin to question your competitiveness in your market. The new or modified supply chain is supposed to connect your killer product with the market's insatiable demand. But your orders are sporadic. And you are almost out of cash. Finally, there is a serious negotiation for a large sale. The customer wants 10 times your current volume. The customer wants to change a product feature. The customer wants delivery inside of lead time. The customer wants a deep volume discount…and Sales agrees to it all!

The proper way to address such a supply chain challenge is to dissect the customer requirement into bite-size pieces. "Ten times the volume" begs the question, "When?" Your customer also has a finite capacity to absorb your product. If such a large order is spread over weeks and months of delivery, then the true increase in throughput may be much smaller. Where do you have to increase network capacity to respond? What is the longest lead time material to hit the schedule? If "wants to change a product feature" is driven by programming a firmware change, then development and testing lead times are key. If a part value change or part substitution is involved, then maybe first shipments go without the change until parts can be expedited to the factory. "Wants delivery inside of lead time" begs the question how many units can be delivered from inventory and current production. Then, how long will it be before the factory can ramp to the required level of throughput? "Wants a deep volume discount" should trigger an analysis of the breakpoint volumes for the most expensive commodities used to build the product. Perhaps, the total order volume gives you the ability to renegotiate pricing with some key suppliers. When all is said and done, you may find that the fulfillment of such an order, while not easy, is less of a stretch than you previously thought.

Shooting from the Hip

In the heat of battle, some organizations will jeopardize profit to make their revenue target. Sales will lobby to reduce the selling price to match a competitor's price and make their revenue target at a reduced gross margin. While the period revenue target may be achieved, the cash flow generated from accounts receivable 30 days in the future may be insufficient to cover the inventory investment and period expenses in that timeframe. This is particularly problematic if the organization wants rapid growth.

In the heat of battle, some organizations will jeopardize cash flow to make their profit target. Purchasing will exercise volume discounts to drive down material costs and reduce COGS. This leads to an inflated inventory investment. While the period profit target may be achieved, the accounts payable 30 days in the future will consume a disproportionate amount of working capital in that timeframe. Again, this is particularly problematic if the organization wants rapid growth.

Normal Response Strategies

Once you get beyond the diagnostics and tune-up at the start-up of a new or modified supply chain, you need to be watchful for operating scenarios that require a change to your response. With the supply chain in full operation, you can change scheduling, capacity, and pricing before resorting to more radical changes. Here is the set of normal response strategies.

- *The responsive strategy: customer-initiated scheduling change*—This is the normal "small-signal" delivery strategy to meet daily customer orders with different dates, different quantities, different product mix, different ship-to locations, and different transport modes. The stimulus is customer initiated. The response is through normal operations planning and execution. Your response requires no change to either the network container or the product contents.

- *Information technology system maintenance and upgrades*—Over time, without regular maintenance and systematic upgrades, your information system will degrade in its ability to support your supply chain operation. You need to budget both people's time and dollars to prevent this from happening. Software license renewals, hardware upgrades, application software patches and upgrades, periodic password revisions, antivirus and malware protection upgrades, periodic retraining, etc., all need your attention.
- *The supply flexible strategy: match supply with demand*—This is a "large-signal" capacity strategy. Manufacturing enterprises are excellent at managing capacity and inventory to match supply with demand, especially when the demand is perishable. The stimulus is initiated from within the supply chain network. Your response requires detailed knowledge of the network constraint and how the network constraint may move with changes in product mix. The network container is modified by increasing capacity at the constraint.
- *Continuous quality improvement*—As more of your product is delivered into the market, you will learn more about customer acceptance and the product's fitness for use. Quality-driven product changes need to be made as any latent design defects become apparent in the field. Supplier, factory, and distribution processes need to be continuously monitored with process deviations and worn tooling being addressed immediately. Drive the root causes for returns, scrap, and no-turn inventory out of your supply chain.
- *The demand flexible strategy: match demand with supply*—This is a "large-signal" pricing strategy. Service enterprises are excellent at managing product pricing to match demand with supply, especially when the supply is perishable. The stimulus is initiated from within the supply chain network. Your response requires detailed knowledge of the fixed and variable cost structures in your network. The product content is modified by applying dynamic pricing across specific combinations of product and delivery channel.
- *Continuous sustainability initiative*—Explore each new opportunity for the use of sustainable raw materials and packaging in your products, for comparing the carbon footprint of your processes, for reducing emissions through your choice of logistics connections, and for environmentally responsible handling, recycling, and disposal of product and process waste.

Resource Management during Periods of Rapid Growth

There may be times when your business experiences explosive growth. While this might sound like a good problem to have, these are not necessarily good times. You will have two key resource management challenges. First, your ability to generate cash flow will become the limiting factor in your organization's ability to grow. Cash is needed to buy ever-increasing volumes of inventory and to fund ever-increasing levels of accounts receivables for customer credit. Remember that the rate of cash thrown off by business profits lags behind the rate of cash needed to support new growth.

Second, your ability to hire and train new employees will limit your growth. Constraints in labor capacity can be in direct labor as in not enough hours and hands to build any more products. You may be able to move some inventory and outsource a piece of the growing labor capacity issue, until you can build your own workforce. Constraints in labor capacity can also be in indirect labor as in not enough order processing, support engineering, or installation services. These roles are harder to fill. Once delivery performance and customer service response times begin to slip, your competitors will step in and gobble up the market opportunity that you created.

Resource Management during Periods of Rapid Decline

There may be times when your business experiences heart-wrenching decline. This can be a very nasty time. While the two top resource management challenges are the same, as in cash and people, the circumstances are decidedly different. It is no longer the case that you cannot get cash quickly enough; now, it is the case that you cannot get cash at all. You experience a liquidity crisis. All your sources for purchasing credit and debt lending dry up. You are forced to shed what you can for the business to stay afloat. Your cash budget becomes a run-out model to predict when the business will run out of cash.

On the people side of the ledger, you enter a period of continuous reorganization. Company-paid employee benefits are eliminated. Departments are consolidated, and people with duplicate responsibilities are let go. Hierarchical organizations are flattened, with previous managers taking on positions as common laborers with a reduction in pay. Employees on the bottom rungs are shed, beginning with those having the least seniority. In such times, it is essential to protect those employees having the critical skills needed to keep the business running until the economy turns around.

Abnormal Response Strategies to External Events and Threats

There are many other forces external to your supply chain that demand your attention but that you cannot control. Accidents, acts of war, competitive threats, corporate actions, criminal intent, cyber-crime, economic conditions, environmental threats, international trade sanctions, legal actions, political actions, the regulatory landscape, relationship events, social media threats, technological advances, etc., all collide with the normal operation of your supply chain. What, besides running out of cash, can drive you out of business? To what degree can you quickly shift from being responsive to being flexible to being agile before your supply chain breaks beyond repair? Great businesses start with plan A then quickly move to plan B or

Table 12.2 Separate What You Can Control from What You Cannot Control

Can Control the Consequence	*Cannot Control the Consequence*
Diagnostics to tune supply chain performance • Throughput • Cost structure • Inventory investment Managing lumpy cash flow	
Normal operations • Address change by scheduling and execution • Maintain and upgrade the information system • Continuous quality improvement • Continuous sustainability initiative	
Can change the product contents • Feature set • Price point • Delivery	Cannot change the product contents to regain competitiveness because of external forces.
Can change the network container • Adjust delivery channel • Adjust direct material/direct labor costs • Adjust inventory placement and mix	Cannot change the network container to regain competitiveness because of external forces.
Can change the business model • Market segment/product value proposition	Cannot change the business model to regain competitiveness because of external forces.
	Run out of cash at start-up and cannot recover from a cash liquidity crisis.

plan C or plan D before they achieved the right match between their target customers, their product contribution, and the competitive landscape. The main supply chain construction question is this: to what degree does the network container, the product contents, or both, have to be changed to track your business moves from plan A to plan B to plan C to plan D?

- *The agile strategy: radical change to both the network and the product*—This is the adaptive strategy. The degree of change is at the fringes of your control.
- *In risk management, the consequence is more important than the cause*—The consequence is whether or not the supply chain is flexible enough and risk tolerant enough for your organization to stay in business. The consequence is the calendar time duration to recovery.
- *Focus on what you can control rather than generating high anxiety over things you cannot control*—Table 12.2 presents a framework to help you determine what you can and cannot control when facing external events and threats.

The remainder of this chapter looks at three broad considerations to make your new or modified supply chain work in a robust and risk-tolerant manner.

- Forces that drive unanticipated product change.
- Forces that drive unanticipated network change.
- Forces that drive unanticipated change to the business model.

Change the Product...If You Can

During 2011, a third-party satellite service provider unexpectedly changed the downlink frequency to its satellite modem to avert deteriorating atmospheric conditions. As a result, fleet operations managers lost contact with thousands of mobile containers scattered across the United States. The satellite modem had been designed with two downlink frequencies that could be switched in the event of atmospheric noise. While the switching feature was programmable, the modems had been operated on the primary frequency for several years. The modem was embedded in a telematics product fitted to each container. There were two generations of telematics products in the field. The satellite downlink frequency was not remotely programmable in the first-generation product, but it was in the second-generation product. The telematics company was challenged with three groups of products: new second-generation production on the factory floor and in inventory, second-generation product installed in the field, and first-generation product installed in the field. Engineering was able to quickly develop and test a firmware fix to switch frequencies. Once released, the firmware fix was immediately implemented in the factory and on all second-generation telematics products. But it was particularly painful and expensive to track down the first-generation telecom products to dispatch field technicians to make on-site repairs. If the downlink had been permanently lost, then the telematics company would have been out of business. The supply chain network did not have to be changed. Product sales mostly recovered because the telematics product's value proposition was hard to match, and the telematics company had been highly responsive during this emergency. Fleet operations were completely restored over a period of weeks. [Author's note: This incident occurred while the author was director of supply chain.]

Change the Product Feature Set

Whether reacting to an unexpected external threat or just moving the business from plan A to a more workable plan B, you can sometimes change the feature set of your product content without changing the network container. External events force product changes all the time. The following list of product feature changes comes from the electronics industry, yet many of these approaches are applicable to other products from other industries. A product design that can accommodate some of these strategies is a more robust, more risk-tolerant product design.

- *Features defined in firmware*—A feature defined in firmware adds value without adding cost or causing the product bill of materials to change.
- *Remote programming of new features*—Many of today's wireless devices can be reprogrammed and upgraded remotely using the same hardware platform.
- *Features designed to be postponed*—Postponement requires some design effort. Postponement with some parts value changes may enable additional product capabilities beyond the initial feature set.
- *Plug-in compatible upgrades*—The base product is designed to accept expected future upgrades of key components from your current supply base. Examples include expected footprints for faster microprocessors and deeper memories.
- *Scalable product performance*—The product is designed as a scalable family. For example, a family of 40-watt power supplies with the same package dimensions might include a 5-volt/8-ampere model, a 10-volt/4-ampere model, a 40-volt/1-ampere model, and a 100-volt/400-milliamp model.
- *Features designed and catalogued, but never built*—This includes catalog combinations of product or system components that are designed and tested through computer simulation to work together but are never produced in volume unless ordered by a customer.
- *Features removed by depopulating component parts*—An initial product offering with a superset of features can be slimmed down by removing components once customer preferences are known.
- *Product quality improvement*—While product quality is not a feature per se, cleaning up a known quality defect to make a product feature more reliable has competitive implications.
- *Component substitution to comply with new regulatory requirements*—It may be possible to substitute components built from older technology with components built from newer technology to comply with new regulations. Examples include Conflict Minerals and California's CARB clean air standards. Component substitutions, particularly ones that involve a different technology, may also require changing the network supply base.
- *Component substitution for sustainability*—It may be possible to substitute components that meet sustainability standards for those that do not. Examples include surface mount components that can be attached

using nonleaded solder and packaging made from biodegradable plastics. Component substitutions may also require changing the network supply base.

Change the Product Price Point

Weak demand is the scourge of many businesses. At best, it keeps business revenue stagnant; at worst, it can lead to a failed business. Just as important is the idea that both capacity and inventory are perishable. Capacity is perishable because while not being used to generate revenue, that calendar time can never be recovered. This is easily demonstrated in service industries such as airlines, hotels, and rental cars. These industries have huge investments in airplanes, real estate, and fleets of cars. Every day that an airline seat, a hotel room, or a rental car goes unused, their capacity to generate revenue is lost forever. Inventory is perishable both for obvious spoilage reasons in the case of food and for nonobvious reasons, including latent quality issues, next-generation upgrades, and aging. For these reasons, distributors and factories have learned to use dynamic pricing to change the price point of their products to shape demand. Where Chapter 10: "Inventory Management" is about matching supply to demand, dynamic pricing is about matching demand to supply. And this is not just a play on words.

You can change the price point of your product content without changing the network container. Dynamic pricing seeks to increase product volume through product price reduction and focused market segmentation, while it conserves the product contribution margin (CM). Dynamic pricing has three components:

1. *Product contribution margin computed from a breakeven analysis*

   Product fixed and variable costs must be well understood. Fixed cost does not change with changes in the volume of products shipped. Variable cost changes in direct proportion to changes in the volume of products shipped. Do not attempt dynamic pricing without a firm grasp of the cost structure of your business. The relationship of fixed cost, variable cost per unit, breakeven volume, and breakeven price per unit is given in Equations 12.1 and 12.2 below.

$$\text{Breakeven volume} = \frac{\text{Fixed cost}}{\text{Breakeven price/unit} - \text{Variable cost/Unit}} \tag{12.1}$$

$$\text{Breakeven price/unit} = \frac{\text{Fixed cost} + (\text{Variable cost/unit}) \times (\text{Breakeven volume})}{\text{Breakeven volume}} \tag{12.2}$$

When the unit volume sales of a product exceed its breakeven volume, the product revenue covers all of its fixed cost, all of its variable cost plus a profit margin. When product volume equals the breakeven volume, the product's contribution to profit is zero. When product volume is less than the break-even volume, the product contribution is a loss. The product's *contribution margin* is given by Equations 12.3 and 12.4 below.

$$\text{\$CM/Unit} = \text{\$Selling price/unit} - \text{\$Variable/unit} \tag{12.3}$$

$$\text{\$Total contribution} = \text{\$CM/unit} \times \text{Unit volume} \tag{12.4}$$

2. *Market segmentation*

   The market is segmented, subsegmented, and temporally segmented to identify homogeneous pricing opportunities. Temporal segmentation means that the perishability of the capacity or inventory asset is tied to a date or an event fixed in time, for example, a contract termination date, a holiday sale date, or the wheels-up date and time for a scheduled flight. The purpose of this additional market segmentation is to identify a nearly homogeneous group of buyers willing to pay a particular price by that date due to their circumstance.
3. *Pricing to maintain the contribution margin*

   Dynamic pricing answers the question of how much a product's price can be reduced. The purpose is to drive more unit volume sales through a more focused market segmentation and the product's price reduction. In tough times, the coverage of variable cost is decreased through a reduction in product pricing, while the demand volume increases such that the product's CM remains intact. Dynamic pricing works only if you are starting from a product volume that exceeds breakeven volume and a product CM that exceeds zero. Equations 12.5 and 12.6 below show the change as a percentage.

$$\text{\% Breakeven sales change} = \frac{-\text{\$Delta price change} \times 100\%}{\text{\$CM} + \text{\$Delta price change}} \tag{12.5}$$

Note: An increase in Delta price change is (+); a decrease in Delta price change is (–); these +/– signs are in addition to the +/– signs of Equation 12.5.

$$\text{Units of breakeven sales change} = \text{\% Breakeven sales change} \times \text{Breakeven volume} \tag{12.6}$$

A Dynamic Pricing Example

The Witt Florist Shop on Seventh Street is a small family-owned business. It has maintained a reputation for excellent service and fresh flowers for over 25 years. The florist buys and transports flowers six days a week from a local flower auction. The florist delivers its floral arrangements using its own panel truck. It will deliver and pick up rented vases and stands after a funeral or wedding or other special engagements. The florist takes orders over the Internet, from the international Florist's Transworld Delivery (FTD) network of florists, by phone, and from walk-ins. It accepts all major credit cards, wire transfers, checks drawn on commercial banks, and cash. Figure 12.1 is the supply chain echelon map for the Witt Florist Shop.

The Witt Florist Shop thinks of its business in terms of selling into three separate demand channels and buying from a supply base with two key suppliers. Figure 12.2 shows the pricing method used at each of the florist's buy/sell interfaces.

1. *Sell to opportunistic demand*—These are local customer and FTD orders driven by special occasions such as Valentine's Day, holidays, Mother's Day, birthdays, hospital visits, etc. The florist uses dynamic pricing for these customers.
2. *Sell to periodic demand*—These are standing orders from three local funeral homes for a limited variety of large floral arrangements. While the florist knows the average number of arrangements ordered per year by each funeral home, the exact timing of the orders varies widely. The florist uses contract pricing for these customers.
3. *Sell to regular demand*—These are weekly orders from four churches and five restaurants scattered around the community. The churches order medium-sized three-piece settings, while the restaurants order small sized 10- to 18-piece settings. The florist uses fixed pricing for these customers.
4. *Buy from daily flower auction*—Flowers are purchased daily at the flower auction. Dynamic pricing is set by the auctioneer.
5. *Buy from garden supply distributor*—Various other supplies are purchased from a distribution. The distributor sells items at a fixed price.

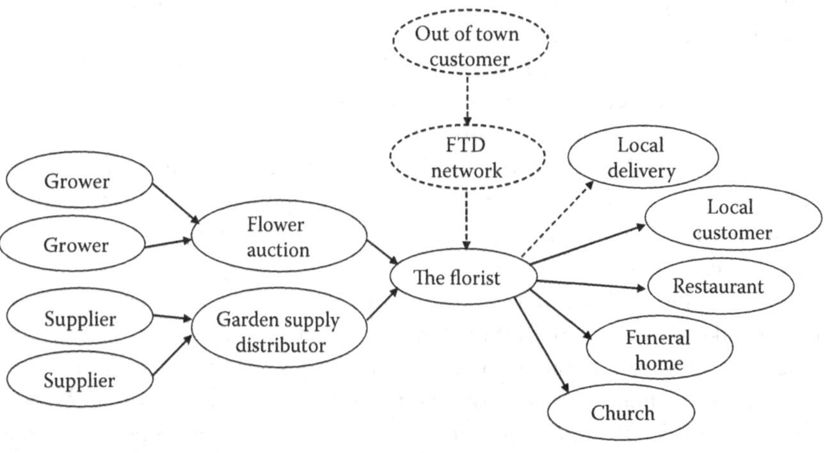

Figure 12.1 Witt Florist Shop supply chain echelon map.

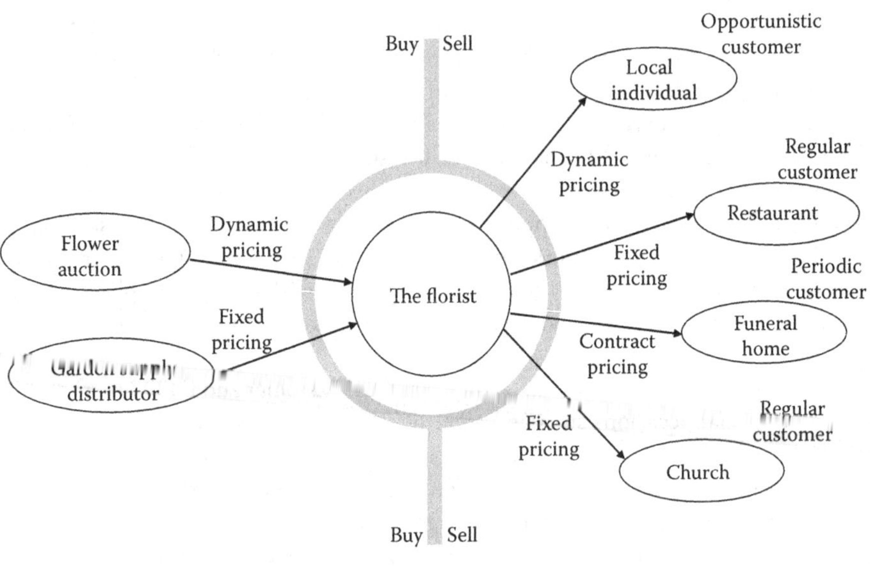

Figure 12.2 Florist's buy and sell pricing arrangements.

Over the years, the Witt Florist Shop has kept good track of its financial records and has a good understanding of its fixed cost, variable cost, and contribution margin (CM) by demand channel. Table 12.3 shows the relevant information for the "opportunistic," "periodic," and "regular" demand channels. The selling price is the highest in the periodic demand channel because the multiple floral arrangements for a funeral home are each large and complex. The largest CM has traditionally come from the opportunistic demand channel in part because this demand channel has the highest unit volume.

Lately, the florist business has slowed because of the economy. The business has been forced to reduce its pricing to break even for its regular demand channel of church and restaurant customers to not lose them. But demand is still weak. This is a family business, and management does not want to lay off any of its employees. With the Easter holidays approaching, management wonders how a reduction in pricing for the opportunistic demand channel might increase its unit volume.

The Witt Florist Shop currently sells products in this channel for $95/unit with a breakeven volume of 100 units/month. First, the market is more carefully segmented as (1) fresh floral arrangements with vases, (2) delivered to individuals within a 10-mile radius of the florist shop, and (3) price reduction available when ordered two weeks before Easter. The last segmentation is the temporal segmentation driven by the holiday. Second, the florist runs the calculations from Equations 12.5 and 12.6 for various price reductions, and it settles on a price that appears

Table 12.3 Florist's Demand Channels

Monthly Fixed Cost	*Monthly Variable Cost/ Unit*					
$12,000	$250					
Fixed Cost	*Per Unit Variable Cost*	*Per Unit Selling Price*	*Per Unit CM*	*Per Unit Breakeven Price*	*Breakeven Volume*	*Total Contribution*
Opportunistic demand—dynamic pricing						
$5,000	$25	$95	$70	$75	100 units	$7,000
Periodic demand—contract pricing						
$3,000	$125	$550	$425	$500	8 units	$3,400
Regular demand—fixed pricing						
$4,000	$100	$220	$120	$200	40 units	$4,800

competitive for a unit volume increase that appears practical. The florist decides to reduce its pricing to $79.99/unit from $95/unit.

$$\%\ \text{Breakeven sales change} = \frac{-(-\$15.01)\times 100\%}{\$70.00+(-\$15.01)} = \frac{+\$15.01\times 100\%}{\$54.99} = +27.3\%$$

Notice how the +/– signs in Equation 12.5 and the negative sign signaling a reduction in price are handled.

$$\text{Unit breakeven sales change} = +27.3\% \times 100 \text{ units} = +27 \text{ units}$$

Therefore, the Witt Florist Shop will have to sell at least 27 more floral arrangements to customers in the opportunistic demand channel at this reduced price to maintain its CM. The florist will attempt to match demand to supply through a reduced product price and more focused marketing and sales before Easter.

Change the Network...If You Can

Custom parts manufactured with plastic injection molding involve the selection of the right plastic resin, the design of the part to fit the product, and the design of the tooling used to produce the part. The resin selection, the part design, and the tool design were done in-house and owned by the company. The tool was made by a third party, owned by the company, and loaned to an injection molder to produce the part.

Late one Friday afternoon, Jack, one of our buyers, asked to borrow a company procurement card. This was highly unusual. He said he had to rent a truck right away and would return the procurement card on Monday. When pressed, Jack said that he had just received a phone call from his contact at our injection molder advising him off the record that the company was going into receivership Monday morning. The production facility would be padlocked sometime that weekend. This injection molder had in its tool inventory our one-of-a-kind plastic tooling used to mold the outside enclosure for a key product line and big revenue generator. The company owned the tool, and the product line was low on inventory. In the extreme, if Jack had not been able to secure the tool that Friday night, then product delivery interruption, loss of customers, and loss of revenue could have been catastrophic. Fortunately, the tool was able to be moved to another company that operated a compatible injection molding machine.

Ensure Continuity of Supply

Whether reacting to an unexpected external threat or just moving the business from plan A to a more workable plan B, you can sometimes change the network container without changing the product contents. External events force changes to the network container all the time. Supply interruptions that impact delivery lead time are frequent, including weather-related delays, suppliers refusing to deliver until a payment is settled, union strikes, dock worker strikes, tractor-trailer fires, etc. The following list of minimal network changes can often provide continuity of supply.

- *Continuously monitor availability and pricing of key raw materials*—Do not be caught short when raw material prices spike and/or raw material goes on allocation.
- *Substitute a supplier*—Inventory items are supplied by sole source, single source, or multiple source suppliers. Items that are single source and multiple source already have substitute suppliers identified.
- *Parallel factories for increased capacity*—Some industries such as apparel require very high volumes at one time. The supply chain network is operated with a number of parallel factories, making the same products to cover peak periods.
- *Substitute a logistics provider*—If you are willing to trade off transit time with cost, there are always logistics alternatives. Within the same transportation mode, some carriers are proven to be more reliable than others. Take a close look at intermodal alternatives for medium and long-haul transport.

- *Relocate a distributor for better geographical coverage*—If your delivery performance lags around the edges of your distributor's area coverage, you may be able to shift distributor locations for better overall performance.
- *Build or buy buffer inventory*—When you know you are facing a network transition, building or buying a limited buffer inventory can be a good solution before closing down the "as-is" network.
- *Practice redundant information technology networks, backup, and recovery*—Identify in a sister division, another company or purchase identical server and networking equipment that can be quickly brought online. Maintain up-to-date source files, backup database files, and an auxiliary source of power. Document your information system disaster recovery plan and practice it at least once a year.
- *Continuous supply chain sustainability improvement*—Improving sustainability in your supply chain can reduce the risk of supply allocation and supply interruption.

Trade Information for Inventory

Much of the recent information technology evolution has to do with making information ever more visible and ubiquitous at ever-decreasing cost. Information visibility enables everyone connected to the information system to be able to see everything. Ubiquity is the degree to which everyone related to the supply chain network is connected to the information system. One particularly interesting technology is voice recognition/voice synthesis, where part numbers, inventory locations, and other operational directives are translated and communicated in the native tongue of the employee doing the work.

Supply chain network construction often requires the cobbling together of a modern enterprise resource planning (ERP) system at one trading partner with a legacy system at another trading partner. Specialized warehouse management systems, transportation management systems, and advanced planning and scheduling systems often augment demand planning and fulfillment. Transparent information sharing requires expensive customized midware programs that are difficult to maintain. Information sharing gets reduced to a least common denominator among the hardware and software system components in the interconnected network. The information flow often does not reach every raw material supplier or every customer along the edges of the supply chain network. The information is not ubiquitous.

Gaps exist especially for tracking and tracing inventory within transient inbound, midbound, and outbound logistics paths. There are now ever more sophisticated technologies being applied to fill such gaps. Bar-code labels containing a few data characters have morphed into universal product code (UPC) labels, 2D bar coding, and radio frequency identification (RF-ID) tags that point to data files and databases containing enormous amounts of information. Global positioning by satellite (GPS) location devices have been combined with remote sensors and wireless communications packages that ride along with inventory from its origin to its destination. The "Internet of Things" is beginning to provide the means for end-to-end visibility in supply chain networks. For example, the automotive industry tracks engine blocks all the way through the factory to a completely customized automobile sitting in the dealer's inventory. The pharmaceutical industry tracks product from source to destination to prevent counterfeit products from being injected into their supply chains.

Trading information for inventory is one powerful concept for making your network lower cost and more robust. Here are four examples.

- *Cross-dock*—A cross-dock is essentially a switch in the logistics path. A cross-docking facility looks a little like a distribution center except that it has many receiving docks, many shipping docks, and no storage area. Suppose you had a truckload of freight going from Sacramento, California, to Atlanta, Georgia, a distance of 2,521 miles on Interstate 80, with some of the freight destined for Cleveland, Ohio, an additional 704 miles on Interstate 75. Instead, you might cross-dock in St. Louis, Missouri, by swapping part of your load with a truck headed for Cleveland and taking on additional pallets headed for Atlanta. Your trailer remains full, but now it has a mixed load all headed for Atlanta. Another full truckload travels the 559 miles on Interstate 70 to Cleveland. Your truck travels a total of 2,521 miles from Sacramento to Atlanta instead of 3,225 miles ending in Cleveland. If you have the routing information, you can make the switch decreasing in-transit time, decreasing in-transit inventory and lowering freight cost.
- *Mixed stock keeping unit (SKU) pallet*—Single SKU pallets arriving at a distribution center from the factory typically hold more products than a single retail store delivery can handle. However, if the distribution center has the information to repack pallets with mixed SKUs based on the stocking orders of single retail stores, then full pallet loads can be delivered to the retail store at a lower freight cost.
- *Postponement*—Postponement is a great strategy for dealing with mix uncertainty. Instead of investing in and stocking a maximum quantity of inventory of every product combination, postponement completes product assembly within distribution. Generic assemblies are shipped to distribution at a forecast rate. The distributor's purchasing buys and stocks a mix of the maximum quantity of each unique item that may be postponed. This postponement stock takes up much less cubic volume and is a fraction of the inventory investment. When the distributor has the configuration information from a real customer order, the generic assembly is combined with a specific postponement component. The completed product is validated and shipped immediately.
- *Risk pooling*—Risk pooling is a strategy that combines safety stocks for independently demanded products, normally held downstream in the store

echelon, upstream in a combined inventory in the distribution echelon. Based on mathematical probabilities, risk pooling can significantly reduce the total safety stock inventory investment. The upstream risk pool is the root mean squared (RMS) combination of the formerly downstream individual statistical safety stocks. Risk pooling works only if you have the information that shows that customer demand from each store is independent of the demand from the other stores and that the distributor's delivery lead time to the store can be competitive against market requirements.

Temporary Disaster Recovery through Redundancy

People, process, inventory, and information are the bare essentials of your network container. It is good business practice to build redundancy around each of these.

- *People*—Key skills need to be cross-trained to other employees. It is not good enough to just shadow the trainer. The student must be given opportunities to practice on the job what he or she has been taught. Disaster is known to strike only when your key people are out sick, traveling, or on vacation.
- *Process*—Identify which processes are common to other similar businesses and which processes are unique to your business. If possible, make arrangement to back up the unique processes. Invest in an inventory of critical spare parts to keep key production equipment running. For example, perhaps an equipment supplier would be willing to let you run a piece of demo equipment under an unusual circumstance. Or perhaps another company would allow you to run a second shift or a weekend operation at their facility under emergency circumstances such as a fire at your plant.
- *Inventory*—Identify which materials are garden variety inventory and which are long-lead-time inventory. Make arrangements with your supplier to hold a specified quantity of safety stock at their location. This safety stock should be rotated through the supplier's next shipment to you and the safety inventory immediately replenished with new production.
- *Information systems*—Completely redundant, identical hardware and software should be located at a geographically distant location. It does no good if the backup data center is in the same flood plain as the factory, just as it does no good if the backup disc is in the same office as the original. It is essential to have a written disaster recovery plan and a switchover practice run twice a year.
- *Information access*—Just as business is even more dependent upon global Internet connections, denial of service attacks, hacking, malware, and Trojan Horse attacks have become prevalent on the Internet. Keep a clean, protected backup of your business data that gets refreshed daily. Periodically exercise the procedure to recover your operating data from the backup.

Change the Business Model...If You Can

Changing the business model means making significant change to both the network container and the product contents at the same time. This requires a reapplication of the Supply Chain Construction Blueprint because of the interactions between the network and the product. Changing the business model is a radical, risky step that may mean that your business is on the brink of failing.

When all is said and done, each link in the supply chain can work only if there is cash liquidity to buy and sell. When any trading partner runs out of cash and has burned their ability to borrow against credit, the link seizes up. If that link happens to be a sole source supplier, the factory, or the key distributor, their bankruptcy will cause the business to fail. Cash is king.

Risk Management

This chapter has covered a lot of ground before getting to the topic of risk management. This is because effective risk management is grounded in having a viable, well-oiled supply chain. You have to thoroughly understand the degree to which you can manipulate the network container and its product contents before you can imagine alternative responses to an unforeseen external event or threat that is outside your control. Your ability to fix any loss of continuity of supply for your customer and any illiquidity of cash for your business becomes a question of your time to recovery. A few hours, maybe even a few days, may be tolerable. Many weeks or months probably mean your business is lost.

How to Build a Risk-Tolerant Supply Chain

Follow these seven steps, in order, to build a flexible and risk-tolerant supply chain.

1. Complete the current supply chain construction project.
2. Perform diagnostics to achieve the intended performance.
3. Under normal circumstances, do not sacrifice profit for revenue.
4. Under normal circumstances, do not sacrifice cash flow for profit.
5. Change the product, not the network, or change the network, not the product.
6. If both the product and network have to be changed, open a new supply chain construction project.
7. Use environmental scanning and scenario planning to manage ongoing risk.

What is so extreme as to force you to change your business model? The number of external events and threats outside of your control that can impact your business numbs the mind. Risk management boils down to the three step process shown below. What is hard is your ability to devote resources and time management discipline to address environmental scanning and scenario planning. You have a choice. Either the business can spend a little time and resource on risk management on a regular basis or the business can become all consumed when a crisis strikes.

1. *Identify the source* of potential disruption through environmental scanning.
2. Assess the *probability* and *severity* of the risk.
3. Use scenario planning to develop contingency plans to *mitigate* and *manage* the risk.

Environmental Scanning

Supply chain risk management involves environmental scanning for potential risks and scenario planning to thwart probable supply chain disruption. Environmental scanning and scenario planning are limited only by your imagination and the amount of business resources you are willing to invest.

External events and threats can be classified into sets such as accidental, acts of war, competitive, counterfeiting, criminal, economic, environmental, extreme weather, health, insurance, legal, political, regulatory, relationship, sustainability, technological, world trade, etc. Each set would then contain lists of possibilities. For example, a set for business regulations might include ISO9000, ISO14000, C-TPAT, Sarbanes-Oxley, Conflict Minerals, OSHA, FINRA, import/export quotas and embargoes, software licensing, intellectual property registration, and more. Which of these might impact your supply chain and, therefore, your ability to do business? Which of these might change in the near future? If you are unfamiliar with these regulations, the Internet, beginning with http://www.wikipedia.org, is a great tool to use to become educated about what might be relevant to your business situation. Environmental scanning means that you periodically take the time to look outside your business to see what threats may be looming around the corner and to assign a probability of occurrence. Additionally, there comes a time in the natural life cycle of any business that individual products, individual services, individual trading partner relationships, and/or entire supply chain networks get terminated. An environmentally responsible, human resource responsible approach should be part of your supply chain planning from the start.

Here is one reasonable, workable approach. Encourage all employees to identify potential risks to the business. Accumulate everyone's inputs and suggestions. Have someone group the inputs and make copies for the entire management team. Pull together a cross-functional management team meeting at least once a quarter for a brainstorming meeting. Document a highly likely threat from the environmental scan and develop your response scenario during this meeting. Over time, document these pairs of environmental scanning threats and matching response scenarios in a three-ring binder titled "Risk Management." Build funding for some of the identified contingencies into your annual investment budgeting. Organize an employee cell phone communications chain, train first aid responders, and set up procedures with the local police, fire protection, and HAZMAT authorities. Should the same or a somewhat related crisis really happen, major portions of the scenario plan you have already worked out become the basis of your actual response.

Scenario Planning

The one-story factory is situated along a picturesque stream near stands of tall, old pine trees. The stream is a runoff from a dammed lake several miles away. To get to the factory, employees and carriers follow the access road crossing a low bridge into the parking lot. The bridge and the access road on the far side of the stream are maintained by the county. A high-voltage power line runs alongside the access road to the factory. The factory pumps well water for site use using an electric pump. Figure 12.3 is a hand drawn site map.

At their quarterly risk management meeting, the cross-functional management team decides that extreme weather at the factory is a highly probable threat that could disrupt the supply chain. The team reviews all the various accumulated

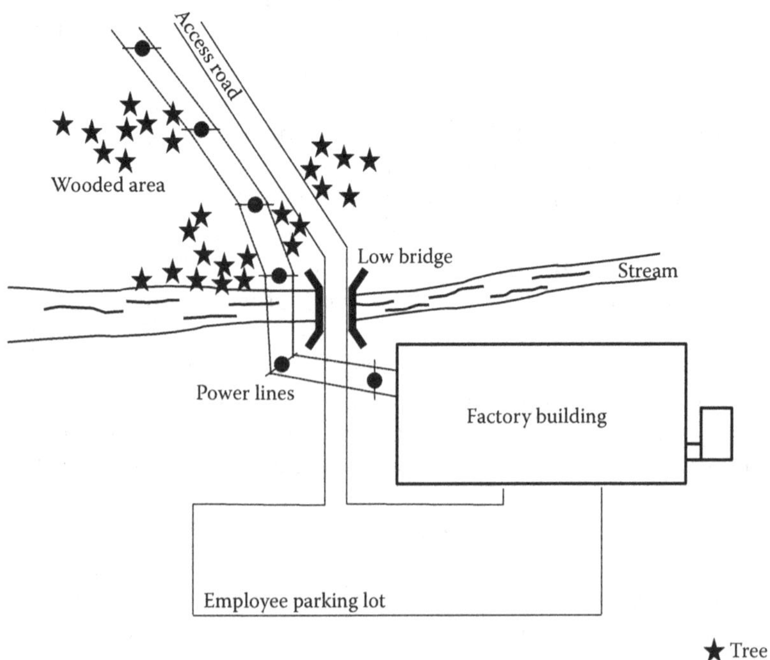

Figure 12.3 Example hand drawn factory (or supplier or distributor) site map.

employee inputs related to "extreme weather" and decides to build their likely scenario around "flooding" and "high winds damage." They brainstorm a set of consequences and the probability of occurrence (low, medium, or high) for each. Next, they go line by line, imagining the severity of the consequence (low, medium, or high), possible contingency actions, and the probable time to recover. Table 12.4 documents their scenario plan.

Table 12.4 Example Scenario Plan

Environmental scan	Shifting national weather patterns seem to be bringing more frequent, more intense storms to the Northeast.		
Scenario description	Extreme weather threat to the factory.		
Threat	*Consequence and Probability*	*Contingency Plan*	*Severity and Time to Recover*
1. Flooding The stream overflows its banks, flooding the factory floor and parking lot. Debris hits the bridge, causing structural damage.	Employee safety with impassible roads. (High)	Employees told to stay home.	(Med) Hours→days
	Key employees cannot get into the factory. (Med)	Position small boats on both sides of stream.	(Low) Hours
	Some inventory gets ruined. (High)	1. Keep all inventory off the floor. 2. Move inventory offsite before stream floods. 3. Keep safety stock of long lead time items at supplier.	(Med) 1. Before the flooding 2. Before the flooding 3. Days to take delivery
	Production equipment gets ruined. (High)	1. Sandbag the building. 2. Build moat around specific equipment. 3. Disconnect power.	(High) Days→weeks for water to recede

(*Continued*)

Table 12.4 (Continued) Example Scenario Plan

Threat	*Consequence and Probability*	*Contingency Plan*	*Severity and Time to Recover*
	The info system server gets destroyed. (Med)	1. Position server and all IT equipment well off the floor. 2. Quick disconnect and hand truck to move the server.	(Med) Day→weeks to access factory cabling Weeks to take delivery on new server Days to load software
	Bridge damaged; truck traffic blocked. (Low)	Wait for county to repair the bridge.	(High) Months→years
2. High winds damage The wind downs trees, which take down the power line and fall across the access road.	Employees cannot use the access road. (Med)	Hike around the downed trees and power lines.	(Low) Hours
	Power loss shuts down the info system. (High)	Invest in battery backup and backup generator.	(High) Hours
	Power loss shuts down production. (High)	1. Work from inventory. 2. Move production to another site temporarily.	(High) Days to weeks for utility company to repair lines
	Power loss disrupts factory lighting. (High)	Use daylight and emergency generator to continue work.	(Med) Hours
	Power loss disrupts water supply. (High)	1. Use stream water to flush toilets. 2. Use bottled water for drinking.	(Med) Hours

(*Continued*)

Table 12.4 (Continued) Example Scenario Plan

Investment priorities	1. Purchase and install an emergency generator and fuel supply. 2. Move all inventory and computer equipment two feet off the floor. 3. Stock sand bags and shovels.

Each risk management meeting has three outcomes. First, it adds a page of environmental scanning and scenario planning to the Risk Management binder. Second, it prioritizes some small investments the business can make over the next several months to improve the supply chain's risk tolerance. Third, it raises awareness among the management team as to what kinds of risk the business cannot withstand without significant outside assistance.

Remember: In risk management, the consequence is more important than the cause.

In Summary

This final chapter presents processes and techniques to make your newly constructed supply chain flexible and risk tolerant. It details the completion of a supply chain construction project, addresses normal operating responses to small demand, addresses abnormal operating responses to dynamic orders and weak demand, and discusses the risk management of external events and threats. For your supply chain construction project to succeed long-term, the resulting supply chain must provide customers with continuity of supply and the company with cash liquidity.

Epilogue

The functional vice presidents had just finished with the celebratory luncheon for the launch of the UPS product line. The Supply Chain Construction Project Team was applauded, their task now completed. The VPs adjourned to their regular two o'clock executive staff meeting.

"I hope we're not premature in dismissing the project team," remarked Alice, the VP of Finance.

"We all agreed to this timing," said Herb, the VP of Engineering. "They have each done a great job. They are some of our best employees, and they are sorely needed on other projects."

"I'll second that!" said Tom, the VP of Manufacturing. "Not everyone could finish such a supply chain project with all its challenges on time and on budget."

"The revenue ramp is well below our projection," countered Alice.

"Remember, we said all along that it's going to take a few months for Computer Products to gain traction in the market with their new line of servers," said Jerry, the VP of Marketing. "Meanwhile, when it comes to stand-alone UPSs, our competitor APC might look like the 500 pound gorilla in the market. They must have an 80% market share. But we are selling a systems solution and not stand-alone battery backup."

"Changing the subject…how do you think our employees really view the new product line?" George, the VP of Quality and executive champion to the Supply Chain Construction Project Team, suddenly asked.

"Why do you ask?"

"Well, I have heard some rumblings in the past couple of weeks," said George. "Some people are really disappointed that we cannot manufacture the new products here. They are afraid their jobs here are no longer secure."

"They may be right," said Steve, the chief executive officer. "Corporate was not pleased with the projected return on this program, especially when the revenue projection was cut midproject. We have just one year to achieve $16 million to $18 million in sales, or the conversation will be about exiting the UPS business."

Bibliography

The following list represents four decades of supply chain relevant books.

Aiello, J.L. 2008. *Rightsizing inventory.* Boca Raton, FL: Auerbach Publications.

Alber, K.L. and W.T. Walker. 1998. *Supply chain management: Principles and techniques for the practitioner.* Alexandria, VA: APICS Educational & Research Foundation.

APICS. 2000. *Advanced supply chain management reprints.* Alexandria, VA: APICS.

APICS. 2010. *APICS dictionary, Thirteenth edition.* Chicago: APICS.

Ayers, J.B. 2001. *Handbook of supply chain management.* Boca Raton, FL: St. Lucie Press.

Ayers, J.B. 2004. *Supply chain project management: A structured collaborative and measurable approach.* Boca Raton, FL: St. Lucie Press.

Ballou, R.H. 2004. *Business logistics/supply chain management, Fifth edition.* Upper Saddle River, NJ: Pearson Prentice Hall.

Beckhard, R. and R.T. Harris. 1987. *Organizational transitions: Managing complex change, Second edition.* Reading, MA: Addison-Wesley Publishing Company.

Bolstorff, P. and R. Rosenbaum. 2003. *Supply chain excellence: A handbook for dramatic improvement using the SCOR model.* New York: AMACOM.

Bowersox, D.J., D.J. Closs, and O.K. Helferich. 1986. *Logistical management: A systems integration of physical distribution, manufacturing support, and materials procurement, Third edition.* New York: Macmillian Publishing Company.

Burt, D.N., W.E. Norquist, and J. Anklesaria. 1990. *Zero base pricing™: Achieving world class competitiveness through reduced all-in-costs.* Chicago: Probus Publishing Company.

Chopra, S. and P. Meindl. 2001. *Supply chain management: Strategy, planning and operation.* Upper Saddle River, NJ: Prentice Hall.

Cook, T.A., R. Alston, and K. Raia. 2012. *Mastering import & export management, Second edition.* New York: AMACOM.

Crandall, R.E. and W.R. Crandall. 2014. *Vanishing boundaries: How integrating manufacturing and services creates customer value, Second edition.* Boca Raton, FL: CRC Press.

Crandall, R.E., W.R. Crandall, and C.C. Chen. 2015. *Principles of supply chain management, Second edition.* Boca Raton, FL: CRC Press.

Friedman, T.L. 2005. *The world is flat: A brief history of the twenty-first century.* New York: Farrar, Strauss, and Giroux.

Gattorna, J. 2006. *Living supply chains: How to mobilize the enterprise around delivering what your customers want.* Harlow, UK: Prentice-Hall Financial Times.

Goldratt, E.M. and J. Cox. 1984. *The goal: Excellence in manufacturing.* Croton-on-Hudson, NY: North River Press.

Handfield, R.B. and E.L. Nichols, Jr. 2002. *Supply chain redesign: Transforming supply chains into integrated value systems.* Upper Saddle River, NJ: Financial Times Prentice Hall.

Hayes, R.H., S.C. Wheelwright, and K.B. Clark. 1988. *Dynamic manufacturing: Creating the learning organization.* New York: The Free Press.

Helfert, E.A. 1997. *Techniques of financial analysis: A practical guide to managing and measuring business performance, Ninth edition.* New York: McGraw-Hill.

Hickman, T.K. and W.M. Hickman, Jr. 1992. *Global purchasing: How to buy foreign market goods and services.* Homewood, IL: Business One Irwin.

Kaplan, R.S. and D.P. Norton. 1996. *The balanced scorecard.* Boston: Harvard Business School Press.

Kepner, C.H. and B.B. Tregoe. 1981. *The new rational manager.* Princeton: Kepner-Tregoe.

LaMarsh, J. 1995. *Changing the way we change: Gaining control of major operational change.* Reading, MA: Addison Wesley Publishing Company.

Levinson, M. 2006. *The box: How the shipping container made the world smaller and the world economy bigger.* Princeton: Princeton University Press.

Locke, D. 1996. *Global supply management: A guide to international purchasing.* Chicago: Irwin Professional Publishing.

Macfarlane, W.N. 1977. *Principles of small business management.* New York: McGraw-Hill.

Macy, B. 2014. *Factory Man: How one furniture maker battled offshoring, stayed local and helped save an American town.* New York: Little, Brown, and Company.

Martin, A.J. 1993. *DRP: Distribution resource planning: The gateway to true quick response and continuous replenishment.* Essex Junction, VT: Oliver Wight Publications.

Mather, H. 1987. *Bills of materials.* Homewood, IL: Dow Jones-Irwin.

McCormack, K.P. and W.C. Johnson, with W.T. Walker. 2003. *Supply chain networks and business process orientation: Advanced strategies and best practices.* Boca Raton, FL: St. Lucie Press.

McNally, R. 2000. *Atlas of the world: Millennium edition.* New York: Metro Books.

Mullins, J. 2010. *The new business road test: What entrepreneurs and executives should do before writing a business plan, Third edition.* London: Financial Times Prentice Hall.

Nagle, T.T. and R.K. Holden. 2002. *The strategy and tactics of pricing: Guide to profitable decision making, Third edition.* Upper Saddle River, NJ: Prentice Hall.

Nelson, C.A. 2000. *Import export: How to get started in international trade, Third edition.* New York: McGraw-Hill.

Novak, S. 2006. *The small manufacturer's toolkit: A guide to selecting the techniques and systems to help you win.* Boca Raton, FL: Auerbach Publications.

Orlicky, J. 1975. *Materials requirements planning.* New York: McGraw-Hill.

Peterson, R. and E.A. Silver. 1979. *Decision systems for inventory management and production planning.* New York: John Wiley & Sons.

Plenert, G.J. 2014. *Supply chain optimization through segmentation and analytics.* Boca Raton, FL: CRC Press.

Plossl, G.W. 1973. *Manufacturing control: The last frontier for profits.* Reston, VA: Reston Publishing Company.

Plossl, G.W. and O.W. Wight. 1967. *Production and inventory control: Principles and techniques.* Englewood Cliffs, NJ: Prentice-Hall.

Poirier, C.C. 2003. *The supply chain manager's problem-solver: Maximizing the value of collaboration and technology.* Boca Raton, FL: St. Lucie Press.

Porter, M.E. 1980. *Competitive strategy: Techniques for analyzing industries and competitors.* New York: The Free Press.

Preiss, K., S.L. Goldman, and R.N. Nagel. 1996. *Cooperate to compete: Building agile business relationships*. New York: Van Nostrand Reinhold.

Proud, J.F. 1994. *Master scheduling: A practical guide to competitive manufacturing.* Essex Junction, VT: Oliver Wight Publications.

Reinfeld, N.V. 1982. *Production and inventory control.* Reston, VA: Reston Publishing Company.

Ritterskamp, J.J. 1987. *Purchasing manager's desk book of purchasing law.* Englewood Cliffs, NJ: Prentice Hall.

Rummler, G.A. and A.P. Brache. 1990. *Improving performance: How to manage the white space on the organization chart.* San Francisco: Jossey-Bass.

Schlegel, G.L. and R.J. Trent. 2015. *Supply chain risk management: An emerging discipline.* Boca Raton, FL; CRC Press.

Schonsleben, P. 2012. *Integral logistics management: Operations and supply chain management within and across companies, Fourth edition.* Boca Raton, FL: CRC Press.

Schragenheim, E. and H.W. Dettmer. 2001. *Manufacturing at warp speed: Optimizing supply chain financial performance.* Boca Raton, FL: St. Lucie Press.

Senge, P.M. 1990. *The fifth discipline: The art & practice of the learning organization.* New York: Doubleday/Currency.

Simchi-Levi, D., P. Kaminsky, and E. Simchi-Levi. 2000. *Designing and managing the supply chain: Concepts, strategies and case studies.* New York: Irwin McGraw-Hill.

Smith, B.T. 1991. *Focus forecasting and DRP: Logistics tools of the twenty-first century.* New York: Vantage Press.

Stevenson, W.J. 2009. *Operations management, Tenth edition.* New York: McGraw-Hill Irwin.

Treacy, M. and F. Wiersema. 1995. *Discipline of market leaders: Choose your customers, narrow your focus, dominate your market.* Reading, MA: Addison-Wesley Publishing Company.

Walden, J.L. 2009. *Modeling and benchmarking supply chain leadership: Setting the conditions for excellence.* Boca Raton, FL: CRC Press.

Walden, J.L. 2006. *Velocity management in logistics and distribution: Lessons from the military to secure the speed of business.* Boca Raton, FL: St. Lucie Press.

Walker, W.T. 1985. *Managing the growing plant: A dynamic systems approach.* Englewood Cliffs, NJ: Institute for Business Planning.

Walker, W.T. 1997. "Chapter 21: Logistics planning." In Greene, J. H. Editor. *Production & inventory control handbook, Third edition.* New York: McGraw-Hill.

Walker, W.T. 2005. *Supply chain architecture: A blueprint for networking the flow of material, information, material and cash.* Boca Raton, FL: CRC Press.

Wight, O.W. 1974. *Production and inventory management in the computer age.* Boston: Cahners Books.

Wight, O.W. 1981. *MRPII: Unlocking America's productivity potential.* Williston, VT: Oliver Wight Limited Publications.

Index

Page numbers ending in "f" refer to figures. Page numbers ending in "t" refer to tables.

C

E

F

G

H

I

K

L

O

P

Q

R

S

Printed in the United States
by Baker & Taylor Publisher Services